Pioneering Portfolio Management

An Unconventional Approach to Institutional Investment

DAVID F. SWENSEN

THE FREE PRESS
New York   London   Toronto   Sydney

fP

THE FREE PRESS
A Division of Simon & Schuster, Inc.
1230 Avenue of the Americas
New York, NY 10020

The author gratefully acknowledges permission from Miles Morland to reprint
an extensive quote in chapter 9.

THE FREE PRESS and colophon are trademarks
of Simon & Schuster, Inc.

Designed by Deirdre Amthor

Manufactured in the United States of America

20 19 18 17 16 15 14

Library of Congress Cataloging-in-Publication Data

Swensen, David F.
    Pioneering portfolio management : an unconventional approach to institutional
    investment / David F. Swensen.
        p. cm.
    Includes index.
    1. Portfolio management. 2. Investments. I. Title.

    HG45529.5 .S94 2000
    332.6—dc21   99-087064

ISBN 0-684-86443-6

For Tory, Alex, and Tim

Acknowledgments

The ideas and influence of Dean Takahashi, my friend for twenty-three years and my colleague for twelve years, touch every page of this book. In fact, the approach to investing I describe here really represents joint intellectual property, formed through more than two decades of spirited discussions of issues large and small. As Dean would be the first to remind you, all of the good ideas belong to him; I take sole responsibility for any errors, omissions, ill-formed notions, and fuzzy concepts.

Charles Ellis inspired (and goaded) me to write this book, both through his example in writing *Winning the Loser's Game* and his persistence in sending countless letters, often ending with a friendly, "How's da book?" As a member of Yale's Investment Committee, Charley's eloquent parables illuminate critical issues, providing a gentle education for me and my associates. His influence permeates the book.

James Tobin bears more responsibility than anyone else for the happy professional position in which I find myself. As my teacher, dissertation adviser, and friend at Yale, Jim provided the intellectual framework for my approach to understanding economics and finance. After I settled into a Wall Street career, he gently reminded me that my planned two years in New York had turned into six, engineered my return to Yale to manage her endowment, introducing me to the job that I love. Without Jim's many important interventions in my life, this book would not exist.

Paula Volent's cheerful assistance with research and structure provided the means to bring the book from an idea to reality. Signing on for a six-month stint after her graduation from Yale's School of Management, she ended up devoting a full year and a half of extraordinary effort to the project, uncovering countless gems to enliven otherwise dry concepts. Her unfailingly enthusiastic efforts provided essential underpinnings to the exhilarating creative process that resulted in this book.

Dean, Charley, Jim, and Paula provided numerous thoughtful comments on drafts of my manuscript. The final product benefits greatly from their collective assistance.

●   ●   ●

New Haven
October 1999

Contents

Foreword: Tobin's Friend   xi

1. Introduction   1
2. Endowment Purposes   8
3. Investment and Spending Goals   25
4. Investment Philosophy   52
5. Asset Allocation   100
6. Portfolio Management   132
7. Traditional Asset Classes   155
8. Alternative Asset Classes   204
9. Investment Advisers   248
10. Performance Assessment   293
11. Investment Process   320

Notes   345
Index   355
About the Author   365

Foreword: Tobin's Friend

Jim Tobin grew up during the Great Depression in Champagne, Illinois, where his father went each day to the public library to read the *New York Times*. He learned that Harvard University had decided to reach out beyond New England for students, and Illinois was one of seven Midwestern states selected for special effort in the Harvard recruiting plans, which included several generous National Scholarships. He suggested to his son, "You might apply."

Jim Tobin did apply, proved to be a first-rank scholar and went on to earn his Ph.D., when economics at Harvard was going through a revolutionary reconsideration, shifting its orientation away from deductive "reasoning" from declared truths over to a rational commitment to empirical analysis of real world data.[1]

Harvard would prove to be an exciting environment for undergraduate and doctoral students as gifted and engaged as Jim Tobin. Filled with the excitement of realizing how useful and how intellectually absorbing a career in economics could be, Tobin accepted a faculty appointment at Yale. He held his position at Yale for nearly four decades,[2] with intellectual distinction, great personal warmth, and important influence on many, many students. At Yale, Tobin headed the celebrated Cowles Foundation for Economic Research, taught and advised students (many of whom went on to careers of great distinction in business, government, and academia), and earned a Nobel Prize. Among his many Ph.D. advisees at Yale, he developed a deep "father-son" friendship with David Swensen, who was headed for a career on Wall Street.

Jim Tobin made two enormously important contributions to Yale's very successful endowment management. First, he led a team that designed the smoothing, inflation-responsive spending rule that would link the endowment fund with the university's annual budget in a rational, continuously adaptive process that works—and is being increasingly adopted by others. (Yale's endowment currently provides 20 percent of the University's annual budget.) Second, with his colleague and later Provost Bill Brainard, Jim Tobin recommended David Swensen to the Yale administration and persuaded Swensen to abandon his promising career on Wall Street and take up the task of managing Yale's endowment. This would lead to Swensen's designing the architecture for the overall portfolio, crystallizing investment objectives and policies for each component and then selecting and supervising dozens and dozens of investment managers tasked with implementing the endowment's investment strategies.

Yale's endowment was just over $1 billion when David Swensen arrived in 1985; it's over $7 billion now. During the intervening 15 years—within a rigorous, risk-controlled portfolio structure that has very little in bonds, relies almost entirely on outside managers and, during the longest and strongest bull stock market in American history, has been quite deliberately and substantially underinvested in publicly-traded U.S. equities—David Swensen and his team have achieved an annualized rate of return for Yale's endowment superior to 96 percent of endowments and 98 percent of such institutional funds as pensions.

Public interest naturally centers on David Swensen's fine results— observers conventionally citing the unconventional structure of the portfolio and the superior returns realized, but usually overlooking the complementary strength of the long- and short-term controls used to avoid, minimize, and manage risk.

Those closer to Yale will recognize that David Swensen's risk-controlling portfolio structure and persistent discipline have enabled the endowment to provide more and more funding for Yale's educational program. Yale's endowment has not only increased quite wonderfully in market value, but has also enabled the Yale Corporation to increase with prudence the rate of annual spending—not once, but twice—because of the structural strength and resilience built into the endowment's portfolio. All told, the dollars flowing each year from Yale's endowment to the University have increased over David Swensen's 15 years from $45 million to $280 million.

The timing couldn't be better: Yale is experiencing a great renaissance under the gifted leadership of President Richard C. Levin and his extraordinary colleagues. And as the Medicis knew so well, any renaissance is costly.[3]

Most of the Western world's great educational and cultural institutions—universities, colleges, libraries, museums, and foundations—depend, to varying degrees, on their endowments and the spendable funds they produce. Usually, the difference between "mediocre" and "excellent" is that margin of assured fiscal strength that only an endowment can produce. In this way, our society depends on endowments for that vital margin of fiscal strength that facilitates institutional excellence. Yale's leadership in endowment management—a leadership Yale cheerfully shares with Harvard, Princeton, and Stanford—is important far beyond the university campus and well beyond the Yale community.

At Yale, superior endowment management has generated the vital extra funding that has enabled President Richard Levin and the Yale Corporation to assure "need-blind" admission and to lead the way in limiting annual increases in tuition. These policies contribute importantly to Yale being a first-choice college for our future leaders to study and mature. And in a "virtuous circle," wonderful students attract, stimulate, and reward great teachers to come to Yale. When Yale set a record by raising $1.7 billion to support its educational mission, the University's alumni and friends were obviously encouraged to be particularly generous by the fine investment record of the Yale endowment.

These lofty consequences are clearly important to David Swensen and his team over the long run, but their real work is also very "daily." They meet regularly with nearly 100 current investment managers; analyze many, many potentially interesting proposals; conduct due diligence on scads of prospective new managers; examine each manager's investment performance versus expectations; and run Monte Carlo simulations to "stress test" the portfolio under various possible market scenarios to work out the probable impact of both intended and unintended risks. This rigorous process of operational management enables Yale to sustain its long-term investment policy commitments through market disruptions, because they are so soundly documented and carefully conceived. The clarity of policy also enables Yale to take swift, bold action when opportunities present themselves.[4]

The operational framework within which David Swensen and his team work each day is the lineal descendant of a conceptual framework that was originated at Yale (and Stanford, MIT, and Chicago) and became known as Modern Portfolio Theory. This conceptual framework, converted into rigorously defined investment policies, gives structural strength to the present portfolio and consistency to its path through time and through markets' turbulence. The discipline to make hundreds of day-to-day decisions in the "real" world to convert this conceptual framework into a very large portfolio of very real investments that fulfill the promise of the theory is the "bottom-up" complement to the "top-down" concept and theory. If nothing is so useless as an "ivory tower" academic theory that goes unused, nothing is so very practical as the theory that works. At Yale, as David Swensen and his team keep demonstrating, the theory works very well.

One of the many ways in which Yale is special among great universities is the traditionally collegial process of decision making. So David Swensen is not alone: He has a committee of trustees and investment experts to work with, and on campus, he's in the proverbial "goldfish bowl." An engaging, warm personality and a first-class mind are wonderfully helpful, but could be insufficient in successfully working with a committee of bright, informed volunteers who are keen to "make a difference." In managing his several constituencies, David Swensen is stellar.

One secret in Yale's success has been David Swensen's ability to engage the committee in *governance*—and not in investment *management*. Contributing factors include: selection of committee members who are experienced, hard-working, and personally agreeable; extensive documentation of the due diligence devoted to preparing each investment decision; and full agreement on the evidence and reasoning behind the policy framework within which individual investment decisions will be made. As a result, the whole investment committee is always conceptually "on board" with overall policy, before turning to specific investment decisions. This preempts *ad hoc* decision making by individuals determined to be "helpful." Of course, good results and careful adherence to agreed and articulated policies help too. But the decisive factor is the great confidence David Swensen has earned by constant fidelity to purpose, rigorous rationality, and open, full review of all investment decisions with staff, investment managers, and members of his committee.

Clearly a descendant of Norway, David Swensen is a man with a deep sense of mission to serve. Personally modest, in a sober Scandinavian way, Swensen is frequently enthusiastic about the achievements of others—particularly successful investment managers. He teaches a popular undergraduate course on investing and a rigorous investment seminar at Yale's School of Management. He lives by *both* aspects of being a "man of principle": on the one hand, devoting quality time to his children and to members of his staff (and to his continuing close friendship with mentors like Jim Tobin); and on the other hand, being almost prim in his insistence on the proper behavioral integrity of the managers and the deals in which Yale invests. Significantly, his moral gyroscope has enabled him to see and make unusual investment decisions that have proven financially beneficial to the University.

Finally, David Swensen has made it fun to work on investing for Yale—recruiting a team of exceptionally talented Yale graduates, who in their first professional jobs, get a wide exposure to the world of investing; early responsibility for enquiry, analysis, and decisions; and an exemplary exposure to teamwork at work. David Swensen's "alumni" have gone on to important endowment management posts at the Carnegie and Rockefeller Foundations, as well as Duke and Princeton universities. As Churchill observed, "People like *winning* very much." Sharing the joys of victory and the discipline necessary to sustain championship performance, David Swensen infuses the process of investing with a sense of the important mission of enabling Yale's faculty, students, and administration to aspire and to achieve.

David Swensen was reluctant to write this book when the idea was first proposed to him. His reasoning illustrates the remarkable integrity of the man. First, he worried that his writing the story would draw attention to him individually and away from his team—and particularly from his senior colleague and friend, Dean Takahashi. He also worried that a "how-to" book might make it look "too easy." He was concerned that other institutions (particularly those with smaller endowment funds) might be attracted by the impressive results achieved in the past several years for Yale. But they might not have the internal staff or the organizational structure and discipline required to sustain commitments through the good *and* bad markets that will be encountered in the future. He knows sustained commitment is necessary for success with out-of-the-mainstream portfolio structures.

Fortunately, David Swensen was persuaded to go ahead with the book. He has a lot to show us and we all have a lot to learn as he shares many of the lessons taught by his experience.

Consider this: Over and above the investment returns earned by the average endowment, the incremental investment results achieved by David Swensen and his team have added well over $2 billion to Yale's endowment and comfortably more than $100 million this year to Yale's annual budget. How many can aspire to make as much of a real difference to an important institution as does David Swensen in his value-added work for Yale?

Charles D. Ellis

Pioneering Portfolio Management

1
Introduction

This book provides readers with a window on the world of institutional funds management, drawing on my fourteen years of experience in managing Yale's endowment, which totaled $7.2 billion at June 30, 1999. During my tenure the university pioneered the move away from heavy reliance on domestic marketable securities, emphasizing instead a collection of asset classes expected to provide equity-like returns driven by fundamentally different underlying factors. Aside from reducing dependence on the common factor of U.S. corporate profitability, the asset allocation changes ultimately exposed the portfolio to a range of less efficiently priced investment alternatives, creating a rich set of active management opportunities.

In spite of a systematic reduction in exposure to domestic equities during one of the greatest bull markets ever, the Yale endowment produced extraordinary returns. Measured from the bottom of the U.S. market in 1982, Yale's return of 16.9 percent per annum stands in the top 1 percent of institutional funds. Stated differently, had the university generated returns equivalent to the average for institutions of higher education, endowment assets would be $3.3 billion lower as of June 30, 1999. Yale's strong investment results stem from disciplined implementation of equity-oriented asset allocation policies, combined with successful exploitation of attractive active management opportunities.

The World of Endowment Management

The fascinating activity of endowment management captures the energy and imagination of the many talented individuals who have accepted responsibility for stewardship of institutional assets. Investing with a time horizon measured in centuries to support the educational and research mission of society's colleges and universities creates a challenge guaranteed to engage the emotions and intellect of fund fiduciaries.

Aside from the appeal of the eleemosynary purposes that endowments serve, the investment business contains an independent set of attractions. Populated by unusually gifted, extremely driven individuals, the institutional funds management industry provides a nearly limitless supply of products, a few of which actually serve fiduciary aims. Identifying the handful of gems in the tons of quarry rock provides intellectually stimulating employment for the managers of endowment portfolios.

The knowledge base that provides useful support for investment decisions knows no bounds. A rich understanding of human psychology, a reasonable appreciation of financial theory, a deep awareness of history, and a broad exposure to current events all contribute to the development of well-informed portfolio strategies. Many practitioners confess they would continue to work without pay in the endlessly fascinating money management business.

The book begins by painting the big picture: discussing the purposes of endowment accumulation and examining the goals for institutional portfolios. Articulation of an investment philosophy provides the underpinnings for developing an asset allocation strategy—the fundamentally important decision regarding the portion of portfolio assets devoted to each type of investment alternative.

After establishing a framework for portfolio construction, the book investigates the nitty-gritty details of implementing a successful investment program. A discussion of portfolio management issues examines situations where real-world frictions might impede realization of portfolio objectives. Chapters on asset class management provide a primer on investment characteristics and active management opportunities, followed by an outline of performance evaluation issues and tools. The book closes with some thoughts on structuring an effective decision-making process.

The linearity of the book's exposition of the investment process masks some complexities inherent in the portfolio management challenge. For example, asset allocation relies on a combination of top-down assessment of asset class characteristics and bottom-up evaluation of asset class opportunities. Since quantitative projections of returns, risks, and correlations describe only part of the scene, investors supplement the statistical overview with a ground-level understanding of specific investments. Because bottom-up insights into investment opportunity provide information important to assessing asset class attractiveness, effective investors evaluate portfolio alternatives with simultaneous consideration of top-down and bottom-up factors. By beginning with an analysis of the broad questions regarding the asset allocation framework and narrowing the discussion to issues involved with managing specific investment portfolios, the book lays out a neat progression from macro to micro, ignoring the complex simultaneity of the asset management process.

Rigorous Investment Framework

Three themes surface repeatedly in the book. The first theme centers on the importance of taking actions within the context of an analytically rigorous framework, implemented with discipline and undergirded with thorough analysis of specific opportunities. In dealing with the entire range of investment decisions from broad-based asset allocation to issue-specific security selection, investment success requires sticking with positions made uncomfortable by their variance with popular opinion. Casual commitments invite casual reversal, exposing portfolio managers to the damaging whipsaw of buying high and selling low. Only with the confidence created by a strong decision-making process can investors sell speculative excess and buy despair-driven value.

Establishing an analytically rigorous framework requires a ground-up examination of the investment challenge that the institution faces, evaluated in the context of the organization's specific characteristics. All too often investors fail to address an institution's particular investment policy needs, opting instead to adopt portfolio structures similar to those pursued by comparable institutions. In other cases, when evaluating individual investment strategies, investors make commitments based on the identity of the co-investors, not on the merits of the proposed transaction. Playing follow the leader exposes institutional assets to substantial risk.

Disciplined implementation of investment decisions ensures that investors reap the rewards and incur the costs associated with the policies that the institution adopts. Among the many important investment activities that require careful oversight, maintaining policy asset allocation targets stands near the top of the list. Far too many investors spend enormous amounts of time and energy constructing policy portfolios, only to allow the allocations they established to drift with the whims of the market. The process of rebalancing requires a fair degree of activity, buying and selling to bring underweight and overweight allocations to target. Without a disciplined approach to maintaining policy targets, fiduciaries fail to achieve the desired characteristics for the institution's portfolio.

Making decisions based on thorough analysis provides the best foundation for running a strong investment program. The tough competitive nature of the investment management industry stems from the prevalence of zero-sum games, where the amount by which the winners win equals the amount by which the losers lose. Carefully considered decisions provide the only intelligent basis for profitable pursuit of investment activities, ranging from sweeping policy decisions to focused security selection bets.

Agency Issues

A second theme concerns the prevalence of agency issues that interfere with the successful pursuit of institutional goals. Nearly every aspect of funds management suffers from decisions made in the self-interest of the decision makers, not in the best interest of the fund. Culprits range from trustees seeking to make an impact during their term on an investment committee, to portfolio managers pursuing steady fee income at the expense of investment excellence, to corporate managers diverting assets for personal gain. Differences in interest between fund beneficiaries and those responsible for fund assets create potentially costly wedges between what should have been and what actually was.

The wedge between principal goals and agent actions causes problems at the highest governance level, causing some fiduciary decisions to fail to serve the interests of a perpetual life endowment fund. Individuals desire immediate gratification, leading to overemphasis of policies expected to pay off in a relatively short time frame. At the same time, fund fiduciaries hope to retain power by avoiding controversy, pursuing only conventional investment ideas. By operating in the institutional mainstream of short-horizon, uncontroversial opportunities, committee members and staff ensure unspectacular results, while missing potentially rewarding longer-term contrarian plays.

Relationships with external investment managers provide a fertile breeding ground for conflicts of interest. Institutions seek high risk-adjusted returns, while outside investment advisers pursue substantial, stable flows of fee income. Conflicts arise since the most attractive investment opportunities fail to provide returns in a steady, predictable fashion. To create more secure cash flows, investment firms frequently gather excessive amounts of assets, follow benchmark-hugging portfolio strategies, and dilute management efforts across a broad range of product offerings. While fiduciaries attempt to reduce conflicts with investment advisers by crafting appropriate compensation arrangements, interests of fund managers diverge from interests of capital providers even with the most carefully considered deal structures.

Most asset classes contain investment vehicles exhibiting some degree of agency risk, with corporate bonds representing an extreme case. Structural issues render such bonds hopelessly flawed as a portfolio alternative. Shareholder interests, with which company management generally identifies, diverge so dramatically from the goals of bondholders that lenders to companies must expect to end up on the wrong side of nearly every conflict. Yet even in equity holdings where corporate managers share a rough coincidence of interests with outside shareholders, agency issues drive wedges between the two classes of economic actors. In every equity position, public or private, management at least occasionally pursues activities providing purely personal gains, directly damaging the interests of shareholders. To mitigate the problem, investors search for managements focused on advancing stock owner interests, while avoiding companies treated as personal piggy banks by the individuals in charge.

Every aspect of the investment management process contains real and potential conflicts between the interests of institutional funds and the interests of the agents engaged to manage portfolio assets. Awareness of the breadth and seriousness of agency issues constitutes the first line of defense for fund managers. By evaluating each participant involved in investment activities with a skeptical attitude, fiduciaries increase the likelihood of avoiding the most serious conflicts with institutional fund goals.

Active Management Challenges

The third theme relates to the difficulties of managing investment portfolios to beat the market by exploiting asset mispricings. Both market timers and security selectors face intensely competitive environments in which the majority of participants fail. The efficiency of marketable security pricing poses formidable hurdles to investors pursuing active management strategies.

While private markets provide a much greater range of mispriced assets, investors fare little better than their marketable security counterparts as the extraordinary fee burden typical of private equity funds almost guarantees delivery of disappointing risk-adjusted results. Active management strategies, whether in public markets or private, generally fail to meet investor expectations.

In spite of the daunting obstacles to active management success, the overwhelming majority of market participants choose to play the loser's game. Like the residents of Lake Wobegon who all believe their children to be above average, all investors believe their active strategies will produce superior results. The harsh reality of the negative-sum game dictates that in aggregate, active managers lose to the market by the amount it costs to play, in the form of management fees, trading commissions, and dealer spread. Wall Street's share of the pie defines the amount of performance drag experienced by the would-be market beaters.

The staff resources required to create portfolios with a reasonable chance of producing superior asset class returns place yet another obstacle in the path of institutions considering active management strategies. Promising investments come to light only after thorough culling of dozens of mediocre alternatives. Hiring and compensating the personnel needed to identify out-of-the-mainstream opportunities imposes a burden too great for many institutions to accept. The alternative of trying to pursue active strategies on the cheap exposes assets to material danger. Casual attempts to beat the market provide fodder for organizations willing to devote the resources necessary to win.

Even with adequate numbers of high-quality personnel, active management strategies demand uninstitutional behavior from institutions, creating a paradox that few can unravel. Establishing and maintaining an unconventional investment profile requires acceptance of uncomfortably idiosyncratic portfolios, which frequently appear downright imprudent in the eyes of conventional wisdom. Unless institutions maintain contrarian positions through difficult times, the resulting damage imposes severe financial and reputational costs on the institution.

• • •

Although the investment lessons in this book focus on the challenges and rewards of investing educational endowment funds, the ideas described here address issues of value to all participants in financial markets. Whether considering mutual fund investments to finance a child's college education or venture capital commitments to support a corporation's pension plan, chances for investment success increase with an understanding of mistakes to avoid and an appreciation of strategies to emphasize.

Beyond the pragmatic possibility of improving investment skill, students of finance might enjoy the book's exploration of the thought process underlying the management of a large institutional fund. Because fund managers operate in an environment that requires insights into tools ranging from the technical rigors of modern finance to the qualitative judgments of behavioral science, the funds management problem spans an improbably wide range of disciplines, providing material of interest to a broad group of market observers.

2
Endowment
Purposes

Institutions accumulate endowments for a number of purposes. A significant level of endowment support for university operations enhances institutional autonomy, providing an independent source of revenues, which reduces dependence on government grants, student tuition, and alumni donations. Financial stability increases with the level of sustainable endowment distributions, facilitating long-term planning and increasing institutional attractiveness to important constituencies. Finally, since colleges and universities tend to exhibit striking similarity in revenue sources, better-endowed institutions enjoy an incremental income stream, providing the means to create a superior teaching and research environment.

Institutions without permanent financial resources support day-to-day operations with funds from transient sources, limiting the ability of the organization to shape its future. Governmental grants expose colleges and universities to a host of regulations concerning matters far afield from the direct purpose of the activity receiving financial support. Gifts from alumni and friends often contain explicit or implicit requirements, some of which may not be completely congruent with institutional aspirations. In an organization's early years, when any source of income might represent the difference between survival and failure, institutions prove particularly vulnerable to the strings attached to external income flows.

Universities frequently make long-term commitments as part of the regular course of operations. For example, awarding tenure to a faculty member represents a financial obligation that might span decades. Funding such an enduring obligation with temporary sources of funds exposes the institution (and the individual) to the risk of disruption in revenue flows. The permanent nature of endowment funds matches nicely the long-term character of tenure commitments.

Different institutions necessarily understand the mission of endowment funds in differing fashions. In fact, individuals within institutions frequently debate the relative importance of the purposes endowment funds are to satisfy. Often the debate revolves around the permanency of endowed funds, raising the issue of current needs versus future obligations. Should endowment funds be used to remedy deficiencies in an institution's physical plant? Do short-term operating shortfalls justify extraordinary distributions from endowment? Such questions concern the fundamental character of endowment assets.

Many constituencies answer questions regarding purposes of endowment with a decidedly short time horizon. Students generally prefer expanded levels of support today, expecting that higher expenditures would translate into better, less expensive education. Faculty recognize that greater current resources provide the wherewithal to pursue a more comprehensive set of scholarly activities, and administrators see enhanced financial flows as the means to relax the binding constraint of budgetary discipline.

Other interested parties take a longer view. Donors generally embrace a long-term orientation, having decided to provide permanent support through endowment funds instead of opting to contribute temporary funding for current operations. In the final analysis, trustees face a difficult-to-resolve tension between the desire to support the institution's current programs and an obligation to preserve assets for future generations.

Understanding the purposes of accumulating assets represents the first step in the investment process. Permanent funds provide institutions with greater independence, increased financial stability, and the means to create a margin of excellence. Focusing on the fundamental purposes of an endowment provides a firm foundation for developing a sensible investment process.

MAINTAIN INDEPENDENCE

Endowment accumulation facilitates maintenance of institutional autonomy, since reliance on impermanent income sources to support operations exposes institutions to the strings attached by providers of funds. For example, when the government provides grants to support specific research projects, university-wide activities frequently face requirements and regulations, even though the affected operations may be far removed from the grant beneficiary. Similarly, universities relying on donor gifts for current use often find that benefactors demand a significant voice in the institution's activities. Even universities that rely heavily on tuition income from students may be constrained by that dependency, perhaps by responding to current trends and fashions to attract sufficient numbers of students to maintain operations. Particularly in the cases of reliance on development activity and tuition income, greater institutional needs correspond to greater degrees of external influence.

Universities benefit from a certain amount of sensitivity to government policy, donor wishes, and student desires. However, such influences detract from the ability of trustees to define institutional direction. Ultimately, universities must be accountable to their constituencies without being held hostage by them.

Obviously, donors to endowment attach meaningful restrictions to gifts, stipulating that funds provide permanent support for designated purposes. Occasionally requirements conflict with institutional goals, as might be the case when an endowment supports a field of study long since abandoned by scholars. More frequently, endowment gifts provide unrestricted support or fund activities central to organizational aspirations, such as teaching and financial aid. Although donors exercise considerable influence in negotiating the initial terms of an endowment gift, after establishing the fund, donor influence wanes.

Overreliance on short-term sources of income requires institutions to respond to a combination of explicit and implicit pressures. The institution benefiting from a stable stream of endowment income stands a greater chance of maintaining independence from external pressures. Support of the operating budget by endowment fosters greater academic freedom, allowing trustees the flexibility to chart an independent course.

Yale and Connecticut

The survival of the fledging Yale in the early eighteenth century depended on generous legislative and financial support from the Colony of Connecticut. In October 1701 the General Assembly of the Colony of Connecticut approved a proposal put forth by five Connecticut ministers to charter a college: "Wherein Youth may be instructed in the Arts and Sciences who thorough the blessing of Almighty God may be fitted for Publick employment both in Church and Civil State." Support for Yale included grants of land, special grants for construction or repair of college buildings, authorization for lotteries, duties on rum, and the exemption of ministers, ministers' tutors, and students from taxes. Brooks Mather Kelley, in his *Yale—A History,* estimates that "throughout the eighteenth century, Connecticut's contribution amounted to more than one half the total gifts to the college."[1]

The Colony's support came with a price. For instance, in 1755, the General Assembly voted to refuse the annual grant to Yale, ostensibly because of wartime expenditures, but in fact to retaliate for a controversial position taken by Yale president Thomas Clap concerning the religious character of the college. In 1792, in exchange for renewed financial support, the governor, lieutenant governor, and six legislators became fellows of the Yale Corporation. The presence of the state-appointed representatives on the Yale governing board caused frequent discord and conflict, with disagreements ranging from the proper religious faith of the faculty to the General Assembly's rights in reforming abuses in the running of the college.

State-appointed representatives on the Yale Corporation served until the termination of support for Yale in 1871, which resulted in the withdrawal of the state senators from the Yale Corporation.[2] With the replacement of the six legislators by fellows elected by Yale's alumni body, control became more firmly centered in the college. Yale's experience mirrored national trends. With the end of the Civil War and the rise of Darwinism and laissez-faire philosophies, the previous view of the major role of the state in the support of private education had shifted. As historian Frederick Rudolph noted, "A partnership in public service, which had once been essential to the colleges and inherent in the responsibilities of government. . . . [became] insidious or . . . forgotten altogether." Fortunately for Yale, this withdrawal of public support was replaced by organized alumni support.[3]

The appointment of elected officials to the university's governing board in exchange for financial support illustrates in the starkest fashion the loss of control associated with reliance on external sources of funds. Although the nearly eighty years of direct state control over Yale's governance represents an extreme case, more subtle issues of outside influence continue to test the wisdom of trustees. Balancing the legitimate interests of providers of funds in having a voice with the need of private institutions to maintain ultimate control poses a difficult challenge to fiduciaries responsible for managing educational organizations.

Federal Support for Academic Research

The benefits and dangers of reliance on governmental support shaped private educational institutions throughout their history. Many scholars credit the influx in the 1960s of federal dollars for research in higher education with the rise to preeminence of the American research university. The costs of this support to the administrative flexibility of the universities became painfully evident in the 1970s.

In their extensive study of the American research university, Hugh Graham and Nancy Diamond note that federal support for research resulted in "increased congressional involvement, an emphasis on targeted research, and a general trend toward government regulation of the private sector."[4] During the late 1960s and early 1970s federal regulation of universities slowly but steadily embraced issues such as hiring, promotion, and firing of university personnel (including faculty); research; admissions; toxic waste disposal; human and animal subjects of research; access for the disabled; wage and salary administration; pensions and benefits; plant construction and management; record keeping; athletics; fund raising; and, in some cases, curricula.[5]

With this new web of federal regulation came increased costs and bureaucracy for the universities. In a widely quoted claim, Harvard president Derek Bok noted that compliance with federal regulations at Harvard consumed over sixty thousand hours of faculty time and cost almost $8.3 million in the mid-1970s. A 1980 study found that meeting regulatory costs absorbed as much as 7 to 8 percent of total institutional budgets.[6]

More important than the out-of-pocket costs of compliance with government regulations, the reduction in administrative flexibility posed a significant threat to institutional governance. In his *Report of the President for 1974–1975,* Yale president Kingman Brewster stated, "The experience of recent years gives fair warning that reliance upon government support for *any* university activity may subject the entire university to conditions and requirements which can undermine the capacity of faculty and trustees to chart the institution's destiny."

When well-endowed institutions accept external financial support, compliance with the accompanying requirements influences university policies on the margin, generally posing no significant threat to the integrity of the institution. The greater the independent flow of financial resources from endowment assets, the greater the ability of an institution either to avoid external funds with onerous requirements or to negotiate changes mitigating undesirable regulations. In cases where organizations lack substantial independent means, external funds providers carry the potential to reshape the institution, threatening to alter the fundamental character of the college or university.

University of Bridgeport

In the early 1990s, severe financial distress caused the University of Bridgeport to lose its independence after a desperate fight to survive. From a peak of more than nine thousand students in the 1970s to fewer than four thousand in 1991, declining enrollment created budgetary trauma, forcing the school to consider radical measures. In spite of the institution's dire straits, in October 1991, the University of Bridgeport rejected an offer of $50 million from the Professors World Peace Academy, an arm of the Reverend Sun Myung Moon's Unification Church. Preferring to pursue independent policies, the institution's trustees elected to take the drastic step of eliminating nearly one-third of its ninety degree programs, while petitioning a judge to dip into restricted endowment funds to meet payroll costs.

After running out of options in April 1992, the trustees of the university reversed course, ceding control to the Professors World Peace Academy in exchange for an infusion of more than $50 million over five years. As board members associated with the Unification Church took control, the sixty-five-year-old institution received a new mission: to serve as "the foundation of a worldwide network of universities striving for international harmony and understanding."[7]

Three years later, the Reverend Sun Myung Moon received an honorary degree from the University of Bridgeport, which recognized him as a "religious leader and a man of true spiritual power."[8] During Reverend Moon's appearance on campus, he took credit for the fall of communism and promised to resolve conflicts in the Middle East and Korea. Claiming that "the entire world did everything it could to put an end to me," the Reverend Moon said, "Today I am firmly standing on top of the world."[9] According to the *New York Times,* the speech provided further evidence to critics that the "once sturdy university" had sold its independence for an infusion of capital from "a religious cult with a messianic and proselytizing mission."

The University of Bridgeport's demise resulted from a number of factors, yet a more substantial endowment might have allowed the institution to maintain its independence. The lack of a stable financial foundation exposed the university to wrenching change, causing varying degrees of distress among important institutional constituencies.

External support for colleges and universities frequently comes with collateral requirements designed to influence institutional behavior. In extreme cases, governments and donors seek to change the fundamental character of an organization. The greater the extent to which endowment funds provide current support for operations, the greater the ability of an institution to pursue its own course.

PROVIDE STABILITY

Endowments contribute to operational stability by providing reliable flows of resources to operating budgets. Nonpermanent funding sources may diminish or disappear, as government policies change, donor satisfaction diminishes, or student interest wanes. By reducing variability in university revenues, endowments serve to promote long-term planning while strengthening the viability of the institution from an operating perspective.

Yale and Josiah Willard Gibbs

Yale's history is riddled with instances of budgetary problems due to fluctuating current income. On numerous occasions, the university operated at a deficit, forcing faculty to forgo full salaries. In an extreme example, the "greatest scholar Yale has ever produced or harbored," Josiah Willard Gibbs, renowned for his seminal research and experiments in physics and engineering, received an appointment as professor of mathematical physics without salary in 1871, indicating "not any lack of esteem for Gibbs, but rather the poverty of Yale." In 1880, officials at Johns Hopkins University attempted to woo Gibbs with an offer of a $3,000 salary. Professor James Dwight Dana, a well-known geologist and mineralogist, convinced Yale president Noah Porter to provide Gibbs a salary of $2,000 with a promised increase as soon as funds were available. In a letter to Gibbs, Dana implored the brilliant professor to stay loyal to Yale: "I do not wonder that Johns Hopkins wants your name and services, or that you feel inclined to consider favorable their proposition, for nothing has been done toward endowing your professorship, and there are not here the means or signs of progress which tend to incite courage in professors and multiply earnest students. But I hope nevertheless that you will stand by us, and that something will speedily be done by way of endowment to show you that your services are really valued. . . . Johns Hopkins can get on vastly better without you than we can. We can not."[10]

Gibbs eventually received Yale's prestigious Berkeley fellowship for postgraduate scholarship, endowed in 1731 by George Berkeley with the gift of a ninety-six-acre farm in Newport, Rhode Island. Funded by income from the farm, the fellowship supported some of Yale's most illustrious graduates, including Eleazer Wheelock, the first president of Dartmouth College, and Eugene Schuyler, the first American to hold the Ph.D.

Today, from an individual scholar's perspective, endowed chairs serve largely to confer honor on particularly distinguished faculty members; in Gibbs's era receiving support from the endowment conferred not only prestige but also greater financial stability. The ability of an institution to promise ongoing financial support created an important competitive edge in recruiting and retaining faculty.

Stanford University

Endowment distributions occasionally provide more than year-to-year stability in funding operations. Well-endowed institutions have the wherewithal to weather episodes of severe economic stress, while those with meager resources face substantial financial trauma more directly.

In 1991, Stanford lost significant amounts of financial support from the federal government in a controversy over cost recoveries that the university claimed in connection with federally sponsored research activity. Stanford allegedly overbilled the government, seeking reimbursement for headline-grabbing charges associated with the seventy-two-foot yacht *Victoria,* a nineteenth-century Italian fruitwood commode, and a Lake Tahoe retreat for university trustees.[11] Primarily as a result of the "continued impact of the disputes with the federal government," the university posted a 1992 operating deficit in excess of $32.5 million, representing nearly 3 percent of revenues.

Facing projected deficits aggregating $125 million over three years, Stanford sought to "finance the expected losses while expense reduction programs were implemented." A critical component of the "financing" plan involved increasing the endowment payout rate from 4.75 percent to 6.75 percent for 1993 and 1994, releasing a projected incremental $58 million to support operations during Stanford's period of adjustment.

The combination of increased endowment spending, budgetary reductions, and borrowing placed the university on firm financial footing. In 1995, basking in the glow of a substantial operating surplus, Stanford lowered the payout rate to 5.25 percent, nearly returning to the "customary rate of 4.75 percent."[12] The extraordinary increase in the endowment spending rate provided a cushion for Stanford's operations, allowing the university to deal with a sudden, significant loss of funds with minimal disruption.

Although Stanford benefited from temporary increases in payout rates, the use of permanent funds to finance temporary operating shortfalls carried substantial costs. In the five years following Stanford's extraordinary payout rate increase, strong investment returns led to more than a doubling in asset values. Certainly, with twenty-twenty hindsight, the university would have benefited by using much lower-cost external borrowing to fund the budget deficits, leaving the payout rate at its "customary" level of 4.75 percent. Considering the longer-term impact of withdrawal of permanent funds only reinforces concerns regarding the ultimate cost of unusually high rates of spending from endowment.

• • •

Reliable distributions from endowment create an important measure of stability for educational institutions. Under normal circumstances, greater levels of endowment serve to improve the quality of an organization's revenue stream, allowing heavier reliance on internally generated income. When faced with extraordinary financial stress, endowment assets provide a cushion, perhaps by paying out unusually large distributions, giving the institution an opportunity to address the disruptive fiscal issues. Alternatively, the financial strength represented by a sizable endowment creates borrowing capacity, allowing an institution to address temporary shortfalls with short-term financing. Stability emanating from a substantial endowment creates a superior everyday budgetary environment, while enhancing an institution's ability to deal with unusual financial trauma.

CREATE A MARGIN OF EXCELLENCE

Endowments provide the means for an institution to establish a superior educational environment, affording the opportunity to create a margin of excellence. On the margin, endowment income attracts better scholars, provides superior facilities, and funds pioneering research. Although more money does not necessarily translate directly into educational excellence, incremental funds provide the means for the faculty, administration, and trustees to develop an unusually strong educational institution.

Endowments and Institutional Quality

Endowment size correlates strongly with institutional quality. A survey of major private research universities, categorized as Research Universities I: Private Institutions by the Carnegie Foundation for the Advancement of Teaching, shows that larger, better-endowed organizations score more highly in the *U.S. News and World Report* rankings of educational institutions.[13] The Carnegie Foundation attempts to classify colleges and universities according to their missions, clustering institutions with similar programs and purposes.

Public universities fall outside the study group because budgetary issues for state-supported institutions differ significantly from those of private universities. For example, government appropriations play a much greater role for public institutions than for private. If public authorities wish to support institutions at a particular level, changes in levels of endowment income might be offset by altering levels of state support for the university. Strong endowment distributions may correspond to weak state subventions, while poor levels of endowment support may elicit higher levels of state contributions. Public institutions face investment and spending problems that differ fundamentally from the endowment concerns of private universities.

Major private research universities have strikingly similar tuition streams. In 1996, among the top twenty research universities in the survey, undergraduate tuition ranged from $18,800 to $23,100, an extremely tight band. Among the top five institutions, tuition charges fell in an even narrower band, from $21,300 to $23,100. Price discrimination, at least with respect to posted tuition levels, does not exist among leading universities.

The Carnegie universities operate substantial enterprises, with 1997 revenues ranging from $286 million to nearly $2.2 billion, averaging $985 million. To put the revenue numbers in a corporate context, twelve of twenty-eight institutions run budgets sufficiently large to rank among the Fortune 1000 companies.[14]

Grants and contracts provide the largest single source of income to research universities, accounting for more than 30 percent of revenues. Student income supplies 21 percent of cash flow, investment income 10 percent, and contributions 6 percent. The catch-all remainder, totaling 33 percent, includes auxiliary services income, hospital operations, and clinical services.

Measurement issues complicate the assessment of the relationship between endowment size and institutional quality. While quantification of financial assets poses little problem, reducing the characteristics of a complex, multifaceted institution to a single number proves next to impossible. Nonetheless, a cottage industry of pundits, led by *U.S. News and World Report,* produces widely followed annual ratings of colleges and universities.

In part because of the impossibility of making precise distinctions where none exist, the ratings engender controversy. In its evaluation, *U.S. News and World Report* assesses academic reputation, student retention, faculty resources, admissions selectivity, financial wherewithal, graduation rates, and alumni giving support.[15] Combining measures such as SAT scores, class size, and graduation rates, the publication fashions a ranking scheme of colleges and universities. While the precise order causes much debate, the general conclusions make intuitive sense.

Dividing the Carnegie universities into quartiles according to their academic ranking allows examination of the relationship between investment income and institutional quality. Focusing on quartiles deemphasizes the rank order of institutions and reduces the impact of the inevitable errors made when attempting to make apples-to-apples comparisons of individual institutional financial and quality data. Table 2.1 lists (alphabetically) the institutions falling into each particular group.

Quality ranking and endowment size exhibit a strong correlation, with top-quartile institutions benefiting from endowments averaging $4.5 billion, in contrast to the bottom-quartile average of $690 million. Moving from one quartile to the next, a clear step pattern emerges in endowment size.

Examining levels of endowment per student tells the same story. Top-quartile universities enjoy more than $300,000 in endowment assets for each full-time-equivalent student. After dramatic declines to approximately $130,000 for the second quartile and just over $100,000 for the third quartile, bottom-quartile institutions average only $54,000 per student. Endowment size correlates clearly and strongly with institutional quality.

The degree to which investment income supports research institu-

Table 2.1 Endowment Size Correlates Strongly with Institutional Quality

Carnegie Foundation Research Universities, Private Institutions (I)

Institution		Average Size of Endowment	Endowment per Student	Average Age of Institution
Top Three	Harvard University Princeton University Yale University	$7.20 billion	$502,000	304 years
First Quartile	California Institute of Technology Duke University Harvard University Massachusetts Institute of Technology Princeton University Stanford University Yale University	4.46 billion	305,000	226 years
Second Quartile	Brown University University of Chicago Columbia University Cornell University Johns Hopkins University Northwestern University University of Pennsylvania	1.95 billion	130,000	164 years
Third Quartile	Carnegie Mellon University Emory University Georgetown University University of Rochester Tufts University Vanderbilt Washington University	1.54 billion	102,000	140 years
Fourth Quartile	Boston University Case Western Howard University New York University University of Southern California University of Miami Yeshiva University	690 million	54,000	133 years
Average		2.36 billion	219,603	167 years

Sources: Financial data from individual institution annual reports as of June 30, 1997, with the exceptions of Stanford, Emory, Northwestern, and New York University as of August 31, 1997; California Institute of Technology as of September 30, 1997; and University of Miami as of May 31, 1997. Quartile distinctions reflect an average of five years of rankings by U.S. News and World Report.

tions' budgets varies dramatically. As shown in Table 2.2, top-quartile universities enjoy average support of nearly 17 percent of revenues. In contrast, bottom-quartile institutions receive less than one-third the relative support, with investments contributing approximately 4 percent of income.

Since higher-quality institutions tend to be larger, greater relative levels of investment income support translate into dramatically greater numbers of dollars. Top-quartile institutions support operations with an average draw of $187 million, while lower-quartile universities receive only $33 million.

Student charges provide the complement to investment income. As institutional quality increases, budgetary dependence on student charges decreases. Top-quartile institutions rely on student income for 15 percent of revenues, while bottom-quartile universities obtain 31 percent of revenues from such charges, a spread of 16 percent. Interestingly, that spread nearly matches the 13 percent gap between investment income support for top- and bottom-quartile universities. One possible explanation for this relationship would be that universities use investment income to reduce costs for students, with wealthier institutions providing greater amounts of financial aid than their less well-endowed counterparts. In fact, per capita student income exhibits a remarkably consistent pattern across the quartiles, ranging from $14,600 for the top quartile to $13,400 for the bottom quartile. The superior explanation corresponds to the conclusion that better-endowed universities use their financial strength to create a richer educational environment.

Other major revenue categories show no particular pattern. Contributions provide reasonably consistent levels of current support, varying from 4 to 6 percent of revenues. Grants and contracts exhibit no definable trend, as proportions of revenue range from 19 to 36 percent.

Although endowment size clearly correlates with institutional quality, the direction of causality remains unclear. Did higher-quality institutions attract higher levels of endowment support, creating a self-reinforcing virtuous cycle? Or did larger endowments provide the resources required to build superior institutions, facilitating the creation of a margin of excellence? Regardless of the direction of causation, greater financial resources provide institutions the ability to acquire better faculties and better facilities, creating the potential for a superior educational environment.

Table 2.2 Endowment Income Provides More Support for Higher-Quality Institutions

Carnegie Foundation Research Universities, Private Institutions (I)

Institution	Average Total Revenues	Student Income	Grants/ Contracts	Contributions	Investment Income	All Other
Top Three	Harvard University Princeton University Yale University	$1.02 billion	18%	27%	6%	25%	25%
First Quartile	California Institute of Technology Duke University Harvard University Massachusetts Institute of Technology Princeton University Stanford University Yale University	1.11 billion	15	36	6	17	27
Second Quartile	Brown University University of Chicago Columbia University Cornell University Johns Hopkins University Northwestern University University of Pennsylvania	1.26 billion	17	29	6	7	41

Third Quartile	Carnegie Mellon University Emory University Georgetown University University of Rochester Tufts University Vanderbilt Washington University	793 million	17	19	6	7	52
Fourth Quartile	Boston University Case Western Howard University New York University University of Southern California University of Miami Yeshiva University	774 million	31	27	4	4	33
Average		985 million	19	29	5	10	39

Sources: Financial data from individual institution annual reports as of June 30, 1997; with the exceptions of Stanford, Emory, Northwestern, and New York University as of August 31, 1997; California Institute of Technology as of September 30, 1997; and University of Miami as of May 31, 1997. Quartile distinctions reflect an average of five years of rankings by U.S. News and World Report.

CONCLUSION

Endowments serve a number of important purposes for educational institutions: allowing greater independence, providing operational stability, and facilitating educational excellence. Institutions of higher education best serve society as independent forums for free and open inquiry, promoting unfettered pursuit of ideas regardless of convention or controversy. The strings attached to sources of outside financial support contain the potential to create institutional sensitivities, limiting healthy debate and impairing the ability of scholars to meet society's needs.

For established institutions, endowment support enhances operating independence and stability on the margin. Sizable reserves of permanent funds allow trustees to be less tolerant of government interference or unreasonable donor requirements. Large endowments enable administrators to smooth the impact of financial shocks, buffering operations against disruptive external forces.

For less established institutions, endowments sometimes determine the difference between survival and failure. In the decade ending 1996, more than four hundred colleges and universities failed or merged, representing approximately 11 percent of the total number of institutions of higher education in the United States.[16] Strikingly, of the institutions that disappeared, only nine boasted endowments sufficiently large to participate in a prominent annual survey of endowed institutions.[17] Even a modest endowment makes a significant difference.

Particularly for larger institutions, providing the means to produce a margin of excellence constitutes a critical function of an endowment. Because of an underlying similarity in college and university operating revenue sources, better-endowed institutions enjoy an incremental source of funds, available for deployment to create a superior educational environment. By contributing to the excellence of superior colleges and universities, endowments play an important role in the world of higher education.

Understanding the purposes driving endowment accumulation represents an important first step in structuring an investment portfolio. By defining the reasons that endowments exist, fiduciaries lay the groundwork for articulation of specific investment goals, shaping in a fundamental manner the ultimate spending policy and asset allocation process.

3
Investment
and Spending Goals

Endowment managers pursue the goals of preserving purchasing power of assets and providing substantial flows of resources to the operating budget. If fiduciaries produce spending and investment policies that deal successfully with the tension between the goals, the institution benefits from a sustainable contribution from endowment assets to support academic programs. The combination of asset preservation and budgetary support, if achieved, can satisfy in perpetuity the purposes of endowment accumulation: maintaining independence, providing stability, and creating a margin of excellence.

Benjamin Franklin suggested that death and taxes represent life's only certainties. Managers of endowment assets suspend those certainties: most educational institutions aspire to exist in perpetuity, and most endowment assets enjoy exemptions from taxes. The perpetual nature of colleges and universities makes endowment management one of the investment world's most fascinating endeavors. Balancing the tension between preserving long-run asset purchasing power and providing substantial current operating support provides a rich set of challenges, posing problems unique to institutions of higher education.

Purchasing-power preservation represents a long-term goal, spanning generations. Successfully managed endowments retain forever the ability to provide a particular level of institutional support, justifying the classification of endowment funds as permanent assets. Pursuit of long-term asset preservation requires seeking high returns, accepting the accompanying fundamental risk and associated market volatility.

Stable operating support constitutes an intermediate-term goal, reflecting a shorter-term budgetary planning cycle. Since academic programs contract only with great difficulty, institutions rely on receiving reasonably predictable flows of funds from endowment to support operations. Supplying stable distributions to finance current operations requires dampening portfolio volatility, suggesting lower levels of fundamental risk with the accompanying reduced levels of expected returns.

The high-risk, high-return investment policy best suited to serve asset preservation conflicts with the low-risk, low-return investment approach more likely to produce stable distributions to the operating budget. By specifying the trade-off between the desire for purchasing-power preservation and the hope for stability of flows to fund operations, spending policies determine the degree to which endowments meet the needs of current and future generations.

INVESTMENT GOALS

Yale professor emeritus James Tobin captures the essence of the investment problem facing fiduciaries:

> The trustees of an endowed institution are the guardians of the future against the claims of the present. Their task is to preserve equity among generations. The trustees of an endowed university like my own assume the institution to be immortal. They want to know, therefore, the rate of consumption from endowment which can be sustained indefinitely. . . . In formal terms, the trustees are supposed to have a zero subjective rate of time preference.
>
> Consuming endowment income so defined means in principle that the existing endowment can continue to support the same set of activities that it is now supporting. This rule says that the current consumption should not benefit from the prospects of future gifts to endowment. Sustained consumption rises to encompass and enlarge the scope of activities when, but not before, capital gifts enlarge the endowment.[1]

Tobin's concept of intergenerational equity comports with the goals of purchasing power preservation and stable operating budget support. By preserving endowment assets adjusted for inflation, the institution retains the ability to "support the same set of activities that it is now supporting." In supplying a stable flow of resources, the endowment provides continuity of support, avoiding disruptive interruptions in distributions to academic programs.

Gifts and Endowment

When making an endowment gift, donors expect to provide permanent support for the institution. If financial managers maintain only the nominal value of gifts, inflation ultimately reduces the impact of the fund to insignificance. Yale's oldest surviving endowment fund dedicated to the support of teaching, the Timothy Dwight Professorship Fund, established in 1822, entered the university's books at a historical cost basis slightly in excess of $27,000. Because price levels rose more than twenty-one-fold in the intervening 177 years, a 1998 distribution from an endowment of $27,000 pales in comparison to an 1822 distribution from the same size fund. While during the Dwight Professorship's existence, the fund grew more than seven times to nearly $200,000, the current value falls short of the inflation-adjusted target by nearly two-thirds. Although the university continues to benefit from the endowment in the late twentieth century, after accounting for inflation the fund fails to provide the same level of support available to the early nineteenth-century Yale. While fiduciary principles generally specify only that the institution preserve the nominal value of a gift,* to provide true permanent support institutions must maintain the inflation-adjusted value of a gift.

Explicitly stating that new gifts "enlarge the scope of activities," Tobin recognizes a principle important to endowment benefactors. Some institutions factor gifts into spending considerations, targeting a consumption level equal to the portfolio's expected real return *plus*

---

*Section 2 of the Uniform Management of Institutional Funds Act (UMIFA), which has been adopted in forty-six states and the District of Columbia as of October 15, 1999, reinforces this obligation by requiring that an institution maintain the historic dollar value of an endowment gift. Some states have strengthened this law to include preservation of purchasing power.

new gifts. Harvard University, in fashioning its spending policy, assumes that "university expense growth would exceed [the long-term inflation] rate by two points."[2] Yet the institution's targeted reinvestment rate offsets only the general level of inflation, not the higher university expense growth. Obviously, supporting the "same set of activities" requires keeping pace with university expense growth, not general inflation, rendering the reinvestment rate inadequate to its purpose. To maintain endowment purchasing power, Harvard articulates a goal of accumulating sufficient new capital gifts to offset the difference between the general inflation rate and university expense growth. In so doing, the university explicitly employs new gifts to replenish inflationary losses.[3]

A policy of using new gifts to offset part of the inflationary impact on asset values fails to "enlarge the scope of activities" supported by endowment. If a fund devoted to supporting a chair in the economics department loses purchasing power, why should a benefactor establishing a chair in the law school replenish the loss? From a bottom-up basis, each individual endowment fund deserves to retain purchasing power of assets through time.

Trade-off Between Today and Tomorrow

Fund managers charged only with preserving portfolio purchasing power face a straightforward task, particularly when measured over a reasonably long time horizon. By investing in a portfolio of risky assets with returns expected to correlate with price level changes, investors create portfolios likely to beat inflation in the long run. Such a single-minded focus on asset preservation fails to meet institutional needs because simply accumulating a portfolio of assets with stable purchasing power provides little, if any, benefit to the academic enterprise.

Endowment assets benefit educational institutions by generating substantial reliable distributions to support operations. Providing generous predictable spending flows poses little problem for fund managers operating with an intermediate time horizon. By holding assets that promise low levels of volatility, managers create a stable portfolio allowing budget planners to forecast payouts with reasonable certainty. Unfortunately, low-risk investment portfolios deliver returns insufficient to preserve purchasing power. Exclusive pursuit of stable support for current operations favors today's generation of scholars over tomorrow's beneficiaries.

A clear, direct trade-off exists between preserving assets and supporting operations. To the extent that managers focus on maintaining purchasing power of endowment assets, great volatility affects the flow of resources delivered to the operating budget. To the extent that managers emphasize providing a sizable and stable flow of resources to the operating budget, substantial volatility influences the purchasing power of endowment assets.

Consider two extreme policies used to determine the annual spending from an endowment. On one hand, spending each year only the real returns generated by the portfolio places maintenance of asset purchasing power at center stage. Assume that a particular year produces investment returns of 10 percent and inflation of 4 percent. Distributing 6 percent of assets to the operating units provides substantial support to operations, while reinvesting 4 percent in the endowment offsets inflation and maintains purchasing power. The following year, in an environment with 2 percent investment returns and 7 percent inflation, the institution faces a serious problem. Compensation for inflation requires a 7 percent reinvestment in the endowment, but the fund generated a return of only 2 percent. The endowment manager cannot go to the operating units and ask for 5 percent rebates to maintain the purchasing power of the portfolio. At best, the institution can declare no distribution, hoping to generate positive real returns in following years to replenish lost purchasing power and provide operational support. From an operating budget perspective, a policy that places year-by-year maintenance of asset purchasing power above all else proves unacceptable.

The other policy extreme, pursuing a goal of providing completely stable flows of resources to the operating budget, requires spending a fixed amount increased each year by the amount of inflation. In the short term, the policy provides perfectly predictable distributions from the endowment to the operating budget. Although under normal market conditions such a policy might not harm the endowment, when faced with a hostile financial environment, serious damage results. In a period of high inflation accompanied by bear markets for stocks and bonds, spending at a level independent of the value of assets creates the potential to damage the endowment fund permanently.

Spending policies specify the trade-off between protecting endowment assets for tomorrow's scholars and providing endowment support for today's beneficiaries, allowing fiduciaries to determine the relative importance of the two fundamental goals. Cleverly crafted rules for determining annual endowment distributions reduce the tension between the objectives of spending stability and asset preservation, increasing the likelihood of meeting the needs of both current and future generations.

SPENDING POLICY

Spending policies resolve the tension between the competing goals of preservation of endowment and stability in budgetary support. Sensible policies cause current-year spending to relate to both prior-year endowment distributions and contemporaneous endowment values, with the former factor reducing fluctuation in operating budget flows by providing a core on which planners can rely and the latter factor protecting purchasing power by introducing sensitivity to market influences.

Yale's Spending Policy

Created by economists James Tobin, William Brainard, Richard Cooper, and William Nordhaus, Yale's policy relates current-year spending to both the current endowment market value and the previous level of spending from endowment. Under Yale's rule, spending for a given year equals 70 percent of spending in the previous year, adjusted for inflation, plus 30 percent of the long-term spending rate applied to the endowment's current market level. Since previous levels of spending depend on previous endowment market values, current spending can be expressed in terms of endowment levels going back through time. The resulting lagged adjustment process averages past endowment levels with exponentially decreasing weights.

Figure 3.1 shows weights applied to endowment values of previous years (ignoring the inflation adjustment). Multiplying the weights by the endowment values for the respective years and summing the results determines spending for the current year. Note that years further in the past have less influence on the calculation than more recent years. In contrast, a simple four-year average would apply equal 25 percent weights to each of the four most recent years.

By reducing the impact on the operating budget of inevitable fluctuations in endowment value caused by investing in risky assets, spending rules that employ an averaging process insulate the academic enterprise from unacceptably high year-to-year swings in support. Because sensible spending policies dampen the consequences of portfolio volatility, portfolio managers gain the freedom to accept greater investment risk with the expectation of achieving higher return without exposing the institution to unreasonably large probabilities of significant budgetary shortfalls.

By doing a particularly effective job of smoothing contributions to the operating budget, Yale's elegant spending rule contributes an important measure of flexibility to the university's investment policy. Instead of a simple averaging process that unceremoniously drops the oldest number in favor of the new, Yale's exponentially declining weights gradually squeeze out the influence of a particular year's endowment value. The superior smoothing characteristics reduce the transmission of investment volatility to the operating budget, allowing pursuit of portfolio strategies promising higher expected returns.

**Figure 3.1 Yale's Spending Policy Insulates
Budget from Market Fluctuations**

Influence of Past Endowment Levels in Determining Current Spending

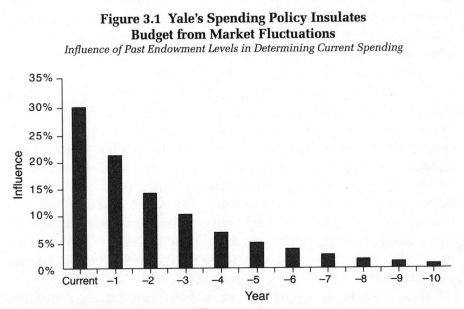

Source: Yale University Investments Office.

Other Spending Policies

In the past, most institutions followed a practice of distributing for current expenditure only income generated in the form of interest, dividends, and rents. Yale, which in 1965 began spending "a prudent portion of the appreciation in market value," noted two reasons for changing policy:

> First, it is only by coincidence that Yield will be a correct balance between the present and the future. . . . Second, when Yield is the sole measure of what can be spent for present needs, a situation of annually increasing needs, such as has obtained for many years and seems likely to continue for many more, forces investment policy to seek to improve current Yield. But this, in turn, under market conditions prevailing most of the time since World War II, could only be done at the loss of some potential Gain.[4]

Concerns about invading principal no doubt underlie the policies of institutions that base spending on the income generated by a portfolio. As Yale recognized, the distinction between current income and capital appreciation proves too easily manipulated to provide a sound foundation for spending policy. Consider, for example, the spending implications of discount, par and premium bonds with comparable levels of sensitivity to changes in interest rates.

Although the bonds in Table 3.1 exhibit remarkably similar investment attributes, spending implications differ dramatically for an institution pursuing a policy of consuming all current income. The zero coupon bond provides no current cash flow, the par bond generates a 6 percent yield, and the premium bond pays out a well-above-market rate of 12 percent. Naturally, holding low coupon bonds leads to lower current spending and higher future portfolio value, while the opposite consequences stem from owning high coupon bonds. Fortunately, income-based spending rules determine spending for far fewer institutions today than in the late 1980s, when nearly one in five educational institutions followed a policy of spending portfolio yield.[5]

Today, nearly seven of ten educational institutions determine spending by applying a prespecified percentage to a moving average of endowment values. Including past endowment values provides stabil-

**Table 3.1 Otherwise Similar Bonds Generate
Dramatically Different Cash Flows**

Coupon, Duration, Price, and Yield for Three Different Types of Bonds

	Coupon	Duration[a]	Price	Yield
Zero coupon	0%	10 years	55.4	6%
Par	6	10 years	100.0	6
Premium	12	10 years	166.5	6

[a]*The maturity of the zero coupon bond is 10 years, the par bond 15 years, and the premium bond 18 1/2 years.*

ity, because those past values in part determined the previous year's spending. Incorporating the current endowment value ensures that spending will be sensitive to market conditions, avoiding the potential for damage caused by spending at levels unrelated to endowment value.

Some institutions spend a prespecified percentage of beginning endowment market value, thereby transmitting portfolio volatility directly to the operating budget. At the opposite end of the spectrum are those colleges and universities that spend a prespecified percentage of the previous year's spending, potentially threatening endowment purchasing-power preservation.

A number of institutions decide each year on an appropriate rate, or have no established rule. This superficially appealing practice fails to instill the financial discipline provided by a rigorous spending rule. In the absence of a well-defined spending policy, budgetary balance becomes subject to manipulation. Spend enough to bridge the gap between revenues and expenses to establish a balanced budget. Spend less to create a deficit. Spend more to fashion a surplus. Balance, distress, and prosperity rest in the hands of the spending committee. Fiscal discipline disappears.

Target Spending Rate

Specification of the target rate of spending lies at the core of determining the degree of intergenerational equity. Spending at levels inconsistent with investment returns either diminishes or enhances future endowment levels. Too much current spending causes future endowment levels to fall; too little current spending benefits future students at the expense of today's scholars. Selecting a distribution rate appropriate to the endowment portfolio increases the likelihood of achieving a successful balance between demands of today and responsibilities to tomorrow.

Target spending rates among endowed institutions range from a surprisingly low 1.25 percent to an unsustainably high 10.0 percent. More than 90 percent of institutions employ target rates between 4.0 percent and 6.0 percent, with nearly half using a 5.0 percent rate.[6] The appropriate rate of spending depends on the risk and return characteristics of the investment portfolio, the structure of the spending policy, and the preferences expressed by trustees regarding the trade-off between stable budgetary support and asset preservation.

Analysis of investment and spending policies leads to the conclusion that distribution rates for educational institutions generally exceed the return-producing capacity of endowment assets. According to a series of simulations, the average endowment faces a nearly 20 percent probability of a disruptive intermediate-term decline in operating budget support. More troubling may be the more than 50 percent long-run likelihood of losing one-half of endowment purchasing power.* High probabilities of intermediate-term spending volatility and long-term purchasing power trauma indicate an inconsistency between expected portfolio returns and projected spending rates. Institutions faced with likely failure to meet the central goals of endowment accumulation need to consider reducing spending levels or increasing expected portfolio returns.

Endowment spending policies balance the competing objectives of providing substantial stable budgetary flows to benefit today's scholars and preserving portfolio assets to support tomorrow's academicians. Responsible fiduciaries face the challenging task of evaluating the ability of investment and spending policies to meet the long-term goal of purchasing power preservation and the intermediate-term goal of stable operating budget support. Employing the tools of portfolio construction and spending rules, trustees ultimately select policies

---

*The simulations assume returns consistent with the average endowment asset allocation as reported in the 1998 NACUBO Endowment Study, employing a spending rate of 5 percent applied to a five-year moving average of endowment values. The intermediate-term spending decline consists of a 25 percent real decline over five years. The time horizon for evaluating purchasing power preservation is fifty years. (NACUBO stands for National Association of College and University Business Officers.)

based on preferences regarding the trade-off between the central goals of endowment accumulation.

PURCHASING POWER EVALUATION

Preserving purchasing power requires that each gift to endowment forever maintain its ability to "support a specific set of activities." In aggregate, then, after deducting spending distributions, endowment assets must grow by the rate of educational inflation and increase by the amount of new gifts.

Appropriate measurement of inflation allows assessment of the continuing ability to consume a basket of goods and services peculiar to higher education. Since budgets of colleges and universities differ dramatically from those of individuals and from the economy as a whole, inflation measures appropriate to individuals (the Consumer Price Index) or the broad economy (the GNP deflator) work less well for higher education.

The Higher Education Price Index (HEPI) measures costs specific to educational institutions. Heavily weighted toward salaries and other personnel costs, over a thirty-six-year period educational costs advanced at a rate approximately 1 percent per annum in excess of the GNP deflator. Lack of productivity gains in education accounts for the greater inflation in academic costs. Because good teaching requires intensive interaction between teacher and student, "efficiency" cannot be improved without impairing the product. For example, applying technology by using video terminals to replace in-person lectures diminishes the educational experience. Similarly, increasing class sizes improves productivity in a superficial sense, but undoubtedly reduces quality at the same time. As long as productivity gains disproportionately benefit the rest of the economy, costs for higher education can be expected to grow at a rate higher than the general level of inflation.

Yale's Endowment Purchasing Power

Figure 3.2 illustrates the Yale endowment's purchasing power from 1950 to 1998. The analysis begins in 1950 because the university lacks clean data on gifts, spending, and investment performance prior to that date. Throughout much of the twentieth century, financial statements recorded only book values of financial assets, providing little information for students of markets. Unit accounting, which enables institutions to distinguish between various inflows and outflows, gained wide acceptance in the early 1970s, causing earlier data to be disentangled only with great difficulty.

Purchasing power analysis starts with the 1950 endowment value and subsequent inflation rates. Increasing the 1950 portfolio value by the amount of inflation in each year creates a purchasing power target for the beginning portfolio of assets. Since gifts "enlarge the scope of activities" supported by endowment, each year the purchasing power target increases by the amount of new gifts, thereafter appropriately adjusted for inflation.

Note the importance of new gifts to the endowment, with roughly two-thirds of 1998's targeted value stemming from gifts made since 1950. In other words, in the absence of new gifts over the past forty-

**Figure 3.2 Endowment Values Fluctuate Around
Purchasing Power Target**

Yale University Endowment Growth versus Inflation, 1950–1998

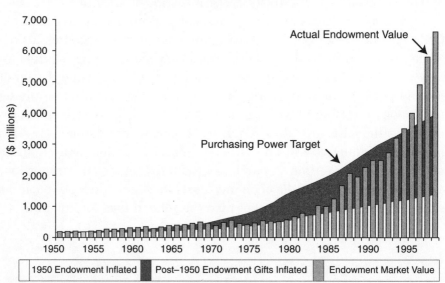

Sources: Yale Financial Statements. Higher Education Price Index data from Research Associates of Washington.

eight years, Yale's endowment would likely total only about one-third of today's value.

A comparison of actual endowment values with targeted levels illustrates the degree of success in meeting purchasing power goals. Based on the June 30, 1998 market value of $6.6 billion relative to the purchasing power goal of $4.1 billion, Yale appears to have succeeded admirably in increasing asset values.* Yet the bottom-line success includes periods in which the overall picture appeared far less rosy.

The 1950s witnessed a rough balance between endowment growth and purchasing power preservation, with a surplus of approximately 17 percent shown by 1959. After keeping pace through most of the 1960s, the endowment began to suffer as inflationary pressures grew, setting the stage for serious problems. During the 1970s, disastrous markets for financial assets and high inflation caused the endowment to end the decade 56 percent below its target level. By 1982, Yale's endowment reached a low point, with assets representing only 42 percent of the targeted purchasing power goal. Fortunately, the 1980s bull market reversed the problems of the 1970s, ultimately allowing the 1994 endowment to achieve the targeted level of the 1950 endowment inflated and adjusted for gifts. Extraordinary market returns subsequently boosted the June 30, 1998, endowment to a 60 percent surplus over the target.

Recent dramatic increases in endowment purchasing power cause some to question whether by accumulating assets, Yale's fiduciaries favor future generations of scholars at the expense of the current generation. While the question of the appropriate spending level generates constant debate, the current increase in assets results from a combination of strong markets and reasonable spending rules, creating a cushion that will be drawn down in tough times to come.

Dramatic swings in purchasing power relative to targeted levels come as little surprise to veteran market observers. In 1982, Yale's endowment registered a nearly 60 percent deficit versus the desired level. Sixteen years later, in a nicely symmetric move, the portfolio

---

*In fact, a significant portion of Yale's increase in purchasing power appears to result from value added in the investment process. Over the last two decades, the longest period for which reliable data are available, Yale's portfolio increased by approximately $3.5 billion relative to the average result achieved by colleges and universities.

shows a 60 percent surplus. Although market swings cause institutions to feel alternately poor and rich, sensible portfolio managers base investment and spending decisions on assumptions regarding long-term capital market characteristics. Evaluating purchasing power preservation requires appreciation of the positive and negative consequences of market volatility, considered within the perspective of a distinctly long time frame.

Changing Spending Rates

Human nature reacts to unexpectedly handsome investment returns by looking for ways to consume new-found wealth. Responding to strong markets by increasing spending rates creates the potential for long-term damage to endowment. First, increases in the rate of spending following extraordinary investment returns puts the institution at risk of consuming part of the cushion designed to protect against a less robust future. Second, increases in spending soon become part of an institution's permanent expense base, reducing operational flexibility. If the rate of spending rises in a boom, an institution facing a bust loses the benefit of a cushion and gains the burden of a greater budgetary base.

Target spending rates lie at the core of fiscal discipline, leading responsible fiduciaries to alter rates with great reluctance. Rather than seeing strong recent performance as an encouragement to increase payouts, skeptical managers wonder about the sustainability of past good fortune and prepare for the possibility of a less rewarding future. Only fundamental improvement in an institution's investment and spending policies, not recent prosperity, justifies altering target spending rates.

Evaluating maintenance of purchasing power requires an extremely long time horizon. Reacting to a decade of disastrous losses by reducing payout formulas or responding to a decade of extraordinary returns by increasing distribution rates contains the potential to harm the academic enterprise. Bear market-induced cuts in programs and bull market-driven expansions of offerings needlessly buffet the institution, causing the endowment to fail in its mission of buffering university operations from financial market volatility. Responsible fiduciaries look past the inevitable short-run swings in endowment value caused by market gyrations, keeping attention firmly focused on the long-run preservation of asset purchasing power.

SPENDING SUSTAINABILITY EVALUATION

Providing a substantial, sustainable flow of resources to support the academic enterprise represents a critical goal for stewards of endowment assets. To "support the same set of activities" throughout time, distributions must grow by at least the rate of inflation in the goods and services consumed by endowed institutions. When new gifts "enlarge the scope of activities," distributions from endowment must increase to support and sustain the new activities.

In contrast to the long-term nature of the purchasing power preservation goal, providing a sustainable flow of support to the operating budget constitutes an intermediate-term objective. Since large fluctuations in endowment flows wreak havoc with a budgetary process that thrives on stability, endowment managers strive to deliver reasonably predictable distributions to support operations.

Yale's Endowment Distributions

A spending sustainability analysis, portrayed in Figure 3.3, mirrors the purchasing power evaluation illustrated earlier. Beginning with 1950 spending from endowment as a base, the targeted spending levels increase each year by inflation and by the amount of spending allocated from new gifts. For purposes of analysis, 4.5 percent represents the assumed spending rate on new gifts, a level consistent with Yale's long-run spending pattern.

Over the nearly half-century covered in the spending analysis, Yale managed to increase or maintain nominal spending year-in and year-out. Unfortunately, after two decades of keeping pace with the inflation-adjusted target, the university's actual spending leveled off and fell short of ever increasing targets, unable to keep up with the virulent inflation of the 1970s. Beginning in the mid-1980s, spending flows grew rapidly, posting sizable real gains and closing the gap between actual distributions and inflation-adjusted goals. In spite of extraordinary growth in the 1980s and 1990s, not until 1996 did Yale's spending from endowment exceed the inflation-adjusted target.

The two-year lag between the endowment's recapture of the 1950 gift-adjusted purchasing power level in 1994, and the spending flow's achievement of the same goal in 1996, stems largely from the dampen-

Figure 3.3 Spending Flows Fail to Provide
Consistent Support for Operations
Yale University Spending Growth versus Inflation, 1950–1998

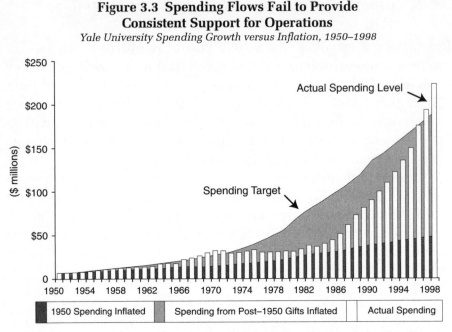

Sources: *Yale University Financial Statements. Higher Education Price Index data from Research Associates of Washington.*

ing effect of the spending policy's smoothing mechanism. As spending rose rapidly from the mid-1980s throughout the 1990s, the averaging process implicit in the spending rule kept endowment distributions from adjusting fully to the endowment's price appreciation.

More evidence of the impact of the smoothing mechanism lies in the spending level for 1998. Although applying the target spending rate of 5 percent to the endowment's $6.6 billion value results in a projected distribution of $330 million, the actual spending level for 1998 amounts to only $220 million. As time passes, the spending rule causes actual payouts to move toward the targeted level, implying that if Yale maintains a $6.6 billion endowment, spending will reach $330 million within a few years.

While current beneficiaries of endowment distributions sometimes complain about the lag between endowment growth and spending increases, the smoothing mechanism performs a necessary function in muting the transmission of volatility in endowment values to spending flows. Yale's policies appear to dampen volatility effectively, since the dispersion of year-over-year percentage changes in endowment value (12.3 percent standard deviation) exceeds by a fair margin the dispersion of changes in spending level (6.9 percent standard deviation). Effective spending rules allow assumption of greater investment risk without transmitting the associated volatility to budgetary distributions.

At times, even the most effective set of policies provides little protection in turbulent markets. The greatest failure in providing stable budgetary support occurred in the 1970s. Operating in an environment where the rate of inflation exceeded returns on every domestic asset class, endowment managers faced a grim set of choices.

In spite of beginning the decade with actual spending comfortably ahead of the adjusted 1950 target level, actual spending by 1980 amounted to less than one-half the inflation-adjusted goal. In the face of hostile financial market conditions from 1970 to 1980, the university managed only to maintain the nominal payout, which proved woefully inadequate in the face of the decade's inflation. Although nominal spending flows began to rise after 1980, the target level rose faster, causing actual spending at 1984's nadir to represent only 44 percent of the goal.

Viewed from the perspective of individual, but not independent, five-year periods, Yale experienced real spending declines of more than 25 percent six times in a succession of miserable years from 1971 to 1981. Such significant drops represent a failure to provide a stable flow of resources from endowment to support operations.

The ultimate test of the effectiveness of endowment investment and spending policies lies in providing stable, substantial, sustainable flows of resources to support operations. Although at times financial market conditions preclude reasonable satisfaction of endowment objectives, investors who fashion a sensible package of asset management and distribution policies increase the likelihood of achieving reasonable balance between the competing goals of protecting endowment assets from inflation-induced erosion and providing high, reliable levels of current budgetary support.

FOUNDATION INVESTMENT GOALS

A number of characteristics separate academic institutions from other not-for-profit investors. Endowment managers control both the disposition of assets, by determining the portfolio allocation, and the specification of liabilities, by defining the spending policy. The lack of constraints on investment and spending strategies provides great flexibility for fiduciaries, increasing the likelihood of meeting institutional goals.

While academic institutions benefit enormously from high levels of distributions from permanent funds, in the event of a serious disruption in endowment support, other revenue sources necessarily play a greater role in the budgetary base. Endowment distributions generally support only a modest portion of educational institution operating budgets, with major research universities relying on endowment payout to fund approximately 10 percent of expenditures.[7] For most such institutions, a significant decrease in spending from endowment poses difficult problems but fails to threaten institutional viability.

Colleges and universities also benefit from the generosity of alumni and friends, with gifts to endowment providing an important source of permanent support for academic programs. In difficult times, inflows from donors contain the potential to dampen shortfalls in endowment support for operations.

On the surface, foundations seem to share many characteristics with educational endowments. Along with their counterparts at colleges and universities, trustees of foundation assets often ignore Ben Franklin's certainties of life, enjoying favorable tax status and operating with a perpetual horizon. For many foundations, however, permanency constitutes a choice, not an obligation. If a foundation pursues a mission with a particular sense of urgency—for example, funding research to cure a terribly virulent disease—the trustees may decide to expend all available resources in an attempt to reach the goal with deliberate speed. Even without a time-sensitive mission, spending at rates designed to extinguish foundation assets constitutes a legitimate option for trustees.

Foundations generally exercise complete control over asset allocation policies, similar to the flexibility educational institutions enjoy. On the spending side, however, foundations must achieve a minimum payout of 5 percent of assets to support charitable purposes, or face tax penalties. The mandated distribution level causes foundations to face an investment problem materially different from the challenge facing educational endowment managers.

Foundations rely almost exclusively on investment income to support operations. The ten largest grant-making foundations receive essentially 100 percent of total revenues from investment portfolios, with only occasional relatively small infusions from other sources. Although grant programs grow and shrink somewhat more readily than do academic operations, foundations require reasonably stable flows of funds to avoid disruption in supporting programs, particularly when activities involve multiyear commitments. The great reliance of foundations on distributions from investment assets requires structuring portfolios with lower-risk profiles.

Finally, foundations generally receive few new gifts to support operations. In fact, many large foundations follow policies of refusing to accept gifts. While the impact of annual giving on endowment assets sometimes seems nearly inconsequential, gifts to endowment play a startlingly significant role when measured over reasonable stretches of time.

The Impact of Gifts

Examining the experience of Harvard, Yale, and the Carnegie Institution over the course of the twentieth century provides insight into the importance of donor support. The Carnegie Institution of Washington, one of Andrew Carnegie's many philanthropies, pursues pure, cutting-edge scientific research in astronomy, plant biology, embryology, and earth sciences. Establishing the institution in 1902 with a $10 million gift, Carnegie increased the endowment by $2 million in 1907 and $10 million in 1911. Carnegie's $22 million endowment nearly equaled Harvard's 1910 fund balance of $23 million and vastly exceeded Yale's $12 million.

Over the course of the past nine decades, the Carnegie Institution endowment more than kept pace with inflation, with June 30, 1998, assets of $420 million, comfortably ahead of the $360 million needed to match the rise in price levels. But the formerly comparable Harvard endowment, now at $12.8 billion, and the previously smaller Yale endowment, currently at $6.6 billion, dwarf the Carnegie fund. While differences in investment and spending policies no doubt explain some of the gap, absence of continuing gift inflows constitutes the fundamental reason for Carnegie's failure to keep pace with Yale and Harvard. The existence of a substantial source of external financial support constitutes a significant difference between the endowment funds supporting universities and foundations.

In desiring to supply a stable flow of operating income, hoping to exist forever, and wishing to comply with minimum IRS distribution requirements, foundation fiduciaries face a fundamentally conflicting set of goals. Without the ability to tap other revenues sources, institutions feel the impact of poor investment results unattenuated by a safety net of external sources of support. Short-term stability in distributions argues for a less volatile portfolio, while long-run maintenance of purchasing power and high payout rates point toward a higher risk allocation. In general, foundations appear to opt for lower-risk portfolios, sensibly providing stable flows of resources to support the institutional mission. As a result, the foundation community may be spending at rates inconsistent with preservation of capital, suggesting that in the long run, the role of most foundations will diminish as purchasing power erodes.

In spite of superficial similarities, endowments and foundations differ in important ways, including the amount of control over spending streams, the degree of programmatic reliance on portfolio distributions, and the availability of continuing external support in the form of gifts. While endowments and foundations share some important investment characteristics, dissimilarities between the two types of funds lead to articulation of meaningfully different purposes and goals. That investment objectives of such closely related organizations differ so significantly highlights the importance of careful consideration of the relationship between investment funds and institutional objectives. The basic framework of understanding the raison d'être of a fund and expressing its aspirations serves as an important starting point in the funds management process.

THE SKEPTICAL VIEWPOINT

In a healthy academic community, few significant issues exist without controversy. In the case of endowments, debate generally centers around intergenerational issues, with current beneficiaries usually suggesting that endowment payout levels provide insufficient support for university operations.

Henry Hansmann, holder of the Sam Harris Endowed Chair in the Yale Law School, goes beyond the issue of distribution rates, questioning the advisability of any endowment accumulation. In an August 2, 1998, *New York Times* interview, Hansmann suggests that "a stranger from Mars who looks at private universities would probably say they are institutions whose business is to run large pools of investment assets and that they run educational institutions on the side that can expand and contract to act as buffers for investment pools."[8] Hansmann suggests that trustees pursue a "real objective" of accumulating a large and growing endowment, viewing the educational operations as a constraint to unfettered financial asset accumulation. Administrators and faculty seek endowments to provide job security, a light workload, and a pleasant physical environment, while alumni focus on reputational capital, hoping to bask in the reflected glory of a wealthy educational institution.

In a working paper entitled "Why Do Universities Have Endowments?" Hansmann characterizes the 1960s as "boom years for higher education," while he notes in the early 1970s "hard times hit" as "private demand declined, government supply abruptly stopped its upward trajectory, and energy costs skyrocketed."[9] Recognizing that "universities found themselves squeezed between costs that were continuing to rise and income sources that were shrinking," Hansmann observes "little affirmative evidence that universities in fact viewed their endowments as buffers for operating budgets."[10]

Yale's Endowment Buffer

Hansmann need not look far for evidence. His employer, Yale University, used endowment spending policy to dampen growth in the boom times of the 1960s and cushion the financial trauma of the 1970s. During the 1960s, Yale released an average of 4.4 percent of the endowment to support the academic enterprise. Strong budgetary results and superior investment performance accompanied endowment distributions that provided support at levels consistent with long-term sustainable rates.

In contrast, during the 1970s, spending from endowment averaged 6.3 percent as Yale sought to offset, at least in part, the impact of hostile economic forces. In spite of following a policy that released support for the operating budget at unsustainable rates, Yale posted deficits in every year of the decade. The policy of "leaning against the wind" cost the endowment dearly; the purchasing power of assets declined by more than 60 percent between 1968 and 1982, in spite of the infusion of substantial amounts of new gifts.

The historical record indicates that Yale uses endowment assets to shield the operating budget from disruptive fluctuations in income streams. Sustainable spending rates in the range of 3.8 percent to 4.4 percent in the 1950s, 1960s, 1980s, and 1990s correspond to reasonably stable operating environments. In contrast, the deficit-plagued 1970s saw spending peak at an unsustainably high rate of 7.4 percent in 1971. Without extraordinary endowment support in the 1970s, Yale's operational troubles would have been magnified, perhaps causing long-term damage to the institution.

Not only does historical experience suggest that Yale employed endowment assets to insulate academic programs from economic stress, but the very nature of the university's spending policy places budgetary stability in a prominent place. Each year Yale spends 70 percent of last year's spending increased by inflation plus 30 percent of the current year's target spending level. By placing a substantial emphasis on budgetary stability, the university expresses a strong preference for using the endowment to reduce the impact of financial shocks.

Spending Policy Extremes

Examining Yale's spending decisions in the context of policy extremes favoring spending stability and endowment preservation, respectively, highlights the university's substantial bias toward providing reliable support for operations. If universities treated academic operations as a sideshow to endowment accumulation, spending distributions would correspond to levels consistent with maintenance of asset purchasing power. In the extreme case, institutions would distribute only returns in excess of inflation, placing preservation of investment assets above even a modicum of stability in supporting academic programs. At the other end of the spectrum, if universities focus exclusively on consistent payouts from endowment, spending would rise with inflation, tracing a pattern independent of fluctuations in the market value of endowment assets.

Figure 3.4 illustrates the spending patterns resulting from two extreme spending policies. The first panel shows the constancy of maintaining inflation-adjusted real spending, while the second depicts the volatility implicit in a policy of targeting endowment stability. Note that an exclusive focus on endowment purchasing power stability fails to allow any distribution to support operations in more than one-half of the simulated periods.

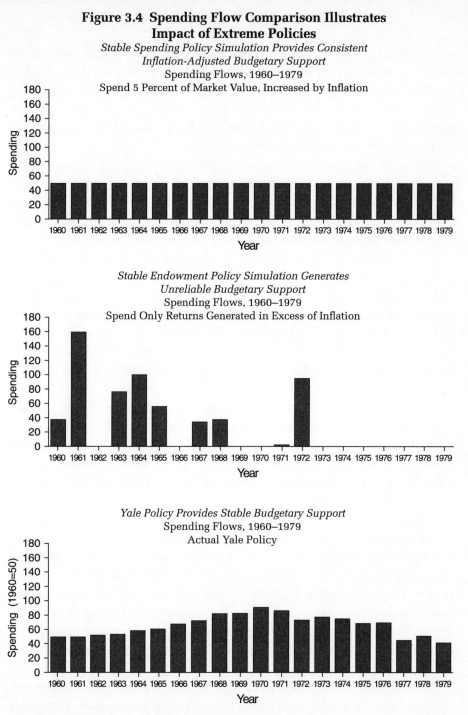

**Figure 3.4 Spending Flow Comparison Illustrates
Impact of Extreme Policies**

*Stable Spending Policy Simulation Provides Consistent
Inflation-Adjusted Budgetary Support*
Spending Flows, 1960–1979
Spend 5 Percent of Market Value, Increased by Inflation

*Stable Endowment Policy Simulation Generates
Unreliable Budgetary Support*
Spending Flows, 1960–1979
Spend Only Returns Generated in Excess of Inflation

Yale Policy Provides Stable Budgetary Support
Spending Flows, 1960–1979
Actual Yale Policy

Note: Data are adjusted for inflation. Hypothetical portfolio has starting value of $1000 and is readjusted to an asset allocation of 60 percent stocks and 40 percent bonds yearly. Actual Yale experience includes impact of new gifts while simulations do not.

Figure 3.5 shows the impact of the extreme spending policies on endowment levels. In pursuing stable spending flows, as illustrated in the first panel, enormous volatility in real endowment values enters the picture. In contrast, focusing on preserving endowment purchasing power promotes stability in asset values, as depicted by the relatively smooth pattern in the second panel.

Policies designed to provide a constant level of inflation-adjusted support for operations, illustrated in the top panels of Figures 3.4 and 3.5, depend on benign financial environments to operate successfully. Consider the dramatically different results from simulations conducted using financial data from the 1960s and the 1970s.

The 1960s provided substantial rewards to investors. Stocks returned 7.8 percent per annum and bonds 3.5 percent annually in an environment where inflation grew by only 2.5 percent per year. Investors pursuing stable spending policies did little damage to endowments, causing a purchasing power decline of only around 10 percent.

Economic and financial conditions in the 1970s posed grave threats to endowed institutions, as high inflation and poor marketable securities returns exacted a terrible toll on investment portfolios. Inflation, consuming 7.4 percent annually, exceeded returns on domestic stocks at 5.9 percent per annum, bonds at 7.0 percent, and cash at 6.3 percent. Investors found no place to hide. Simulations show that in 1970, if a traditional portfolio followed a stable spending policy, more than 60 percent of the purchasing power of a fund would be lost by the end of the decade.

Policies focused solely on endowment preservation, shown in the middle panels of Figures 3.4 and 3.5, fail to release any distribution to the operating budget in twelve of twenty years between 1960 and 1979, highlighting the impracticality of a single-minded focus on asset protection. Even in the hospitable environment of the 1960s, investment results provided no support for current operations in three of ten years. So hostile were the 1970s that even with only one meaningful distribution to the budget, stable endowment policies failed to preserve assets, as purchasing power declined by nearly 24 percent.

Yale's policies, as reflected in spending flows and endowment levels depicted in the bottom panel of the two figures, track the stable spending policy much more closely than the stable endowment policy. Similar to other endowed institutions, in the 1970s Yale experienced an extraordinary decline in endowment purchasing power as the instit-

Figure 3.5 Endowment Level Comparison Illustrates Impact of Extreme Policies

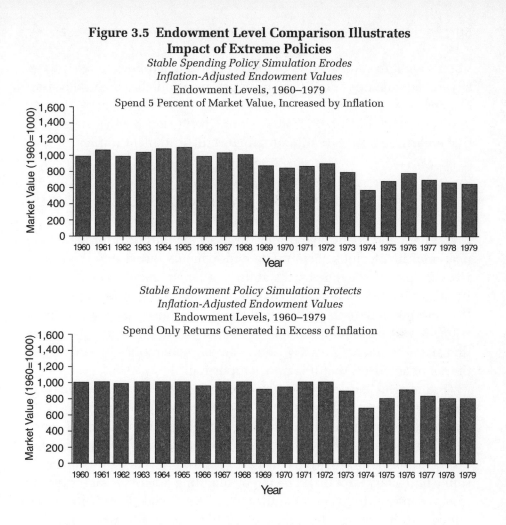

Stable Spending Policy Simulation Erodes
Inflation-Adjusted Endowment Values
Endowment Levels, 1960–1979
Spend 5 Percent of Market Value, Increased by Inflation

Stable Endowment Policy Simulation Protects
Inflation-Adjusted Endowment Values
Endowment Levels, 1960–1979
Spend Only Returns Generated in Excess of Inflation

Yale Policy Favors Budgetary Flows at the Expense of Endowment Preservation
Endowment Levels, 1960–1979
Actual Yale Experience

Notes: Data are adjusted for inflation. Hypothetical portfolio has starting value of $1,000 and is readjusted to an asset allocation of 60 percent stocks and 40 percent bonds yearly. Actual Yale experience is indexed to 1000 in 1960 to facilitate comparison with the simulations, but includes the impact of new gifts while simulations do not.

ution sought to supply flows of funds critical to supporting the university's academic mission. By spending at unsustainably high rates, purchasing power of assets declined dramatically, dropping more than 40 percent during the 1970s. Yale's actions belie Hansmann's suggestion that endowment preservation dominates institutional thinking.

CONCLUSION

Investment and spending policies support the purposes for which educational institutions accumulate endowments, providing the framework for producing increased stability, independence, and excellence. By achieving the long-term goal of purchasing power preservation and the intermediate-term goal of substantial stable budgetary support, colleges and universities meet economist James Tobin's requirement that an endowment "preserve equity among generations by supporting the set of activities that it is now supporting."[11]

Fiduciaries face a challenge in balancing the conflicting goals of preserving assets and supporting current operations. Spending policies resolve the tension by specifying the relative importance of sensitivity to current endowment market values (contributing to asset preservation) and sensitivity to past spending levels (contributing to stable budgetary support). The target spending rate plays an important role in determining a fund's ability to meet the objective of intergenerational equity, with rates that are too high favoring current scholars and rates that are too low favoring tomorrow's.

Donors to endowment expect to provide permanent support to a designated activity, requiring endowment managers to maintain each specific fund's ability to purchase the associated goods and services throughout time. Rates of inflation that educational institutions face exceed general price-level increases, since productivity gains generally fail to benefit the human resource-dependent academic enterprise, increasing the difficulties inherent in maintaining endowment purchasing power. New gifts do not relax the pressure to maintain asset values, as contributions to endowment expand the set of activities funded by an institution's permanent funds, enlarging the size of the portfolio to be preserved.

The process of articulating purposes and defining goals benefits fund managers of all stripes, allowing each investor to express institution-specific traits. Even in the case of institutions as similar as endowments and foundations, differences in institutional character cause purposes to vary leading to the expression of investment goals that accommodate the particular institution's specific opportunities and constraints.

By providing the ultimate test of the desirability of various investment and spending policies, investment goals supply an essential foundation for the funds management process. Investment objectives influence the philosophical tenets that underlie the creation of investment portfolios, generating important guidance for fund managers. In the final analysis, investors evaluate combinations of portfolio asset allocations and spending policies in terms of the ability to meet institutional goals, placing articulation of objectives at the heart of the investment process.

4
Investment
Philosophy

Successful investors operate with a coherent investment philosophy that they apply consistently to all aspects of the portfolio management process. Philosophical principles represent time-tested insights into investment matters that rise to the level of enduring professional convictions. The central tenets of an investor's approach to markets emanate from fundamental beliefs regarding the most effective way to generate investment returns to satisfy institutional goals.

Investment returns stem from decisions regarding three tools of portfolio management: asset allocation, market timing, and security selection, with investor behavior determining the relative importance of each.* Careful investors consciously construct portfolios to reflect the expected contribution of each portfolio management tool.

Asset allocation, the starting point for portfolio construction, involves defining the asset classes that constitute the portfolio and determining the proportion of the fund to be invested in each class. Typical institutional asset classes include domestic equities, foreign equities, fixed income, real estate, and private equities. The policy portfolio describes the target allocation to each of the asset classes employed by the fund.

Market timing consists of short-run deviation from the long-term policy targets. For example, assume that a fund's long-term targets are 50 percent stocks and 50 percent bonds. A fund manager who believes stocks are temporarily cheap and bonds expensive might weight the portfolio 60 percent to stocks and 40 percent to bonds on a tactical basis. The return resulting from the overweighting of stocks and underweighting of bonds constitutes the return attributable to market timing. *(continued)*

The Role of Asset Allocation

Many investors believe that natural law dictates that policy allocation decisions dominate portfolio returns, relegating market timing and security selection actions to secondary status. In an oft-cited 1991 study, "Determinants of Portfolio Performance," Gary Brinson, Brian Singer, and Gil Beebower conclude that more than 90 percent of variability of institutional portfolio performance stems from asset allocation policy with less than 10 percent of return variation explained by market timing and security selection. Moreover, the overwhelming positive contribution to returns results from policy asset allocation. Market timing and security selection make marginal, often negative, contributions to returns.[1]

Investors often treat asset allocation's central role in determining portfolio returns as a truism. It is not. The Brinson, Singer, and Beebower study describes investor behavior, not finance theory. Imagine a buy-and-hold portfolio consisting of one (particularly idiosyncratic) stock; portfolio returns follow largely from security selection. Or consider the strategy of aggressively day-trading bond futures; market timing dominates returns.

Obviously institutional portfolios usually consist of more than one stock and rarely engage in day-trading strategies. Instead, investors hold broadly diversified portfolios and avoid market timing, causing portfolio asset allocation targets to be the most important determinant of investment results. Given the difficulties in timing markets and selecting portfolios of securities that will outperform, such behavior provides a rational foundation for investment management. By avoiding extreme portfolio shifts and holding diversified portfolios, investor behavior causes asset allocation to account for the largest share of portfolio returns.

(continued)
Security selection derives from active management of the portfolio. If a manager creates portfolios that faithfully replicate the markets (i.e., passive portfolios), that manager makes no active bets. To the extent that a portfolio differs from the composition of the overall market, active management accounts for a portion of investment results. For example, security selection return for the U.S. equity asset class of a specific portfolio would be the difference between returns from the U.S. equity portfolio's securities and returns from the overall domestic equity market, as defined by a benchmark index of U.S. equities such as the S&P 500 or Wilshire 5000.

Recognizing that decisions regarding the relative importance of as-set allocation, market timing, and security selection lie within an in-vestor's purview serves as an important starting point for policymakers. Instead of passively accepting the overwhelming importance of asset al-location, knowledgeable investors treat each source of return as a signif-icant independent factor in generating portfolio returns. In articulating a philosophy regarding the respective roles of asset allocation, market timing, and security selection, investors determine the fundamental character of an investment portfolio.

By choosing to place asset allocation at the center of the investment process, investors define a decision-making framework grounded in the relative stability of long-term policy actions. Focus on asset alloca-tion relegates market timing and security selection decisions to the background, reducing the degree to which investment results depend on mercurial, unreliable factors. For sensible investors, defining an in-stitution's policy portfolio constitutes the central activity of invest-ment management. As such, the core tenets of investment philosophy permeate asset allocation discussions, allowing investors to express firmly held beliefs in concrete terms.

Selecting the asset classes for a portfolio constitutes a critically important set of decisions, contributing a large measure to a portfolio's success or failure. Identifying appropriate asset classes requires focus on functional characteristics, considering potential to deliver returns and mitigate portfolio risk. Commitment to an equity bias enhances return-generating potential, while pursuit of diversification reduces portfolio risk exposure. Thoughtful, deliberate focus on asset alloca-tion dominates the agenda of long-term investors, providing a frame-work for all other portfolio activity.

The principles of equity ownership and diversification underlie asset allocation deliberations of serious long-term investors. Both his-torical experience and finance theory point to the conclusion that owning equities provides higher returns than owning bonds. Investors seeking to provide high levels of sustainable operating support natu-rally gravitate toward substantial allocations to equity assets. At the same time, risks associated with concentrating portfolios in a single asset type give investors pause, causing prudent market participants to diversify portfolio exposures. Maintaining an equity bias and fol-lowing diversification principles provide the foundation for building strong investment portfolios.

The Role of Market Timing

Market timing, according to Charles Ellis, represents a losing strategy: "There is no evidence of any large institutions having anything like consistent ability to get in when the market is low and get out when the market is high. Attempts to switch between stocks and bonds, or between stocks and cash, in anticipation of market moves have been unsuccessful much more often than they have been successful."[2]

Market timing causes portfolio characteristics to deviate from those embodied in the policy portfolio, producing inevitable differences in risk and return attributes. If market timing involves betting against the stock market by reducing equity holdings and increasing cash positions, long-run expected portfolio returns decline as the market timer's position decreases risk levels. Because such activity lowers anticipated returns, market timers must succeed substantially more than 50 percent of the time to post a winning record. The wind in the speculator's face, combined with transactions costs and market impact, provides a high hurdle for those who would beat the market by holding excessive cash positions.

Market timers increasing the risk profile of a portfolio by over-weighting a risky asset at the expense of lower-risk positions face a different challenge. Fiduciaries must consider the advisability of moving risk beyond policy portfolio levels. If riskier portfolios produce expected results consistent with institutional goals, portfolio managers ought to consider adopting a higher-risk policy portfolio. If the market timer's enhanced risk gives fiduciaries pause, then prudence demands rejecting even temporary moves to increase risk. Serious investors avoid timing markets.

The Role of Security Selection

In efficient markets, active portfolio management, like market timing, tends to detract from aggregate investment performance. In the context of relative performance, security selection constitutes a zero-sum game. Since IBM represents a finite, measurable proportion of the market value of the U.S. equity market, investors can hold an overweight position in IBM only when other investors hold a corresponding underweight position. The active manager who overweights IBM creates market impact and incurs transaction costs in establishing the position; on the other side of the trade are other active managers underweighting IBM, incurring those same transactions costs and creating market impact. Only one of those positions can be right when measured by IBM's subsequent performance. The amount by which the winners win equals the amount by which the losers lose. Since active managers pay a high price to play, in the aggregate active investors will lose by the amount it costs to play the game in the form of transactions costs, fees, and market impact.

In less efficient markets, active management produces potentially sizable rewards. In fact, passive replication of benchmark returns proves impossible in private markets, such as venture capital, leveraged buyouts, and oil and gas. Even were the "market" return obtainable, investors may well prefer to pursue more selective approaches. For many recent periods, purchasing the "market" result in private equity would have produced mediocre returns relative to less risky marketable security alternatives.

An inverse relationship exists between efficiency in asset pricing and appropriate degree of active management. Passive management strategies suit highly efficient markets, such as U.S. Treasury bonds, where market returns drive results and active management adds less than nothing to returns. Active management strategies fit inefficient markets, such as private equity, where market returns contribute very little to ultimate results and investment selection provides the fundamental source of return.

Active managers willing to accept illiquidity achieve a significant edge in seeking high risk-adjusted returns. Because market players routinely overpay for liquidity, serious investors benefit by avoiding overpriced liquid securities and locating bargains in less widely followed, less liquid market segments.

Pursuit of value-oriented strategies enhances opportunities to achieve security selection success. Value can be purchased, by identifying assets trading below fair value, or created, by bringing unusual skills to improve corporate operations. Value investors operate with a margin of safety unavailable to less conservative investors.

The degree of active management opportunity in various asset classes provides important input into the portfolio management process. Emphasizing inefficiently priced asset classes with interesting active management opportunities increases the odds of investment success. Intelligent acceptance of illiquidity and a value orientation provide a sensible, conservative foundation for portfolio management.

•   •   •

In structuring portfolios, investors make choices, either explicitly or implicitly, regarding the respective roles and impact of asset allocation, market timing, and security selection decisions. A strong portfolio management framework rests on asset allocation decisions, incorporating a bias toward equity assets with an appropriate level of diversification. Since market timing actions generally prove unrewarding and always cause portfolios to deviate from desired characteristics, serious investors avoid meaningful deviations from asset allocation targets. Security selection decisions, while extremely difficult, contain the potential to add value to portfolio returns. Investors increase the likelihood of success by pursuing excess returns where the degree of opportunity appears largest, accepting reasonable degrees of illiquidity, and maintaining a value orientation.

ASSET ALLOCATION

Thoughtful fiduciaries place asset allocation at the heart of the investment process, emphasizing policy portfolio decisions over market timing and security selection activities. Satisfaction of long-term institutional goals depends in large part on the underpinnings of successful asset allocation: equity bias to provide high returns, and diversification to produce an acceptable level of risk.

Equity Bias

Successful investors approach markets with a strong equity bias, since accepting the risk of owning equities rewards long-term investors with higher returns. High returns contribute mightily to meeting the goals of purchasing power preservation and provision of sustainable operating budget support. In fact, the tension between the conflicting goals of preserving assets and spending for operations can be relaxed only by increasing investment returns.

Table 4.1 Equities Generate Superior Returns in the Long Run
Wealth Multiples for U.S. Asset Classes and Inflation,
December 1925–December 1998

Asset Class	Multiple
Inflation	9 times
Treasury bills	15 times
Treasury bonds	44 times
Corporate bonds	61 times
Large-capitalization stocks	2,351 times
Small-capitalization stocks	5,117 times

Source: Ibbotson Associates, Stocks, Bonds, Bills and Inflation, 1999 Year Book *(Chicago: Ibbotson Associates, 1999).*

Finance theory indicates that acceptance of greater risk leads to the reward of higher expected returns. In a happy coincidence, historical data, collected by Roger Ibbotson and Rex Sinquefield, support the theoretical conclusion. Consider the wealth multiples for investments in various U.S asset classes and inflation outlined in Table 4.1.

The U.S. Experience

The data indicate that a dollar invested in treasury bills at the end of 1925, with all income reinvested, would have grown fifteen times by December 31, 1998. At first glance, having multiplied the original investment by a factor of fifteen appears satisfactory. However, given that 60 percent of the increase would have been lost to inflation, the result is not particularly impressive. The low return of treasury bills should not come as a surprise. On at least two measures, treasury bills have been close to risk free. Investors face virtually no credit exposure because the U.S. government represents perhaps the most creditworthy entity in the world. In addition, treasury bills have provided a hedge against inflation, with returns that closely track price increases. The price of these attractive characteristics has been an extremely low real return. Thus, at least with twenty-twenty hindsight, treasury bills would not have been an appropriate investment for an institution investing to earn substantial after-inflation returns.

Moving further out the risk spectrum, the same dollar invested in longer-term government bonds at the end of 1925 would have multiplied forty-four times by the end of 1998. Government bonds share with treasury bills extremely high credit quality. Unlike shorter-term instruments, however, bonds have a highly uncertain real return. Twenty-year bonds, which are used in the Ibbotson-Sinquefield analysis, face two decades of inflation rates, unknown and unknowable at the time of purchase. Not only do real returns vary greatly, nominal returns also fluctuate over holding periods of less than the term to maturity. The higher risks of longer-term bonds have been rewarded with higher returns, although such returns still do not provide meaningful support for an institution that consumes only after-inflation returns.

Corporate bonds provide an alternative to investment in government securities. Over the seventy-three-year period, corporate bonds provided a wealth multiplier of 61, exceeding the multiple of 44 for default-free government bonds. The incremental return reflects compensation for credit risk and call risk embodied in corporate obligations.* In essence, high-grade corporate bonds are a hybrid instrument, containing predominantly bondlike characteristics combined with some equity risk and some optionality.

The 15 multiple for investing in treasury bills, the 44 multiple for investing in treasury bonds, and the 61 multiple for investing in corporate bonds represent long-term rewards for lending money. Loans are relatively low-risk assets. In the case of treasury obligations, the full faith and credit of the U.S. government stand behind the commitment to pay interest and return principal in a timely manner. In the case of corporate bonds, the instruments have a senior claim on the assets of a corporation. That is, payments on bonds must be made before distributions to the owners of a company, its equity holders.

Obviously, as residual claimants, equity holders face substantially greater risks than do bondholders. In individual cases, when corporate income fails to meet fixed obligations, equity owners may be wiped out (although this is an extreme circumstance). In aggregate,

---

*Call risk represents the risk that an issuer will redeem its bonds at a fixed price prior to maturity. Bondholders generally suffer when issuers call bonds, since calls usually form part of a transaction designed to decrease funding costs through substitution of lower cost debt.

stock markets may underperform less risky bond markets for years at a time. In spite of (or perhaps because of) these risks, over long periods of time, equities in the United States have outperformed fixed income investments by staggering margins.

A dollar invested in common stock at the end of 1925 would have multiplied 2,351-fold during the seventy-three-year holding period. An enormous difference exists between the return expected from the conservative investment in cash (fifteen times) or government bonds (forty-four times) and that expected from taking the greater risk in owning equity securities (2,351 times).

The long-term benefit of owning equities increases as investments move further out the risk continuum. When investors assume more risk by investing in smaller-capitalization equities, the dollar grows 5,117 times during the period, a staggering amount relative to returns for other asset classes. Although controversy surrounds the methodology used by Ibbotson-Sinquefield's measurement of returns for small stocks, their work gives some sense of the long-term rewards for accepting greater risk.

Although the Ibbotson-Sinquefield data show persuasive results, considering longer periods of time produces even more dramatic conclusions. Wharton professor Jeremy Siegel, in his book *Stocks for the Long Run*, examines investment returns from 1802 to 1992. By using Ibbotson's recent data to extend Siegel's return series, a dollar in the U.S. stock market over the nearly two centuries from 1802 to 1998 grows to $9.86 million. During the same period, cash investments generate only $3,847. The return-generating power of equity investment over long periods of time dominates the multiples obtained by investing in bills and bonds as shown in Table 4.2.

As a footnote, gold "bugs" will be disappointed to learn that their favorite precious metal returned a multiple of only 12, trailing by a large margin the returns of even relatively low-risk treasury bills and failing to match the fourteen-fold impact of inflation.

These findings suggest that long-term investors maximize wealth by investing in high-return, high-risk equity rather than buying debt instruments of governments and corporations. As with many other broad generalizations, this seemingly obvious conclusion requires further examination.

Table 4.2 Equities Provide Astonishing Results in the Very Long Run
Wealth Multiples for U.S. Asset Classes and Inflation,
December 1802–December 1998

Asset Class	Multiple
Inflation	14 times
Treasury bills	3,847 times
Treasury bonds	9,950 times
Large-capitalization stocks	9,856,849 times

Sources: Ibbotson Associates, Stocks, Bonds, Bills and Inflation. 1999 Yearbook *(Chicago: Ibbotson Associates, 1999); Jeremy Siegel,* Stocks for the Long Run *(New York: Richard D. Irwin, Inc., 1994).*

Other Countries' Experiences

Market studies focusing only on returns for securities in the United States miss important information. Recent academic work on investor experience in other countries reduces confidence in the long-run superiority of equity investing.[3] At the turn of the twentieth century, active stock markets existed in Russia, France, Germany, Japan, and Argentina, all of which have been interrupted "for a variety of reasons, including political turmoil, war, and hyper-inflation. Obviously, these markets provide little grist for the mill of long-term capital market studies. Even the most continuous of markets, those in the United States and United Kingdom, were shut down for several months during World War I."[4] Studies of long-term returns in the United States ignore the fact that investors in foreign markets experienced less favorable outcomes, with sometimes dramatically worse results.

In addition to the possibility that enthusiasm for equities might be based on parochial experience, survivorship bias might inflate perceptions of historical returns.* One study suggests that "the 4.3 percent real (long term) capital appreciation return on U.S. stocks is rather exceptional, as other markets have typically had a median return of only 0.8 percent."[5] Were this conclusion to influence expectations for long-

---

*Survivorship bias occurs when data samples exclude markets (or investment funds or individual securities) that disappear. Since lower-returning, higher-risk markets (or investment funds or individual securities) tend to fail at a higher rate than their higher-returning, lower-risk counterparts, the data sample of survivors describes an environment that overstates the real-world return and understates the real-world risk.

run equity returns, the case for stock investments becomes considerably less compelling.

Ultimately the argument for an equity bias in a long time horizon investment portfolio rests on more than historical experience. Finance theory sensibly teaches that acceptance of greater risk accompanies an expectation of greater return. While future returns might not be as robust as they have been for U.S. equity investors, long-term investors will be well served with an equity bias.

Diversification

Although historical market return studies indicate that high levels of equity market exposure benefit long-term investors, the associated risks come through less clearly. Significant concentration in a single asset class poses extraordinary risk to portfolio assets. Fortunately, diversification provides investors with a powerful risk management tool. By combining assets that vary in response to forces that drive markets, more efficient portfolios can be created. At a given risk level, properly diversified portfolios provide higher returns than less well-diversified portfolios. Conversely, through appropriate diversification, a given level of returns can be achieved at lower risk. Harry Markowitz, pioneer of modern portfolio theory, maintains that portfolio diversification provides investors with a "free lunch," since risk can be reduced without sacrificing expected return.

Yale and the Eagle Bank

An extraordinary example of the risk in portfolio concentration comes from a catastrophic event in the early history of the Yale endowment. An overwhelmingly large, ill-advised investment in a single bank nearly bankrupted the college, with consequences that lasted for decades.

In 1811, Yale College treasurer James Hillhouse and his illustrious colleagues, Eli Whitney, William Woolsey, and Simeon Baldwin, were successful in acquiring a charter for the formation of the Eagle Bank of New Haven. At that time, only one other bank served New Haven's healthy economy and developing merchant class. Hoping to pursue a mission of fostering industry and commerce, the Eagle Bank at its opening commanded significant public confidence.

William Woolsey, a shrewd and experienced merchant and banker, served as the bank's first president, returning to New Haven from a lucrative business career in New York as a speculative sugar trader, hardware merchant, and merchant banker. With Woolsey at the helm and a roster of New Haven's finest citizens as founders, the financial officers at Yale were so convinced of the soundness of the bank that they applied for a special dispensation from the State of Connecticut to invest more than the statutory limit of $5,000 in the stock of any one bank. Yale not only invested far in excess of the limit, the trustees also leveraged the college's investment with borrowed funds. In 1825, with the exception of a few shares in municipal projects, the entire endowment was invested in the Eagle Bank.

Sadly, Yale's confidence was misdirected. Upon William Woolsey's return to his business ventures in New York in 1825, he selected George Hoadley, a Yale graduate, practicing lawyer, and mayor of New Haven, to succeed him as bank president. The illustrious founders of the bank were too busy with other endeavors to oversee Hoadley. In September 1825, after Hoadley had loaned out nearly the entire value of the bank in inadequately collateralized loans, the bubble burst, and the Eagle Bank declared bankruptcy. Yale College lost over $21,000, bringing the total value of the endowment down to $1,800. Unpaid debts for the college at the time amounted to well over $19,000, causing Yale president Jeremiah Day to obtain emergency sources of financing. The collapse of the bank was catastrophic to New Haven, precipitating a depression in the local economy. George Hoadley quietly moved to Cleveland, Ohio, in disgrace, where he finished out his days as a justice.

The Clark Foundation and Avon

While Yale's early nineteenth-century portfolio exhibited unusual concentration, similar situations exist today. Of the ten largest foundations in the United States, four hold more than 50 percent of assets in a single stock. Oblivious to the measure of good fortune that contributed to the undiversified portfolio's rise to the top of the charts, trustees use past success to justify continuing to concentrate assets in one security.

For each institution with a wildly successful concentrated portfolio, other institutions with undiversified holdings languish in obscurity. Unfortunately, many single-stock foundation officials ultimately experience the costs of holding radically undiversified portfolios.

Even when investors make good-faith efforts to diversify, results sometimes disappoint. In the early 1970s, trustees of the Edna McConnell Clark Foundation decided to reduce exposure to Avon Products, the company that provided the wherewithal to establish the institution. By selling shares of Avon to fund a diversified external equity manager, the trustees hoped to reduce heavy dependence on the fortunes of a single security. The timing of the decision made exquisite sense, as prices of Avon and other members of the "Nifty Fifty" had climbed to unprecedented heights in an extraordinary bull market for large-capitalization growth stocks.*

The trustees chose J. P. Morgan to manage the portfolio, selecting the era's dominant money management firm. Pursuing a strategy that had served the firm and its clients well, Morgan promptly diversified the foundation's assets into other high-quality growth stocks. But by exchanging one member of the Nifty Fifty for others of the same cohort, the Clark Foundation's portfolio received little protection from the subsequent dramatic collapse of the valuation bubble in quality growth stocks.

Yale's experience with a single security—shares of the Eagle Bank—and the Clark Foundation's ill-fated investments in the Nifty Fifty provide cautionary tales regarding portfolio concentration. Diversification matters, and true diversification requires owning assets that respond differently to fundamental forces that drive markets.

Stocks and the Great Crash

Even large market segments sometimes produce risks too great for investors to bear. Consider the wealth multiples for small-capitalization stocks around the time of the Great Crash in October 1929 shown in Table 4.3. According to these data, small-stock prices peaked in No-

---

*A phenomenon of the early 1970s, the Nifty Fifty consisted of approximately fifty high-quality growth stocks. Investors believed these securities faced such extraordinary prospects that some called them "one-decision" stocks, selling being out of the question.

vember 1928. Had a dollar been invested at that time, it would have declined 54 percent by December 1929, an additional 38 percent by December 1930, an additional 50 percent by December 1931, and a final 32 percent by June 1932. From November 1928 to June 1932, market action nearly destroyed the original investment.

No investor, institutional or individual, can tolerate that kind of trauma. During this period, as market forces turned dollars into dimes, investors sold small-capitalization stocks, placed the proceeds in treasury bills, swearing never to invest in the equity market again. Of course, selling equities in June 1932 represented precisely the wrong response. An investment at that time in small-capitalization stocks would have grown 29,238-fold by December 31, 1998.

The sense of the skepticism with which investors viewed stocks in the 1930s runs through Robert Lovett's "Gilt-Edged Insecurity," which appeared in the April 3, 1937, edition of the *Saturday Evening Post*. Lovett began his examination of historical market returns by suggesting that his readers "consider the absurdity of applying the word security to a bond or a stock." Lovett's analysis showed that an investor buying "100 shares of each of the more popular stocks" at the turn of the century would have turned nearly $295,000 into just $180,000 by the end of 1936. He concluded by warning his readers to remember "(1) that corporations . . . die easily and frequently; (2) to be extra careful when everything begins to look good; (3) that you are buying risks and not securities; (4) that governments break promises just as businesses do; and (5) that no investments worth having are permanent."[6] Lovett's commentary vividly illustrates why so few investors came up with the dime to invest in small stocks in June 1932.

Table 4.3 High-Risk Assets Hit Occasional Air Pockets
Wealth Multiples for Small Capitalization Equities,
November 1928–June 1932

Date	Multiple
November 30, 1928	1.00 times
December 31, 1929	0.46 times
December 31, 1930	0.29 times
December 31, 1931	0.14 times
June 30, 1932	0.10 times

Source: Ibbotson Associates, Stocks, Bonds, Bills and Inflation: 1999 Yearbook *(Chicago: Ibbotson Associates, 1999).*

Diversifying Strategies

Institutions generally respond to the risk in stocks by holding as much domestic equity as tolerable, mitigating portfolio volatility by adding significant amounts of bonds and cash to the mix. At June 30, 1998, the average educational endowment held 53 percent in domestic equity, 23 percent in domestic fixed income, and 4 percent in cash, for a total of 80 percent in domestic marketable securities.[7]

The large concentration of assets in bonds and cash, with fully 28 percent of the average portfolio in these low-return assets, creates significant opportunity costs. Instead of owning equity assets where dollars in the past seventy-three years grew more than 2,300-fold, investors diversifying with fixed income assets held positions that grew 44-fold with treasury bonds and 15-fold with cash.

The outsized exposure of more than 80 percent to securities of the U.S. market, with fully half of assets invested in domestic equities, violates sensible diversification principles. Committing more than 50 percent of a portfolio to a single asset type, domestic stocks, exposes investors to unnecessary risk. The consequences of a domestic equity concentration might be exacerbated by significant correlation between domestic stocks and bonds. Interest rates play an important role in equity valuation. Increasing (decreasing) rates may cause bond prices and stock prices to decline (rise) simultaneously, eliminating or reducing the hoped-for diversification effects. Under such circumstances, an average educational institution investor has four-fifths of the portfolio driven by the same economic factor.

By identifying high-return asset classes, not highly correlated with domestic marketable securities, investors achieve diversification without the opportunity costs of investing in fixed income. The most common high-return diversifying strategy for a U.S. investor involves adding foreign equities to the portfolio. Other possibilities for institutions include real estate, venture capital, leveraged buyouts, oil and gas participations, and absolute return strategies.* If these asset classes provide high equity-like returns in a pattern that differs from the return

---

*Absolute return strategies are commitments to event-driven investments in merger or bankruptcy situations and to value-driven investments in long/short or market-neutral strategies. See page 205 for a full description of the asset class.

pattern of the core asset (U.S. domestic equities), investors create portfolios that offer both high returns and diversification. Although on an asset-specific basis, higher expected returns come with the price of higher expected volatility, diversification provides investors with a mechanism to control risk. Such diversification represents "a free lunch" because risk decreases without sacrificing expected returns.

• • •

The combination of an equity bias and appropriate diversification provides a powerful underpinning for establishing policy asset allocation targets. Responding to the tenets of equity bias and diversification, investors begin by identifying a variety of high-expected-return assets that derive returns in ways fundamentally dissimilar from one another. By creating portfolios of a variety of asset types, investors diminish the risk that undiversified exposure to a single market will cause significant damage. If the strategy succeeds, portfolios generate high expected returns with low levels of risk.

MARKET TIMING

Explicit market timing lies on the opposite end of the spectrum from disciplined portfolio management practices. J. M. Keynes wrote in a Kings College Investment Committee memo that "the idea of wholesale shifts is for various reasons impracticable and indeed undesirable. Most of those who attempt to, sell too late and buy too late, and do both too often, incurring heavy expenses and developing too unsettled and speculative a state of mind."[8] Deliberate short-term deviations from policy targets introduce substantial risks to the investment process.

On the surface, arguments used to attack market timing sound uncomfortably similar to those advanced when making asset allocation decisions. For example, market timing might be rejected because it requires making a few, focused undiversifiable bets. Or difficulty in timing markets stems from the insurmountable challenges of identifying and predicting the multitude of variables that influence securities markets. While these factors apply to both market timing and policy asset allocation, differences in time frame fundamentally separate one from the other.

Market timing, by definition a bet against long-term policy targets, requires being right in the short run about factors that investors reasonably deal with in the long run. Making concentrated bets against the institution's adopted asset allocation, market timers run the risk of inflicting serious damage by holding a portfolio inconsistent with long-term objectives.

Tactical Asset Allocation

In the 1950s, many investors played a market timing game with stock and bond yields, based on "practically an article of faith that good stocks must yield more income than good bonds."[9] When dividend yields on stocks exceeded bond yields by a fair margin, investors viewed stocks as attractive, overweighting equities relative to bonds. Conversely, when bond yields neared stock yields, investors favored bonds. History provided a solid foundation for the strategy: "Only for short periods in 1929, 1930, and 1933 [had] stocks yielded less than government bonds."[10] This valuation-based technique worked well until 1958, when stock yields last exceeded bond yields. As the yield advantage of bonds increased relative to stocks, market timers became more invested in fixed income at the expense of stock positions. Of course, investors incurred significant opportunity losses while futilely waiting for stock yields to signal a buying opportunity. Ultimately the obvious failure of the market timing technique forced its practitioners to identify alternative pursuits.

A modern, somewhat more sophisticated version of the 1950s yield game, tactical asset allocation (TAA), moves assets above and below policy weights based on recommendations of a quantitative model. After gaining institutional favor based on strong performance during the crash of 1987, TAA's appeal waned, as successes of the late 1980s faded from memory. Although TAA's recommendations stem from sensible quantitative disciplines, the system suffers from the faults of other market timing mechanisms.

A notable problem with standard three-way (stock, bond, and cash) TAA relates to the resolution of model-identified "mispricings."

TAA models tend to prefer cash when short-term interest rates equal or exceed long-term rates, that is, in flat or inverted yield curve environments.* When TAA holds significant cash positions, investors receive meaningful protection in environments where interest rates increase. The increase in rates causes bond prices to decline, which may have a negative influence on stock prices as well. (Although the relationship between stocks and bonds is complex, higher interest rates lead to lower stock prices, all else being equal.) By holding cash, TAA practitioners protect portfolio assets from declines in bond and stock prices.

In contrast, if investors hold cash as the yield curve moves down sharply, portfolios might sustain irreversible opportunity losses. Downward shifts in the yield curve result from bond rallies, which could cause stocks to rally. TAA investors, stuck with substantial cash positions, receive modest income returns, while bonds and stocks post significant gains. In this example, losses are irreversible in the sense that while cash originally appeared to be the "cheapest" asset class, an across-the-board decline in rates resolved cash's cheapness in a fashion that provided little or no benefit to holders of cash. Handsome returns to holders of bonds and stocks make the relatively paltry cash returns a particularly bitter pill for TAA investors to swallow.

Because cash represents a poor asset class for investors with long time horizons, market timing strategies employing cash pose particularly great dangers to endowment assets. If investors mistakenly overweight cash and underweight higher expected return assets, subsequent rallies in long-term asset prices might cause permanent impairment of value. While less severe damage may result from mistakes made in timing one high-expected-return asset class relative to another, the ultimate consequences depend on disciplined contrarian responses to initial market timing losses. Such discipline might be a lot to expect from parties engaged in market timing in the first place.

*Yield curves represent graphically the relationship between yield and term to maturity for bonds with the same credit quality. Normal yield curves slope upward with higher yields for longer maturities. Flat yield curves reflect constant yields, regardless of maturity. Inverted yield curves depict environments where short-term rates exceed longer-term rates.

Rebalancing and the 1987 Market Crash

While relatively few investors admit to explicit pursuit of market timing strategies, most portfolios suffer from drift as market forces cause
actual allocations to differ from target levels. Circumstances surrounding the market crash in 1987 illustrate the meaningful costs incurred
by failing to conduct disciplined rebalancing activity in the face of
dramatic market moves.

During the period surrounding the 1987 stock market collapse, endowment portfolios exhibited aspects of disciplined rebalancing, allocation drift, and purposeful market timing. In June 1987, the average
endowment invested slightly more than 55 percent of assets in domestic equities and committed almost 37 percent to bonds and cash.[11] The
midsummer allocations marked the end of a period of extraordinary
portfolio stability; between June 1985 and June 1987 stock allocations
ranged from 55.0 to 55.4 percent, and fixed-income allocations ranged
from 36.7 to 36.9 percent. It appears that in the two years prior to June
1987, endowment investors engaged in rebalancing activity, offsetting
market-induced asset allocation drift. Since equities outperformed
bonds by a margin of 70 to 25 percent for the two-year period, only by
leaning against the bull market wind could investors file three consec-
utive reports indicating essentially constant allocations to domestic
marketable asset classes.

After the October 1987 crash, portfolio stability disappeared as
market forces drove down allocations to stocks and pushed up allocations to bonds. Responding to the collapse in prices with fear, the average endowment manager exacerbated market-induced dislocation
by selling stocks and purchasing bonds. From June 1987 to June 1988,
equity holdings declined from 55.3 to 49.1 percent, more than can be
explained by the market drop during the year. Roughly offsetting the
equity decline, fixed income increased from 36.7 to 41.9 percent of
portfolio assets, as fearful managers sought to reduce portfolio risk.
On average, educational institutions bought high and sold low, following a poor recipe for investment success.

By reallocating more than 5 percent of assets from domestic stocks
to bonds and cash in the aftermath of the 1987 market crash, endowment investors incurred significant opportunity costs as the market
staged a reasonably rapid recovery. Even in the face of stronger prices,

fear of the U.S. stock market persisted; endowment bond and cash allocations remained above the precrash level until 1993. College and
university portfolios maintained lower risk levels for years after the
stock market crash.

A charitable interpretation of postcrash equity sales lies in the
possibility that institutions inadvertently allowed equity allocations
to drift above desired levels in the strong stock market of the early
1980s. Perhaps the 1987 crash highlighted the degree to which equities dominated institutional portfolios, causing fiduciaries to sell
stocks to reach a lower desired portfolio risk profile. If so, postcrash
reductions in equity allocations represent a belated, costly, inelegant
response to excessive portfolio risk.

Another fundamental justification for reduced equity holdings
concerns the possibility that the 1987 crash caused investors to believe that risk characteristics of equities differed from previous assumptions. Perhaps past assessments of stock market variability
materially understated true risk. Maybe equity returns exhibit more
frequent extreme moves than market participants previously believed.
Certainly the unprecedented market collapse forced investors to re-
assess the character of equity return patterns, possibly contributing to
a portfolio shift from equities to less risky assets.

Unfortunately for those seeking a reasonable explanation for institutional behavior, increases in stock allocations during the 1990s argue against interpreting November and December 1987 sales as a
rational portfolio adjustment. Investors motivated by greed held high
allocations going into the crash, only to reduce holdings significantly
thereafter. As confidence returned, equity allocations began to rise, reversing the allocation decisions made only a short time before.

With the benefit of hindsight, postcrash equity purchases made
enormous sense, enriching those with the courage to go against the
crowd. While near-term profitability of postcrash equity purchases illustrates a positive aspect of rebalancing activity, investors face the possibility of confusing the important risk control function of rebalancing
with the unreliable return-oriented activity of "buying the dips."

In fact, the apparently easy money made by buying common
stocks in late 1987 encouraged investors to follow a policy of buying
the dips with increasing enthusiasm. As the bull market continued its
run through the 1990s, the public saw every modest decline in stock

prices as an opportunity to buy equities "on sale." Did investors learn an important rebalancing lesson from the 1987 stock market crash, or did the relatively quick rebound in prices point market participants in the wrong direction?

Drawing conclusions from the 1987 stock market crash about the easy profits gained from buying the dips places far too much weight on a shaky foundation, since the extraordinary circumstances surrounding the October break in markets constitute a unique occurrence. The extreme one-day decline of 23 percent in the S&P 500 represents a 25-standard-deviation event, an occurrence so rare in normally distributed variables that the event defies imagination.* Basing future behavior on the 1987 crash and subsequent market recovery exposes investors to the danger that less-extreme market declines contain far less information regarding future price behavior.

Investors hoping to profit in the short run from rebalancing trades face nearly certain long-run disappointment. Over long periods of time, portfolios allowed to drift tend to contain ever increasing allocations to risky assets, as higher returns cause riskier positions to crowd out other holdings. The fundamental purpose of rebalancing lies in controlling risk, not enhancing return. Rebalancing trades keep portfolios at long-term policy targets by reversing deviations resulting from asset class performance differentials. Disciplined rebalancing activity requires a strong stomach and serious staying power. Conducted in a significant bear market, rebalancing appears to be a losing strategy as investors commit funds to assets showing continuing relative price weakness.

Contrast the positive experience of rebalancing investors in 1987 with the fate investors suffered in the bear market of 1973 and 1974. Price declines required purchases of equities, followed by further declines that impaired asset values, requiring further purchases. Losses

---

*In a normally distributed variable, a one-standard-deviation event occurs approximately one out of every three trials, a two-standard-deviation event occurs one of every twenty trials, and a three-standard-deviation event occurs one out of a hundred trials. An eight-standard-deviation event occurs once every six trillion years, based on a 250-business-day year. The frequency of a 25-standard-deviation event requires descriptive capabilities beyond my capacity.

incurred on rebalancing trades prove particularly painful as investors second-guess the wisdom of buying into a bear market. For investors seeking to maintain long-term targets in the early 1970s, two years of nearly uninterrupted price deterioration produced a troubling environment of relentless incremental losses.

Rising equity prices provide a similar set of challenges. In a sustained bull market, rebalancing appears to be a losing strategy as investors constantly sell assets showing relative price strength. Years go by without reward other than the knowledge that the portfolio embodies the desired risk-reward characteristics.

The alternative of not rebalancing to policy targets causes portfolio managers to engage in a peculiar trend-following market-timing strategy. Like many other contrarian pursuits, rebalancing frequently appears foolish as momentum players reap short-term rewards from going with the flow. Regardless of potentially negative reputational consequences, serious investors maintain portfolio risk profiles through disciplined rebalancing policies, avoiding the sometimes expedient appeal of market timing strategies.

Burton Malkiel, in *Managing Risk in an Uncertain Era*, writes that "we are particularly averse to the suggestions that a university try to move in and out of the stock market according to its capacity to forecast market trends. Investors who wish to play this timing game must possess an unusual degree of prescience about the course of the general economy, corporate profits, interest rates, and indeed the entire set of international economic, political, and social developments that affect the securities market. The existence of such omniscience, to say the least, is hard to document."[12] More succinct advice to those who must time markets comes from remarks attributed to a nineteenth-century cotton trader: "Some think it will go up. Some think it will go down. I do, too. Whatever you do will be wrong. Act at once."

Market timing explicitly moves the portfolio away from long-term policy targets, exposing the institution to avoidable risks. Because policy asset allocation provides the central means through which investors express return and risk preferences, serious investors attempt to minimize deviations from policy targets. To ensure that actual portfolios reflect desired risk and return characteristics, avoid market timing and employ rebalancing activity to keep asset classes at targeted levels.

SECURITY SELECTION

Security selection captures the imagination of most market participants, leading many to subtract value by overusing ultimately futile
active management strategies. By focusing on less efficient markets,
and pursuing less liquid, value-oriented opportunities, investors increase the odds of winning the loser's game.

Market Efficiency

Investors wishing to beat the market by actively managing portfolios
face daunting obstacles. Although no market prices assets precisely at
fair value all of the time, most markets price assets reasonably efficiently much of the time, providing few opportunities for easy gains.
Moreover, active management costs increase the hurdle for success as
investors pay management fees, incur transactions costs, and create
market impact. Intelligent investors approach active strategies with a
healthy sense of skepticism.

Markets with inefficiently priced assets ought to be favored by active managers; markets with efficiently priced assets should be ap-
proached by active managers with great caution. Unfortunately, no
clear measures for pricing efficiency exist. In fact, financial economists engage in a quasi-religious debate regarding efficiency, with one
end of the spectrum represented by those who believe in the impossibility of finding risk-adjusted excess returns and the other by those
who concede the existence of active management opportunities.

Degree of Opportunity

In the absence of direct measures of market efficiency, active manager
behavior provides clues about the degree of opportunity in various
markets. In markets with limited opportunities for active management, managers deviate little from the market portfolio, tending to obtain market-like returns. Why do managers in efficient markets tend to
hug the benchmark? In a world of efficiently priced assets, consider
the business consequences to investment managers holding portfolios

that differ markedly from the market portfolio. Substantial deviations in security holdings cause portfolio results to vary dramatically from the benchmark. Underperforming managers lose clients, suffering a punishing loss in assets. While overachievers may temporarily gain clients (and public adulation), because markets price securities efficiently, success will be transitory. If markets present no mispricings for active managers to exploit, good results stem from luck, not skill. Over time, managers in efficient markets gravitate toward closet indexing, structuring portfolios with only modest deviations from the market, ensuring both mediocrity and survival.

In contrast, active managers in less efficient markets exhibit greater variability in returns. In fact, many private markets lack benchmarks for managers to hug, eliminating the problem of closet indexing. Inefficiencies in pricing allow managers with great skill to achieve great success, while unskilled managers post commensurately poor results. Hard work and intelligence reap rich rewards in an environment where superior information and deal flow provide an edge.

The degree of opportunity for active management (at least as measured by manager behavior) relates to the distribution of actively managed returns in a particular asset class. Any measure of dispersion ought to provide some sense of where active management opportunities lie. The spread in returns between the first and third quartiles in collections of actively managed portfolios illustrates the notion that more efficiently priced assets provide less opportunity for active managers and that less efficiently priced assets provide more opportunity.

Table 4.4 shows active manager returns for various asset classes for the decade ending December 31, 1997. U.S. Treasury securities, arguably the most efficiently priced asset in the world, trade in staggering volumes in markets dominated by savvy financial institutions. Since nobody (possibly excepting the Federal Reserve) knows where interest rates will be, few managers employ interest rate anticipation strategies. Without potentially powerful differentiating bets on interest rates, institutional portfolios tend to exhibit market-like interest rate sensitivity, or duration. As a result, managers generally limit themselves to modest security selection decisions, causing returns for most active managers to mimic benchmark results. The spread between first- and third-quartile results for active managers measures an astonishingly small 1.2 percent per annum for the decade.

Large-capitalization equities represent the next rung of the efficiency ladder, with a range of 2.5 percent between top and bottom quartiles. Stocks provide more difficult pricing challenges than bonds. Instead of discounting relatively certain fixed income cash flows, valuation of equities involves discounting more-difficult-to-project corporate earnings. The greater volatility in equity markets also contributes to the wider active manager spread. Less efficiently priced international equities show a range of 2.9 percent per annum over the decade. The progression of degree of opportunity across types of marketable securities makes intuitive sense.

The radical break comes when moving from liquid public to illiquid private opportunities. Real estate, venture capital, and leveraged buyouts exhibit dramatically broader dispersions of returns. For the ten-year period, real estate returns show a range of 4.7 percent between the first and third quartiles, while leveraged buyouts and venture capital exhibit even more extreme 13.0 and 21.2 percent per annum spreads.

Selecting top-quartile managers in private markets leads to much greater rewards than in public markets. In the extreme case, choosing a first-quartile fixed-income manager added only 0.5 percent per annum relative to the median result. In contrast, the first-quartile venture capitalist added 12.7 percent per annum relative to the median, providing a much greater contribution to portfolio results. Ironically, identifying superior managers in the relatively inefficiently priced private markets proves less challenging than in the efficiently priced marketable securities markets.

Active Manager Returns

Regardless of the scope of active management opportunities, investors face serious headwinds. As shown in Table 4.5, in the two most significant institutional asset classes, domestic fixed income and domestic equity, fee-adjusted median manager returns fall short of benchmark results. In the extremely efficiently priced U.S. bond market, the median fixed income manager loses twenty-five basis points per year net of fees relative to the benchmark, while a first-quartile manager beats the market by a mere twenty-five basis points

**Table 4.4 Dispersion of Active Management Returns
Identifies Areas of Opportunity**

Asset Returns by Quartile, Ten Years Ending December 31, 1997

Asset Class	First Quartile	Median	Third Quartile	Range
U.S. fixed income	9.7%	9.2%	8.5%	1.2%
U.S. equity	19.5	18.3	17.0	2.5
International equity	12.6	11.0	9.7	2.9
Real estate	5.9	3.9	1.2	4.7
Leveraged buyouts	23.1	16.9	10.1	13.0
Venture capital	25.1	12.4	3.9	21.2

Sources: Data for marketable securities are from the Piper Managed Accounts Report *of December 31, 1997. The data for real estate are from Institutional Property Consultants. The venture capital and leveraged buyout data are from Venture Economics. Venture capital and leveraged buyout data represent returns on funds formed between 1988 and 1993, excluding more recent funds so that immature investments will not influence reported results.*

per annum.* Active fixed income management represents a classic loser's game. Before engaging in active bond management, investors should ponder Warren Buffett's famous dictum: "Remember, if you are at a poker table and can't identify the patsy, you are the patsy."

Domestic equity markets produce similar, albeit slightly more hopeful, results. With fee adjustments, the median active manager gives up about thirty-five basis points per year relative to the benchmark. A first-quartile manager adds more value, however, exceeding the benchmark by eighty-five basis points per annum net of fees.

In the case of domestic marketable securities, both the scope of opportunity (represented by the first- to third-quartile spread of active manager results) and the deficit of median returns relative to the benchmark tell the same story. Avoid active management, or undertake active strategies with great caution and realistic expectations.

Foreign equities tell a somewhat different story. Median manager results exceed benchmark returns by a meaningful margin, exceeding the hurdle by an impressive 3.8 percent per year. Why might the opportunity for active management be greater in foreign stocks?

Consider the markets in which the various securities trade. Domestic fixed income operates in a market dominated by institutions.

*A basis point is 1/100 of 1 percent.

The returns contained in the active manager universe likely represent the results of sophisticated investors trading against one another. Traders gain an advantage with extraordinary difficulty. As a result, active managers post results in a narrow range, with the median manager losing relative to the benchmark. The highly efficient, competitive fixed income market stands at one end of the continuum.

International equities, with an astonishing positive spread relative to the benchmark, stand at the other end of the continuum. In these markets, institutional fund managers systematically generate excess returns at the expense of less sophisticated players. Many in the funds management industry believe that even rudimentary application of investment techniques to foreign markets leads to reasonable excess returns. Foreign investors trading in their local markets likely provide the other side of the money-making trades. As markets evolve, the edge that active managers currently enjoy will no doubt diminish. But as long as the patsies remain visible, it pays to play the game.

Before crowing too loudly about the international success of active management, consider the role of the Japanese market. The astonishing degree of success that foreign equity managers enjoy stems in large part from a near-universal underweighting of Japan over the past decade, prompted by that country's late 1980s bubble valuations. As a result, 100 percent of active managers tracked by a major consulting firm beat the standard foreign equity benchmark, with the overwhelming portion of incremental active performance stemming from the reduced Japanese country allocation. Obviously foreign equity manager results for the recent past are mightily influenced by the Japanese opportunity. Without such an obvious bet, active managers will have a much more difficult time beating the index. Perhaps the conditions contributing to the success of active foreign managers relate more to the Japanese bubble than to the richness of the foreign market opportunity.

Greater inefficiency in the market environment may not lead to greater average success. Private markets provide a case in point. Median results for venture capital and leveraged buyouts dramatically trail those for marketable equities, despite the higher risk and greater illiquidity of private investing. Over the decade ending December 1997, deficits relative to the S&P 500 amounted to 5.9 percent annually for venture capital and 1.4 percent annually for leveraged buyouts, numbers that would be higher after risk adjustment. In order to

Table 4.5 Efficiently Priced Markets Beat the Average Active Manager
Median Returns Relative to Benchmark, Ten Years Ending December 31, 1997

Asset Class	Median Return	Benchmark˙	Estimated Fees	Fee Adjusted Gain (Deficit)
U.S. fixed income	9.2%	9.1%	35 basis points	(25 basis points)
U.S. equity	18.3	18.0	65 basis points	(35 basis points)
International equity	11.0	6.5	75 basis points	375 basis points

Sources: Data on fees are from Cambridge Associates, Inc. Investment Manager Database, rounded to the nearest 5 basis points. Benchmarks for asset classes are as follows: Lehman Brothers Government Corporate Bond Index for U.S. fixed income, the S&P 500 Index for U.S. equity, and the MSCI EAFE Index for International equities.

justify including private equity in the portfolio, investors must believe they can select top-quartile managers. Anything less fails to compensate for the time, effort, and risk entailed in the pursuit of nonmarketable investments.

Survivorship Bias

Although comparisons of active management returns to benchmark results already paint a bleak picture, managers hoping to beat the market face a challenge even greater than suggested by a first reading of the data. Survivorship bias causes active managers as a group to appear more successful than reality indicates, since databases frequently contain only the strong (survivors), having purged the weak (failures).

Errors of underinclusion and overinclusion bias manager performance data, limiting the usefulness of consultant reports in understanding active management results. Underinclusion occurs when managers disappear without a trace; overinclusion results when new entrants contribute historical results to the database.

Compilations of return data sometimes include only results of managers active at the time of the study. Discontinued products and discredited managers disappear, coloring the return data with an optimistic tint. Were the generally poor results of nonsurvivors included in the database, the challenge of beating the market would appear even more daunting.

Even if the data gatherer undertakes to include results of failed managers, the figures provide reasonable guidance only when considering returns on a year-by-year basis. Problems arise when examining results spanning several years since managers disappear during any given multiple-year period, forcing even the most diligent database gurus to drop any partial reports. Because managers tend to disappear after posting poor relative results, most multiple-year comparisons suffer from return inflation driven by the superior results of survivors.

Small-Capitalization Growth Managers. Examination of the survival, failure, and disappearance of a cross-section of active managers over a number of years provides some clues to the seriousness of the survivorship issue. In a thorough analysis of the collection of small-capitalization growth products included in one consultant's database from 1992 to 1997, managers left the pool at a surprisingly high rate.[13] In 1992, eighty-eight investment managers reported returns. Five years later, fewer than half of the original participants remained; thirty-one managers ceased reporting, and seventeen managers underwent reclassification.

The thirty-one nonreporting managers generally produced substandard results, averaging seventh-decile performance for the three years prior to departure. Although determining the precise reasons for manager disappearance constitutes an inexact science, examination of a number of investment industry references indicates that eight managers ceased operations, eleven managers discontinued small-capitalization growth products, and twelve managers continued to manage small-growth products, but stopped reporting results.[14]

In addition to the thirty-one products that left the consultant's universe, a further seventeen funds classified as small-capitalization growth in 1992 underwent reclassification over the subsequent five years. Because prior to changing categories funds exhibited near-median performance, reclassification in this specific case exerted little systematic influence on the database. In nine cases, funds moved from small capitalization to mid-capitalization, with eight in the growth category and one in value. The large-capitalization growth category claimed seven funds, while the "other" category took one.

Regardless of the reasons for disappearing from the small-growth company manager universe, as shown in Figure 4.1, the attrition of forty-eight out of eighty-eight funds from 1992 to 1997 altered the characteristics of the database in fundamental fashion. Lack of data on poorer-performing funds created a false picture of active manager results, systematically inflating the reported numbers. Losing data from funds for any reason diminished the value of year-to-year comparisons, because 1992's cohort differed from 1993's, 1994's, 1995's, 1996's, and 1997's, with the gap between appearance and reality widening with each successive year.

The disappearance of managers from a database over time creates a problem of underinclusion, tainting results with survivorship bias. When specific investment vehicles cease to exist, the pool shrinks regardless of the compiler's diligence. However, when investment managers stop reporting results to certain firms, more thoroughness in collecting numbers mitigates the problem. Had the consultant examined publicly available sources, the database might have included results from twelve small-capitalization growth funds that continued to exist but stopped reporting results.

Figure 4.1 Survivorship Bias Clouds Comparisons
Small-Capitalization Growth Equity Managers
1992 Performance Data as Reported, 1992–1997

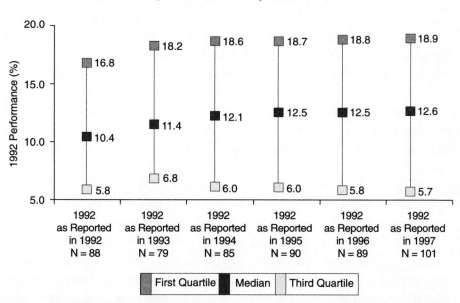

Source: Pensions and Investments' Performance Evaluation Report (PIPER), Managed Accounts Report, *1992–1997. Note: N represents the number of investment management firms reporting results in a particular year.*

Aside from the return inflation caused by underinclusion, the potential exists for overinclusion to exert further upward pressure on reported results. For example, the consultant's compilation of investment rankings routinely adds managers, including not only current information on returns but also the past performance records of the newly added firms. In the case of small-stock growth funds, 101 managers reported 1992 results in 1997 in contrast to the eighty-eight managers reporting 1992 results in 1992. Since only forty managers consistently reported returns for the five years from 1992 to 1997, more than sixty firms entered the small-stock growth category during the period. Many of the new entrants provided historical results, dutifully added by the consultant to the existing database. As a result, in 1997, of the 101 firms that reported figures for 1992, only forty actually represented part of the 1992 cohort, with the others entering after the fact. Obviously firms posting mediocre returns face little likelihood of joining a database. Since only successful managers rise to the level necessary to gain the attention of the consulting industry, adding complete records of new entrants produces an upward bias in reported results.

International Equity Managers. Figure 4.2 illustrates the magnitude of survivorship bias in the consultant's 1992 international equity data set, measured over a six-year period. The first column shows figures for 1992 reported after the close of that year. The second column contains data for 1992 as reported one year later. Note that the number of accounts increases from 120 to 165 as firms enter the performance charts, exerting a strong upward bias to the reported numbers. In just one year, the 1992 median return jumped from −6.4 percent to −5.4 percent, as new firms with strong records entered the data set.

By the end of 1997, after a net addition of 74 international equity firms, the 1992 median return reached −4.1 percent, fully 2.3 percentage points above the originally reported level. Imagine the reaction of a manager with a 1992 return of −6.2 percent. In 1992, that result placed the manager just in the top half of active managers, more or less equivalent to a gentleman's C. In 1997, without any action on the part of the manager, the grade for 1992 changed to failing as the "new and improved" data indicated that more than 60 percent of international portfolios beat the hapless manager's result.

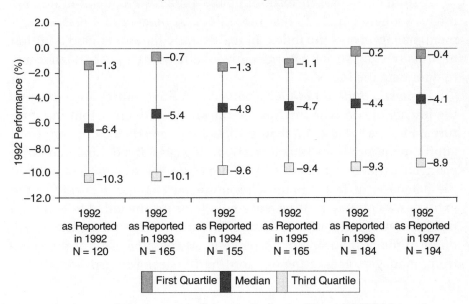

**Figure 4.2 Performance Hurdles Increase as Time Passes
International Equity Managers**
1992 Performance Data as Reported, 1992–1997

Source: *Pensions and Investments' Performance Evaluation Report (PIPER),* Managed
Accounts Report, *1992–1997. Note:* N represents the number of investment management
firms in the PIPER database in a particular year.

Small-Capitalization Value Managers. Survivorship bias punishes
individual managers as decile ranking demarcations creep ever upward with the addition of new managers reporting superior results. In
contrast, as the "quality" of manager returns increases through time,
to the casual observer markets appear easier to beat. As shown in Figure 4.3, the data set compiled after 1992's year-end shows the majority
of small-capitalization value managers failing to beat the Russell 2000,
a small-company index. In fact, the passive alternative of 18.4 percent
exceeded the median active small-capitalization value manager result
by one-half of 1 percent.

By 1997, after a doubling in number of small-capitalization value
managers posting results for 1992, more than half of the newly constituted group beat the index. The one-half of 1 percent margin by which
1997's active managers bested the benchmark mirrored the original
deficit, a swing of one full percentage point. The changing picture of
active management results caused by survivorship bias represents a

material influence in a business where mere basis points sometimes separate success from failure.

A student of markets examining the 1992 results reported in 1997 might wrongly conclude that more than 50 percent of 1992's investment managers beat the index. In reality, only the subsequent addition of firms posting strong returns allowed a majority of active managers to dominate the index.

Domestic Bond and Stock Managers. A final impression concerns the impact of survivorship bias on the shape of the distribution of returns. Figures 4.4 and 4.5 display data for domestic fixed income and equity managers from 1992 to 1997. In the case of fixed income, little changed as large numbers of benchmark-hugging managers entered the database. In fact, the most pronounced changes occurred at the extremes. Managers posting extremely poor results failed to enter the database proportionally, causing the ninety-fifth percentile break point to move from 4.7 to 5.4 percent. At the other end of the spectrum, managers generating extraordinarily strong returns also failed

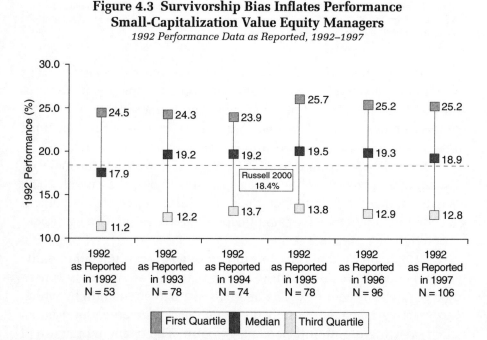

Figure 4.3 Survivorship Bias Inflates Performance
Small-Capitalization Value Equity Managers
1992 Performance Data as Reported, 1992–1997

Source: Pensions and Investments' Performance Evaluation Report (PIPER), Managed Accounts Report, *1992–1997. Note:* N represents the number of investment management firms in the PIPER database in a particular year.

to maintain pro-rata representation, leading the fifth percentile break point to decline from 10.7 to 10.3 percent. It appears that fixed income managers entered the manager universe by producing index-like results, fattening the heart of the return distribution.

In contrast, producing strong results led to inclusion in the domestic equity database. As the number of managers more than doubled from 1992 to 1997, every distribution break point increased, reflecting the superior results generated by the new entrants. The pattern of continuous "improvement" of domestic equity results repeated itself with small-capitalization value, small-capitalization growth, and international equity. While a limited set of observations fails to support broad conclusions, it seems as if investors in the more efficiently priced fixed income asset class engaged middle-of-the-road managers, while investors in the less efficient equity markets sought more adventuresome managers. In any event, when evaluating historical active management records, survivorship bias influences, sometimes dramatically, the reported level and shape of return distributions.

Figure 4.4 Benchmark-Hugging Bond Managers Survive
Domestic Fixed Income Managers
1992 Performance Data as Reported, 1992–1997

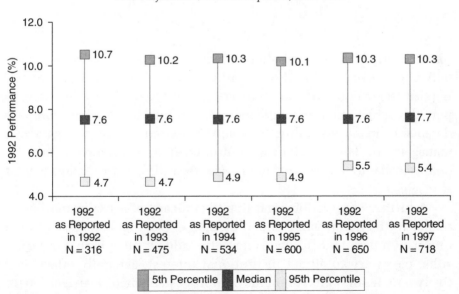

Source: Pensions and Investments' Performance Evaluation Report (PIPER), Managed Accounts Report, *1992–1997. Note:* N represents the number of investment management firms in the PIPER database in a particular year.

Figure 4.5 Strong-Performing Equity Managers Enter the Database
Domestic Equity Managers
1992 Performance Data as Reported, 1992–1997

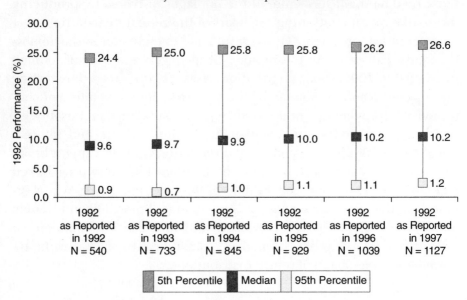

Source: Pensions and Investments' Performance Evaluation Report (PIPER), Managed
Accounts Report, *1992–1997. Note:* N represents the number of investment management
firms in the PIPER database in a particular year.

• • •

Survivorship bias in distributions of active manager returns fundamentally alters investor attitudes toward active management. Data indicating that the majority of managers beat the index encourage investors to
play the active management game, while numbers showing a prepon-
derance of managers failing to match index returns discourage active
management. The positive bias introduced by survivorship bias no
doubt leads to excessive confidence regarding active management
strategies.

A further observation regarding the efficacy of active management
relates to the dollar value added by market-beating strategies. Simple
return numbers tend to overstate value added since early strong results, necessary to attract institutional interest, generally affect relatively small amounts of money. More established managers with
greater funds under management tend to produce less eye-catching re-

sults. Because investment management return compilations weight each manager equally, the new managers (presumably with smaller portfolios) exert disproportionate influence in the manager rankings. No doubt a dollar-weighted evaluation of active management provides less encouragement to those hoping to beat markets than does the standard equal-weighted analysis.

Active portfolio management faces high hurdles, requiring that investors approach potential strategies with great skepticism. In the world of marketable securities, passive management provides the obvious alternative to active management strategies. If investors undertake active approaches, focusing on less efficient markets increases chances for success. Issues of survivorship bias cloud understanding of historical records, causing general problems in evaluating the efficacy of active management strategies and specific problems in assessing individual manager performance. In private markets, the passive alternative of attempting to replicate market returns makes little sense, since investors face a broad range of opportunities and market-like results will likely disappoint. Sensible investors engage in active management with reasonable caution and realistic expectations.

Liquidity

Active managers pursuing inefficiencies frequently gravitate toward relatively illiquid markets, since rewarding investments tend to reside in dark corners, not in the glare of floodlights. Such out-of-the-way, undiscovered opportunities receive little attention from Wall Street, which thrives on markets that generate large trading volumes.

Market players seek liquid positions, allowing immediate disposition of yesterday's loser and rapid acquisition of today's hot prospect. Speculators and asset gatherers pay a premium price for liquid assets, expecting markets to accommodate reversal of a trade with immediacy and little or no impact on price.

By avoiding the highly liquid securities favored by market players, serious active investors focus on much more interesting opportunities. In embracing less liquid assets, investors often identify opportunities to establish positions at meaningful discounts to fair value.

Full Faith and Credit Obligations

The most actively traded treasury bonds, so-called on-the-run issues, command a price premium, generally yielding as much as 5 to 10 basis points less than off-the-run bonds. Based on current issuance patterns by the government, on-the-run offerings carry terms to maturity of two, three, five, ten, and thirty years. When the treasury auctions a new ten-year bond, market attention shifts from the old ten-year instrument to the new. Since the premium enjoyed by on-the-run issues relates solely to superior market liquidity, a characteristic that disappears when a new issue supplants the old, the price premium disappears for the old on-the-run.

Regular opportunities exist to purchase full faith and credit instruments of the U.S. government at spreads of 40 to 50 basis points above otherwise comparable but more liquid treasury issues. Because such offerings tend to contain structural complexities, cautious investors undertake careful due diligence before committing funds. Moreover, opportunities tend to be relatively small, requiring portfolio managers to "fill a bathtub with a teaspoon." Dogged pursuit of unusual, illiquid securities results in the accumulation of an attractively priced portfolio of high-quality assets.

Markets occasionally offer extraordinary opportunities to investors willing to accept illiquidity. In the aftermath of a market panic in the fall of 1998, less frequently traded assets provided enormous returns relative to highly liquid positions. On November 12, 1998, an intermediate-term off-the-run treasury issue, the 5 7/8s of February 2004, yielded 18 1/2 basis points more than the current, or on-the-run 4 1/4s of November 2003.

Beyond the extremely high reward for accepting modest illiquidity in an off-the-run issue, investors willing to invest in a private placement backed by the full faith and credit of the United States faced incredible opportunity. Issued by the Overseas Private Investment Corporation, an agency of the United States devoted to promoting economic growth in developing nations, securities with an effective maturity date of March 2004 carried a spread of more than 100 basis points over the comparable on-the-run treasury issue. Receiving a full percentage point in yield over treasuries for simply bearing the illiquidity of a private placement raises serious questions about the rationality of market participants.

Emerging Market Debt

In the emerging markets, U.S. dollar–denominated debt of sovereign issuers frequently trades at a substantial premium to nondollar debt of the same issuer. This phenomenon presents itself most dramatically in times of crisis, as investors place extraordinary value on the greater liquidity of U.S. dollar–denominated instruments. To arbitrage this discrepancy, investors require only a set of currency forward contracts to eliminate the foreign exchange risk between the two instruments. Arbitrageurs can buy the relatively cheap nondollar debt, sell the relatively expensive dollar debt, and eliminate currency risk with forward foreign exchange transactions. Investors paying a premium for dollar-denominated debt provide a free lunch to more patient investors.

Throughout 1998, investors found some extraordinary opportunities amid dislocations caused by the collapse in Asian markets. While the successful resolution of many investments depended on market recovery, other positions promised almost certain rewards to investors. Samsung, a highly leveraged Korean diversified electronics manufacturer, issued debt in a variety of currencies, including U.S. dollars, Korean won, Japanese yen, and German marks. Dollar-denominated bonds generally traded at premium prices, reflecting superior liquidity characteristics. In the fall, pricing discrepancies reached an extreme with Samsung 9.75 percent dollar bonds due May 2003 trading at a yield to maturity of 16 percent (approximately 1,200 basis points over U.S. Treasuries), and Samsung 3.3 percent yen bonds due April 2003 trading at a yield of 18 percent (approximately 1,700 basis points over Japanese government bonds). Investors could create a stream of dollar cash flows by buying the relatively cheap yen bond and swapping all future yen flows for dollars. By using the forward currency markets to translate the Samsung yen cash flows into dollars, investors created a synthetic dollar asset with a yield to maturity of 21 percent. The spread between the synthetic bond yield and the Samsung dollar bond yield of 16 percent created an opportunity for arbitrageurs to purchase the relatively cheap synthetic dollar asset cash flows and sell the relatively expensive dollar bond, locking in the profit represented by the yield spread.* If spreads narrow,

---

*Execution of the Samsung corporate bond arbitrage requires a short sale of the relatively expensive dollar bonds. Short sellers must borrow bonds to

(continued)

the investor unwinds the trade with a profit; if not, the investor collects a stream of payments until the bonds mature. By applying modest amounts of leverage to the trade, investors could expect holding period returns in the neighborhood of 24 percent; without leverage the position carried an 18 percent return.

Sallie Mae Stock

Different classes of equity frequently trade at prices reflecting, inter alia, liquidity differences. The Student Loan Marketing Association ("Sallie Mae"), established in 1973 to provide liquidity for entities involved in programs supporting the credit needs of students, originally raised equity capital from institutions participating in the federal government's Guaranteed Student Loan Program. In 1983, creation of a new class of more broadly held nonvoting stock increased the company's equity base, funding a corporate growth program designed to meet the needs of hundreds of thousands of students. In spite of the voting rights vested with the original shares, the newly issued nonvoting stock traded at a premium generally ranging between 15 and 20 percent, a spread that market participants attributed to the illiquidity of the original shares.

In an attempt to reduce the discount, Sallie Mae made regular offers to convert the cheaper, less liquid voting stock to the more expensive, more liquid nonvoting stock. The discount persisted despite annual conversion of between 28 and 41 percent of shares tendered from 1984 to 1989. Curiously, a substantial number of voting shareholders failed to take advantage of the opportunity. During the final tender offer in March 1989, at the height of market participant familiarity with the program, of the 8.7 million shares outstanding, 1.5 million shares ignored an offer of $91.875 in cash for shares trading at $83.50, exhibiting behavior difficult to reconcile with notions of market efficiency. In 1991 Congress authorized cre-

(continued)   consummate the transaction. One risk in executing the arbitrage lies in losing the "borrow," causing the investor to unwind the short position prematurely. In well-functioning capital markets, maintaining short positions poses little problem; however, in well-functioning capital markets, nearly identical streams of cash flows (as represented by the Samsung bonds) do not trade at substantially different prices.

ation of a single class of stock for Sallie Mae, eliminating the discount and removing a trading opportunity for arbitrageurs willing to play in less liquid markets.

Illiquidity's Attractions

Illiquidity accompanies several characteristics prized by serious investors. Less information tends to be available on illiquid securities, creating an opportunity to be rewarded for uncovering nuggets of data relevant to valuation. Highly liquid large-capitalization stocks receive widespread coverage, generating enormous amounts of publicly available information. As of December 1998, Microsoft, the largest stock by capitalization, received coverage from forty Wall Street analysts. The company was mentioned 19,899 times in the *Wall Street Journal* alone in 1998. In contrast, Micro Linear, the five-thousandth company by market capitalization, had only three research analysts. *Wall Street Journal* references totaled thirty-four. Table 4.6 shows the direct relationship between company size and public scrutiny.

While Microsoft operates a complex set of businesses, superficially presenting a great opportunity for research, security analysts actually face a tough challenge in developing an edge in light of competition from other analysts devouring mountains of publicly available information. With Micro Linear, the bottom-up stock analyst finds greater opportunity. Information will no doubt be harder to obtain, but its value will be enhanced by its proprietary nature.

Obviously, private markets present more extreme information advantages. Wall Street research analysts do not follow private companies. Press coverage tends to be less intense, in part because less information becomes public through government-mandated regulatory filings. The lack of easily obtainable information about private companies poses a challenge and creates an opportunity. Superior information flows lie at the heart of private investing, contributing to the results of all successful partnerships.

Illiquidity induces appropriate long-term behavior. Rather than relying on liquid markets to trade out of mistakes, investors in illiquid securities enter into long-term arrangements, purchasing part ownership in a business with which they have to live. As a consequence, in-

Table 4.6 Large Companies Receive More Intense Research Scrutiny

Small Companies Offer Opportunities to Develop an Information Edge

	Capitalization Rank	Average Market Capitalization	Average Number of Analysts	Average Number of Wall Street Journal Citations
Microsoft General Electric Intel Wal Mart Stores Exxon	1–5	$274.8 billion	45	8,968
Chevron Unilever Gillette McDonald's General Motors	50–54	52.6 billion	40	3,812
United Technologies Suntrust Banks Automatic Data Processing National City Corporation Dayton Hudson	100–104	24.2 billion	26	638
Shared Medical Systems Skytel Communication Olin Corporation Ohio Casualty Maxtor Corporation	1,000–1,004	1.3 billion	20	96
Micro Linear Corporation RIBI Immunochemical S&K Famous Brands TCSI Corporation Burnham Corporation	5,000–5,004	47.0 million	3	39

Sources: Bloomberg; Wall Street Journal; *Dow Jones New Service.*

Note: Data as of December 31, 1998, except for Wall Street Journal citations which represent calendar year 1998 data.

creased care, thoroughness, and discipline represent hallmarks of successful investors in less liquid assets.

Liquidity's Ephemeral Nature

Investors prize liquidity because it allows trading in and out of securities. Unfortunately, liquidity tends to evaporate when most needed.

The crash of October 1987, described in the *Report of the Presidential Task Force on Market Mechanisms,* provides a case in point:

> As the rate of decline accelerated on October 19, the efficiency with which the equity market functioned deteriorated markedly. By the late afternoon of October 19, market makers on the major stock exchanges appear to have largely abandoned serious attempts to stem the downward movement in prices. In the futures and options markets, market makers were not a significant factor during that time. . . . Price changes and trading activity were highly erratic from late Monday afternoon through most of the day on Tuesday, October 20, as market makers were overwhelmed by selling. . . . Realistically, in the face of October's violent shifts in selling demand for equity-related securities, a rational downward transition in stock prices was not possible. Market makers possessed neither the resources nor the willingness to absorb the extraordinary volume of selling demand that materialized.[15]

Just when investors most needed liquidity, it disappeared.

J. M. Keynes argues in *The General Theory of Employment, Interest and Money* that "of the maxims of orthodox finance none, surely, is more anti-social than the fetish of liquidity, the doctrine that it is a positive virtue on the part of investment institutions to concentrate their resources upon the holding of "liquid" securities. It forgets that there is no such thing as liquidity of investment for the community as a whole."[16]

Keynes toyed with the idea of reducing market liquidity to increase the prevalence of long-term investing. In *The General Theory* he wrote, "The spectacle of modern investment markets has sometimes moved me towards the conclusion that to make the purchase of an investment permanent and indissoluble, like marriage, except by reason of death or other grave cause, might be a useful remedy for our contemporary evils. For this would force the investor to direct his mind to the long-term prospects and to those only."[17]

Investors should pursue success, not liquidity. If private, illiquid investments succeed, liquidity follows as investors clamor for shares of the hot initial public offering. In public markets, as once-illiquid stocks produce strong results, liquidity increases as Wall Street recognizes progress. In contrast, if public, liquid investments fail, illiquidity follows as interest dries up, with trading disappearing almost completely when a company declares bankruptcy. Portfolio managers should fear failure, not illiquidity.

Value Orientation

Consistent investment success follows most reliably from pursuing value-based strategies, in which investors acquire assets at prices below fair value, "buying dollars for fifty cents." Investors wishing to implement value-oriented programs require unusual skill, intelligence, and energy. Without a significant edge relative to other market participants, investors face likely failure. Moreover, value opportunities tend to be out of favor with mainstream investors, demanding courage of conviction to initiate and maintain contrarian positions.

Margin of Safety

Renowned investor Benjamin Graham distills the central tenet of value investing into a single concept, margin of safety—the cushion in value created by owning shares of a company with "expected earning power considerably above the going rate for bonds." Graham notes,

> The margin-of-safety idea becomes [most] evident when we apply it to the field of undervalued or bargain securities. We have here, by definition, a favorable difference between price on the one hand and indicated or appraised value on the other. That difference is the safety margin. It is available for absorbing the effect of miscalculations or worse than average luck. The buyer of bargain issues places particular emphasis on the ability of the investment to withstand adverse developments. For in most such cases he has no real enthusiasm about the company's prospects. True, if the prospects are definitely bad the investor will prefer to avoid the security no matter how low the price. But the field of undervalued issues is

drawn from the many concerns—perhaps a majority of the total—for which the future appears neither distinctly promising
nor distinctly unpromising. If these are bought on a bargain basis, even a moderate decline in the earning power need not
prevent the investment from showing satisfactory results. The
margin of safety will then have served its proper purpose.[18]

In today's highly efficient securities markets, few opportunities exist to acquire assets at less than a fair price. Even with twenty-twenty
hindsight, investors seldom know whether positions entered the portfolio below intrinsic value. Adjusting for risk and assessing the impact
of subsequent external events, positive or negative, complicate evaluation of the initial acquisition decision. Because of the difficulty of
proving the efficacy of value-investing strategies, investors accept the
approach almost as an article of faith.

Perhaps the most compelling argument for value-based investment approaches rests on contrarian principles. Markets frequently
move to extremes, with high valuations for the popular and low valuations for the out of favor. By looking for opportunity in neglected securities, contrarian investors increase the likelihood of identifying
profitable investments.

Yet mindless contrarian investing poses dangers to portfolios.
Sometimes popular companies deserve premium valuations. Sometimes out-of-favor companies fail to recover, justifying the market's
discounted valuation. Identifying out-of-favor assets serves as a starting point for serious investors, leading to further analysis. Only if
such analysis justifies expectations of superior future performance
should investment be contemplated.

The naive strategy of purchasing stocks with low ratios of price-to-
earnings or price-to-book represents mindless contrarianism. Simply
selecting the cheapest stocks, measured relative to current earnings or
book value, neglects important factors such as the quality of a business's management and future earnings prospects.

Historically, naive value strategies have delivered superior rates
of return while exposing investors to relatively high levels of fundamental risk.[19] Jeremy Grantham of Grantham, Mayo, Van Otterloo
warns of the "sixty year flood," which may wipe out years of gains
garnered by simply purchasing the cheapest stocks. True value can be

acquired by purchasing assets at prices below fair value, a forward-looking concept that incorporates anticipated cash flows adjusted for the level of risk.

Value investors need not limit choices to low-growth or distressed companies. Even high-growth industries contain companies with appealing valuations. One technology stock manager, when attending industry conferences, avoids the rooms crowded with analysts pursuing the "flavor of the month." Instead, operating out of the mainstream, he pursues companies that cannot attract an audience. While many find the concepts of value and technology strange bedfellows, combining the two creates a powerful combination. Value investors seek to purchase companies at a discount to fair value, not to purchase distressed assets per se.

Benjamin Graham recognized that careful investors might identify value in unusual precincts. He writes:

> The growth-stock approach may supply as dependable a margin of safety as is found in the ordinary investment—provided the calculation of the future is conservatively made, and provided it shows a satisfactory margin in relation to the price paid. The danger in a growth-stock program lies precisely here. For such favored issues the market has a tendency to set prices that will not be adequately protected by a *conservative* projection of future earnings. The margin of safety is always dependent on the price paid. It will be large at one price, small at some higher price, nonexistent at some still higher price. If, as we suggest, the average market level of most growth stocks is too high to provide an adequate margin of safety for the buyer, then a simple technique of diversified buying in this field may not work out satisfactorily. A special degree of foresight and judgment will be needed, in order that wise individual selections may overcome the hazards inherent in the customary market level of such issues as a whole.[20]

While Graham recognizes the occasional opportunity to identify growth stocks exhibiting a margin of safety, value-oriented investors choosing among out-of-favor securities face a richer set of attractive portfolio alternatives.

Contrarian Investing

Superb opportunities to purchase assets at prices significantly below fair value tend to be hidden in deeply out-of-favor market segments. At market bottoms, the broad consensus so loathes certain asset types that investors brave enough to make commitments find their sanity and sense of responsibility questioned. In fact, Keynes wrote of the contrarian investor that "it is in the essence of his behavior that he should be eccentric, unconventional, and rash in the eyes of average opinion."[21] Managers searching among unloved opportunities face greater chances of success, along with almost certain tirades of criticism in the event of failure.

The real estate market in the early 1990s provided obvious opportunities to acquire dollars at a discount. In January 1994, Yale participated in the purchase of a real estate asset with a lease that promised a rate of return of 14.8 percent. Over the term of the lease, the return would be fully realized in cash, paying back the entire investment along with a profit and leaving a valuable asset in the partnership's possession upon expiration of the lease. Even without ascribing any residual value to the property, the real estate return of nearly 15 percent exceeded by dramatic margin comparable returns on treasury notes of approximately 5.75 percent. Based on these facts, the transaction may or may not have represented good value. Perhaps the risk of nonperformance by the tenant justified the large spread between the lease payments and the riskless treasury rate. In reality, the responsibility of the U.S. government for lease payments rendered the quality of the rental stream equivalent to the treasury note. Rarely do investors face clearer opportunities to buy dollars at a discount. (Ironically, the opportunity to purchase a risk-free stream of cash flows at a bargain price came from an agency of the U.S. government, the Resolution Trust Corporation (RTC). While the RTC generally did an effective job of disposing of assets, attractive deals occasionally presented themselves.)

The opportunity to purchase real estate assets at bargain basement prices had its seeds in the excesses of the late 1980s. Real estate was an institutional favorite, topping the list of categories to be increased in asset allocation studies. Investors characterized regional malls as "irreplaceable assets" with "monopoly positions," purchasing them at cash yields below 5 percent. Downtown office buildings were treated with similar reverence.

In the early 1990s the story changed dramatically. The overbuilding, overleveraging, and overpaying of the previous decade became apparent as real estate prices went into free fall. Regional malls, in reverse evolution, became dinosaurs, threatened by competition from power centers and other new retailing concepts. Central business district office buildings too were headed for extinction, as working at home was about to replace commuting to the city.

Value-oriented investors recognized that circumstances were not as good as they seemed in the 1980s and were not as bad as they appeared in the early 1990s. By simply looking at the relationship between market value and replacement cost, an investor would be a late 1980s seller and an early 1990s buyer. Buying low and selling high beats the alternative.

Tobin's q

J. M. Keynes in *The General Theory* articulated this concept of value: "There is no sense in building up a new enterprise at a cost greater than that at which a similar existing enterprise can be purchased; whilst there is an inducement to spend on a new project what may seem an extravagant sum, if it can be floated off . . . at an immediate profit."[22] James Tobin and William Brainard formalized this concept as q, the ratio of market value to replacement cost.

In equilibrium, under a reasonable set of conditions, Tobin-Brainard q equals one as the market value of assets equals replacement cost. If market value exceeds replacement cost, a q greater than one encourages entrepreneurs to create companies, offering them for sale at an immediate profit in the public markets. If replacement cost exceeds market value, a q of less than one leads managers to acquire corporate assets in the public market instead of building enterprises from the ground up. Value investors thrive in environments where q measures less than one.

• • •

Value investing provides a sturdy foundation for investing portfolios of assets as the acquisition of assets below fair value provides a margin of safety for investors. In many instances, value investing proves fundamentally uncomfortable, as the most attractive opportunities frequently lurk in unattractive or even frightening areas. Value acquisition strategies provide a measure of control to investment managers, reducing dependence on the vicissitudes of the market for investment returns and serving to mitigate risks.

CONCLUSION

Investment philosophy defines an investor's approach to generating portfolio returns, describing in the most fundamental fashion the tenets that permeate the investment process. Market returns stem from three sources—asset allocation, market timing, and security selection—with each source of return providing a tool for investors to use in attempting to satisfy institutional goals. Sensible investors employ the available tools in a manner consistent with a well-defined, carefully articulated investment philosophy.

Investor behavior causes policy asset allocation to dominate portfolio returns, since institutions tend to hold stable commitments to broadly diversified portfolios of marketable securities. Creating a diversified portfolio with equity-oriented asset classes that behave in fundamentally different fashion provides important underpinning to the investment process.

Market timing causes investors to hold portfolios that differ from policy targets, jeopardizing a fund's ability to meet long-term objectives. Often driven by fear or greed, market timing tends to detract from portfolio performance. Many institutions practice an implicit form of market timing by failing to maintain allocations at long-term policy targets. Risk control requires regular portfolio rebalancing, ensuring that portfolios reflect institutional preferences.

Active security selection plays a prominent role in nearly all institutional investment programs despite the poor relative results posted by most investors. Fund managers increase the probability of success by focusing on inefficient markets, which present the greatest range of opportunities. Accepting illiquidity pays outsized dividends to the patient long-term investor, while approaching markets with a value orientation provides a margin of safety. Even if investors approach active management programs with intelligence and care, efficiency in pricing assets creates great difficulty in identifying and implementing market-beating strategies.

5
Asset
Allocation

Asset allocation exemplifies the importance of combining art and science in portfolio construction, as either informed judgment or quantitative analysis alone fails to produce consistently successful results. Seat-of-the-pants decisions lack rigor, omitting information valuable to the investment process. On the other end of the spectrum, mechanistic application of quantitative tools produces naive, sometimes dangerous, conclusions. Marrying the art of seasoned judgment with the science of numeric analysis creates a powerful approach to allocating portfolio assets.

Defining and selecting asset classes constitute initial steps in producing a portfolio. Many investors simply allocate among the asset classes popular at the time in proportions similar to those of other investors, creating uncontroversial portfolios that may or may not address institutional needs. By relying on the decisions of others to drive portfolio choices, investors fail to consider the function of particular asset classes in a portfolio designed to meet specific goals.

Asset Classes and Fashion

The asset classes from which investors structure portfolios change over time. Snapshots of Yale's portfolio throughout the past 150 years provide an impression of the evolution of asset class categorization. Real estate constituted nearly half of the 1850 portfolio, with "bonds and notes mostly secured by mortgages" and stocks making up the remainder. At the turn of the twentieth century, dominant asset class categories included mortgage bonds, railroad bonds, and real estate, with relatively small allocations to "stocks in sundry corporations" and "corporation bonds other than railroad." In the 1950s, the university held domestic bonds, domestic common stocks, preferred stocks, and real estate.

Just as sartorial fashion changes, investment fashions ebb and flow. Railroad bonds earned special consideration in asset allocation discussions in the late nineteenth and early twentieth centuries because of the dominant role railroads played in the developing U.S. economy. Investors willingly lent money for hundred-year terms, ostensibly to secure rail companies, knowing that even if a particular concern failed, valuable rail-bed right of way provided unimpeachable security.

Imagine the surprise of a 1890s-vintage portfolio manager upon learning the fate of the Lehigh Valley Railroad 4 1/2s due in 1989. Offered at 102 1/2 in January 1891 by the distinguished syndicate of Drexel & Co. of Philadelphia, J. P. Morgan & Co., and Brown Bros. & Co. of New York, the bonds attracted little notice for the next four decades; required payments arrived in full and on time. Widespread economic distress in the 1930s hurt the Lehigh Valley, leading to relief in the form of the 1938 Debt Adjustment Plan. Initial concessions failed to put the rail line on sound financial footing, leading to further negotiations, which resulted in the 1949 Debt Adjustment Plan. Restructuring proved insufficient to solve the Lehigh Valley's woes, culminating in failure to meet the October 1, 1970, interest payment. Bondholders, beneficiaries of a first lien on 14.4 miles of track (7.9 miles from Hazle Creek Junction to Hazleton, Pennsylvania, and 6.5 miles from Ashmore to Highland Junction, Pennsylvania) received little comfort from the security interest, seeing the obligations trade as low as 5 percent of face value in 1972. Although not all railway debt suffered the fate of the Lehigh Valley bonds, railroad obligations generally failed to meet expectations.[1]

Railroad bonds no longer constitute a separate institutional asset class, since the rail industry proved less enduringly robust than investors of the 1890s believed. In contrast to heavy concentration in railway debt, investors allocated relatively little to domestic common stocks, missing an opportunity to create portfolios with superior return potential. Twenty-twenty hindsight provides obvious conclusions regarding what would have produced profits in the past. The basic challenge for investors lies in fashioning portfolios that succeed in the environment to come.

Investors begin by selecting asset classes that promise to meet fundamental investment goals. Institutional portfolios require assets likely to generate equity-like returns, such as domestic and foreign equities, absolute return strategies, and private equities. To mitigate equity risks, portfolios include assets such as fixed income and real estate. By understanding and articulating the role played by each asset class, investors avoid making allocations based on the fashion of the day.

Asset Class Definition

Purity of asset class composition represents a rarely achieved ideal. Carried to an extreme, investors define dozens of asset classes, creating an unmanageable multiplicity of alternatives. While market participants disagree on the appropriate number of asset classes, fewer tend to be better. Portfolio commitments must be large enough to make a difference. Committing less than 10 percent of a fund to a particular type of investment makes little sense; the small allocation holds no potential to influence overall portfolio results. Investors trade off the benefits of precise definition of an asset class with the costs of employing large numbers of classes.

Functional attributes play the dominant role in defining asset classes, with structural and legal characteristics taking secondary positions. Asset class distinctions rest on broad sweeping differences in fundamental character: debt versus equity, private versus public, liquid versus illiquid, domestic versus foreign, inflation sensitive versus deflation sensitive. Ultimately investors attempt to group like with like, creating relatively homogeneous groups of investments that provide fundamental building blocks for the portfolio construction process.

Fixed income represents an interesting case. If investors want fixed income assets to provide a hedge against financial accidents, then only high-quality, long-term, noncallable bonds satisfy the requirement. Although legally and structurally, below-investment grade bonds (aka junk) belong to the fixed income family, they lack important crisis-hedging attributes. Junk bonds contain equity-like risks, as payments depend mightily on the financial health of the issuer. Even if the high-yield obligor meets contractual obligations, holders may lose bonds through a mandatory call, as lower interest rates or improved corporate health allow issuers to redeem bonds at a fixed price prior to maturity. Ironically, holders of junk bonds may lose if corporate prospects deteriorate—or if they improve! In either circumstance, below-investment-grade bonds provide little protection against a period of severe financial distress.

Government bonds dominate portfolios designed to hedge against financial trauma, providing high-quality portfolio protection. Not all treasury issues make the grade, however. The recently issued Treasury Inflation-Protection Securities (TIPS) have no place in a properly defined fixed income portfolio. Traditional fixed income assets respond to unanticipated inflation by declining in price, as the future stream of fixed payments becomes worth less. In contrast, inflation-indexed bonds respond to unexpected price increases by providing a higher return. When two assets respond in opposite fashion to the same critically important variable, those assets belong in different asset classes.

Many investors include foreign bonds in portfolios as part of a broadly defined fixed income asset class or in a separate allocation. Neither choice makes fundamental sense. Foreign bonds have no role in a fixed income portfolio designed to protect against deflation or financial trauma. Investors cannot know how foreign bonds might respond to a domestic financial crisis, since conditions overseas may differ from the environment at home. Moreover, foreign exchange translations may influence returns in a substantial, unpredictable manner. As a separate asset class, high-quality foreign bonds hold little interest. The combination of low, bondlike expected returns and foreign exchange exposure negate any positive attributes associated with nondomestic fixed income. If investors pay the price (in terms of low expected returns) by buying bonds for disaster insurance, the payoff must be clear and direct.

Careful investors define asset classes in terms of function, relating security characteristics to the role expected from a particular group of investments. In the case of fixed income, introduction of credit risk, call risk, and currency risk diminish disaster-hedging attributes. Yet in reaching for return or seeking an easy way to beat the benchmark, most institutional portfolios contain disproportionate allocations to bonds lacking the purity of U.S. Treasury obligations. The net result creates a portfolio that meets neither the goal of producing equity-like returns nor the goal of protecting against market trauma.

Judgment plays a critical role in defining and shaping asset classes. Although the asset allocation process necessarily involves quantitative tools, unless statistical analysis rests on reasonable judgment, the resulting portfolio stands little chance of meeting institutional needs.

QUANTITATIVE AND QUALITATIVE ANALYSIS

Establishing policy asset allocation targets requires a combination of quantitative and qualitative inputs. Financial markets invite quantification. Return, risk, and correlation lend themselves to numerical measurement. Statistical methods allow analysis of possible portfolio combinations through a number of frameworks, including the capital asset pricing model (CAPM), arbitrage pricing theory (APT), and modern portfolio theory (MPT). Quantitative analysis provides essential underpinnings to the portfolio structuring process, forcing investors to take a disciplined approach to portfolio construction. Systematic specification of inputs for an asset allocation model clarifies the central issues in portfolio management.

Nobel laureate Harry Markowitz developed mean-variance optimization, one of the most useful and most widely used analytical frameworks. The process identifies efficient portfolios, which for a given level of risk have the highest possible return. Using inputs of expected return, expected risk, and expected correlation, the optimization process evaluates various combinations of assets, ultimately identifying superior portfolios. Those portfolios that cannot be improved on represent the efficient frontier, a set of points from which rational investors will choose.

Identifying Efficient Portfolios

The mere phrase *mean-variance optimization* intimidates many investors, conjuring images of complicated quantitative methods beyond the grasp of the intelligent laypublic. In fact, the optimization process rests on several relatively basic concepts, allowing even casual students of finance to comprehend the model.

Identifying efficient portfolios constitutes the core mission of mean-variance optimization. An efficient portfolio dominates all others producing the same return or exhibiting the same risk. In other words, for a given risk level, no other portfolio produces a higher return than the efficient portfolio. Similarly, for a given return level, no other portfolio exhibits lower risk than the efficient portfolio. Note that the definition of efficiency relates entirely to risk and return. Mean-variance optimization fails to consider other asset class characteristics.

Practitioners generally assume that normal, or bell-curve-shaped, distributions describe asset class characteristics, allowing complete specification of the distribution of returns with only a mean and a variance. Although using normal distributions facilitates implementation of mean-variance analysis, security returns may include significant nonnormal characteristics, limiting the value of the conclusions.

Correlations specify the manner in which returns of one asset class tend to vary with returns of other asset classes, quantifying the diversifying power of combining asset classes that respond differently to forces that drive returns. Correlation supplies a third means through which asset class characteristics influence portfolio construction, supplementing the return and risk factors.

After describing the set of investible asset classes, the search for efficient portfolios begins. Specifying a given risk level, the model examines portfolio after portfolio, ultimately leading to identification of a combination of assets producing the highest return. The superior portfolio takes a place on the efficient frontier, as the process continues by identifying the highest return portfolio for a range of risk levels.

At its core, mean-variance optimization represents a simple process. Employing capital markets characteristics described in a rigorous fashion, a quantitative model uses "brute force" iterative techniques to search for efficient portfolios. When considering combinations of assets lying on the efficient frontier, investors choose from a superior set of portfolios.

Limitations of Mean-Variance Analysis

Unconstrained mean-variance runs usually provide solutions unrecognizable as reasonable portfolios. Richard Michaud, in his critique of mean-variance optimization, writes, "The unintuitive character of many 'optimized' portfolios can be traced to the fact that mean-variance optimizers are, in a fundamental sense, 'estimation-error maximizers.' . . . Mean-variance optimization significantly overweights (underweights) those securities that have large (small) estimated returns, negative (positive) correlations and small (large) variances. These securities are, of course, the ones most likely to have large estimation errors."[2] Although Michaud's comments pertain to a portfolio of securities, his critique applies equally to a portfolio of asset classes.

Other fundamental problems limit the usefulness of mean-variance analysis. Evidence suggests that distributions of security returns might not be normal, with markets exhibiting more extreme events than would be consistent with a bell curve distribution. Richard Bookstaber, managing director at Salomon Smith Barney, states that a "general rule of thumb is that every financial market experiences one or more daily price moves of four standard deviations or more each year.* And in any year, there is usually at least one market that has a daily move greater than ten standard deviations."[3] If extreme price changes occur substantially more frequently than predicted by a normal distribution, some extremely important events fail to influence conclusions generated from quantitative analysis. In fact, investors may care more about extraordinary situations, such as the 1987 stock market crash, than about outcomes represented by the heart of the distribution.

The way in which asset classes relate to each other may not be stable. Most investors rely heavily on historical experience in estimating quantitative inputs, yet continuous structural evolution would be sufficient to cause historical correlations to be of questionable use in building portfolio allocations. Even more disturbing, market crises tend to cause otherwise distinct markets to behave in a similar fashion. In October 1987 equity markets all over the world collapsed, disappointing those portfolio managers hoping that foreign diversification might cushion a drop in domestic equity prices. Although correlations between global stock markets prior and subsequent to October 1987 measured substantially less than one, the behavior of markets in the period immediately surrounding the 1987 crash caused many investors to wonder what happened to the hoped-for diversification.

Mean-variance optimization assumes that expected return and risk

---

*Normally distributed variables generate a four-standard-deviation event once every 15,780 trials. Based on a 250-day year, a four-standard-deviation event occurs once every sixty-three years.

completely define asset class characteristics. The framework fails to consider other important attributes, such as liquidity and marketability. In fact, the inclusion of less liquid assets in a mean-variance framework raises material issues. Most frequently, mean-variance optimization involves analysis of annual series of return and risk data. The analysis implicitly assumes an annual rebalancing of portfolio allocations. That is, if stocks have moved above target and bonds below, then on the relevant anniversary date, investors sell stocks and buy bonds, restoring target allocations. Clearly, less marketable assets, such as private equity and real estate holdings, cannot be rebalanced in a low-cost, efficient manner. The inability to manage private assets in a manner consistent with model assumptions reduces the applicability of mean-variance optimization conclusions.

Another problem associated with using annual periods in mean-variance optimization relates to investor time horizon. The period of analysis corresponds to investor time frames, with one-year analysis implying a fairly short investment horizon. One-year treasury obligations typically represent the riskless asset, providing investors with an absolutely certain return over a twelve-month period. For longer-term investors, returns on one-year instruments embody significant risk. Since future reinvestment rates for short-term obligations remain unknown at the time of initial commitment, holding-period returns depend on future interest rate levels. An investor in one-year bills with an intermediate horizon—say, five years—faces four future reinvestment rates to generate a holding-period return. Simply buying a five-year note involves far less risk than a strategy of rolling one-year instruments. Unfortunately, running optimizations with a five-year investment period proves impractical, as the limited number of independent historical data points provides insufficient support for developing sensible capital markets assumptions, particularly for nontraditional assets.

In the final analysis, both the fundamental shortcoming and the basic attraction of quantitative analysis stem from reducing a rich set of asset class attributes to a neat, compact package of precisely defined statistical characteristics. Because the process involves material simplifying assumptions, adopting the unconstrained asset allocation point estimates produced by mean-variance optimization makes little sense.

Qualitative Judgments

The limitations of mean-variance analysis argue for inclusion of qualitative considerations in the asset allocation process. Judgment might be incorporated by applying reasonable constraints to particular asset class allocations. For example, prospective allocations to private equity could logically be limited to a modest increase over the current portfolio. Since illiquidity and lumpiness of opportunities limit prudent expansion of private equity holdings, incremental changes make sense.

A similar, albeit less persuasive, argument might be made for constraining allocations to marketable securities. Incremental moves create less market impact, limiting potential disruption to internal or external managers of securities.

Gradualism represents a virtue in and of itself. Substantial uncertainty surrounds the asset allocation process. Keynes's "dark forces of time and ignorance" cloud the future, causing even the most thoughtful estimates of capital markets characteristics to prove unreliable.[4] Deciding to make radical changes based on highly uncertain data places too much weight on a shaky foundation. Limiting asset allocation responses by constraining asset class movements represents a sensible modification of the optimization process.

Care must be taken, however, to avoid using asset class constraints simply to fashion a reasonable-looking portfolio. Taken to an extreme, placing too many constraints on the optimization process causes the model to do nothing other than reflect the investor's original biases, resulting in the GIGO (garbage in/garbage out) phenomenon well known to computer scientists.

Quantitative modeling proves most helpful in focusing investor attention on potentially rewarding asset allocation changes. By analyzing portfolios using mean-variance optimization and measuring the degree to which existing asset class allocation levels limit moves desired by the optimizer, investors understand the direction quantitative analysis suggests moving the portfolio. Attractive asset classes strain at the constraints, while unattractive holdings may not even reach current allocation levels. The degree to which the optimizer "likes" a particular asset class suggests increasing or decreasing allocations, providing a starting point for qualitative assessment of the quantitative conclusion. Using market judgment to modify and interpret mean-variance results improves the asset allocation process.

CAPITAL MARKET ASSUMPTIONS

Return and risk expectations constitute the heart of any quantitative assessment of portfolio alternatives. While historical experience represents a reasonable starting point in developing a set of forward-looking data, investors seeking to create truly useful conclusions must move beyond simply plugging historical numbers into the mean-variance optimizer.

Developing a set of quantitative inputs for portfolio optimization poses some difficult issues. Most troubling may be the forward-looking nature of the estimates. While past patterns provide important input for assumptions about the future, historical data must be modified to produce a set of numbers consistent with expected market realities. Thoughtful investors strike a balance between respect for history and concern for analytical consistency.

Situations where historical capital market data require adjustments abound. Mean reverting behavior in security prices implies that periods of abnormally high returns follow periods of abnormally low returns, and vice versa. Jeremy Grantham, a prominent money manager, believes that reversion to the mean constitutes the most powerful force in financial markets.[5] If prices tend to revert to the mean, then return expectations must be adjusted to dampen expectations for high fliers and boost forecasts for poor performers.

Data covering specific periods frequently suggest counterintuitive results. Relatively risky asset classes may show returns below those of obviously lower-risk investments. Assets that have little in common may move together for no apparent reason. Adjusting assumptions to reflect appropriate risk and return relationships proves critical to sensible quantitative analysis.

Structural changes in markets force analysts to weight recent data more heavily, deemphasizing numbers reflecting earlier, sometimes dramatically different environments. Introduction of new classes of securities, such as U.S. Treasury issuance of thirty-year bonds beginning in February 1977, may alter asset class characteristics in so fundamental a manner as to render earlier data far less valuable in reaching conclusions regarding future asset class behavior.

Perhaps the greatest value lies in producing a set of reasonable forecasts of expected relative returns for various asset classes. Developing capital markets assumptions with reasonable relative relationships enables identification of a set of sensible portfolio alternatives. Even if point estimates of risk and return variables fail to represent reality fairly, insofar as inputs stem from well-grounded interrelationships, the mean-variance optimization process produces valuable insight into efficient portfolio alternatives.

Unfortunately, point estimates of asset class returns prove necessary for some purposes. In evaluating the ability of various portfolio combinations to support specified return requirements, the specific levels of forecast returns come into play. When deciding whether a portfolio can reasonably produce returns sufficient to satisfy a 4 percent, 4 1/2 percent, or 5 percent target rate of spending, fiduciaries face the difficult challenge of relying on forecasts of future capital markets returns. Predicting the level of future investment returns represents one of the investment world's greatest challenges.

In running mean-variance optimization, data on expected returns provide the most powerful determinant of results, demanding the greatest share of quantitative modeler's attention.[6] Forecasts of variances constitute the second most significant collection of variables, while assumptions regarding correlations prove least critical to the process. Fortunately, the most intuitive variables—expected returns and variances—prove to be more important to the model than the less intuitive correlations.

Marketable Security Characteristics

Based on the availability of a lengthy series of high-quality data, past returns for domestic stocks and bonds provide a sensible starting point. Choosing an appropriate time period to examine poses interesting trade-offs. On the positive side, a long time series provides a robust picture of asset class returns and interrelationships with other asset classes. On the negative side, a long time series includes results from periods with fundamentally different structural characteristics. For instance, Jeremy Siegel's *Stocks for the Long Run* begins its study of U.S. equity and bond market returns with data from the turn of the nineteenth century. During significant portions of Siegel's study period, the United States constituted an emerging market, no Federal Reserve System operated, and no long-term government bonds existed.

What relevance does the level of stock and bond returns from the nineteenth century have to expectations for stock and bond returns today?

Recognizing the arbitrary nature of choosing any particular subset of data to use as a foundation for estimating future returns, one sensible starting point involves using the landmark Ibbotson-Sinquefield data series, first published in 1976.[7] Beginning at the end of 1925, the period contains a sufficient number of observations to provide a rich set of data, but encompasses a short enough span to limit the impact on markets of significant structural changes in economic and financial conditions.

Using Table 5.1's historical data as a foundation, the following discussion illustrates some factors considered in creating a coherent set of capital markets assumptions, presented in Table 5.2. Since prudently managed endowments consume only postinflation returns, all capital markets data reflect an appropriate inflation adjustment.

Domestic Bonds

Domestic bond market returns provide a reasonable starting point for building a matrix of capital markets assumptions. Over the long sweep of time, as fixed income investors found returns eroded by spells of unanticipated inflation, bonds provided mediocre real returns of 1.2 percent per annum with risk of 6.5 percent. The October 1979 Federal Reserve decision to target monetary aggregates instead of interest rates caused bond markets to trade with greater volatility, resulting in higher subsequent real returns, albeit with higher risk. Placing more weight on recent experience leads to an assumed expected return of 2 percent with risk of 10 percent.

Marketable Equities

Discussion of the difference in expected returns for bonds and stocks, or the risk premium, occupies many volumes of finance journals. Even while recognizing the complexities surrounding discussion of the risk premium, asset allocators must deal with the issue explicitly or im-

Table 5.1 Historical Capital Markets Data Provide a Starting Point for Quantitative Analysis

Historical Data Inflation Adjusted Using the Higher Education Price Index

	U.S. Bonds	U.S. Equity	Developed Equity	Emerging Equity	Absolute Return	Real Estate	Private Equity	Cash
Observations	72	72	38	13	20	21	16	72
Arithmetic return	1.2%	9.2%	6.3%	11.1%	17.6%	3.5%	19.1%	-0.4%
Standard deviation	6.5	21.7	18.9	27.9	11.8	5.1	20.0	4.1
Growth rate	1.0	7.0	4.7	7.7	17.0	3.4	17.5	-0.5

Sources: U.S. bonds: Lehman Brothers Government Bond Index (1973–1997) and Ibbotson Intermediate Term Government Bond Index (1926–1972). U.S. equity: 70 percent weight on the S&P 500 (1926–1997) plus 30 percent weight on the Russell 2000 (1979–1997) or DFA Small Companies Deciles 6–10 (1926–1978). Developed equity: Capital International data (1960–1977) and Adjusted MSCI-GDP EAFE Index (1978–1997). Emerging equity: IFC Emerging Markets Index (1985–1997). Absolute return: Yale Absolute Return Portfolio (1991–1997), and Weighted Average Composite of Cambridge Associates' Data and other reported returns for Absolute Return Managers (1978–1990). Real estate: NCREIF FRC Index (1977–1997). Private equity: Yale Private Equity Portfolio (1982–1997).

Table 5.2 Quantitative Model Inputs Rely on Modified Risk and Return Assumptions

Model Data Inflation Adjusted Using the Higher Education Price Index

	U.S. Bonds	U.S. Equity	Developed Equity	Emerging Equity	Absolute Return	Real Estate	Private Equity	Cash
Expected return	2.0%	6.0%	6.0%	8.0%	7.0%	4.0%	12.5%	0.0%
Standard deviation	10.0	20.0	20.0	30.0	15.0	15.0	25.0	5.0
Expected growth	1.5	4.1	4.1	3.9	6.0	2.9	9.8	(0.1)

Source: Yale University Investments Office.

plicitly. The historical risk premium of 8.0 percent appears to be excessive, resulting in large part from the extraordinary recent performance of U.S. equities. Moreover, examination of time series of equity and bond returns leads to the conclusion that the risk premium has declined through time. Combining mean-reverting tendencies with the observation that the equity risk premium seems to decline secularly justifies an assumption for U.S. equity returns of 6 percent real, with a standard deviation of 20 percent.

Making geographic distinctions among various equity markets poses interesting analytical questions. Approaches range from global, to regional, to individual country allocations. A global equity asset class fails to recognize the critical contribution that currency movements make to investment returns, while individual country asset classes create too many variables for reasonable analysis. Separating domestic equities from foreign, with a further distinction between developed and emerging markets, groups assets with respect to important differentiating characteristics.

Developed economies tend to share similar economic and market fundamentals. In the long run, stock markets in Germany, Japan, and the United Kingdom ought to generate returns similar to those of the United States, while exposing investors to similar risk levels.* Assumed foreign developed market return levels of 6 percent with risk of 20 percent matches expectations for U.S. equities, while corresponding closely to historical levels for developed foreign markets.

Relative to other marketable equities, emerging markets embody substantially greater fundamental risks, causing investors to anticipate higher rewards and higher volatility. Expected real returns of 8 percent compensate holders of emerging market equities for accepting increased risk of 30 percent standard deviation of returns.

---

*Large differences between returns from U.S. and foreign equities provide further support for reducing domestic equity return expectations. The extraordinary bull market in U.S. equities caused the S&P 500 to outpace foreign equities (as measured by the Morgan Stanley Capital International Europe Australia Far East benchmark) by a margin of 17.7 percent versus 13.8 percent for the period from 1979 to 1998. Operating under the premise that developed economies ought to be expected to produce similar returns requires either upward adjustment of historical foreign return data or downward adjustment of historical domestic return data.

Alternative Asset Characteristics

Nontraditional asset classes provide interesting challenges. Unlike traditional marketable securities, alternative assets exist outside established markets. No benchmark returns provide guidance to investors seeking to model asset characteristics. Past data, limited in scope, generally describe active manager returns, with results inflated by substantial survivorship bias. The lack of reliable historical information on which to base forecasts requires thinking about alternative asset classes from a fundamental perspective in making estimates of expected return and risk.

Absolute Return

Absolute return investing, first identified as a distinct asset class by Yale University in 1990, relies on active management for its very existence.* Dedicated to exploiting inefficiencies in pricing marketable securities, absolute return managers attempt to produce equity-like returns uncorrelated to traditional marketable securities through pursuit of investments in event-driven and value-driven strategies. Event-driven strategies, including merger arbitrage and distressed security investing, depend on the completion of a corporate finance transaction such as a merger or corporate liability restructuring. Value-driven strategies employ offsetting long and short positions to eliminate market exposure, relying on market recognition of mispricings to generate returns. Generally absolute return investments involve transactions with relatively short time horizons, ranging from several months to a year or two.

Based on historical data, observers might conclude that absolute return investing produces returns in the neighborhood of 20 percent per annum. Consultants brandish long lists of hedge funds with impressive historical records, showing high returns with low risk and little correlation to traditional marketable securities. Since investors taking no market risk earn a money market rate of return, if a manager constructs a market-neutral portfolio in an environment with a 4 percent cost of funds, 20 percent returns imply excess returns of 16 per-

*For a full description of the absolute return asset class, see pages 205–216.

cent! The high observed incremental return stems from survivorship bias, a case of past performance raising the profile of successful firms, while less successful firms languish in obscurity. Bottom-up consideration of the types of activities pursued by absolute return managers leads to more realistic expectations of future performance.

Modeling absolute return risk and return expectations requires thorough understanding of manager strategies. In value-driven transactions, managers often take long and short positions in marketable equities, creating two opportunities to generate excess returns. Assume that a manager producing top-decile performance in domestic equities generates approximately 3 percent excess returns.* Applied to both sides of the portfolio, long and short, gross returns total approximately 10 percent, resulting from adding a 4 percent short-term rate of return to a 3 percent alpha for long positions and 3 percent alpha for short positions. Based on past experience, producing 3 percent excess returns represents a heroic achievement, suggesting that this analysis relies on aggressive assumptions. After paying 20 percent incentive compensation, the investor nets approximately 8 percent. On a bottom-up basis, justifying return expectations of 20 percent proves difficult. In fact, the long/short investor needs to produce excess returns of more than 10 percent on both sides of the portfolio to deliver 20 percent net returns to investors. Producing such performance over extended periods of time would literally put a manager "off the charts."†

Historical absolute return data suffer from extreme survivorship bias, causing forward-looking assumptions to differ dramatically from past statistics. The combination of actual experience and consultant data presented in Table 5.1 shows a staggering 17.6 percent return

*Excess return, or alpha, represents the risk-adjusted incremental return for an active strategy relative to the market.
For the ten years ending December 31, 1997, top-decile equity manager beat the market by 3.1 percent per year according to data compiled by PIPER.
†Interestingly, fifth-percentile performance relative to the median for one year ending December 31, 1997, amounts to nearly ten percentage points. In contrast, fifth-percentile incremental performance for ten years totals less than five points per year. Perhaps stellar short-run performance attracts attention, causing investors to expect the sustained extraordinary performance necessary for absolute return managers to generate 20 percent net returns. More realistic, albeit still aggressive, expectations result from considering incremental returns generated by longer-term superior performance.

with unbelievably low volatility of 11.8 percent. If credible, the absolute return numbers indicate returns nearly double those of domestic equities with a risk level of nearly one-half. Using a conservative approach to determine absolute return asset class characteristics, the model assumes expected returns of 7 percent real with risk of 15 percent. Even with this substantial adjustment, the numbers suggest that absolute return investments will generate higher returns than domestic stocks with less risk.

Real Estate

Real estate markets provide dramatically cyclical returns. Looking in the rear-view mirror in the late 1980s, investors generated wild enthusiasm for real estate as historical statistics dominated numbers for traditional stocks and bonds. A few years later, after the market collapse, those same investors saw nothing other than dismal prospects for real estate. Poor returns nearly eliminated interest in real estate as an institutional investment asset. Reality lies somewhere between the extremes of wild enthusiasm and despair.

Real estate embodies characteristics of both debt and equity. Lease payments, the contractual obligations of tenants, resemble fixed income instruments, while the property's residual value contains equity-like attributes. In some extreme cases, real estate investments become completely bondlike. For example, properties subject to long-term, triple-net leases provide cash flows identical to fixed income instruments. In contrast, some real estate consists almost entirely of residual value. For example, hotel properties, with daily "leases," provide nearly pure equity characteristics. Most real estate, falling in the middle portion of the continuum, contains elements of debt and equity.

As in the case of absolute return data, historical real estate volatility numbers require dramatic modification. With equity risk at 20 percent and bond risk at 10 percent, observed real estate risk of 5.1 percent seems inconsistent with the asset class's fundamental characteristics. Because real estate data come predominantly from infrequently conducted appraisals, reported returns fail to capture true economic volatility. Not only does infrequent sampling reduce opportunity to observe price fluctuations, the appraisal process tends to perpetuate whatever biases influenced past appraisals.

Assumed real estate risk and return characteristics lie between attributes for debt and equity. Expected real estate returns of 4 percent lie between bond returns of 2 percent and stock returns of 6 percent. Expected real estate risk of 15 percent lies between bond risk of 10 percent and stock risk of 20 percent. Developing capital markets assumptions by evaluating fundamental asset class characteristics allows investors to create a reasonable framework for portfolio assessment independent of cyclical market conditions.

Private Equity

Private equity consists predominantly of venture capital and leveraged buyout participations, assets that respond to market influences in a manner similar to marketable equities. In fact, both venture and buyout investments resemble high-risk equity assets, raising the possibility of classifying the private assets with marketable securities.

Private managers pursuing purely financial strategies lay the weakest claim to managing a separate asset class. In the buyout arena, simply adding leverage to a company's balance sheet does little to distance the private investment from the public corporation. In the case of venture investing, a provider of mezzanine equity finance owns assets nearly identical to small-capitalization, publicly traded equity securities. Since fundamental characteristics of private investments created through financial engineering suggest strong similarity to marketable security counterparts, the argument for segregating such private assets rests primarily on differences in liquidity.

A stronger justification for treating private equity as a distinct asset class stems from value-added management by investment principals. To the extent that venture capitalists contribute to the process of bringing a company from an idea to a reality, generating tens of millions of dollars in revenues and employing hundreds of individuals, value creation occurs independent of market activity. A buyout specialist contributing expertise leading to meaningful operating improvements generates similarly noncorrelated returns. Superior potential for value creation, combined with liquidity and structural differences, supports treatment of private equity as a distinct asset class.

Historical data provide limited guidance in fashioning forward-looking capital markets assumptions. Infrequent marks-to-market cause private assets to appear less volatile than the underlying reality. Start-up companies held in a venture capitalist's partnership receive only occasional valuations, leading to relatively low levels of observed risk. Subsequent to an initial public offering, when a company begins day-to-day trading, measured volatility increases dramatically. Obviously true risk tends to decrease as companies mature, suggesting that observed volatility levels understate risk for privately held assets.

Guidance for specifying private equity risk and return attributes comes from the expected relationship with domestic equity investments. Illiquidity and higher risk in private assets demand a substantial premium over domestic equity's expectations of 6 percent returns with 20 percent risk. Assuming that private equity investments generate 12.5 percent returns with a risk level of 25 percent represents an appropriately conservative modification of the historical record of 19.1 percent returns with a 20.0 percent risk level.

Correlation Matrix Assumptions

The correlation matrix represents the most difficult set of mean-variance optimization variables to specify. Less intuitive than either means or variances, correlations indicate the degree to which asset class returns tend to move with one another.

Considering the relationship between bond and stock returns in various economic scenarios highlights the difficulties in specifying correlations. Under normal circumstances bond returns exhibit high positive correlation to stock returns. If interest rates fall, bond prices rise as a result of the inverse relationships between prices and yields. When interest rates decline, stock prices tend to rise as investors subject future earnings streams to lower discount rates. Strong, positive correlation between stocks and bonds in normal environments produces little diversifying power when combining the assets.

In the case of unanticipated inflation, bonds suffer. Inflationary price increases erode purchasing power of fixed nominal bond payments, causing investors to push bond prices down. While inflation may have negative short-term consequences for stocks, in the long run stocks react positively to inflation.[8] With unexpected inflation, the long-term correlation between stocks and bonds proves to be low, providing substantial diversification to the portfolio.

In a deflationary environment, stocks perform poorly as economic woes cause earnings to suffer. In contrast, bonds provide handsome returns since fixed payments appear increasingly attractive as price levels decline. During periods of deflation, low or negative correlation between stocks and bonds helps to diversify portfolio assets.

Data specification techniques for quantitative models tend to evolve. When Yale began employing mean-variance optimization in 1986, unadjusted historical data provided risk and return assumptions. By 1987, expected return data reflected adjustments designed to create internally consistent assumptions. In 1988, risk levels underwent the same type of scrubbing directed to return data. Finally, in 1994, the correlation matrix received judgmental modification to incorporate more consistent future expectations. Table 5.3 shows an unadjusted set of historical data, and Table 5.4 depicts a modified set of correlation assumptions. As investors accumulate experience with implementing quantitative models, the process becomes more intuitive, increasing the richness of the analysis and conclusions.

• • •

Producing a reasonable set of capital markets assumptions provides the basis for serious quantitative portfolio analysis. Developing sensible relative relationships produces a group of efficient portfolios, helping investors select superior asset allocation strategies. The more difficult to estimate specific levels of future returns provide necessary input in assessing the capacity of portfolios to support specified spending levels. Regardless of the ultimate utility of the model output, the process of creating capital markets assumptions provides investors with a rigorous disciplined framework in which to analyze investment issues.

Misuse of Mean-Variance Optimization

Despite mean-variance optimization's potential for positive contribution to portfolio structuring, dangerous conclusions may be reached if poorly considered forecasts enter the modeling process. Some of the most egregious errors committed with mean-variance analysis involve inappropriate use of historical data. Consider allocations to real estate in the late 1980s. Real estate provided extremely strong returns during

Table 5.3 Historical Correlation Matrix Provides a Starting Point for Defining the Relationship Between Asset Classes

Historical Correlation Matrix

	U.S. Equity	U.S. Bonds	Developed Equity	Emerging Equity	Absolute Return	Private Equity	Real Estate	Cash
U.S. equity	1.00							
U.S. bonds	.06	1.00						
Developed equity	.48	.25	1.00					
Emerging equity	.14	.04	.35	1.00				
Absolute return	.28	.15	.16	.36	1.00			
Private equity	.30	(.17)	.19	(.13)	.29	1.00		
Real estate	.13	.03	.30	(.21)	.06	.08	1.00	
Cash	(.09)	.70	.08	(.56)	(.08)	.01	.35	1.00

Sources: U.S. equity: 70 percent weight on the S&P 500 (1926–1997) plus 30 percent weight on the Russell 2000 (1979–1997) or DFA Small Companies Deciles 6–10 (1926–1978). U.S. bonds: Lehman Brothers Government Bond Index (1973–1997) and Ibbotson Intermediate Term Government Bond Index (1926–1972). Developed equity: Capital International data (1960–1977) and Adjusted MSCI-GDP EAFE Index (1978–1997). Emerging equity: IFC Emerging Markets Index (1985–1997). Absolute return: Yale Absolute Return Portfolio (1991–1997), Weighted Average Composite of Cambridge Associates' Data and other reported returns for Absolute Return Managers (1978–1990). Private equity: Yale Private Equity Portfolio (1982–1997). Real estate: NCREIF FRC Index (1977–1997).

Table 5.4 Modified Correlation Matrix Reflects Assumptions About Future Interrelationships

Modified Correlation Matrix

	U.S. Equity	U.S. Bonds	Developed Equity	Emerging Equity	Absolute Return	Private Equity	Real Estate	Cash
U.S. equity	1.00							
U.S. bonds	.45	1.00						
Developed equity	.60	.30	1.00					
Emerging equity	.30	.20	.50	1.00				
Absolute return	.30	.35	.30	.30	1.00			
Private equity	.40	.25	.25	.10	.25	1.00		
Real estate	.15	.25	.20	.10	.40	.15	1.00	
Cash	.00	.50	.00	.00	.00	.00	.20	1.00

Source: Yale University Investments Office.

the 1980s with relatively low volatility and relatively low correlation to traditional marketable securities. Not surprisingly, naive application of mean-variance analysis led to recommendations of extraordinary allocations to real estate.

The spring 1988 *Journal of Portfolio Management* study by Paul Firstenberg, Stephen Ross, and Randall Zisler, "Real Estate: The Whole Story," concluded that institutional allocations to real estate should be increased dramatically from the then current average of under 4 percent of portfolio assets. The authors based their conclusions on data showing government bonds with returns of 7.9 percent and risk (standard deviation) of 11.5 percent, common stocks with returns of 9.7 percent and risk of 15.4 percent, and real estate with returns of 13.9 percent and risk of 2.6 percent. Although for purposes of their study, the authors increased real estate risk levels from historical levels to more reasonable levels, their mean variance results were anything but sensible. Efficient portfolio mixes included between 0 and 40 percent in government bonds, between 0 and 20 percent in stocks, and between 49 and 100 percent in real estate. Fortunately, the authors tempered their enthusiasm, taking the "pragmatic perspective . . . that pension funds should seek initial real estate allocations of between 15 to 20 percent."[9]

The mean-variance optimizer favored real estate because of past high returns, past low risk, and past low correlation with other asset classes. The risk premium for real estate exceeded that for stocks by 2.9 percent and that for bonds by an even greater margin. Although historical real estate risk levels measured only 2.6 percent standard deviation of returns, Firstenberg used a valuation model to justify increasing risk levels to 11.3 percent, slightly below the assumed volatility of government bonds. The authors' favored real estate time series exhibited negative correlation with both domestic stocks (−0.26) and government bonds (−0.38). When the highest returning asset class exhibits the lowest risk and negative correlation with other asset classes, mean-variance optimizers reach the obvious conclusion, emphasizing that asset class in the portfolios.

The fundamental flaw in Firstenberg stems from failure to examine real estate return assumptions critically. Why should real estate be expected to return more than stocks or bonds? Why should real estate have lower risk than both stocks and bonds? Why should real estate exhibit negative correlation with stocks and bonds? Real estate contains characteristics of both debt and equity. The stream of contractual lease payments resembles fixed income, while the residual value is equity-like. Hence, return and risk expectations logically flow from and fall between those for stocks and bonds. Similarities in factors driving valuations of real estate and traditional marketable securities lead to the conclusion that correlations might be expected to be positive, albeit less than one. Instead of focusing only on adjusting the risk level of real estate, Firstenberg and his coauthors should have adjusted return and correlation levels as well.

Had an investor overweighted real estate in 1988, portfolio results would have disappointed because both stocks and bonds dramatically outperformed real estate in subsequent years. From 1988 to 1997, real estate returned an annualized 4.4 percent, with stocks and bonds generating annual results over the same period of 18.0 percent and 8.3 percent, respectively. When relying on historical data, real estate appears most attractive just when future prospects prove bleakest.

Investors relying on backward-looking data in cyclical markets invite whipsaw. In the early 1990s, after a period of disastrous real estate performance, the asset appeared less appealing as poor results dampened historical returns. Investors employing the Firstenberg approach increased real estate holdings in the late 1980s and avoided real estate investing in the early 1990s. In the deeply cyclical real estate market, historical data suggest high allocations at market peaks (when returns have been high and risks low) and low allocations at market troughs (when returns have been low and risks high). Making money by buying high and selling low proves difficult for even the most nimble investors.

TESTING THE ALLOCATION

For many investors, defining the efficient frontier represents the ultimate goal of quantitative portfolio analysis. Choosing from the set of portfolios that lie on the frontier ensures that given the underlying assumptions, no superior portfolio exists. Unfortunately, the mean-variance optimization approach provides little useful guidance in choosing a portfolio. Academics suggest specifying a utility function, choosing the portfolio at the point of tangency with the efficient frontier. Such advice proves useful only in the unlikely event that investors find it possible to articulate a utility function in which utility relates solely to the mean and variance of expected returns.

Structuring a mean-variance-efficient portfolio fails to finish the task at hand. After defining the efficient frontier, investors must determine which combination of assets best meets the goals articulated for the endowment fund. Successful portfolios must satisfy the two goals of endowment management: preservation of purchasing power and provision of substantial, sustainable support for operations. To assess the ability of a portfolio to meet these goals, quantifiable tests must be fashioned.

Preserving purchasing power represents a long-term goal. The contract that an endowed institution makes with donors requires that a gift to endowment support the designated purpose in perpetuity. Evaluating success or failure in meeting the endowment preservation goal requires a long-term measure, spanning generations. For example, failure to maintain endowment value might constitute losing one-half of the purchasing power over fifty years.

Providing stable operating budget support represents an intermediate-term goal. Because university operations require stable sources of support, dramatic short-term declines in endowment income prove difficult to accommodate. Spending trauma could be defined by a one-quarter reduction in real endowment distributions over five years.

Unfortunately, a clear, direct trade-off exists between preserving purchasing power and supplying stable support for operations. The challenge for investors lies in selecting the portfolio best suited to satisfy, to the extent possible, both goals. Fashioning quantitative tests of performance relating to the two goals facilitates portfolio choice.

Although obvious obstacles prevent reaching agreement on precise definitions of failure to preserve endowment assets and failure to provide stable operating budget support, obtaining reasonable consensus on the rough equivalence of the two measures proves essential for evaluating trade-offs between the two goals. The process of considering trade-offs requires investors to treat the quantitatively defined goals as reasonably similar in importance.

Simulating the Future

Once goals have been quantified, statistical simulations provide a mechanism for evaluating investment and spending policies. Investors begin by identifying a spending policy, specifying a target rate and an averaging process. The spending policy remains constant as various investment portfolios undergo the simulation process.*

Simulations rely on the capital markets assumptions employed in mean-variance optimization. Random selections from distributions for each asset class determine portfolio returns for the initial period. The spending rule dictates the amount withdrawn from endowment, leaving the residual to be invested in the second period. After rebalancing the portfolio to long-term policy weights, repeating the process provides data on endowment value and spending level for the subsequent year. The process continues, in this case for fifty years, creating a time series of spending and portfolio data.

The simulation process described above creates one specific fifty-year path, a far from robust test of portfolio characteristics. To increase the information content of the test, analysts conduct literally thousands of simulations, providing reams of data on future spending and endowment levels. Examining the collective results allows calculation of probabilities of failure to preserve assets and failure to provide stable budgetary support.

Interpreting the simulated results requires a combination of quantitative and qualitative judgment. Some portfolios fall from consideration on the basis that they are dominated by others that have lower probabilities of failing to meet each of the goals. Other portfolios fail because they satisfy one goal at the expense of the other. Once investors eliminate clearly inferior portfolios, qualitative judgment enters the picture in assessing more subtle trade-offs between reducing risk on one measure while increasing risk on another. In the final analysis, portfolio selection involves careful subjective assessment of trade-offs between conflicting goals.

One significant benefit of running simulations lies in the direct link between the quantitative analysis and the goals articulated for endowment management. Mean-variance optimization, run in isolation, produces a set of efficient portfolios. The fund manager, faced with these efficient combinations of assets, has little idea which portfolio might best address the fund's needs. How should investors choose be-

---

*The simulation process also proves useful in evaluating spending policies. By keeping constant the investment portfolio, various spending rates and averaging processes might be tested.

tween Figure 5.1's portfolio A, with an expected return of 5.9 percent
and standard deviation of 9.5 percent, and portfolio B, with an expected return of 7.3 percent and standard deviation of 12.5 percent?
Finance theory suggests that a utility function might be employed to
identify the appropriate asset allocation. Since few market participants would have any idea of how to specify such a function, this
technique proves remarkably unhelpful.

In contrast, simulation data address directly the issue facing portfolio managers, describing the trade-off between the conflicting goals of
endowment management. Figure 5.2 shows the set of choices identified through a program of simulations. In selecting either portfolio A
with 3.2 percent probability of intermediate-term spending instability
and 14.8 percent probability of long-term purchasing power impairment, or portfolio B with 4.8 percent probability of spending instability
and 8.7 percent probability of purchasing power impairment, investors
express preferences on the trade-off between two goals central to an endowment's mission. Instead of wondering about the impact on institutional goals of the interaction between a specified spending policy and
a particular portfolio, investors examine the degree to which spending
and investment policies serve articulated goals. Simulations build on

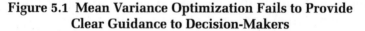

**Figure 5.1 Mean Variance Optimization Fails to Provide
Clear Guidance to Decision-Makers**

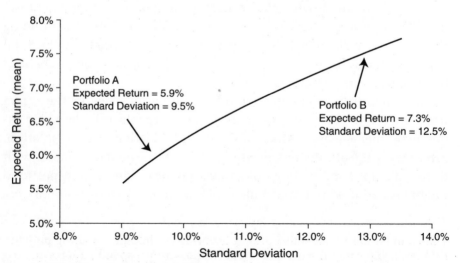

Source: Yale University Investments Office.

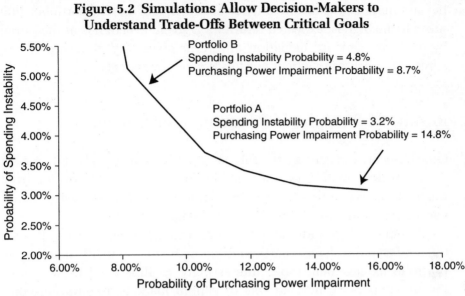

**Figure 5.2 Simulations Allow Decision-Makers to
Understand Trade-Offs Between Critical Goals**

Source: *Yale University Investments Office.*

the foundation of mean-variance optimization, allowing direct assessment of goals identified by fund fiduciaries.

Simulations liberate mean-variance analysis from another of its practical limitations: the use of one-year investment periods. Theoretically, mean-variance optimization ought to be conducted for periods commensurate with the investment horizon of the investor. Three-year, five-year, or even ten-year periods would be appropriate for most institutional funds. Unfortunately, data limitations force the use of annual periods. Reasonably long time series of data do not exist for many asset classes, including foreign equities, real estate, venture capital, and leveraged buyouts. Without a long time series, investigators lack a sufficient number of independent three-year, five-year, or ten-year data points to draw robust conclusions. Although forward-looking estimates of the relevant inputs do not require history, few investors exhibit sufficient boldness to specify longer-term capital markets characteristics without the assistance of a reasonable time series of historical data.

Forward-looking simulations address the problem. The intermediate-term issue of providing stable operating budget support can be analyzed in an intermediate-term context. The long-term issue of preserving purchasing power can be evaluated in a long-term context. By employing simulations, the mean-variance abstraction of a set of portfolios that provide the highest expected return for a given level of risk as measured by one-year standard deviation of returns gives way to concrete measures of the degree to which portfolios meet investor goals.

Results of Disciplined Portfolio Management

Questions arise regarding the robustness of conclusions based on a set of institution-specific capital markets assumptions. While far from dispositive, examining the results of portfolios managed using mean-variance optimization provides some insight into the answer.

Among college and university endowments, Yale, Harvard, Princeton, and Stanford have a particularly long history of using quantitative portfolio management tools. Interestingly, as illustrated in Table 5.5, the independently derived sets of capital markets assumptions produce reasonably similar results. Although minor variations in conclusions result from differences in data inputs among the four institutions, specific portfolio recommendations tend to be supported by all four sets of assumptions.

The largest university endowments pursue asset allocation strategies dramatically different from those of other educational institutions. A comparison of the average asset allocation of a broad universe of colleges and universities with the large institutions shows striking patterns. Yale, Harvard, Princeton, and Stanford exhibit substantially greater diversification than the average endowment. Domestic equities dominate most endowment portfolios, averaging 45 percent of assets, while the better-diversified large institutional portfolios commit only 27 percent to domestic equities. Domestic bonds account for 22 percent of the average endowment's portfolio in contrast to an allocation of 10 percent by Yale, Harvard, Princeton, and Stanford. Private assets, including venture capital, leveraged buyouts, and real estate, which barely register among the broad group of educational institutions, accounting for less than 10 percent of assets, play an important role for the major endowments, with an allocation in excess of 28 percent. Disciplined quantitative modeling techniques encourages investors to create well-diversified portfolios.

The major university endowments pursue higher return strategies,

Table 5.5 Large University Endowments Pursue More Diversified Investment Approaches

Target Asset Allocation, Expected Return, and Standard Deviation of Yale, Harvard, Princeton, and Stanford Universities, Compared to University Mean, June 30, 1997

	Yale	Harvard	Princeton	Stanford	Large Institution Mean	General College and University Mean
Domestic equity	22.5%	36.0%	20.0%	30.0%	27.1%	45.3%
Domestic fixed income	12.5	10.0	10.0	9.0	10.4	21.5
Foreign equity	12.5	29.0	20.0	23.0	21.1	17.3
Private assets	32.5	25.0	25.0	30.0	28.1	9.6
Other marketable assets	20.0	0	25.0	8.0	13.3	6.3
Expected return	7.2	6.6	6.7	6.4	6.7	5.0
Standard deviation	12.5	13.8	11.8	12.4	12.6	12.8

Sources: Expected return and risk data rely on Yale University Investments Office capital market assumptions. General College and University Mean data are from the National Association of College and University Business Officers (NACUBO) 1997 Endowment Study.

causing expected returns for the funds to exceed the average by 1.7 percent, an enormous increment relative to a baseline expected return of 5.0 percent. In spite of producing greater expected returns, large institution portfolio risk levels actually fall slightly below risk estimates for the less well-diversified endowments. Employing rigorous quantitative portfolio analysis contributes to the construction of diversified, high-return portfolios.

CONCLUSION

Built on the philosophical principles of equity orientation and diversification, asset allocation decisions provide the framework that supports creation of effective investment portfolios. Placing policy allocation targets at the center of the process lends a measure of stability to funds invested in an uncertain world.

Purely statistical descriptions of various asset allocation alternatives provide little guidance for decision makers. The widely used Markowitz mean-variance optimization process produces a set of efficient portfolios, fully described by two parameters: expected return (mean) and expected risk (standard deviation). Academics identify optimal portfolios by specifying an institutional utility function that produces a point of tangency with the mean-variance efficient frontier. Even in the unlikely event that the academic approach proves helpful, decision makers wonder how the chosen portfolio will interact with the institution's spending policy.

A number of problems implicit in most applications of mean-variance analysis limit its usefulness in evaluating portfolios of long-term investors. Incorporating sensible qualitative considerations into the asset allocation process represents a critical factor in reaching reasonable conclusions. Informed judgment plays a significant role in selecting and defining asset classes, as well as in constructing a coherent set of capital markets assumptions. Combining powerful quantitative tools and sensible qualitative decisions provides a starting point for asset allocation decisions.

The use of simulations to test portfolios created through mean-variance optimization allows assessment of the effectiveness of investment and spending policies over appropriate time horizons. Employing the same capital markets assumptions used in mean-variance analysis, the simulations allow examination of longer time frames, consideration of interaction between spending and investment policies, and translation of statistical capital market and portfolio characteristics into relevant quantitative criteria for decision makers.

Failure to achieve investment goals defines portfolio risk in the most fundamental way. Goals, and risks following therefrom, must be described in a manner allowing investment fiduciaries to understand trade-offs between various portfolios. By evaluating portfolios in terms of probabilities of maintaining purchasing power and providing stable spending streams, fiduciaries understand and choose among alternatives defined in the context of criteria directly relevant to institutional objectives.

Portfolios generated through this combination of mean-variance optimization and forward-looking simulation suffer from a number of limitations. The results depend on assumptions regarding future returns, risks, and covariances. While precise estimates are certain to be wrong, much of the power of the analysis stems from evaluating easier-to-assess relative relationships among the variables. If the quality of return and risk assumptions represented the greatest hurdles, conclusions reached through quantitative analysis would be quite robust.

More serious problems stem from instability in the risk and covariance characteristics of asset classes. The tendency for markets to move together in times of crisis reduces the value of diversification, at least in the short run. Questions regarding the nature of distributions of security returns and stability of relationships between asset classes pose serious challenges to quantitative modeling of asset allocation. Nonetheless, the process of quantifying portfolio analysis provides discipline lacking in less rigorous approaches to portfolio construction.

A systematic quantitative portfolio construction process lies at the heart of portfolio management activity, providing a disciplined framework within which qualitative judgments inform portfolio decisions. By recognizing and affirming the centrality of policy asset allocation targets, fund managers sensibly focus on the most powerful investment management tool. Ultimately, thoughtful asset allocation work provides the basis for building a successful investment program.

6
Portfolio
Management

The degree of risk assumed in pursuit of investment returns constitutes the core issue in investment management. In a world where risk
correlates with return, investors hold risky assets in pursuit of returns
exceeding the risk-free rate. By determining which risky assets are
held and in what proportions, the asset allocation decision resides at
the center of portfolio management discussions.

The fundamental objective of portfolio management lies in faithful
implementation of long-term policy targets. If investors allow actual
portfolio holdings to differ materially from asset class targets, the resulting portfolio fails to reflect risk and return preferences expressed
through the asset allocation process. By holding assets in proportion to
policy targets, and generating asset class returns commensurate with
market levels, investors achieve investment goals without slippage.

Only the most basic portfolios, consisting entirely of marketable
securities, allow investors to implement investment policies at targeted levels using passive investment vehicles to mirror market returns. Subsequent to establishing initial allocations, conservative
investors maintain targeted levels by following a disciplined program
of rebalancing, using proceeds from selling assets exhibiting relative
strength to fund purchases of assets showing relative weakness. The
existence of low-cost, passive investment vehicles facilitates the
seamless implementation of policy asset allocation targets in marketable security portfolios. Serious pursuit of rebalancing ensures that

portfolios maintain target levels, exposing the fund to the desired risk and return characteristics.

Unfortunately, for all but the simplest structures, the complexities of real-world investing drive a wedge between the easily articulated ideal and the messy reality of implementing an investment program. Investment in illiquid vehicles, pursuit of active management strategies, and existence of explicit or implicit leverage cause actual performance to differ from results expected from rigorous pursuit of the policy portfolio.

Less liquid asset types introduce the likelihood that inability to vary exposure causes actual allocations to deviate from target levels. Shortfalls or surpluses in private assets require offsetting positions in more liquid assets, driving portfolio characteristics away from desired levels. Since by their very nature private holdings take substantial amounts of time to buy or sell efficiently, actual portfolios usually exhibit some functional misallocation. Dealing with the over- or under-allocation resulting from illiquid positions creates a tough challenge for the thoughtful investor.

Even when actual portfolio allocations match long-term targets, active management techniques may cause asset class returns to differ from index returns. If inefficiencies exist in the pricing of individual securities, market participants might be rewarded for uncovering attractive investment opportunities with risk-adjusted excess returns. Portfolio managers willingly accept risks associated with active management, expecting that investment skill will ultimately provide positive results. But because the expected excess returns arrive in unpredictable fashion, if at all, the actively managed asset class might suffer from periods of material underperformance, opening a gap between reality and the hoped-for active management result.

Leverage, both explicit and implicit, poses another challenge to faithful implementation of policy asset allocation targets. By magnifying investment outcomes, both good and bad, leverage fundamentally alters the risk and return characteristics of investment portfolios. Unless fiduciaries pay close attention to investment manager activities, leverage may expose funds to unanticipated outcomes. Inherent in certain derivatives positions, leverage lurks hidden in many portfolios, coming to the light only when investment disaster strikes. More explicit leverage, such as that embodied in security lending programs, contains the potential to alter portfolio risk characteristics in unwelcome ways. Understanding and controlling the degree of risk inherent in particular policies and strategies allow investors to fashion investment portfolios appropriate to their tolerance for risk.

Most market participants treat risk with little sophistication. Portfolio managers spend enormous amounts of time, energy, and resources on asset allocation projects, implement the recommendations, and then let portfolio allocations drift with the markets. Some investors pursue active management programs by cobbling together a variety of specialist managers, without understanding the sector, size, or style bets created by the more or less random portfolio construction process. Other participants hire managers based on strong past performance, forgetting to evaluate the investment program, unaware of hidden leverage likely to provide volatile performance. Recognizing biases created in the portfolio management process allows managers to accept only those risks with expected rewards.

The Greek author Palladas must have had portfolio management in mind when he wrote that "there be many a slip 'twixt the cup and the lip."[1] Asset allocation drift and active management risk contain the potential to create outcomes measurably different from results expected from the policy asset allocation portfolio. Moreover, exposure to implicit and explicit leverage might move portfolios to risk levels materially different from baseline expectations, dramatically altering expected investment outcomes. Disciplined implementation of asset allocation policies avoids altering the risk and return profile of an investment portfolio, allowing investors to accept only those active management risks expected to add value.

Concern about risk represents an integral part of the portfolio management process, requiring careful monitoring at the overall portfolio, asset class, and manager levels. Understanding investment and implementation risks increases the chances that an investment program will achieve its goals.

REBALANCING

Proper use of mean-variance optimization and forward-looking simulations places risk considerations at the heart of the investment management process. By evaluating the likelihood that investment policies fail to meet articulated goals, investors confront directly the critical financial risks facing an institution. The asset allocation targets selected through thoughtful application of quantitative tools and informed judgment define with great precision the portfolio of assets most likely to satisfy institutional needs.

After establishing asset allocation policies, risk control requires regular rebalancing to policy targets. Movements in prices of financial assets inevitably cause asset class allocations to deviate from target levels. For instance, a decline in U.S. stock prices and an increase in bond prices leads stocks to be underweight and bonds to be overweight relative to target, causing the portfolio to have lower than desired expected risk and return characteristics. To restore the portfolio to target allocations, rebalancing investors purchase stocks and sell bonds.

Rebalancing Frequency

Investors debate the frequency with which portfolios should be rebalanced. Some follow the calendar, transacting monthly, quarterly, or annually. Others attempt to control transactions costs, setting broad limits and trading only when allocations exceed specified ranges. Pursuit of continuous rebalancing provides greater risk control with potentially lower costs than either the calendar or trading range approaches.

Continuous rebalancing involves as frequent as daily valuation of portfolio assets. If asset class values deviate by as much as one- or two-tenths of one percent from target values, managers trade securities to achieve targeted levels. Trades tend to be small and accommodating to the market. Since rebalancing requires sale of assets experiencing relative price strength and purchase of assets experiencing relative price weakness, the immediacy of continuous rebalancing causes managers to provide liquidity to the market. In contrast, rebalancing strategies not as responsive to the market require larger transactions, increasing market impact and transactions costs.

To the extent that markets exhibit excess volatility, continuous rebalancing may generate excess returns. Market activity on October 27 and 28, 1997, provides a dramatic example. On October 27, a 6.9 percent drop in stock prices accompanied a rally in the bond market. The following day's reversal saw stocks rebound by 5.1 percent, with bonds suffering from selling pressure. Rebalancing a 60 percent equity and a 40 percent bond portfolio on those two October days added 10 basis points to returns, providing a bonus for an activity dedicated fundamentally to risk control.

Rebalancing facilitates reshaping of marketable security portfolios, allowing alteration of manager allocations without incurring incremental transactions costs. Investors improve portfolio returns by giving funds to managers expected to outperform and withdrawing money from those with less rosy prospects. In the absence of fundamental reasons to change manager allocations, positive results might be expected from following the strategy of withdrawing money from managers posting strong recent performance and supplying money to those with weak numbers. When in doubt, lean against the wind.

Rebalancing and Illiquidity

Owners of private assets must modify rebalancing activity. At any point in time, illiquid holdings of venture capital, leveraged buyouts, and real estate are unlikely to match targeted levels. An amount of assets equivalent to the aggregate illiquid portfolio shortfall (or surplus) must be invested in (or withdrawn from) liquid securities portfolios. Appropriate candidates for investing private asset underallocations include shorter duration and low-risk assets, since funds may be required on short notice to make investments to bring private portfolios closer to target levels. Cash, bonds, and absolute return investments provide reasonable temporary alternatives for private asset underallocations.

The strategy of investing underallocations of private assets in fundamentally similar marketable securities holds superficial appeal. For instance, while attempting to build a venture capital portfolio, allocation shortfalls might be invested in a portfolio of small technology stocks. Unfortunately, the strategy exposes investors to the risk that venture partnerships call funds when technology stocks trade at depressed levels, causing sales to be made at an inopportune time. In the final analysis, private assets constitute a separate asset class because private holdings behave in a fundamentally different fashion from marketable securities, making dependence on high short-run correlation between private and public markets an internally inconsistent, potentially dangerous strategy.

When private allocations exceed target levels, as might be the case when marketable security prices decline relative to private asset values, investors face a difficult problem. Relying on correlations between marketable and private assets poses substantial risks. Yet reducing allocations to lower-risk assets to accommodate excessive levels of private equity increases an already elevated portfolio risk level. Choosing the least bad alternative, investors need to fund over-allocations to private assets by reducing holding of risky marketable assets, thereby controlling overall portfolio risk levels.

Using short-duration, lower-risk assets to substitute for generally higher-return private assets decreases expected portfolio return and risk levels; the opposite result occurs when reducing marketable security positions to accommodate a private equity overweighting. Because differences may be substantial between characteristics of target and actual portfolios, investors must analyze thoroughly the investment and spending implications of both target asset allocations and actual portfolio allocations.

The potential for material differences between actual and target asset allocations argues for gradualism in altering targets for illiquid asset classes. Keeping the reality close to the ideal facilitates analysis of spending and investment possibilities. Avoiding large differences between actual and target allocations reduces the size of the mismatch requiring temporary adjustment in the target for an alternative investment vehicle, limiting the impact of a decision fraught with problems.

Rebalancing ensures that investors face the risk profile embodied in the policy portfolio. Institutions that follow no particular rebalancing policy engage in a peculiar form of market timing. By allowing portfolio allocations to drift with the whims of the market, portfolio risk and return characteristics change unpredictably, introducing more noise into an already highly uncertain process. In fact, over long periods of time, without rebalancing, portfolio allocations move toward the highest return asset, increasing the overall risk level of the portfolio. Ultimately disciplined rebalancing provides risk control, increasing the likelihood that investors achieve investment goals.

ACTIVE MANAGEMENT

After establishing policy asset allocation targets, investors face individual asset class management issues. In the marketable securities arena, passive investment vehicles provide near certainty that investment results mirror market activity. To the extent that investors pursue active strategies, actual results will likely differ from the market, causing asset class characteristics to differ from those modeled. On the private side, lack of passive investment vehicles inevitably causes active results to vary, sometimes dramatically, from benchmarks.

Investing in passively managed vehicles representing individual asset classes effectively eliminates variance from market results. Index funds cost little to implement, present far fewer agency issues than do actively managed portfolios, and promise faithful replication of market portfolios. What explains the fact that few institutional portfolios employ passive management exclusively? Perhaps those few smart enough to recognize that passive strategies provide superior results believe themselves to be smart enough to beat the market. In any event, deviations from benchmark returns represent an important source of portfolio risk.

Investors embarking on active management strategies introduce potential for creating either purposeful or inadvertent portfolio biases. Among the powerful ways in which asset classes might differ from benchmarks are with respect to size, sector, and style. *Size* refers to market capitalization of securities holdings, *sector* concerns the nature of corporate business activities, and *style* relates to the active manager's general approach to investing (e.g., value versus growth).

Deliberate portfolio biases create potential for significant value added. For instance, an investor might believe value strategies to be superior to growth approaches, consciously choosing only managers with a value orientation. Others believe that small-capitalization stocks provide superior stock-picking opportunities, moving portfolios toward an explicit overweighting in securities of smaller companies. Purposeful, thoughtful strategic bets might generate risk-adjusted excess returns for the portfolio.

Such returns do not come without potential costs. Hiring managers specializing in particular market segments sometimes skews portfolio characteristics dramatically. Consequently, managers face the possibility of meaningful underperformance as short-term costs (poor relative performance from small stocks) overwhelm long-term opportunities (less efficient pricing of small-capitalization securities). Strategic portfolio biases add value only if implemented in a disciplined fashion, after thoughtful analysis, with an appropriately long investment horizon.

Some portfolio bets result from sloppy management. If portfolio construction simply involves collecting enough domestic equity managers to fill the slots in the portfolio's roster, the resulting asset class characteristics almost certainly contain significant inadvertent biases. Unintended portfolio bets often come to light only after being directly implicated as a cause for substandard asset class performance.

Completeness Funds and Normal Portfolios

The investment management tools of normal portfolios and completeness funds allow managers to evaluate and control portfolio biases. The use of normal portfolios assists investors in analyzing portfolio bets. A normal portfolio defines the universe of securities from which a manager selects holdings. Because it contains an active manager's investment universe, a normal portfolio represents a fair benchmark for measuring manager performance. If the aggregate of the normal portfolios within an asset class matches size, sector, and style distributions of that asset class, the resulting portfolio contains no deliberate bets relative to these variables. Bets resulting from active manager decisions will still influence portfolio returns, but those bets ought to be welcomed as part of an active management strategy.

If the aggregate of normal portfolios within an asset class fails to match important asset class characteristics, portfolio managers introduce biases. One way to offset inadvertent biases is through the use of completeness funds. A completeness fund represents the portfolio of securities, complementary to the aggregate of an asset class's normal portfolios, which causes the sum of the normal portfolios plus the completeness fund to match relevant asset class characteristics.

By offsetting any gaps left by the aggregate of a fund's normal portfolios, completeness funds cause portfolio returns to be driven by deliberate choice, not inadvertently assumed residual risk. A danger in using completeness funds lies in the imprecision inherent in identifying normal portfolios, which may fail to fill unidentified portfolio gaps or may offset deliberate security selection bets.

Because deviations from asset class characteristics cause performance to differ from the market, fund managers must ensure that deliberate choice, not sloppy construction, drives portfolio structure. Normal portfolios and completeness funds assist investors with asset class management, but precise application of these tools remains a theoretical goal, not a practical reality.

Opportunity and Risk

Strong biases within asset classes may reward strong-willed, adventuresome investors, but they pose serious danger to investors with weak hands. The temptation to fire underperforming managers often proves too great to resist. When underperformance stems from an underlying portfolio bias, the fund exposes itself to a potential whipsaw—firing a manager with the wind in its face and hiring a manager with the wind at its back, all done just as the wind is about to change.

Stocks of cyclical and consumer-oriented companies often exhibit dramatic relative performance differentials. Cyclical stocks consist of securities of economically sensitive companies, such as U.S. Steel and General Motors, which tend to do well in strong economies and poorly in weak environments. Consumer stocks represent more stable, high-quality holdings, including Coca-Cola and Pfizer, companies expected to produce reasonably consistent results regardless of the economic backdrop. In 1992 and 1993, as the economy emerged from the recession of 1990 and 1991, cyclical stocks significantly outperformed consumer-oriented companies. Morgan Stanley price indexes showed cyclical outperformance of 19.1 percent in 1992 and 26.6 percent for for the first ten months of 1993, totaling a staggering 45.7 percent for the twenty-two-month period. Investment managers focused on high-quality consumer stocks faced tough sledding.

A prominent West Coast investment manager with an impressive long-term record from investing in stable consumer growth stocks boasted returns at or near the top of consultant databases for the ten years ending December 31, 1992. The firm's emphasis on consumer stocks caused results to suffer in 1993, losing nearly 15 percent relative to the S&P 500. In spite of the firm's superior long-term record and a clear explanation for underperformance, the adviser suffered asset withdrawals and client defections. Those who sold in late 1993 and early 1994 paid a price. The firm subsequently outperformed the market by a meaningful margin, beating the S&P 500 by almost 5 percent per annum for the four years ending December 31, 1997.

In 1993, the individuals responsible for portfolio decisions had not suddenly become inept. The firm's focus on high-quality growth stocks led to poor results in an environment that favored cyclical companies. Investors recognizing this reality developed the conviction to stay the course, ultimately benefiting from informed perseverance. Investors with weak hands paid a price for untimely exit from a strategy with long-term potential for success.

LEVERAGE

Leverage appears in portfolios explicitly and implicitly. Explicit leverage involves use of borrowed funds for pursuit of investment opportunities, magnifying portfolio results, good and bad. When investment returns exceed borrowing costs, portfolios benefit from leverage. If investment returns match borrowing costs, no impact results. In cases where investment returns fail to meet borrowing costs, portfolios suffer.

Harvard University's endowment employs explicit leverage in two ways. For a number of years in the 1990s the university articulated an unusual asset allocation target of −5 percent to cash, hoping to improve portfolio results by generating returns in excess of borrowing costs. Over long periods of time, Harvard's borrowing strategy promises superior results as portfolio returns should exceed leverage costs represented by cash, the lowest expected return asset class. Of course, if returns fall below the cost of funds, results of a bad year will be made worse. In the case of Harvard's negative allocation to cash, careful and disciplined analysis of portfolio considerations led to the use of leverage.

Harvard's second form of explicit leverage involves borrowing substantial amounts of funds to establish positions exploiting mispricings among securities. At June 30, 1997, the university's nearly $12 billion endowment supported long positions of $29 billion and short positions of $17 billion.[1] By using leverage to magnify security selection bets, Harvard alters fundamental asset class risk characteristics. In contrast to the asset allocation process's direct consideration of the consequences of the negative allocation to cash, by grossing up positions Harvard alters portfolio risk outside of the mean-variance framework. As a consequence of levering the endowment two-and-a-half times, the university dramatically increases risk levels, enhancing positive and negative outcomes alike.

Implicit leverage stems from holding positions that embody greater risk than contemplated by the asset class within which they are categorized. Simply holding riskier-than-market equity securities leverages the portfolio. Unless risk levels of securities within an asset class match asset allocation risk assumptions, the portfolio either becomes leveraged from holding riskier assets or deleveraged from holding less risky assets. For example, the common practice of holding cash in portfolios of common stocks causes the domestic equity portfolio to be less risky than the market, effectively deleveraging returns.

Derivatives provide a common source of implicit leverage. Suppose an S&P 500 futures contract requires a margin deposit of 10 percent of the value of the position. If an investor holds a futures position in the domestic equity portfolio, complementing every one dollar of futures with nine dollars of cash creates a position equivalent to holding the underlying equity securities directly. If, however, the investor holds five dollars of futures and five dollars of cash, leverage causes the position to be five times as sensitive to market fluctuations.

Derivatives do not create risk per se, as they can be used to reduce risk, replicate positions, or increase risk. To continue with the S&P 500 futures example, selling futures against a portfolio of equity securities reduces risks associated with equity market exposure. Alternatively, using appropriate combinations of cash and futures creates a risk-neutral replication of the underlying securities. Finally, holding futures without adequate balancing cash positions increases market exposure and risk. Fiduciaries must understand and control the use of derivatives in investment activity.

Granite Capital

Granite Capital's David Askin suffered devastating losses while pursuing an apparently sophisticated strategy of identifying, hedging, and leveraging pricing anomalies in mortgaged-backed security derivatives. Based on a record of generating mid-teens returns with low variability, Askin attracted funds from an impressive list of investors, including the Rockefeller Foundation and McKinsey & Company. Unfortunately, explicit and implicit leverage caused the firm's entire $600 million portfolio to be wiped out in a matter of weeks.

Askin invested in collateralized mortgage obligation derivatives with exotic names such as super-inverse interest-only strips. As unusual as the names might be, the securities simply represented pieces of pools containing ordinary home mortgages. By combining securities expected to respond in opposite ways to interest rate movements, Askin hoped to be hedged; when rates move, profits on one part of the portfolio would more or less offset losses on the other. If Askin correctly identified pricing anomalies, profits would exceed losses by a margin equal to the mispricing.

Because mispricings in fixed income markets tend to be small, investors frequently use leverage to magnify the portfolio impact of trades. At the time of his denouement, Askin employed leverage of approximately two and one half times, running positions of $2 billion on $600 million of equity.

Askin's portfolio failed to weather the trauma created by the Federal Reserve's decision to increase interest rates in early 1994. What appeared to be well-hedged positions in a benign interest rate environment turned out to be wildly mismatched positions in a bearish bond market. As Askin's portfolio accumulated losses, investment banks that lent money to fund the positions seized the bonds, selling positions to cover their exposure. The combination of poor portfolio structure and leverage led to Askin's downfall.

Askin sustained major losses because his hedges failed to perform.

Had he not been leveraged, he likely would have survived the 1994 interest rate debacle. Losses of 30 percent on a leveraged $2 billion portfolio wiped out $600 million of equity. Losses of 30 percent on a $600 million unleveraged portfolio reduce equity by a painful $180 million, but investors live to fight another day. In fact, subsequent to Askin's demise, prices of the liquidated bonds recovered smartly. But by that time, Askin was no longer a player.*

•   •   •

Leverage magnifies portfolio outcomes, containing the potential to benefit or cause harm to portfolio assets. In extreme cases, inconsistency between the risk profile of asset class characteristics and investment activity leads to significant losses. In less extreme cases, differences in risk profile cause portfolio attributes to vary meaningfully from targeted levels, leading to undesirable deviations from policy goals. Sensible investors employ leverage with great care, guarding against introducing material excess risk into portfolio characteristics.

Security Lending

Some types of leverage, such as negative cash positions and explicit borrowing to increase positions, exhibit themselves openly. Investment staffs prepare papers that investment committees discuss, creating awareness of the general nature and magnitude of the borrowing. Other forms of leverage remain hidden until trouble arises, causing damage to the portfolio too late for corrective action.

Most large institutional investors conduct security loan programs, which involve lending equity and debt securities to third parties, providing modest incremental income to the investor. Security borrowers, generally Wall Street financial concerns, require the loans to create short positions or cover failed trades. The lender receives cash

*Although with an unleveraged portfolio, Askin might not have gone out of business, without leverage Askin never would have been in business. Leverage boosted the underlying returns on his strategy to the mid-teens level necessary to attract investment capital. Without the juiced returns, Askin had no business.

collateral to secure the asset on loan, making that aspect of the transaction quite safe. The lender pays a below-market rate of interest on the cash collateral, expecting to reinvest the cash at a higher rate. This aspect of the transaction takes on the risk characteristics of the reinvestment vehicle. Security lending places the entire amount of the transaction at risk to generate the hoped-for spread between the borrowing and lending rates.*

Because the owner of securities on loan retains ownership, along with the attendant economic consequences, security lending activity provides little disruption to the portfolio. Investors find it easy to forget about security lending, relegating it to back-office status. Security lending rarely appears on investment committee agendas, treated like other functions performed by custodian banks. If considered at all, committees likely view the process as a low-risk method of offsetting a portion of the bank custody fee.

In the 1970s, before pension funds entered the arena, security lending generated handsome returns. Low supply of lendable securities, combined with high demand from Wall Street brokers, created an environment where security lenders paid no interest on cash collateral. Security lenders earned market rates on reinvested collateral, providing spreads that more than compensated for risk levels.

In the 1980s, the entry of massive pools of pension assets into the market increased supply of lendable securities, putting enormous pressure on returns to security lending. In today's highly efficient market for domestic equities and bonds, security lenders generally pay a market-like rate on cash collateral, reinvesting at higher rates only by accepting interest rate or credit risk. The expected return for lending securities consists of the small spread between the borrowing and the lending rates. Meaningful upside does not exist. Downside represents impairment of value of the reinvestment asset.

Returns from security lending activity exhibit patterns characteristic of negatively skewed distributions, along with their undesirable investment attributes. Like other types of lending activity, upside represents a fixed rate of return and repayment of principal, while

---

*Many participants have responded to slim margins in traditional security lending by introducing maturity mismatches to increase lending income and program risk. Others use the cash to pursue more exotic strategies, introducing even greater risk to the lending activity.

downside represents a substantial or total loss. Unless offset by handsome expected rates of return, sensible investors avoid return distributions with a negative skew.

Typical institutional deal structures exacerbate the unimpressive economics of security lending. Custodian banks generally run security lending programs, splitting income with investors on a seventy-thirty or sixty-forty basis, with the larger share accruing to security lenders. Such profit-sharing arrangements cause banks to seek risk, since they share in returns without sharing in losses. The bank gets a good deal, earning a significant share of the profits generated by putting client assets at risk. Investors get a raw deal, earning little in return for exposing portfolio assets to meaningful downside.

The Common Fund

The Common Fund, an organization providing investment services to educational institutions, learned in 1995 that its security lending program managed by First Capital Strategists had incurred estimated losses of $128 million.[2] Transgressions by a rogue trader, Kent Ahrens, caused the losses, which later calculations showed to be nearly $138 million. According to Ahrens, in early 1992 he lost $250,000 on an equity index arbitrage trade. Instead of closing out the position, he tried to offset the loss with speculative trading. After more than three years of deception and fraud, Ahrens's cumulative losses reached a staggering level.

The Common Fund security lending debacle hurt the firm in meaningful ways, tarnishing its sterling reputation and causing large numbers of client defections. At June 30, 1995, the Common Fund had $18.1 billion of marketable equity and fixed income assets under management. One year later, assets amounted to $15.5 billion, a dramatic $5.2 billion, or 25 percent, less than would have been expected had asset levels kept pace with markets.

The First Capital Strategists story tells much more than the tale of a rogue trader. It illustrates the risks in pursuing investment strategies with poor payoff structures, highlights the problems of monitoring certain types of trading activity, and shows the dangers of incentive schemes inappropriate for the nature of the investment activity.

Security lending activity at its best involves "make a little, make a little, make a little . . ." as investors earn small positive spreads on security loans. Unfortunately, to make a little, an investor exposes a lot to risk, creating the possibility of "make a little, make a little, make a little, lose a lot." This negatively skewed return pattern exhibits limited upside (make a little) with substantial downside (lose a lot), representing an unattractive distribution of outcomes for investors.

Decades earlier, security lending returns exhibited more favorable characteristics. In the 1970s when security lenders paid no interest on cash collateral, extremely handsome returns resulted from the activity. Since cash collateral secured the value of the asset on loan and the collateral could be reinvested in treasury bills, security lending participants faced essentially no risk. "Make a little, make a little, make a little" described the activity; "lose a lot" had yet to appear.

Structural changes and increased competition caused security lending risk to increase. As participants began to pay interest on cash collateral, reinvestment risk entered the equation. When security lenders could no longer create positive spreads by simply investing collateral in treasury bills, generating returns required accepting credit risk, interest rate risk, or even more exotic risks.

The Common Fund, through its relationship with First Capital Strategists, accepted these risks with enthusiasm. Table 6.1 outlines the wide range of authorized collateral reinvestment strategies that the Common Fund pursued beginning in the early 1980s. Alternatives ranged from extremely conservative to quite aggressive. Equity index arbitrage, properly implemented, poses little risk to invested assets. On the other end of the spectrum, Mexican broker repurchase agreements embody substantial risks.

Risky "Arbitrages"

By following standard Wall Street practice of referring to many reinvestment strategies as "arbitrages," market participants obtain a false sense of security. *Webster's Dictionary* defines arbitrage as "the often simultaneous purchase and sale of the same or equivalent security (as in different markets) in order to profit from price discrepancies." While occasional mispricings of futures contracts for stocks and bonds relative to cash markets provide fleeting arbitrage opportunities, other so-called arbitrages do not involve "the same or equivalent security," thereby exposing assets to substantial risk.

**Table 6.1 The Common Fund Exposed Participant
Assets to Material Risk**
Approved Investment Strategies, 1994

Equity index arbitrage

Fixed income arbitrage

OTC option arbitrage

Treasury/Eurodollar (TED) spread arbitrage

Dividend reinvestment arbitrage

Corporate restructuring arbitrage (risk arbitrage)

Forward and reverse equity conversions

Convertible security arbitrage

Warrant arbitrage

Equity and corporate bond repurchase agreements

Repurchase agreements with Mexican brokers collateralized with Mexican
 government securities

Matched positions

Triparty repurchase agreements

Interest rate and cross currency swaps

Fixed income securities called for redemption

For example, convertible arbitrage involves owning a convertible bond and selling short the stock of the issuing company to exploit perceived mispricings between the relatively cheap bonds and relatively expensive stock. Implementing convertible arbitrage requires dynamic hedging, which may or may not be feasible, and assumption of unhedgeable residual interest rate and credit risks. Under certain circumstances, convertible arbitrage offers attractive risk-reward relationships. Under no circumstance does convertible arbitrage create riskless returns.

At best, referring to risky strategies as arbitrages represents a Wall Street conceit, an attempt to create an aura of mystery and sophistication surrounding the investment process. At worst, the practice constitutes deceptive advertising, hoping to lessen investor concerns surrounding fundamentally risky activities.

Trading Intensity

A further problem with security lending activity lies in the high level of trading required. Trading-intensive programs range from relatively low-risk security lending to high-risk derivative and commodity strategies. Monitoring high levels of activity poses considerable challenges to the trading organization, the investment manager, and other responsible professionals, such as lawyers and accountants. When investment positions turn over several times daily, supervisors have little recourse but to trust that traders faithfully implement strategies and follow guidelines. Investors have little recourse but to trust that supervisors monitor the process carefully. High levels of trading activity create difficult control issues.

In contrast, long-term investment activity raises fewer monitoring issues. Security positions held for months or years provide far less control risk than positions held for minutes or days. Moreover, the temptation to hide losing tickets in a drawer or violate guidelines to trade out of losses seems more consistent with the speculative mindset of a trader than with the more temperate attitude of an investor. In fact, many of the 1990's most sensational losses resulted from the activity of rogue traders, such as Nicholas Leeson, who brought down Barings PLC; Toshihide Igushi, who caused Daiwa Bank to be exiled from the United States; and Robert Citron, who forced Orange County into bankruptcy. While avoiding trading strategies provides no guarantee against fraud, pursuing longer-term investment programs lessens control risks for fiduciaries.

Deal Structure

Poor deal structure contributed to the dangers of the Common Fund's security lending program. First Capital Strategists earned between 25 and 33 percent of profits generated by putting the Common Fund member institutions' funds at risk. In essence, First Capital flipped coins in a "heads I win, tails you lose" game. Since the firm did not share in losses, employees had strong incentive to recommend and pursue risky, potentially high-return strategies.

Poor incentives provide only a partial explanation of the problem. The Common Fund knowingly participated in First Capital Strategists risk-seeking activity. Prior to the Kent Ahrens debacle, two events brought the risky nature of the reinvestment vehicles to the fore. In August 1987, First Capital incurred a loss of $2.5 million by speculating on an aborted hostile takeover of Caesar's World. While First Capital reimbursed the Common Fund for the loss, the transaction high-lighted risks involved in corporate restructuring "arbitrage." Later, be-ginning in September 1989, First Capital accumulated a position in the ill-fated employee-led attempt to take over United Airlines. Ulti-mately liquidated at a loss of $2.6 million to the Common Fund, the trade caused security lending for fiscal year 1990 to show a loss of $577,600. The Caesar's World and United Airlines incidents forced trustees of the Common Fund to be acutely aware of the risks associ-ated with the firm's security lending program.

In essence, the Common Fund leveraged its assets by participating in security lending, borrowing funds (the cash collateral), and secur-ing the loans with Common Fund member institution stocks and bonds. First Capital invested proceeds from the loans in risky vehi-cles, hoping to generate positive returns. While dangers inherent in trading activities and problems associated with poor deal structure provide the most visible contribution to the Common Fund's disaster, the root of the problem originates with inappropriate use of leverage implicit in the security lending program.

The State of Florida

Sometimes a flawed approach to rebalancing, poor definition of asset class characteristics and ill-considered employment of leverage come to-gether to create a Triple Crown of portfolio management problems. Begin with a policy favoring winners and punishing losers. To the perverse re-turn-chasing rebalancing strategy, add significant mismatch between portfolio holdings and benchmark characteristics. For good measure throw in some leverage to create an extremely volatile combination.

Investment managers pursuing what has worked, as opposed to what will work, set themselves up for failure. In the early 1990s, the state of Florida used a return-chasing strategy in running a $3 billion pool of operating funds. An April 1994 *Barron's* reported: "Florida pits the managers against one another, and the winners get more money while the losers forfeit some." One of Florida's managers, Worth Bruntjen, a fixed income specialist at Piper Capital in Min-neapolis, benefited enormously from the state's program. "'Year after year, Piper has been our top manager,' [Florida State treasurer Tom]

Gallagher says, noting that Bruntjen now [1994] runs $400 million for the state, double that of the nearest competitor."³

"We buy government-agency paper that has a higher interest rate than the 30-year bond but has an average life of only three to five years," said Bruntjen in explaining his strategy.⁴ The "paper" in his portfolio consisted of mortgage derivatives with a bull market bias. Declining interest rates in the early 1990s drove Bruntjen's returns to the top of the charts, causing Morningstar to name this "visionary and guiding force" runner-up in its portfolio manager of the year competition.⁵

Florida's "conservative" operating funds investment grew as Piper Capital racked up impressive bull market returns, with Bruntjen's account peaking at $434 million in January 1994. Unfortunately for Bruntjen's investors, dramatic interest rate increases, beginning in early 1994, caused a spring meltdown in the bond markets. The *Wall Street Journal* described the scene:

> The blood bath in mortgage derivatives is claiming new casualties as investors and dealers continue to rush for the exits, feeding a vicious cycle of falling prices and evaporating demand. The mortgage market has been one of the worst hit by rising interest rates. . . . Even under the best circumstances, [mortgage-backed] bonds are difficult to manage, because their values depend on assumptions about how fast homeowners will prepay the mortgages that back these securities. The recent interest-rate volatility has badly roiled those assumptions, so that in today's market it's almost anyone's guess what "fair" prices of these bonds should be.⁶

The nearly unprecedented carnage in the bond market turned Bruntjen's strategy on its head. Instead of owning long-term yields with short-term duration, "as a result of borrowing and heavy use of derivatives, Bruntjen's funds experienced the volatility of a 30-year treasury bond, not three- to six-year bonds. Bruntjen's aggressive style, making liberal use of borrowed money and significant investments in volatile derivatives like inverse floating-rate bonds and principal-only strips, was perfect for a bull market, but ill-suited to a period of rising rates."⁷

The state of Florida and Piper Capital's other investors suffered.

By September, investment losses had reduced the Piper account by $90 million to $344 million, a disastrous result for a supposedly low-risk strategy. In response, Florida announced its intention to reduce funds invested with Piper Capital by $117.8 million over the next twelve months, faithfully pursuing a program of penalizing "losers."

As a result of reducing Piper Capital's account, Florida missed out on the full force of Bruntjen's rebound. Over the next year, as normalcy returned, his funds dramatically outperformed the market, placing in the top decile of actively managed fixed income accounts.[8] Ultimately Florida exposed itself to a powerful whipsaw, increasing exposure to a winner, only to suffer losses, and reducing exposure to a loser, only to miss full participation in a reversal of fortune.

When active management results appear too good to be true, they probably are. As much as people want to believe that success comes from intelligence and hard work, good fortune generally plays at least a supporting role. Reducing commitments to successful strategies reflects an appropriately humble response to favorable outcomes, dampening the inevitable downward leg of the active management roller-coaster ride.

Perhaps more important, investors must have sufficient confidence in investment strategies to increase commitments when inevitable setbacks occur. Providing additional funds to managers with sub-par results creates an opportunity to increase investment returns by adding to positions at more attractive valuations. If insufficient confidence prevents rebalancing an underperforming manager's account, either the manager or the investment adviser ought to be replaced.

The state of Florida's experience with Worth Bruntjen involves more than a lesson in rebalancing. The securities Piper Capital held bore little relationship to holdings appropriate for conservative operating funds. By straying far afield from a sensible benchmark, Florida exposed the portfolio to unacceptable volatility. Leverage inherent in the derivative-based strategies carried inappropriate risks for conservative operating funds. The leverage magnified positive results, causing the state to increase commitments. When the inevitable exaggerated decline arrived, the state pursued a portfolio-damaging policy of retreat. Florida's investment policy combined perverse rebalancing, assets inappropriate for operating funds, and excessive exposure to leverage, resulting in an investment debacle.

CONCLUSION

Placing asset allocation targets at the center of the portfolio management process increases the likelihood of investment success by ensuring that portfolios rest on the stable foundation of policy targets. Disciplined rebalancing techniques provide the basis for creating portfolios that reflect articulated risk and return characteristics. Less rigorous approaches to portfolio management almost guarantee that asset actual allocation differs from desired levels, leading to outcomes less likely to satisfy institutional goals.

Attractive investment opportunities frequently contain elements of illiquidity, introducing some rigidities into a portfolio's asset allocation. By forcing investors to hold positions inconsistent with targeted levels, illiquid assets force overall portfolio characteristics to deviate from desired levels, creating challenges for disciplined rebalancing activity.

Pursuit of active management introduces friction between investment results and benchmark returns. Sensible investors take great care in identifying portfolio biases, ensuring that differences result from deliberate choice, not an inadvertent consequence of portfolio construction. Use of normal portfolios and completeness funds assists managers in understanding and controlling active management bets embodied in the portfolio.

While successful active management programs eventually create value, investors face the interim possibility of experiencing periods of underperformance. Many sensible investment strategies require time horizons of three to five years, introducing the likelihood that even ultimately successful decisions appear foolish in the short run. When market prices move against established positions, investors with strong hands add to holdings, increasing the benefit from active management. Conversely, sensible investors trim winning positions, preventing excessive exposure to recently successful strategies. Leaning against the wind proves to be an effective risk-control measure.

Leverage contains the potential to add substantial value and create great harm, posing particular danger to investors pursuing long-term strategies. Keynes warns that "an investor who proposes to ignore market fluctuations . . . must not operate on so large a scale, if at all, with borrowed money."[9] Fiduciaries strive to identify and assess sources of explicit and implicit portfolio leverage, seeking to ensure that the leverage influences portfolio characteristics in an acceptable manner.

Many high-profile investment disasters in recent years involve losses stemming from leverage lurking beneath the surface of portfolio management activities. The Common Fund made explicit use of leverage in its risk-seeking security lending program, exposing educational institution assets to high levels of risk in exchange for modest expected returns. David Askin employed explicit leverage on top of the implicit leverage inherent in his mortgage-backed securities derivatives positions, turning an otherwise serious impairment of value into a total wipeout. Avoiding headline-grabbing disaster requires thorough understanding of the sources and magnitude of exposure to leverage in an investment fund.

Serving institutional goals requires disciplined implementation of asset allocation policies, centered around regular rebalancing to ensure that portfolio characteristics match targeted levels. Many activities pursued by institutional fund managers create frictions, causing portfolio results to differ from expectations. Illiquid investments often provide attractive active management opportunities, while posing significant challenges to the rebalancing process. Investors employing active management strategies expose funds to the impact of performance differentials relative to benchmark results. Use of leverage magnifies investment results, potentially altering portfolio characteristics in a manner unanticipated by asset allocation analyses. Sensible investors pursue regular rebalancing strategies, carefully considered active management approaches, and limited leveraging techniques.

7
Traditional Asset Classes

Traditional asset classes—marketable equities and bonds—form the core of most institutional portfolios, providing fundamentally important building blocks for portfolio construction. For institutions unwilling or unable to commit sufficient resources to pursue management-intensive commitments to alternative assets, marketable securities represent the opportunity set available to structure portfolios.

Bonds contribute diversification. Under normal circumstances, the stabilizing influence of bond positions comes at the opportunity cost of low relative returns. When conditions fail to meet expectations, bonds diversify. Unexpected inflation damages fixed income, while unanticipated deflation causes bonds to shine. Bondholders reap the rewards of owning fixed income in times of financial crisis or under conditions of deflationary pressure.

Marketable equities drive investment returns in traditional portfolio schemes, providing the long-run gains necessary to support institutional activities. Ownership of interests in corporate enterprises generates superior results for patient investors with sufficiently long holding periods.

Equity investors face a staggering array of alternatives, ranging from heavily scrutinized large-capitalization domestic securities to much less-well-followed emerging markets shares. By embracing a broad definition of equity markets, from large to small and near to far, fund managers create a diverse, intriguing range of investment opportunities.

The efficiency of pricing in fixed income markets leaves little room for successful active management. Government bonds trade in the most competitive market in the world, allowing no opportunity for active managers to create an edge. Large-capitalization U.S. equities operate in a similarly efficient environment, presenting few, if any, opportunities for value-added management. Smaller-capitalization domestic stocks trade in less efficient markets, affording thoughtful investors the possibility of beating the market. Since the evolution of overseas financial markets lags the development of the U.S. investment industry, less heavily researched foreign securities generally present superior active management opportunities. Emerging markets represent an extreme among equity alternatives, providing substantial numbers of mispricings for hard-working investors to exploit.

Owners of marketable securities incur costs imposed by agency activity, as the stewards of corporate assets pursue self-interest at the expense of providers of debt and equity capital. Bonds exhibit the most extreme misalignment of interests, as most debt issuers benefit by reducing the value of debt obligations, resulting in direct conflict between the goals of borrowers and lenders. Equities provide generally superior coincidence of interests, albeit with potential for poorly incentivized corporate managers to benefit personally at the expense of external shareholders.

Investors employing external managers to run portfolios of marketable securities face agency risks in both the underlying investments and the relationship with the manager. Investment advisers generally receive asset-based fees, encouraging behavior at odds with investor interests. Without explicit performance-based compensation, investment management firms tend to pursue staying-in-business strategies of hugging benchmarks, and cash-flow-generative, asset-gathering activities. Neither closet indexing nor large asset size serves investor goals.

ROLE OF FIXED INCOME

Long-term bonds play a diversifying role in institutional portfolios, providing steady, reliable streams of income to investors. The security provided by bond investments becomes particularly significant in times of financial crisis, when investors embark on a flight to quality, seeking to hold only the most secure, most liquid assets. Similarly, high-quality fixed income instruments perform well in an environment of unanticipated price deflation, when gains generated by bond positions serve to offset declines suffered by holdings of riskier assets.

Under normal economic and financial circumstances, the relatively low volatility of bonds serves to mitigate portfolio risks, although much of the time bond prices correlate with equity prices, limiting the diversifying power of fixed income allocations. The strong, positive connection between bonds and other investment classes stems from the central importance of interest rates in valuing assets. Increases in rates cause discount rates to rise, reducing the present value of future cash flows expected from bonds and equities alike. Decreases in rates lead to the opposite consequence, resulting in increased valuations for both bonds and riskier assets. The normally positive relationship between bonds and riskier investment vehicles diminishes the diversifying value of bond holdings, forcing long-term investors to pay the price of reduced portfolio returns in exchange for short-run dampening of portfolio volatility.

In the case of unanticipated inflation, fixed income positions perform poorly, as increases in the price level erode the value of the fixed nominal coupon flows and principal repayment promised to bond investors. For much of the modern era, fixed income holdings disappointed investors as yields marched ever upward. From 2 percent coupons in the 1950s to 4 percent coupons in the 1960s to 8 percent coupons in the 1970s and 16 percent coupons in the 1980s, bond owners faced a relentless series of inflation-induced price declines. At the same time, equity positions provided superior performance as inflationary increases ultimately enhanced the value of existing corporate assets. Bondholdings perform particularly poorly when price increases exceed expectations.

The role that fixed income plays depends critically on the economic and financial environment that investors face, with bonds exhibiting the strongest diversifying characteristics in periods of unanticipated inflationary or deflationary price changes. Under normal circumstances, investors receive a modest level of portfolio stability from fixed income positions, albeit at the high cost of diverting assets from investment opportunities promising higher returns. When investors experience unanticipated inflation, bonds tend to suffer relative to equity positions, increasing the opportunity costs of owning bonds. In periods of deflation or financial crisis, investors benefit enormously from the protection provided by bonds, justifying inclusion of the generally low expected return asset in well-structured portfolios.

Investors frequently own more fixed income than necessary to protect against hostile financial environments, leading to behavior that undermines the fundamental purpose of holding bonds. Confronted with a larger-than-ideal allocation to fixed income, investment managers often seek to enhance returns by accepting credit, option, and currency risk. Although under normal circumstances, risky bonds might generate superior returns, investors face likely disappointment in times of financial stress. Buying insurance from a fly-by-night insurance company appears sensible until the unreimbursed catastrophe losses overwhelm the previous savings from discounted premium payments. When buying an insurance policy, deal only with the highest-quality providers.

By holding portfolios of high-quality, long-term, noncallable instruments, investors emphasize the attributes of bonds that provide the greatest protection in times of financial crisis. When investors seek refuge from the volatility induced by panics, securities backed by the full faith and credit of the U.S. government outperform risky assets, sometimes dramatically.

Panic of 1998

In the summer and early fall of 1998, the Asian financial crisis painted a bleak backdrop for securities markets. A mid-July slump in equity markets accelerated in August when devaluation and default in Russia contributed to investor anxiety. The near collapse in September of the insanely levered Long Term Capital Management hedge fund fueled bearish sentiment, causing market participants to demand immediate liquidity and safety.

During the worldwide collapse in equity prices, the broad-based Wilshire 5000 declined 22 percent from its all-time peak on July 17 to the market bottom on October 8. As shown in Figure 7.1, a strong preference for quality and size caused large-capitalization stocks to outperform small securities in dramatic fashion, with the S&P 500 outpacing the Russell 2000 by a margin of 14 percentage points, or –19 percent to

–33 percent. Developed foreign and emerging equity returns provided little solace for diversified portfolios, with the markets falling 21 percent and 27 percent, respectively.

Amid the market tumult, long-term treasuries posted solid gains, returning 8 percent and besting the results of every major asset class. Credit risk and optionality dampened the performance of high-quality corporate bonds and mortgages, limiting returns to 5 percent and 2 percent, respectively. Junk bond and emerging debt losses reflected the high degree of equity exposure implicit in risky bond positions, with high yield posting a –7 percent return and emerging markets showing a dismal –24 percent result over the period.

Asset class performance surrounding the 1998 market panic illustrates the superior diversifying power of pure fixed income—long-term, noncallable, default-free issues. Accepting credit and option risk increases expected return under normal circumstances; in times of

Figure 7.1 Treasury Bonds Protect Portfolios in Turbulent Markets
Various Asset Class Returns, July 17, 1998, to October 8, 1998

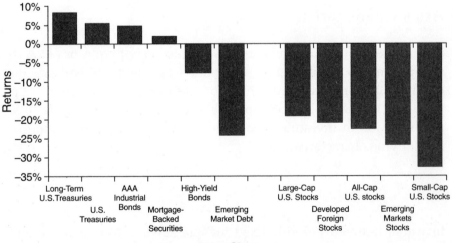

Sources: Long-term U.S. Treasuries: Merrill Lynch U.S. Treasury/Agency 10+ Years Index. U.S. Treasuries: Merrill Lynch U.S. Treasury/Agency Master Index. AAA industrial bonds: Merrill Lynch AAA Industrial Index. Mortgage-backed securities: Merrill Lynch Mortgage Master Index. High-yield bonds: Merrill Lynch High Yield Master Index. Emerging market debt: JP Morgan Emerging Market Bond Index. Large-capitalization U.S. stocks: S&P 500 Index. Developed foreign stocks: MSCI EAFE Index. All-capitalization U.S. stocks: Wilshire 5000 Index. Emerging markets stocks: IFC Global Index. Small-capitalization U.S. stocks: Russell 2000 Index.

crisis, however, investors require the protection provided by positions of U.S. Treasury bonds.

•   •   •

Sensible investors focus on the superior diversifying characteristics of long-term government bonds, holding only the amount necessary to protect portfolios against financial trauma. If portfolios include the minimum allocation necessary to provide insurance against catastrophe, investors free up assets to diversify into alternative asset classes, achieving volatility reduction without sacrificing return. A low allocation to high-quality fixed income reduces the costs associated with holding bonds during normal circumstances and periods of unanticipated inflation, the environments in which fixed income positions tend to impair portfolio performance. Tailoring the bond portfolio to emphasize the essential diversifying characteristics of fixed income increases expected benefits in time of crisis while reducing the long-term costs of holding bonds.

Asset Characteristics

Since the end of 1925, bonds provided investors with returns of 5.2 percent per annum, exhibiting a risk level of 9.2 percent standard deviation of returns. After adjusting for inflation, returns drop to 2.1 percent per year, well below the level of most other investment alternatives. To justify inclusion in investment portfolios, bonds must provide important diversifying characteristics.[1]

Cash

Investors frequently divide fixed income assets into cash and bonds, with the former consisting of instruments maturing within one year and the latter including instruments with more than a year to maturity. For investors with short investment horizons, cash represents the riskless asset, as market participants know nominal and real returns with reasonable certainty. This certainty, however, comes with a high price: historical returns amount to 3.8 percent per annum for cash, which reduces to a paltry 0.7 percent per year after adjustment for inflation.

If investors operate with time horizons of several years, cash constitutes a risky asset. Holding-period returns become uncertain as investors roll over maturing cash instruments into new investments at then-market rates. In contrast, when employing a five-year investment horizon, the five-year zero coupon bond with its fixed nominal return represents the risk-free asset.

Because investors frequently employ one-year horizons when conducting portfolio analysis, cash naturally enters the matrix of capital markets returns, causing many long-term investors to misidentify cash as a riskless asset. If investors conducted analysis over periods consistent with an appropriate investment horizon, cash would appear as a substantially riskier asset.

Some investors argue that cash provides necessary liquidity for endowment funds, ignoring the massive amounts of liquidity resident in institutional portfolios. Interest income, dividend payments, and rental streams provide liquid cash flows, facilitating the ability of the investment fund to meet spending distribution requirements. Natural turnover of assets provides another source of funds. Bonds mature, companies merge, and private assets become liquid, serving as sources of cash flow for the institution. Manager sell decisions create yet another set of liquidity events. Finally, if income flows, natural asset turnover, and manager sales create insufficient liquidity to meet spending requirements, investors retain the ability to direct sales of assets to provide for current consumption. The modest transactions costs incurred in selling assets pale in comparison to the drag on returns created by holding cash as a standard part of an institutional portfolio. Based on delivery of poor real returns and failure to serve as a riskless asset for long-term investors, cash plays no significant role in a well-constructed endowment portfolio.

Duration

Duration measures the effective maturity of a bond, considering the timing and present value of individual cash flows received over the term of the instrument.* Longer-duration bonds exhibit greater sensitiv-

---

*The term *duration* was first used in 1938 by Macaulay, who developed a formula to measure the average economic life of a security. Duration constitutes a weighted average of the proportions of the present value of the expected cash flows from a bond, with each payment weighted by the period in which the payment is expected to be received.

ity to interest rate changes than do shorter-duration bonds. By increasing a portfolio's duration, investors gain greater exposure to interest rate moves, creating a roughly equivalent choice between more assets with lower duration and fewer assets with higher duration. Portfolio managers wishing to reduce the opportunity costs of holding fixed income assets might rely on a small allocation to a long-duration portfolio, hoping to buy the diversifying power of bonds at reduced prices.

Quality

Bonds range in quality from the most secure assets backed by the full faith and credit of the United States to obligations of corporations no longer able to make timely payments. U.S. Treasury bonds represent pure fixed income, providing a certain stream of payments untainted by exposure to credit risk inherent in nongovernment bonds. Even the highest-quality corporate obligations contain elements of equity risk, since a company's ability to meet fixed obligations depends on its continuing corporate health. In the extreme case of bankruptcy, bonds frequently take on pure equity attributes, as control of corporate assets moves from the previous owners to the holders of defaulted debt obligations.

Call Options

Many bonds contain call options, allowing issuers to prepay outstanding obligations at a fixed price. When interest rates decline, previous issuers of callable bonds benefit by redeeming the outstanding issue at a fixed price, refunding the bonds at lower interest costs. If interest rates rise, issuers of callable bonds benefit by securing funding at what in retrospect turn out to be attractive rates. Unless the purchaser of callable bonds receives sufficient compensation for granting the call option, bond issuers create a "heads I win, tails you lose" proposition.

Call options play an important role in evaluating mortgage-backed securities, as borrowers typically have the option to prepay home mortgages at any time. Wall Street technowizards spend countless hours developing models to predict repayment behavior, a critical component in pricing the options embedded in mortgage-backed securities.

Foreign Bonds

The diversification provided by high-quality foreign sovereign fixed income stems almost completely from foreign exchange exposure. If investors hedge currency exposure by using forward foreign exchange contracts to convert coupon and principal payments from foreign currency to dollars, the resulting package becomes identical to a domestic dollar-denominated bond. Because forward foreign exchange contracts derive from interest rate differentials, a full hedge simply causes a foreign bond to take on the interest rate characteristics of domestic bonds. Unless arbitrage opportunities exist, fully hedged foreign bond investing holds little appeal.

Agency Issues

Investors in bonds face the uncomfortable fact that issuers of debt benefit from reducing the value of fixed income obligations. To mitigate the potential diminution in value of bond positions, lenders place contractual limitations on borrower behavior, hoping to force obligors to respect creditor interests. Ultimately contracts provide little security, because self-interest causes corporate managers to find ways to profit at the expense of bondholders.

Bond issuer behavior ranges from generally good deportment needed to maintain consistent access to debt markets to egregious actions designed to make a quick killing. Most frequently, bond issuers gain the upper hand with subtle tactics, such as issuing bonds with company-friendly call provisions. Particularly severe conflicts exist between interests of debt and equity holders in highly leveraged situations, since high costs of debt place great pressure on companies, causing managers to attempt to lessen the burden by pursuing strategies designed to reduce the value of debt obligations. Holders of corporate bonds sit across the table from management, occupying a position on the wrong side of substantial conflict of interests.

Relative to corporate obligations, U.S. Treasury bonds contain fewer alignment-of-interest issues, as the government lacks a strong set of incentives to reduce the value of existing debt obligations. To the extent that domestic entities own government bonds, interest and principal payments simply represent transfers within the country. By impairing the value of treasury issues, the government harms the interests of one set of constituents (bondholders) while advancing the interests of another (taxpayers). Since no clear motivation exists for the government to diminish the value of its debt obligations, holders of U.S. Treasury securities face fewer issues regarding agency costs.

Bonds and the RJR Buyout. An extreme example of management improving its position at the expense of bondholders occurs when a company undergoes a recapitalization or buyout. In such transactions, large amounts of debt replace equity, creating a capital structure with greater leverage. The primary rationale for pursuing recapitalizations and buyouts lies in increasing returns to shareholders. As an inevitable consequence of such transactions, existing debt becomes riskier, increasing its yield and reducing its price. The reduction in value of existing company debt represents a direct wealth transfer from the bondholders to the equity holders of the company.

In October 1988, RJR Nabisco's management proposed taking the company private in a $16.7 billion transaction, beginning one of the strangest chapters in American corporate finance.[2] Public announcement of the deal caused RJR's stock to skyrocket 21 1/4 points to 77 1/8, foreshadowing continued excitement by closing well above the deal price of 75. While stockholders celebrated, owners of RJR bonds saw prices plummet. In the face of conventional wisdom that RJR's size precluded a leveraged buyout, values of the firm's bonds tumbled as much as 15 percent in response to the proposed deal. George Collins, president of T. Rowe Price, reacted: "What a mess. This is ridiculous. The bond holder gets taken to the woodshed and there is no recourse."[3]

For holders of RJR securities, the adventure continued. Equity owners benefited as competition from buyout firm Kohlberg Kravis Roberts (KKR) raised the bid from 75 to 90, then to 92, next to 100, and ultimately to 109. With each increase in bid level came an increase in the amount of debt required to finance the transaction. As the expected debt burden rose, the risks to current bondholders rose concomitantly, reflected in declining prices for RJR bonds.

Prior to the late October bid, R. J. Reynolds Industries Sinking Fund Debentures 7 3/8s due 2001 traded at a price of 87, yielding 9.15 percent. After the buyout bid, the bonds immediately dropped to 82 and continued to decline, reaching a price of 79 5/8 with a yield of 10.34

percent by the middle of the following week. Table 7.1 shows the successive decline in bond prices as bid levels increased. Ultimately, in February 1989 when KKR paid a staggering $109 per share for the company, the RJR 7 3/8s due 2001 traded at 74 3/4, well below the prebid price of 87. The spread over comparable U.S. Treasury issues increased from the original 33 basis points, reflecting the strong investment-grade credit of RJR, to a lower-quality 214 basis points consistent with the bond's newly designated junk grade status.

The loss suffered by the holders of the RJR 7 3/8s of 2001 paralleled losses suffered by RJR's other creditors. Estimating that RJR bonds lost nearly $1 billion in value subsequent to the buyout announcement, in mid-November the Metropolitan Life Insurance Company sued RJR Nabisco, contending that the firm's management "breached a promise not to intentionally destroy investment grade debt, while lining its own pockets." Soaring to rhetorical heights, Met Life chief executive John Creedon suggested that RJR's "wanton destruction of the value of long term debt jeopardizes the very foundation of our capitalist system."[4]

In contrast to Met Life's estimate of a $1 billion loss for bondholders, equity owners faced the happy accumulation of approximately $7 billion of gains from the early stages of the buyout bidding war. Ultimately stockholder value rose a stunning $10 billion from October 1988 to February 1989, creating an enormous windfall for RJR shareholders. The dramatic increase in value stems from a combination of transfer of wealth from bondholders, tax benefits associated with high levels of anticipated interest expense, improved management incentives, and hoped-for efficiency gains in managing the company.

As stock owners gained from the bidding process, bondholders flailed about, attempting to enforce real or imaginary contractual obligations with lawsuits and oratorical bombast. Hurt by an internal study that concluded that bond covenants failed to prevent RJR from accepting a buyout bid, Met Life settled its suit by exchanging pre-leveraged buyout obligations for a package of new securities. Left to manage its impaired position in RJR's bonds, Met Life retained the consolation afforded by the possibility that the insurance company's equity investment in the RJR buyout, made through its partnership with KKR, might produce offsetting profits.

While the RJR buyout provides an extreme example of destruction of bondholder wealth, the transaction highlights the risks of owning

Table 7.1 RJR Stock Soars as Bonds Collapse During Buyout Battle

October 19, 1988–February 8, 1989

Date	Deal Status	Stock Price	Bond Price 7 3/8, 2001	Bond Yield 7 3/8, 2001	Spread over Treasuries
October 19, 1988	Prebid	55 7/8	87	9.15%	33 basis points
October 20, 1988	$75/share, management bid	77 1/8	82	9.94	115 basic points
October 24, 1988	$90/share, KKR bid	84	79 5/8	10.34	151 basis points
November 4, 1988	$92/share, management bid	87	76 1/4	10.94	203 basis points
November 20, 1988	$100/share, management bid	84	79	10.46	141 basis points
November 29, 1988	$109/share, KKR bid	89	78 1/2	10.55	142 basis points
February 8, 1989	Deal closes	100	74 3/4	11.27	214 basis points

Sources: RJR stock, RJR bond, and U.S. Treasury data from Wall Street Journal and Bloomberg.

fixed income assets other than treasuries. By lending money to private companies, bond investors provide funds to managers who stand to benefit by reducing the value of the loan. Entering into arrangements with such a stark misalignment of interests poses an ongoing threat to the corporate bond investor's position.

Active Management

Active management of high-quality fixed income makes little sense, as U.S. Treasury securities trade in the broadest, deepest, most liquid market in the world. On a bottom-up basis, in competing with the world's most sophisticated financial institutions, managers face little prospect of identifying mispriced assets. From a top-down perspective, when dealing with the staggering variety of variables influencing interest rates, managers face almost certain failure in attempting to time markets. Holding a passively managed portfolio of high-quality, long-term, noncallable bonds best serves a fixed income portfolio's fundamental mission.

Fund managers seeking to increase returns often expand the scope of bond portfolios to include corporate obligations, mortgage-backed securities, and foreign-currency-denominated debt. By embracing credit risk, optionality, and currency exposure, investors undermine the fundamental protective character of fixed income holdings. Since in a flight to quality, markets shun all but the most liquid U.S. Treasury obligations, pure fixed income provides portfolios with the highest degree of protection from economic and financial accidents.

Credit risk taints bonds by introducing equity characteristics into expected payment streams, as the value of promised cash flows depends on the issuer's financial health. While under normal circumstances investors benefit from accepting credit exposure, in times of crisis, when bonds play a critical diversifying role, the equity risk inherent in corporate securities reduces the protective value of fixed income holdings.

Call provisions confound the crisis protection characteristics of bonds. Just when investors expect to benefit from a flight-to-quality-induced bond rally, the associated decline in interest rates causes call options to become more valuable, dampening the callable bond's price appreciation potential. In essence, call options exaggerate the negative response of bonds to extreme moves in interest rates, shortening duration when rates decline and lengthening duration when rates increase. Accepting call option risk in fixed income portfolios tends to add value when reality conforms to previous expectations, precisely the environment in which the diversifying properties of fixed income play little role. Bonds without call risk best protect portfolios in times of market trauma.

Foreign bonds hold a superficial appeal, with proponents suggesting that foreign fixed income assets provide important portfolio diversification. Since fully hedged foreign bonds take on the characteristics of domestic bonds, most managers offer unhedged or partially hedged products, exposing investors to the foreign exchange risk inherent in nondollar bonds. Whether the exposure proves profitable depends on the vagaries of unknowable future foreign exchange rate movements. Unfortunately, foreign bonds suffer from the same low expected returns associated with domestic bonds, while lacking the offsetting benefit of protecting portfolios in financial panics.

The fundamental problem with holding nondollar bonds stems from the complete lack of predictability of the response to financial panic or economic trauma. Would deflationary conditions in the United States necessarily coincide with deflation overseas? Even if investors assume that links between various national economies suggest a high likelihood of co-movement, would spot exchange rates allow conversion of foreign bond prices to dollars at attractive rates? In the case of financial trauma, would the flight to quality center on U.S. Treasury securities, or would foreign government securities benefit as well? The degree of potential slippage in response of foreign bonds to domestic economic and financial trauma reduces the protection provided by holding fixed income assets.

Benchmark Games and Active Managers

Actively managed bond portfolios face two levels of agency risk. At the most basic level, borrowers seek to reduce costs of debt funding, a goal at odds with the desire of bondholders to realize high returns. On another level, active portfolio managers usually pursue risk-enhancing management strategies in an attempt to beat an extremely efficient market. In both the financial instrument itself and typical portfolio management strategies, bond owners suffer from lack of coincidence of interests.

The typical profile of actively managed bond portfolios illustrates the benchmark gaming strategy that fixed income managers pursue. Table 7.2 contains the results of a survey of eight of the largest institutional bond managers, responsible for more than $100 billion of fixed income assets. The managers hold portfolios with consistently greater-than-market credit risk, consistently greater-than-market optionality, and market-like interest rate exposure. In other words, bond managers avoid the big bet on interest rates in favor of small bets on credit and option values. Barring unusual credit stress or interest rate volatility, managers reap the benefits for exposing client assets to higher-than-market risk, collecting fees that represent the lion's share of the reward while proudly reporting a set of market-beating returns.

The characteristics of bond portfolios managed by eight firms at one point in time provide insufficient evidence to draw firm conclusions regarding bond manager behavior. Because portfolios change at the whim of the manager, holdings at December 31, 1997 might differ from the positions of several months earlier or several months later. Although a full examination of actively managed bond portfolio allocations requires a time series of portfolio allocation data, a brief look at allocations of a number of large-core fixed income portfolios provides support for the hypothesis that bond managers pursue above-market returns by exposing assets to above-market call and credit risk, not through security selection in the ultraefficient government bond market.

Each of the eight fixed income portfolios underweight treasury and agency issues, with average holdings of less than 26 percent of assets, relative to the Lehman Brothers Aggregate Index level of 49 percent. Managers hold funds garnered from the underweight treasury position in assets with greater credit and call risk by maintaining above-market exposure to mortgage-backed securities and corporate bonds. Mortgages represent 35 percent of active portfolios relative to an index weight of 30 percent, while corporate obligations constitute a larger bet, with a 32 percent allocation relative to the index level of 16 percent.

Returns stemming from the additional credit risk in the actively managed portfolios constitute the source of much of the "value added" by fixed income managers. Because the bulk of the mortgage-backed security universe emanates from agency issuers,[5] nearly 80

**Table 7.2 Active Fixed Income Managers Expose Client Assets
to Above-Market Levels of Risk**

Active Fixed Income Portfolio Composite versus Index

	Lehman Brothers Aggregate Index	Active Portfolio Composite
Type of Asset		
U.S. Treasuries and agencies	49%	26%
Mortgage-backed securities	30	35
Corporate bonds	16	32
Other	5	7
Total	100	100
Quality of Asset		
Treasury and agency	80	40
Investment grade	20	52
Below-investment grade	0	5
Other	0	3
Total	100	100

Sources: Index data are from Lehman Brothers. Active portfolio composite data compiled by the Yale University Investments Office.
Note: Data as of December 31, 1997.

percent of the Lehman Aggregate Index consists of treasury and agency credit quality. The active portfolios hold only half of the index weight in the highest-quality tier of securities with explicit and implicit government backing, as managers choose to overweight lower-quality obligations by holding 52 percent of assets in investment-grade bonds relative to the index level of 20 percent.

Active managers overweight the lowest-quality bonds most aggressively. At 11 percent, holdings of BBB-rated securities, the lowest rung of the investment-grade ladder, represent almost double the index level. Although below investment grade, or junk, bonds do not appear in the Lehman Aggregate Index,[6] managers allocate more than 5 percent of assets to these speculative securities.

In contrast to the large credit bets that managers make with client assets, explicit interest rate bets appear modest. The average duration of 4.74 years for the eight portfolios lies very close to the Lehman Aggregate duration of 4.81 years, with no manager deviating from the benchmark by as much as a year.

Few active managers pursue strategies involving market timing decisions, attempting to shorten portfolio duration in anticipation of interest rate increases and trying to lengthen duration in advance of rate declines. Although the general futility of timing markets causes external advisers to avoid big interest rate bets, the strategy of maintaining stable, market-like duration serves investor interests. With an active duration approach, investors run the risk of owning short-duration assets just as financial panic erupts, dramatically limiting the possible benefits from a flight-to-quality-induced bond market rally. Even if investors justify holding short-term bonds with the most thoughtfully articulated rationale imaginable, the potential costs of undermining the protective role of the fixed income portfolio preclude holding assets other than long-term bonds.

The evidence points to cynical benchmark-gaming behavior on the part of active fixed income managers. Avoiding the loser's game of interest rate anticipation strategies, bond managers add an incremental measure of optionality by overweighting mortgage-backed securities and corporate obligations. In addition to accepting higher levels of option-linked risk, active managers aggressively seek credit risk, hoping to boost returns above benchmark levels. By simply holding greater-than-market allocations to risky securities, bond managers increase expected returns by increasing portfolio risk, doing nothing to add value that justifies charging management fees. On a risk-adjusted basis, investors fare far better with passively managed high-quality bond portfolios.

•   •   •

Portfolios of long-term U.S. Treasury securities promise to generate a steady flow of returns in even the most dire economic and financial circumstances, defining the fundamental justification for including in a portfolio the relatively low expected return asset class of bonds. By introducing deviations from the purity of long-term, default-free government bonds, active managers threaten the ability of fixed income to protect portfolios in times of economic and financial peril. Investors holding a passively managed portfolio of treasury securities know the insurance policy will pay off when needed.

In spite of promising lower returns than most other investment classes, bonds earn inclusion in portfolios by providing protection against the extraordinary circumstances of a financial crisis or economic deflation. Only high-quality, long-term bonds perform well in times of severe stress, allowing investors to view the opportunity costs of holding bonds as an insurance premium incurred to insulate portfolios from extreme conditions. By holding high-quality, long-term, non-callable fixed income assets, investors emphasize unique attributes of bonds, enhancing the ability of portfolios to survive traumatic periods.

ROLE OF MARKETABLE EQUITIES

Equity positions, representing ownership shares of corporate enterprises, generate the returns that drive the results of institutional portfolios. Investors with long time horizons enjoy the opportunity to hold substantial amounts of marketable and private equity, creating portfolios with high levels of expected return.

Equity holdings form the core of institutional portfolios because owning a share of the profits generated by well-run enterprises provides greater expected rewards than does staking a claim to debt service payments promised by the same corporations. Although bond owners occasionally outperform stockholders, sometimes for extended periods, equity positions deliver superior returns over sufficiently long time frames. The portfolio construction process for long-term investors begins with the presumption of a heavy commitment to equities.

As the core institutional asset, marketable equities provide the frame of reference for judging all other assets. The difference between the expected return from stocks and the expected returns from the diversifying assets of bonds and real estate defines the price of obtaining their special portfolio protective attributes. The principal justification for incurring expected opportunity costs by investing in bonds and real estate stems from the diversification they provide when marketable equities perform poorly. At the other end of the return continuum, venture capital and leveraged buyouts claim a place in institutional portfolios by promising returns in excess of marketable equities. As the core asset, equity holdings set the standard for evaluating other assets.

The great obstacle confronting successful implementation of equity-dominated portfolio strategies lies in the desire to emphasize past winners and avoid yesterday's losers. Human nature leads investors to overinvest in marketable equities at market tops and underinvest in stocks at market bottoms. Breaking the cycle of excessive enthusiasm and extreme caution requires investors to behave differently from the crowd.

Placing 50, 60, or 70 percent of assets in marketable equities proves sensible only if investors exhibit staying power, maintaining positions through thick and thin. If fund managers respond to poor market results by selling stocks, or react to strong returns by increasing equity positions, the resulting whipsaw damages the portfolio. Buying high and selling low profits only the brokerage community.

Unfortunately, investors tend to develop conviction based on past performance, emphasizing holdings of assets falling into the category of proven winners. In the late 1990s, domestic equities achieved an almost cultlike status as the only true investment for long-term investors. Since U.S. corporations boast better management than foreign operations, investors saw little reason to venture into developed overseas markets. Because U.S. companies operate in developing countries, dedicated emerging markets exposure became unnecessary. Citing nearly two centuries of results, enthusiasts advocated creating portfolios dominated by U.S. stocks.

The relative performance of U.S. equities in the bull market of the 1980s and 1990s further reinforced the apparent inevitability of achieving superior results through investing in U.S. stocks. Throughout much of the period, diversifying the portfolio by investing in marketable securities other than U.S. stocks created a drag on returns. In fact, measured from the beginning of the bull market in 1982 until 1998, the S&P 500 return of 18.4 percent per annum outpaced 99 percent of institutional portfolios.[7] Trailing ten-year numbers provide even more dramatic evidence of the futility of diversification. U.S. equities continued to outperform 99 percent of institutions, while the diversifying assets of cash, bonds, and foreign equities posted bottom-of-the-barrel results, falling below returns of every major institutional fund. Investors reached the obvious conclusion, anointing domestic stocks as the asset of choice for the long-term investor.

If portfolio management were as straightforward as choosing yesterday's winners, investing would be a simple task. Today's stock market promoters forget that throughout much of the two-century history of domestic equity prices, the United States represented one of many emerging markets. Only with crystal-clear hindsight does the ultimate success of the U.S. stock market appear foreordained. Citing the recent history of return and risk in domestic, foreign, and emerging markets, many observers conclude that U.S. corporate assets represent a dominant alternative, generating higher returns with lower risk. A more thoughtful interpretation of history would encourage investors to examine today's out-of-favor markets in a search for tomorrow's winner.

In an environment where U.S. stocks represent the obvious choice, investors run the risk of elevating expectations for the admittedly important asset to unrealistic levels. If future results fail to conform to the high level of expectations, disappointed investors may respond to the folly of buying high with the equally profound mistake of selling low.

Regardless of occasionally excessive enthusiasm or overblown concern regarding various markets, publicly traded equities represent core holdings for long-term investors, defining the standard for measuring other asset positions. If investors maintain sensible allocations through thick and thin, the long-term rewards for holding equity positions provide handsome levels of support for institutional purposes.

Asset Characteristics

Since the end of 1925, U.S. equities provided investors with returns of 11.0 percent per annum, while exhibiting a risk level of 20.3 percent standard deviation of returns. After adjustment for inflation, returns fall to a still handsome 7.9 percent per year, setting the standard for assets held by long-term investors.[8]

Developed foreign markets produced 12.8 percent per annum returns over the twenty-nine-year life of the Morgan Stanley Capital International Europe Australia Far East (MSCI EAFE) Index, with a volatility of 21.9 percent measured by the standard deviation of returns. Emerging markets investments, with a substantially shorter history, exhibit the unattractive historical characteristics of a lower return of 9.7 percent per annum with a higher risk of 37.7 percent standard deviation of returns. Developed and emerging markets posted 7.6 percent and 6.5 percent per annum returns, respectively, after accounting for inflation.[9]

Market Classification

Faced with tens of thousands of publicly traded companies world-wide, investors confront the problem of developing classification schemes to facilitate asset allocation and portfolio management. A first cut of separating domestic and foreign securities allows investors to segregate the direct influence of foreign exchange rates on the portfolio. Stripped to the bare essentials, domestic and foreign companies represent similar investment opportunities. Fiat, Toyota, and Ford compete head to head in markets all over the world, dealing with similar market dynamics regardless of their country of domicile. From an investor's perspective the fundamental difference in choosing among companies in the global marketplace lies in the currency exposure associated with owning stocks of foreign companies, suggesting a separation of domestic from foreign holdings.

Further division between developed markets and emerging markets allows investors to calibrate exposure to the fundamentally riskier less developed markets. While emerging markets offer the potential to generate premium returns, investors expect the pattern of results to exhibit substantial variability as prices respond to the inevitable string of successes and failures. Differences in fundamental risk characteristics suggest treating emerging markets investments as a distinct pool.

Some investors opt for even finer distinctions in defining portions of a fund's marketable equity exposure. For instance, a regional approach might identify separate allocations for the United States, Asia, Europe, and Latin America, with developed and emerging market distinctions where appropriate. In addition, differences in capitalization size and investment style provide other criteria to define subcategories for marketable equities. By increasing the number of investment categories, investors achieve greater clarity in understanding individual portfolios at the expense of confusion in dealing with a profusion of units requiring care and attention.

Because marketable equities represent a collection of investment opportunities as diverse as the economies of the capitalist world and as broad as the geography of free markets, few generalizations guide investor understanding of equity investment opportunities. Unlike fixed income investors employing the tools of duration, credit quality, and yield to evaluate bond portfolios, equity investors confront a nearly unimaginably broad selection of choices with idiosyncratic characteristics relating to value and growth metrics, company size, industry exposure, and a multitude of other factors. One of the most important variables for investors concerns the relationship between security prices and changes in inflation.

Over long periods of time, domestic stocks tend to track inflation, protecting holders from price-level-induced declines in asset purchasing power. In contrast to the fixed nominal payments promised to holders of bond obligations, equity owners lay claim to the price-level-sensitive residual value of a corporation. Foreign equities provide no similar dependable protection, as returns from overseas markets depend not only on internal macroeconomic conditions but also on the exchange rate used to translate foreign values to domestic currency. Investors seeking long-run protection against inflation emphasize domestic equities.

Corporate profitability constitutes the basic force driving returns to holders of marketable equities. In an environment with perfect alignment of interests, corporate management pursues profit-maximizing strategies, allowing the fruits of success to benefit equity owners directly. In reality, substantial friction frequently exists between the actions of management and the desires of shareholders. Firms often attempt to appease a variety of stakeholders, including employees, the surrounding community, distributors, and suppliers, diverting resources that might otherwise flow to equity owners. While explicit recognition of stakeholder interests may represent good public policy, in many cases satisfying a diverse group of constituencies interferes with reasonable profit-seeking activity.

Shareholders and RJR. Self-interest of company management often represents an even more problematic source of divergent interests. Because of the separation in public markets between ownership by investors and control by management, situations arise where management actions prove inconsistent with investor goals. Conflicts begin with excessive salaries and end with managers diverting corporate assets to satisfy ego-driven desires. The classic example of RJR Nabisco's pre-buyout excesses illustrates aggressive pursuit of selfish individual goals by managers at the expense of satisfaction of legitimate shareholder interests.

The extravagance of F. Ross Johnson's RJR Nabisco begins at the headquarters he created in Atlanta. Moved from Winston-Salem at an estimated cost of $50 million, the new building contained pricey antique appointments purchased "without a budget," according to one vendor.[10] To ferry Johnson, his senior executives, and hangers-on, the company maintained the RJR Air Force, a fleet of ten planes (including two new $21 million G4 Gulfstream jets) manned by thirty-six pilots, and housed in a $12 million complex, featuring a three-story atrium and a walk-in wine cooler. Johnson retained a bevy of star athletes, ostensibly to promote RJR Nabisco products. For catering to Johnson's personal and professional needs, former football greats Don Meredith ($500,000 per year), Frank Gifford ($413,000), and O. J. Simpson ($250,000) joined golfers Ben Crenshaw ($400,000), Fuzzy Zoeller ($300,000), and Jack Nicklaus ($1,000,000), as well as baseball star Don Mattingly ($250,000), in earning more than all but the most senior executives.[11] RJR's opulent headquarters, bloated fleets of corporate jets, and stellar roster of paid retinue provided a means for management to benefit at the expense of shareholders. While the RJR case constitutes an extreme example, the problem exists to lesser degrees throughout much of corporate America.

• • •

Although F. Ross Johnson's excesses at RJR represent an unusual example of management self-aggrandizement, more subtle principal-agent conflicts permeate the marketable equity arena. Grants of options to senior executives appear on the surface to align interests of management and shareholders. By rewarding option program participants with outsized compensation when the company's stock soars, both insiders and external owners benefit. Unfortunately, when stock prices decline, the coincidence of interests breaks down. Shareholders lose real money while managers lose only an opportunity to profit. In fact, the widespread practice of repricing options to reflect lower stock prices frequently eliminates even the minor sting suffered by management. Failing to live up to their billing as aligning management and shareholder interests, the one-way character of options simply serves to increase management compensation at the expense of shareholders living in a two-way world. Although management and shareholder interests frequently diverge, investors retain the ability to invest in shareholder-oriented companies, reducing the degree to which results suffer from corporate managers diverting resources for personal benefit.

The divergence of interests between shareholders and corporate managers poses far less severe problems than the chasm between the goals of bondholders and equity interests. In spite of incurring the inevitable frictional costs, long-term shareholders benefit enormously from exposure to equity markets.

Active Management

Investors evaluating management alternatives for marketable equity portfolios face a spectrum ranging from the generally efficiently priced large-capitalization domestic equities to the frequently mispriced emerging market stocks. Following the principle that active management makes most sense when inefficiencies abound, investors find that passive management of large-capitalization domestic stocks provides a high hurdle for investment advisers' market-beating strategies. The heavily researched, intensively traded environment for sizable public companies leaves little room for active management success.

Because Wall Street finds following smaller companies far less profitable, in terms of both day-to-day trading opportunities and occasional investment banking transactions, investors face the prospect of uncovering some interesting, mispriced investment opportunities. Although success demands hard work, small-capitalization equity managers with an edge have a reasonable shot at generating attractive relative returns.

Foreign equities present an intriguing set of active management opportunities, as even the most advanced marketplaces overseas lag the development of domestic financial markets. Because foreign countries devote far fewer resources to corporate finance and investment management, equivalent levels of investigative effort produce more interesting ideas in foreign than in domestic markets. Although inefficiencies in pricing create opportunities overseas, managers of foreign equities face a formidable task as particular numbers on individual companies and overview data on market valuations tend to be hard to uncover.

The logistics of travel and barriers to easy communication further complicate the life of foreign equity managers. Conducting fundamental research on overseas companies requires significantly more effort than investigating domestic corporations. Aside from dealing with geographic and linguistic hurdles, managers generally lack the day-to-day flow of information on corporate activity available to domestic security advisers. The inefficient market conditions that create the investment opportunity require hard work to exploit.

Hiring managers domiciled overseas might ameliorate some of the logistical problems associated with foreign equity portfolio management. Not surprisingly, identifying attractive candidates poses a problem. Because the lack of market efficiency stems from a paucity of sophisticated local players, investors seeking foreign-domiciled investment advisers find little from which to choose. Even in the United Kingdom, with its relatively advanced financial services industry, large, clubby, bureaucratic organizations dominate the advisory business. Foreign investment advisers tend to lack the sophistication and the edge that result from operating in the ruthlessly competitive U.S. investment management business.

Investors pursuing active management of marketable equities find few opportunities to exploit among larger-capitalization domestic securities, leading prudent investors to passive management of the more efficiently priced assets. Mispricings become more prevalent in the less-well-followed small-capitalization and foreign security markets, with the emerging markets providing the richest set of active management opportunities. By focusing active management efforts in arenas with the greatest degree of opportunity, investors increase the likelihood of producing market-beating results.

Security selection techniques vary widely, providing many possible paths to success or failure. Success favors rigorous, fundamental, bottom-up approaches to assessing forward-looking estimates of investment cash flows. Seeking to acquire assets at below fair value, disciplined investors combine quantitative techniques with informed market judgment, creating concentrated portfolios designed to generate handsome risk-adjusted returns. By identifying a clear, compelling set of strengths prior to initiating a relationship with an active manager, investors increase the likelihood of success.

Money managers operate along a number of important dimensions, each representing a spectrum of choices. For example, managers choose to approach investing somewhere along the bottom-up/top-down continuum. Bottom-up investment involves selecting stocks based solely on the relative attractiveness of individual securities; top-down investing incorporates only high-level macro factors in portfolio structuring. Few managers operate at either extreme, but most managers exhibit distinct biases that influence portfolio outcomes in powerful ways. Other important dimensions of active management include fundamental versus technical, value versus growth, quantitative versus judgmental, and concentrated versus diversified. The positioning of investment management firms along each of these vectors drives portfolio performance in fundamental ways.

Bottom-Up versus Top-Down

Security prices derive from a staggering number of complex factors. Broad macroeconomic factors, such as employment levels and inflation, influence prices at a market level, creating a systematic impact on individual securities. Obtaining an informational advantage in the incredibly multifaceted world of top-down investing requires extraordinary skills. Market participants study and analyze macroeconomic data to such an extent that market prices reflect the current store of knowledge. Even if an investor gleans an important macro insight, success requires more than an accurate prediction. Problems remain in identifying the direction and magnitude of the macro insight's influence on market levels.

Keynes lamented in his famous beauty contest metaphor that "it is not the case of choosing those which, to the best of one's judgement, are really the prettiest, nor even those which average opinion genuinely thinks the prettiest. We have reached the third degree where we devote our intelligences to anticipating what average opinion expects the average opinion to be. And there are some who practice the fourth, fifth and higher degrees."[12] Investments based on sound forecasts of macro variables suffer from the vagaries of price movements related not to how the factor itself performed, but to how it performed relative to how it had been expected to perform.

Along with broad systemic influences, idiosyncratic factors exert nonsystemic forces on a particular security's price. Although managers hoping to identify company-specific opportunities face daunting difficulties, the challenges prove less severe than those faced by macro investors. Given equal intelligence and energy, the company analyst who operates in a more narrowly defined arena more easily obtains important informational advantages than does the market analyst who deals with a multitude of heavily studied macro variables.

While the bottom-up investor faces the expectations-game issues illustrated in Keynes's beauty contest metaphor, company-specific insights provide powerful valuation underpinnings missing in macro analysis. If an analyst correctly foresees product demand beyond the market consensus, when that demand leads to higher-than-expected profitability, earnings surprises drive revaluation of the stock.

In contrast, correct assessment of particular macro variables provides no specific insight into market valuation. Consider the impact of increases in inflation rates on stock prices. Jeremy Siegel observes that in the short run, stock prices tend to react negatively to increasing inflation, presumably because higher inflation leads to higher interest rates. Applying higher discount rates to future earnings streams causes prices to decline.[13]

Paradoxically, Siegel notes that stock prices "provide excellent long-run hedges against inflation."[14] Since shares of stock represent a claim on assets denominated in nominal terms, stock prices ultimately reflect inflationary increases in value. As general inflation influences price levels, the replacement cost of corporate assets increases. Ultimately market values rise as stock prices reflect the increase in the nominal value of goods produced by corporate assets, insulating stock owners from inflationary damage.

Siegel's conclusions create a conundrum. Presumably stock prices decline in the short run because of inflation, and rise in the long run because of inflation. But the long run consists of a series of short runs, leading to a logical inconsistency; inflation influences stock prices negatively and positively.

The macro investor with an accurate forecast regarding higher future inflation rates obtains no special insight into market valuations. Betting on a short-run decline in prices places the investor at odds with expected long-run consequences of inflation. Betting on long-run price increases puts the investor at risk of sustaining serious near-term losses, which may test the patience of even the longest-term investor.

Macro investing involves making judgments not only about extremely difficult-to-forecast variables but also about the expected impact of those macro variables on security prices. The difficulty in making forecasts and assessing impacts makes macro investing extraordinarily treacherous.

The Exceptional Case of Japan. In spite of nearly overwhelming difficulties, top-down investing occasionally yields important insights, providing opportunities to generate excess returns. In environments where market values go to extremes, patient investors with strong nerves stand to benefit. Extraordinary valuations in the Japanese stock market in the late 1980s provided a huge opportunity for top-down analysis.

In the mid-1980s, Japan's equity market lost its moorings. After trading at sometimes scant, but generally understandable, dividend yields ranging from 2 percent to 5 percent for most of the 1970s, starting in 1980 the market's dividend yield began a long stretch of below 2 percent readings, driven by relentless increases in Japanese stock prices.* In 1986, the yield dropped below 1 percent as equity prices continued their meteoric rise. For most of 1987 and 1988, yields registered an astonishingly low one-half of 1 percent, dropping to an extraordinary four-tenths of 1 percent in September 1989. At the market's peak, Japan boasted the largest capitalization of any equity market in the world.

Relative valuations became absurd. At one point during the mania, the market capitalization of one Japanese security, Nippon Telephone & Telegraph (NTT), ranked fourth among countries, behind the United Kingdom and ahead of Canada as shown in Figure 7.2. In other words, an extremely wealthy investor could choose to own all of NTT—a Japanese telephone company—or all of the publicly traded stocks in Switzerland and Australia. Actually, the investor opting to own the two countries' marketable securities would pay about $14 billion less than the cost of purchasing the entirety of NTT.

Grantham, Mayo, Van Otterloo (GMO), a Boston-based money management firm, recognizing the extreme overvaluation, underweighted Japan beginning in 1985. As the bubble grew, GMO systematically reduced exposure to Japan. By late 1988, GMO owned no Japanese stocks in what Jeremy Grantham characterized a "bet-the-firm" position. In 1986, 1987, and 1988 GMO underperformed the for-

---

*The dividend yield serves as a simple proxy market valuation. While determining equity prices involves many more variables, dividend yield provides a reasonable shorthand assessment of market valuation levels.

**Figure 7.2 Nippon Telephone and Telegraph's Peak Market
Capitalization Exceeds Canada's**
Market Capitalization, June 1988

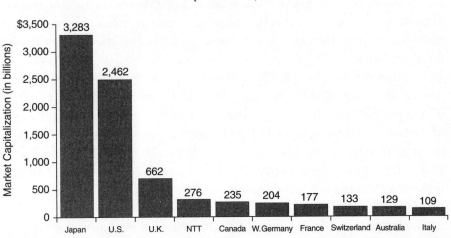

Source: Data from Morgan Stanley Capital International Perspective, June 1988.

eign benchmark by a margin of 110 percent to 172 percent, as Japanese
stock prices continued their relentless upward march. Ultimately
GMO's position generated strong relative performance, when the
Japanese underweighting caused results to exceed benchmark returns
every year from 1989 to 1993, adding a total of nearly 66 percentage
points to relative performance. Over the entire period, an investor in
GMO's foreign equity fund enjoyed a return of 269 percent, vastly outpacing the EAFE result of 200 percent.

The stark return pattern highlights a risk of top-down investing.
Generally the process involves making a handful of undiversifiable
bets, causing relative performance to be extremely volatile. Prudent
investors pursue macro strategies only when circumstances permit extraordinary degrees of confidence and perseverance.

More recently, Cursitor Eaton nearly destroyed its franchise by
making an erroneous, or at least premature, country allocation bet on
Japan. A top-down asset allocator, Cursitor Eaton developed a strong
long-term record by "attempting to identify major disequilibria in
macroeconomic forces leading to shifts in [the] financial markets of
the United States, the United Kingdom, Switzerland, France, Germany, and Japan."[15] The firm's investment approach rested on a strat-

egy of taking big bets and creating portfolios described as "global, concentrated and undiversified by traditional market standards." By making "substantial shifts between major asset classes," Cursitor Eaton's approach appealed to investors hoping to benefit from the firm's independent outlook for cash, bonds, and stocks in the six-country investment universe.

At the end of 1995, trailing ten-year performance of 15.6 percent per annum exceeded the results of the MSCI World Index by a margin of 1.9 percent per annum. Strong performance attracted client assets of more than $8 billion, as well as the attention of investment management giant Alliance Capital. In a deal characterized by Putnam, Lovell as a "'dream team' transaction," Alliance paid in excess of $150 million for a "strong, credible presence in the global asset allocation marketplace."[16]

Unfortunately for Alliance, Cursitor Eaton's concentrated asset allocation bets proved disastrously wrong. Overweighting Japan and underweighting the United States destroyed the firm's record, as American equities benefited from a continuing bull market, while Japanese stocks languished in an environment of economic malaise. Responding to deficits relative to the index of more than twenty points in 1996 and more than seven points in 1997, clients deserted the once-popular manager, causing assets under management to decline from the year-end 1996 level of $8.4 billion to 1998's $1.7 billion.

The withering of Cursitor Eaton's business forced Alliance Capital to write down the value of its investment by more than $120 million in the second quarter of 1997. Continuing client defections led to further financial pain; in the first quarter of 1998, the firm recorded a $10 million provision for buying a minority interest in Cursitor at a price "which will be substantially higher than its fair value."[17] Alliance's dream turned into a nightmare.

Many thoughtful investors shared Cursitor Eaton's 1995 conclusion that U.S. stocks appeared expensive relative to the washed-out valuations accorded Japanese equities. While the firm's conclusion may ultimately prove correct, client time horizons lack sufficient length to benefit from any possible future vindication. The performance of Cursitor Eaton's large and largely undiversifiable bet caused the firm to lose most of its client base, threatening its very existence.

As a consequence of the active management opportunity presented by the extraordinary Japanese overvaluation, according to one consultant's database, in the past ten years only three of sixty-eight active foreign managers failed to beat the most widely used benchmark, Morgan Stanley Capital International's Europe, Australia and Far East Index.[18] The success of foreign equity managers stands in stark contrast to the relative performance deficits posted by median active managers of domestic equities and fixed income. Even considering the universal underweighting of underperforming Japanese equities, the breadth of superior performance defies imagination.

Global Asset Allocation. Notwithstanding the huge relative gains generated by avoiding full exposure to Japan's lost decade, making macro top-down country allocation decisions constitutes an extraordinarily difficult strategy. Under normal circumstances, investors require substantial amounts of information to arrive at fair country valuations. Even after devoting considerable time and effort to the process, the end product generally provides inadequate support for discriminating among reasonably accurately priced developed country markets. Tactical country allocation decisions constitute nothing more and nothing less than market timing, exposing investors to the risks inherent in making large, undiversifiable bets on inadequate information.

Global asset allocation investment mandates take the country allocation strategy several steps further, allowing managers to hold stocks, bonds, and cash in any of a number of markets. Reasoning that if twenty-three developed stock markets in MSCI's World Index represent a good opportunity, then adding twenty-three bond markets and twenty-three cash markets must constitute a great opportunity, market players enthusiastically pursue tactical allocation across a daunting number of markets. Unfortunately, the currently popular investment approach flies in the face of funds management history. In the 1960s balanced mandates dominated the investment scene, populated by managers exercising discretion in distributing assets among U.S equities, bonds, and cash. As a result of disappointing results from the market timing implicit in balanced strategies, investors moved toward developing fixed asset allocation targets, employing specialist firms to manage specific asset class exposures.

By increasing the number of decision variables, market timers increase the chances for failure. If the 1960s-vintage balanced fund managers accumulated a long record of failure in timing three domestic asset classes, why should expanding the practice to a large number of overseas markets increase the likelihood of success for the

1990s-vintage global asset allocators? Driven by the naive enthusiasm of participants like the endowment manager who suggested that global asset allocation provides the opportunity "to beat every benchmark of every asset class in the world," investors in global asset allocation products face near-certain disappointment.

Top-Down Emerging Market Opportunity. Although top-down investors in developed markets face few opportunities to make sensible country bets, investors in emerging markets confront a dramatically different country valuation environment. Swinging from extraordinary enthusiasm to extreme pessimism, emerging markets present opportunities for contrarian investors to take a top-down approach to generating excess returns.

In contrast to the generally fair relative valuations in developed markets, emerging markets swing from one wild extreme to another, allowing profitable trades from purchase of deeply out-of-favor countries and sale of currently hot prospects.[19] Examination of country weightings in the IFC Global Emerging Markets Index provides dramatic evidence of speculative exuberance and pessimistic despair.

In the mid-1980s, as shown in Figure 7.3, Korea and Taiwan accounted for somewhat more than one-fifth of the market capitalization

Figure 7.3 Valuation Swings Provide Country Allocation Opportunities
Role of Korea and Taiwan in the IFC Emerging Markets Index

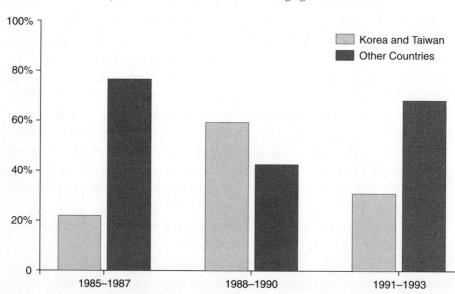

Source: Morgan Stanley Capital International.

of the IFC Index, with aggregate valuations at a reasonable level of 1.7 times book value. After several years of explosive equity market returns for the two markets, during which both Korea and Taiwan posted triple-digit years, the two markets constituted nearly three-fifths of the total emerging markets capitalization, dominating the index. Amid the late 1980s bubble, valuations rose along with prices, with the markets trading at a lofty average of 4.1 times book value. Subsequently the markets collapsed, as investors recognized that the path to maturity contained more than a few pitfalls, causing the weighting of the two countries to fall by nearly one-half. The price decline drove valuations to a more sensible average of 2.1 times book value.

Alternately strong and weak investment performance drove the changing allocations as the Asian powerhouses returned 67 percent per annum from 1986 to 1989, and the ninety-eight-pound weaklings lost 21 percent per annum from 1990 to 1992. During the bull market, Taiwan posted an extraordinary run, chalking up returns of 117 percent, 91 percent, and 98 percent in 1987 through 1989. Korea's series of results from 1986 to 1988 of 75 percent, 32 percent, and 107 percent pales only in comparison to the off-the-charts returns of the Taiwanese market.

The ensuing bear markets destroyed large amounts of financial value, with neither Korea nor Taiwan ever regaining the market peaks of the late 1980s. The decline in prices reduced by an order of magnitude the importance of Korea in the IFC Index, with 1988's dominant 27.5 percent share ultimately reduced to 1997's nearly inconsequential 2.6 percent share. Even a cursory examination of emerging market investment performance identifies a large number of countries exhibiting stupendous increases in price followed by equally spectacular falls from favor.

With such extraordinary swings in relative value, even the most naive valuation model delivers sensible contrarian buy and sell signals, allowing investors to overweight cheap countries and avoid expensive markets. Profit potential in top-down emerging markets country allocation represents the exception that proves the rule.

• • •

Bottom-up investing provides a substantial universe of investment opportunities. Morgan Stanley estimates that the countries included in its All Country World Index contain approximately 34,500 companies, providing fertile ground for the dedicated security analyst.[20] In contrast, the index encompasses only forty-eight countries, giving the top-down analyst far fewer options from which to choose.

Company-specific assessments, while challenging, involve much less complex variables than those influencing macro factors. Obtaining special insight into the earnings outlook for particular companies constitutes an achievable goal. By spending substantial amounts of time, energy, and intelligence, the bottom-up investor creates an informational edge that translates into superior performance based on a strong link between investment thesis and market response. Bottom-up security selection delivers a greater likelihood of investment success than does top-down investing.

Fundamental versus Technical

Technical analysis relies on identifying patterns in past price movements that predict future prices. In spite of staggering amounts of evidence indicating that charts cannot forecast future prices, technicians continue to attract a substantial following. The arrogance of technical analysts exceeds even that of the purist quantitative managers. While quants contend, "It's all in the data," technicians argue, "It's all in past prices."

Beating the market requires much more than knowing where prices have been. Burton Malkiel's *A Random Walk Down Wall Street* identifies three forms of market efficiency: weak, semistrong, and strong. The weak form simply states that knowledge of past price movements provides no help in determining future prices. No credible academic work disputes the validity of the weak form of the efficient markets hypothesis. Malkiel pulls no punches: "Technical rules have been tested exhaustively by using stock price data on both major exchanges going back as far as the beginning of the twentieth century. The results reveal that past movements in stock prices cannot be used reliably to foretell future movements. The stock market has no memory. The central proposition of charting is absolutely false, and investors who follow its precepts will accomplish nothing but increasing substantially the brokerage charges they pay."[21]

The semi-strong form of market efficiency argues that no publicly available information allows generation of risk-adjusted excess returns.

Most active managers attempt to use fundamental information to make superior security choices, hoping to disprove the semi-strong form of market efficiency. Although evidence is mixed, some managers appear to beat the market based on skill in identifying superior portfolios.

The strong form of market efficiency contends that no information—public or private—allows superior security selection. This extreme characterization implies that even material nonpublic information known to corporate insiders provides no advantage in picking stocks. If the strong form of the efficient markets hypothesis holds, then active management strategies make no sense. While markets tend to price securities efficiently, the strong form of the efficient markets hypothesis envisions market mechanisms far different from those that exist today.

The semi-strong form of the efficient markets hypothesis best characterizes most of today's securities markets. The only way for managers to exploit available security mispricings involves intensive application of fundamental analysis. Fiduciaries pursuing excess returns must seek out superior fundamental analysts, avoiding the modern quackery of market technicians.

Value versus Growth

One of the most powerful dimensions along which managers position themselves involves value stock versus growth stock investing. Value investors seek to buy dollars at a discount, constructing portfolios that have high dividend yields, low price-to-earnings ratios, and low price-to-book ratios. In contrast, growth investors seek companies exhibiting strong momentum, whether in earnings or price.

Dramatic differences in performance result from manager orientation toward value and growth. While over the past ten years value managers and growth managers generated roughly equivalent returns, periods of several years exist when one strategy materially outperforms the other. For example, Cambridge Associates data show that for the decade ending December 31, 1997, value strategies returned 17.9 percent per annum relative to 18.2 percent per annum for growth investors. However, from 1989 to 1991, growth outperformed value by a cumulative 24.3 percent, or 7.5 percent per annum, while from 1992 to 1994, value dominated, returning an incremental 8.3 percent, or 2.7

percent per annum.[22] The swing of the pendulum from favoring growth to favoring value provides an opportunity for nimble active managers.

Value Investing and Fundamental Risk. Extreme value strategies expose investors to danger. Deep value investors purchase the most out-of-favor securities, buying stocks that trade at extremely low price-to-book and price-to-earnings ratios. Under normal conditions, a benign economic environment and corporate resilience combine to allow distressed companies to recover, causing value investors to realize handsome returns. The wind at the back of value investors stems from powerful forces causing fundamentals to revert to the mean.

Since deep value stocks generally inhabit out-of-favor industry sectors, capital flows tend to be sparse. Low price-to-book ratios discourage new investment, since as Keynes observed "there is no sense in building up a new enterprise at a cost greater than that at which a similar existing enterprise can be purchased."[23] Rational investors prefer acquiring assets in disfavor through the discounted prices of the stock market, not the full prices of new bricks and mortar.

The lack of investment in neglected industries improves the competitive position of existing assets. Less competition leads to improved profitability, causing prices of out-of-favor stocks to strengthen. Regression to the mean boosts value stock valuations.

While deep value investors tend to perform well over reasonable time frames, adjusting reported performance for risk poses a substantial problem. Deep value portfolios contain lower-quality, fundamentally riskier assets. Returns ought to be higher to compensate for greater underlying risk.

Under conditions of severe economic distress, higher risk levels in value portfolios lead to disastrous investment results. Akin to the damage wrought by the sixty-year flood, severe financial trauma causes widespread damage by meting out extraordinary punishment for weak, lower-quality, deep value securities. Failure rates skyrocket, taking stocks out of the game and eliminating the possibility of recovery. Regression to the mean fails to perform its magic, and value investors suffer permanent losses.

The Great Crash of 1929 illustrates the dangers of holding lower-quality securities. Jeremy Grantham studied the impact of the economic trauma of the early 1930s on value stocks. Dividing the universe of equity securities into quintiles based on 1928 price-to-book ratios, Grantham measured returns from the market peak in 1929 to the trough in 1933. High price-to-book securities, representing higher-quality, growth-oriented stocks, declined a staggering 84.3 percent over the period. Low price-to-book stocks, representing riskier value situations, dropped an even more debilitating 93.0 percent. Stated differently, from the bottom in 1933 to regain 1929 purchasing power, higher-quality stocks required 6.4-fold appreciation and lower-quality securities needed a 14.3-fold increase in value.

Assuming a post-1933 risk premium for value stocks of 2.0 percent per annum, forty-one years would pass before lower-quality stocks caught up with their higher-quality counterparts. If value investors "win a little, win a little, win a little, lose a lot," recovery periods may extend beyond the time horizon of even the most patient investor.

Momentum Strategies and Speculative Excess. On the other extreme, high-growth or momentum portfolios expose investors to different types of risks. Momentum investing represents a hot money game with a goal, described by Keynes, "to beat the gun, . . . to outwit the crowd, and to pass the bad, or depreciating, half crown to the other fellow."[24] Pure momentum investors care little for fundamentals. Strong historical growth attracts attention, with technical chart patterns playing a central role. Riding the wave exhilarates momentum players, as price increases follow price increases.

The "greater fool" concept resides at the center of momentum investing. Fundamentals cease to matter if investors assume someone will pay a higher future price for assets purchased today. The problem for momentum investors arises when fools come to their senses. Momentum works until it stops working. Investors missing the inflection point sustain certain damage.

Momentum investors fail to realize that winds ultimately blow in their face. High-growth stocks trade at high price-to-book and high price-to-earnings ratios. Just as capital avoids the low price-to-book environment of value stocks, capital seeks the high price-to-book world of growth stocks. Keynes noted that "there is an inducement to spend on a new project what may seem an extravagant sum, if it can be floated off on the Stock Exchange at an immediate profit."[25] As capital floods into attractive, high-growth industries, rates of return decline, causing former highfliers to lose altitude, and sometimes to crash spectacularly.

Both extreme growth and extreme value strategies rest on naive foundations, exposing practitioners to serious dangers. Both approaches focus on the past, ignoring forward-looking information important to determining security prices. Value investors examine the relationship between market price and historical cost of assets (book value) or between market price and historical earnings. (Value investors who look at price relative to projected twelve-month earnings move in the right direction, but fail to incorporate expectations regarding earnings flows beyond one year.)

Extreme growth strategies embody similar flaws. Projecting continuation of historical growth rates into the future ignores powerful mean reverting tendencies. Belief in the possibility of safely exiting a roller coaster just before the downward leg of the journey resembles belief in the tooth fairy or Santa Claus. Growth investors lead a vulnerable existence, tempting the fates by trying to beat the gun.

Forward-Looking Investment. Reasonable security selection techniques rely on forward-looking approaches, attempting to uncover what will happen. Purchasers of equities acquire an interest in future corporate profits. The value investor employing a historical price-to-earnings ratio to select stocks fails to incorporate expectational information important to the valuation process. The momentum investor basing investment decisions on past price patterns or past earnings behavior drives a car by looking only in the rear-view mirror.

Between the extremes of pure growth and pure value lie sensible investment strategies focused on fair value. Paying less than a fair price for a handsomely growing stream of future earnings satisfies both value and growth criteria. Or, success might result from purchasing at less than fair value a stream of lower-quality earnings discounted at rates to reflect the fundamental risk of the future cash flows. In both cases, fair value plays a central role in security selection decisions.

Unfortunately, abandoning the simplicity of historical price-to-earnings ratios and charts of past security prices forces the investor into a Keynesian world of "extreme precariousness . . . where knowledge of the factors which will govern the yield of an investment some years hence is usually very slight and often neglible."[26] In this environment, "investment based on genuine long-term expectation is so difficult . . . as to be scarcely practicable. He who attempts it must surely lead more laborious days and run greater risks. . . . Given equal intelligence, he may make more disastrous mistakes." Keynes's litany of obstacles provides a high hurdle for "the long term investor, he who most promotes the public interest."[27]

Although evaluating prospective conditions increases the difficulty of making investment judgments, the rewards of capturing significant insights increase as well. Forward-looking investors place themselves in a position to generate superior returns while contributing to Keynes's "social object of skilled investment [of defeating] the dark forces of time and ignorance which envelop our future."[28]

Quantitative versus Judgmental

At one extreme, quantitative approaches to investment management employ "black boxes"—computer-driven algorithms responsible for portfolio construction. At the other extreme, judgmental investors rely on "gut instinct," managing portfolios by the seat of their pants. Sensible investment operations avoid both extremes, melding reasonably rigorous quantitative disciplines with a substantial dose of informed judgment. Combining hard quantitative inputs with soft qualitative inputs satisfies the notion that successful investment operations incorporate both hard and soft factors.

Pure quantitative investment management suffers from opacity, violating a fundamental requirement of sensible investing. To the extent that results emerge from a mysterious black box, investor faith in the process relies exclusively on superior performance.

As long as the numbers satisfy investors, quantitative managers thrive. When returns falter, investors face a dilemma. Are the poor results an aberration, reflecting a temporary setback expected to be reversed? Or do inadequate returns reflect more fundamental problems, signaling that the quantitative model no longer works? Addressing the dilemma plays a critical role in investment success. If unfavorable market conditions cause temporary underperformance, sensible investors increase exposure to the portfolio, expecting to benefit from purchases made at depressed prices. If, on the other hand, poor model specification accounts for disappointing results, sensible investors eliminate exposure to the portfolio, avoiding further losses.

Quantitative management approaches provide little assistance in resolving the dilemma. The fundamental question for investors concerns the continued viability of the quantitative model. Because fiduciaries operate outside the model-building process, making judgments about the likelihood of the model's producing market-beating portfolios poses a nearly insurmountable challenge.

In fact, quantitative managers face similar tough decisions. Should the existing underperforming model continue to be employed, or would fine-tuning produce superior results? Have increases in market efficiency eliminated the opportunity that the original model exploited? Managers altering models subsequent to a bout of poor returns take the risk of abandoning an approach about to be rewarded. On the other hand, managers stubbornly wedded to a misspecified model expose clients to a dismal future. As "improvements" change the quantitative process, investors wonder whether the changes increase the likelihood of success—or the likelihood of whipsaw.

Barr Rosenberg's Black Box. Barr Rosenberg's credentials suggested a high probability of success in quantitative portfolio management. A 1963 graduate of the University of California at Berkeley with a degree in economics, Rosenberg went on to receive a master's degree in mathematical economics and econometrics from the London School of Economics and a Ph.D. in economics from Harvard University. Rosenberg wrote his Ph.D. dissertation on quantitative models with randomly dispersed parameters, a topic with important implications for research on the covariance of securities returns and portfolio modeling. In 1968 he was appointed professor of finance, econometrics, and economics at Berkeley. The following year he began a quantitative consulting business, providing economic data and modeling services to institutional money management firms. Ultimately this consulting business became BARRA, an internationally recognized enterprise. In 1985, Rosenberg left BARRA to form his own money management firm, Rosenberg Institutional Equity Management (RIEM). Well grounded in academic finance theory and market realities, Rosenberg's skills provided an excellent foundation for building a quantitative investment management business.

RIEM got a fast start. Promising to beat the S&P 500 by an impressive margin of 400 basis points per year, with a relatively low volatility of 6 percent, RIEM set a high hurdle. The firm reached its goal in the first three years, returning 17.3 percent annually relative to 13.3 percent for the S&P 500, beating the benchmark by precisely 4.0 percent per annum.

Rosenberg's aggressive investment goals and early success attracted much attention. A September 1989 *Institutional Investor* cover story gushed about "his team's genius for developing insights into market behavior and building portfolio systems based on those insights."[29] RIEM's principals characterized their firm as an "alpha factory," implying a regularity and predictability of outperformance unheard of in the investment management world.

Assets under management skyrocketed. From three clients and less than $200 million on December 31, 1985, the firm's core equity product grew to more than $8,000 million by the end of 1989. RIEM attracted funds from some of the investment world's premier institutional investors, including Yale, Stanford, Eastman Kodak, General Motors, and the Rockefeller Foundation.

Clients hired RIEM based on confidence in Barr Rosenberg and enthusiasm for his firm's strong track record. No client truly understood the investment process, for the secretive Rosenberg disclosed few details regarding his model's inner workings. Even were he more forthcoming, few clients, if any, could hope to fathom the intricacies of Rosenberg's black box. As long as RIEM delivered strong performance, clients felt little need for more than a superficial sense of the firm's investment model.

After an indifferent 1989, Rosenberg's performance deteriorated sharply, falling to the bottom decile of active managers for 1990 and 1991. Returns for the next six years failed to add value, with the firm posting only two above-median results, neither of which met RIEM's 400 basis point alpha bogey.

Clients deserted in droves, causing assets under management to fall from more than $8,100 million at the 1990 peak to just over $1,600 million at the end of 1997. In one terrible year, 1990, all of the value added by RIEM in the early years disappeared as poor performance affected a significantly larger asset base. A back-of-the-envelope calculation indicates that during its twelve-year history, Rosenberg's core equity product lost $480 million relative to the market. The experience damaged client portfolios, stunting growth of the Rosenberg organization.

The RIEM saga illustrates the difficulties in assessing quantitative investment management opportunities. Barr Rosenberg's impeccable academic and consulting records provided a powerful combination of theoretical and practical experience. Early investment returns supported the notion that RIEM's black box delivered 400 basis points of excess performance with low risk. Yet in spite of superb personal credentials and strong historical performance, RIEM ultimately failed to deliver the goods.

After a number of disappointing years, even Rosenberg's confidence in his model faltered. In 1995, RIEM began articulating a goal of beating "each client's designated benchmark by several hundred basis points," dropping the obviously too aggressive target of 400 basis points. Moreover, the core equity product benchmark became the easier-to-beat Russell 3000, as Rosenberg accepted the futility of exceeding the more efficiently priced S&P 500.

By year-end 1997, assets in the core equity product dropped to $1,600 million. While the absolute magnitude of the decline represents a severe loss, in the context of a bull market for equities, the relative decline constitutes a staggering failure. Had RIEM's 1989 client assets simply matched the S&P 500, the firm would have managed approximately $27,500 million.

The causes of Rosenberg's failure cannot be identified with any precision. If the original model had been left in place, would it have delivered superior results? Did RIEM's "tinkering" improve or debase the model? Were assets under management too much for the strategy? The fundamental opacity of sophisticated quantitative models masks the answers to these important questions.

●   ●   ●

Aside from problems associated with lack of transparency, purely quantitative managers ignore valuable information contained in non-quantifiable factors, such as the drive and personality of a company's senior management. Asked about such omissions, the dyed-in-the-wool quant insists that "it's all in the numbers." Because so much is in the numbers, investment management remains a fundamentally quantitative endeavor. But, since everything is not in the numbers, qualitative judgment remains critical to the investment process.

Combining a quantitative discipline and rigor with a qualitative sense of corporate prospects provides a powerful approach to investment decision making. Resulting portfolio decisions exhibit transparency, allowing investment advisers to explain portfolio decisions to clients. When inevitable stretches of poor performance appear, clients can ascertain whether the shortfall resulted from fundamental mistakes or market noise. If the manager's original thesis remains intact, opportunities may exist to increase positions at more attractive prices. If analytical errors caused poor performance, a less enthusiastic response may be appropriate.

Balancing hard quantitative analysis with soft qualitative judgments provides the greatest opportunity for investment success. The combination employs the broadest range of data, increasing the number of tools available to the investment manager. Moreover, the relative transparency of a blended investment approach allows clients to manage portfolio allocations with greater confidence.

Concentrated versus Diversified

As in other aspects of investment management, agency issues often interfere with the pursuit of marketable equity strategies likely to lead to success. For example, although portfolios concentrated in relatively few positions provide the greatest opportunity to add significant value, most fund fiduciaries and investment advisers seek the comfort of overly diversified portfolios. With a broad-based set of securities, managers reduce deviations from index levels, avoiding embarrassment, or even termination, from posting poor relative results.

Portfolio concentration increases the likelihood of beating the market. Instead of following the maxim, "Don't put all of your eggs in one basket," fiduciaries ought to hire managers who put all of their eggs in one basket, and watch that basket very carefully. Managers with relatively few holdings follow a business model geared toward producing investment returns, not stable fee income. Since diversification reduces the chances of underperforming benchmark returns, fee-maximizing investment advisers tend to become closet indexers, hoping to generate returns sufficiently close to the benchmark to avoid being fired. In contrast, highly concentrated portfolios contain enormous relative performance risks causing the investment adviser to live or die by portfolio results.

Managers of concentrated portfolios require more tolerance than do managers of highly diversified portfolios. Because one or two positions may greatly influence results, portfolio returns may deviate dramatically from benchmark returns. While concentration enhances opportunity for long-term success, less diversified portfolios exhibit greater short-term volatility.

Diversification at the overall fund level mitigates the concentration risk faced by investors. While volatility associated with large security bets inevitably produces occasional disappointments, the impact on investor psychology of underperformance in an asset class comprising 20 or 30 percent of the portfolio pales in comparison to the reaction by fiduciaries when the poor results affect an asset class representing 60 or 70 percent of the portfolio.

Diversification within asset classes dampens the impact of the volatility of a particular manager's account. Most fiduciaries employ multiple managers, obviating the need for any single manager to construct a diversified portfolio. The aggregation of a number of concentrated portfolios contains sufficient diversification to satisfy even the most nervous fiduciary.

Concerns regarding excessive concentration in institutional portfolios represent largely theoretical worries. The common practice of using multiple managers, each constructing a diversified portfolio, often produces an overly diversified aggregate portfolio. In fact, investors run the risk of creating a composite portfolio so diversified that it resembles an index fund. As a result, investors incur high active management fees and implementation costs to construct broadly diversified, high-turnover portfolios, nearly guaranteeing disappointing results. Simply pursuing lower-cost passive management strategies provides a superior alternative to an overly diversified, actively managed portfolio.

Concentrated portfolios benefit from focused attention. Understanding as much as can be understood about a position proves more likely with ten stocks than with eighty, ninety, or one hundred. In 1992, Yale hired Chieftain Capital, an investment management firm running a concentrated portfolio of domestic equities. Typically holding eight to twelve stocks, the managers pride themselves on knowing much more than other investors about individual security holdings. During the initial due diligence process, to check on Chieftain's thoroughness, Yale's Investments Office staff made calls to several Chieftain portfolio company chief executives without identifying the purpose of the call. When asked which security analysts exhibited the most thorough understanding of their companies, the CEOs mentioned one or two employees of Wall Street firms and Glenn Greenberg and John Shapiro, the principals of this low-profile money management organization. By focusing attention on relatively few positions, Chieftain ranked among the most informed analysts in selected securities, obtaining a valuable informational edge.

Wall Street Research. Managers of concentrated portfolios tend to rely primarily on internally generated research, using Wall Street sources as secondary or supplemental sources. Wall Street research suffers from a number of significant problems: it comes from conflicted sources, tends to represent consensus positions, and enjoys wide distribution.

Conflicts abound in Wall Street research operations. Analysts take care not to offend clients, since irritated chief executives rarely choose critical investment banks to lead underwritings or pursue lucrative advisory assignments. In fact, managements sometimes cut off information flows to analysts with the temerity to criticize company strategies.

In many instances, research analysts directly solicit underwriting and advisory business for the security firm's investment banking operations. In such cases conflicts become even more severe, placing the analyst in the irreconcilable positions of objective observer and salesperson. Relying on research produced by investment banking wannabes provides a poor foundation for security selection.

Cowardice in the analyst community leads to the extraordinary result that more than 90 percent of analyst stock recommendations typically fall in the positive and neutral categories. According to Zack's Investment Research, on July 31, 1998, a minuscule 0.7 percent of analyst opinions fell in the bottom rank, as opposed to 31.1 percent in the top tier. Since analyst opinions generally reflect forecast performance relative to the market, roughly equal numbers of strong buys and strong sells would be expected. The investment world of Wall Street analysts exhibits an extraordinary skew. Imagine the shape of the distribution of returns if relative gains on the 61.3 percent of the securities in the top two categories were offset by losses on the 5.7 percent of stocks in the bottom two rungs. The sell candidates face dismal prospects indeed.

Analyst earnings estimates tend to hug the consensus. Going out on a limb, while occasionally rewarding, places the analyst's reputation at risk. Negative consequences stem from the big mistakes, not from the near misses. In fact, some investment managers explicitly exploit the notion that analysts tend to get the direction right, but understate the magnitude of the move. Behavioral influences reduce the value of Wall Street analyst reports.

Even if accurate, Wall Street research provides little edge to its recipients. Reports circulate widely as investment banks attempt to gain the largest advantage possible. The wider the distribution of information, the less value it has, as the implications of the report become incorporated into security prices in short order.

• • •

Evidence from the mutual fund industry indicates that relatively few managers of concentrated portfolios exist. In 1998, of the more than 9,500 funds tracked by Morningstar, a leading provider of mutual fund information, only ten invested in ten or fewer stocks. Even if twenty-stock portfolios qualify as concentrated, the fund numbers increase only to thirty-eight, representing four-tenths of 1 percent of the Morningstar database.[30] While the specific numbers for mutual funds may differ somewhat from the data for institutional portfolios, the lack of concentrated portfolios in the mutual fund industry carries through to practices in the institutional management of marketable securities.

Investment managers seeking an edge need to uncover otherwise hidden insights, relying on proprietary work. Operating in an entrepreneurial environment almost dictates focusing on a handful of securities, since coverage of a broad universe of stocks requires an army of analysts. Deeply researched, concentrated portfolios provide the greatest opportunity for investment success.

CONCLUSION

Marketable securities provide core holdings for the vast majority of institutional funds, frequently representing the only vehicles available for investment by groups without the resources to pursue management-intensive commitments to alternative investment strategies. Although portfolios consisting solely of traditional fixed income and equity holdings face serious limitations with respect to expected return and risk characteristics, thoughtfully structured combinations of marketable asset classes contain the potential to provide reasonable results for disciplined, long-term investors.

In spite of promising lower returns than most other investment classes, bonds earn a place in portfolios by providing protection against the extraordinary circumstances of a financial crisis or economic deflation. Only high-quality, long-term bonds perform well in times of severe stress, allowing investors to view the opportunity costs of holding bonds as an insurance premium incurred to insulate portfolios from extreme conditions. By holding high-quality, long-term, noncallable fixed income assets, investors emphasize the unique attributes of bonds, enhancing the ability of portfolios to survive traumatic periods.

While the volatility reduction produced by fixed income assets improves portfolio risk characteristics, if investors face a stable world in which expectations generally foreshadow reality, bonds end up enhancing return stability at the price of reduced portfolio returns. Under normal financial circumstances, investors achieve portfolio risk reduction without exposing the portfolio to low returning bond investments by diversifying into alternative assets.

Investors employing external bond portfolio managers face two levels of agency risk. At the most basic level, borrowers generally desire to reduce costs of debt funding, a goal at odds with the desire of bondholders to realize high returns. On another level, active portfolio managers usually pursue risk-enhancing management strategies in an attempt to beat an extremely efficient market. In both the financial instrument itself and typical portfolio management strategies, bond owners suffer from a lack of coincidence of interests.

Because traditional investment portfolios contain excessive allocations to fixed income, portfolio managers frequently stretch to improve returns, hoping to benefit from introducing credit risk, optionality, and currency exposure. In moving portfolios away from the bedrock of long-term U.S. Treasury securities, portfolio managers undermine the fundamental function of fixed income portfolios.

Active management of fixed income portfolios generally involves "gaming" benchmarks by constructing portfolios with greater-than-market risk. Disingenuous managers point to higher-than-benchmark returns as signs of management success, pocketing as fees the incremental returns generated by exposing client assets to high levels of credit, call, or foreign exchange risk.

Because fixed income holdings promise lower returns than other investment alternatives, long-term investors hold fixed income assets at the minimum level required to protect portfolios against financial trauma. Sensible bond portfolios contain only high-quality, long-term, noncallable assets, emphasizing characteristics uniquely suited to perform well in times of crisis.

Marketable equities represent the core asset of institutional portfolios, providing the standard for judging all other asset classes. By providing substantial levels of return over extremely long periods of time, equity holdings benefit patient investors willing to hold positions through thick and thin.

Driven by the profitability of corporate enterprises, the residual value claimed by stockholders exhibits strong correlation to movements in the general level of prices. By tending to rise and fall in sympathy with inflation and deflation, movements in stock prices provide a natural hedge for changes in the cost structure of institutional beneficiaries of endowment support.

Although equity ownership provides the bedrock for constructing institutional portfolios, investors often exhibit excessive enthusiasm for equities after extended stretches of superior relative performance. While owning equity securities provides enormous benefits to steadfast investors, the stock market's long-term performance comes with occasionally troubling volatility and sometimes extended spells of miserable returns. By limiting stock market exposure to levels that fund managers can maintain comfortably, investors avoid the whipsaw of buying high and selling low, and ensure receipt of the benefits of long-term exposure to equity markets.

Equity investors face a staggering array of investment alternatives, ranging from high-quality domestic stocks to fundamentally risky emerging markets companies. Domestic holdings provide the most comfortable source of returns, while foreign market securities add diversification and more robust active management opportunities.

The advisability of active management for marketable securities runs the gamut from completely out-of-the-question for fixed income, to questionable for large-capitalization domestic equities, to nearly required for emerging markets positions. By avoiding payment of excessive fees in the futile quest for risk-adjusted excess returns in the bond market, investors obtain a higher likelihood of good results and avoid undermining the fundamental role of bonds. In the equity arena, investors face the challenging task of determining which markets provide sufficient opportunity to warrant the costly undertaking of searching for excess returns. Only in the emerging markets, which reside at the least efficiently priced end of the continuum, do investors find clear justification for active management.

Investment managers approach security selection along a variety of important dimensions. Bottom-up investors choose from a broad array of alternatives, with a rich set of information and reasonable valuation equilibrating mechanisms. In contrast, top-down investors face relatively few opportunities, many of which require more insight and patience than might be reasonably expected from most market participants. Fundamental approaches to investment management involve gathering and analyzing available data with hopes of identifying important information not yet incorporated into the market. Technical tools provide no insight into security prices.

Avoiding the extremes of deep value and momentum-driven growth, managers identify the richest set of opportunities by seeking growth at a reasonable price or value on a risk-adjusted basis. Forward-looking analysis underlies all sensible investment approaches. While investment analysis requires quantitative disciplines, black box investment models fail to meet an investor's requirement for transparency. Purely judgmental approaches to portfolio construction frequently lack the necessary discipline, suggesting the use of a combination of hard and soft factors in the security selection process. Concentrated portfolios provide focused exposure to a manager's best ideas, avoiding the lack of conviction inherent in a diversified portfolio.

The assets in which institutions invest invariably contain opportunities for agents to benefit at the expense of providers of capital. Bonds provide a particularly dramatic example of structural misalignment of interests. One method for management to increase shareholder value lies in reducing the worth of debt obligations. Although bondholders try to limit impairment of debt values by contractually restricting management activity, bondholders ultimately lose as managers respond to economic incentives. Investing in assets managed by individuals with diametrically opposed interests makes little sense.

In every equity position, public or private, management at least occasionally pursues activities providing purely personal gains, directly damaging the interests of shareholders. To mitigate the problem, investors search for managements focused on advancing stock owner interests, while avoiding companies treated as personal piggy banks by the individuals in charge. Although conflicts between shareholders and management appear less severe than differences between bondholders and management, careful investors examine motives of corporate executives with a skeptical eye.

While many portfolios consisting entirely of marketable securities embody the potential to satisfy institutional objectives, investors employing nontraditional asset classes enjoy a more powerful set of tools. By limiting asset choices to traditional alternatives, fund managers miss opportunities to enhance portfolio efficiency by increasing expected returns and reducing anticipated risk.

8
Alternative Asset Classes

Alternative asset classes—absolute return, real estate, and private equity—contribute to the portfolio construction process by pushing back the efficient frontier, allowing the creation of portfolios with higher returns for a given level of risk or lower risk for a given level of returns. Investors treating alternative assets as legitimate tools in the portfolio allocation process reduce dependence on traditional marketable securities, facilitating the structuring of truly diversified portfolios.

As separate asset classes, each alternative investment category adds something distinctive and important to portfolio characteristics. Absolute return and real estate provide diversification, generating returns driven by factors materially different from those determining results of other asset classes. In contrast, private equity investment returns depend on many factors common to the determination of marketable equity returns. Although private investments provide little diversification, well-selected private holdings contain the potential to make a dramatic contribution to portfolio returns.

Alternative asset pricing lacks the efficiency typical of traditional marketable securities, leading to opportunities for astute managers to add substantial value in the investment process. In fact, investors in alternative asset classes must pursue active management since market returns do not exist in the sense of an investable passive option. Even if investors could purchase the median result in real estate, venture capital, or leveraged buyouts, the results would likely disappoint since historical returns tend to lag comparable marketable security results. Only by generating superior active returns do investors realize the promise of investing in alternative assets.

ROLE OF ABSOLUTE RETURN

Absolute return investing, a relatively new asset class, consists of in-efficiency-exploiting marketable securities positions exhibiting little or no correlation to traditional stock and bond investments. Absolute return positions provide equity-like returns with powerful diversifying characteristics.

Although absolute return strategies employ marketable security positions, managers reduce market risk by investing in event-driven or value-driven situations, expected to behave independently of market forces. Event-driven positions depend on the timing of a specific corporate finance transaction, such as the consummation of a merger or the emergence of a company from bankruptcy. Value-driven strategies employ hedged portfolios in which short positions offset long positions, dramatically reducing the investor's systematic risk. Absolute return investments seek to generate high levels of returns, independent of market results, contrasting with the relative, benchmark-beating gains pursued by active marketable security managers.

Event-Driven Investing

Merger arbitrage represents a core event-driven absolute return strategy, with results related to the manager's ability to predict the probability that a deal will close, its likely timing, and the expected value of the consideration for the transaction. Upon announcement of a stock-for-stock deal, the price of the target company's stock generally rises to a level somewhat below the acquirer's offer, creating an opportunity for the merger arbitrageur to profit. Uncertainty regarding the ultimate outcome of the transaction causes many holders to sell, motivated by the concern that gains stimulated by the merger offer might disappear for any of a number of reasons. After careful assessment of deal-specific factors, merger arbitrage investors buy the stock of the target company

and sell shares of the acquiring company, hoping to profit from the closing of the spread when the transaction closes. Because the arbitrageur
holds long positions offset by short positions, the direction of the overall market plays little role in determining returns. Instead, results depend on the merger arbitrageur's ability to assess correctly the factors
relevant to the ultimate conclusion of the transaction.

In the distressed-securities area, event-driven investors look for
opportunity in securities of companies undergoing reorganization. Because of the complexity of the issues surrounding bankruptcy, many
market participants sell positions regardless of price, creating an opportunity for hard-working investors to profit. By assessing the timing
of the company's emergence from bankruptcy and valuing the expected package of securities, players in the distressed-securities arena
generate returns more dependent on events important to the bankruptcy process than on the level of the overall stock market.

Obviously, event-driven strategies lack the power to insulate investors completely from financial market moves. Factors influencing
the stock market may alter the likelihood that a particular merger will
be completed, causing a commonality of influence. To the extent that
investors receive equity interests as part of a package of securities distributed in connection with a company's reorganization, the market
exerts direct influence on the ultimate return to the investment. In
spite of indentifiable links between event-driven investing and market
moves, under normal circumstances event-driven strategies provide
meaningful portfolio diversification.

In times of financial crisis, the correlation between event-driven
strategies and market activity increases to uncomfortable levels. During the stock market crash in October 1987, merger arbitrage positions
fell in step with the general market, providing little protection in the
short run against the dramatic market decline. As time passed, investors recognized that companies continued to meet contractual
obligations, ultimately completing all merger deals previously announced. The return of confidence improved merger arbitrage results,
providing handsome returns relative to the market.

Results of two prominent merger arbitrage firms, which later
formed the base for Yale's absolute return portfolio, illustrate the importance of evaluating performance over reasonable time horizons.
Pursuing the conservative approach of investing only in announced
deals, the two firms reported combined results of –17.9 percent for the

fourth quarter of 1987, somewhat ahead of the S&P 500 return of −22.5 percent but well behind expectations for event-driven strategies. Although no merger deals broke, the market turmoil caused investors to demand higher compensation for merger arbitrage risk, resulting in a dramatic widening of spreads. In the first quarter of 1988 the arbitrage managers rebounded, posting results of 16.3 percent, far ahead of the S&P 500 returns of 5.7 percent. Viewed in isolation, the last quarter of 1987 provided disappointing double-digit losses coincident with the stock market crash, failing to protect the portfolio during the period of crisis. Viewed as a package, the fourth quarter of 1987, with the worst results ever for both firms, and the first quarter of 1988, with the best results ever for both firms, constitute six months of asset preservation, providing meaningful diversification relative to the equity market's losses. Even though for short time periods, diversifying financial assets, including absolute return strategies, may show high correlation to marketable equities, over reasonable investment horizons assets driven by fundamentally different factors produce fundamentally different patterns of returns.

Value-Driven Opportunities

Value-driven absolute return strategies rest on the manager's ability to identify undervalued and overvalued securities, establish positions, and reduce market exposure through hedging activity. If an investor purchases a portfolio of attractively priced stocks and sells short an equivalent amount of expensively priced stocks, the offsetting long and short positions eliminate systematic exposure to the equity market. Results depend entirely on stock picking ability, with the long/short investor enjoying the opportunity to add value with both the long ideas and short ideas. Skillful value-driven managers win on both sides of the portfolio.

While value-driven investment strategies share with event-driven approaches the lack of correlation with traditional marketable securities, investors face a longer time horizon for value-driven portfolios. Expected holding periods for merger arbitrage and distressed securities correspond to the anticipated date of corporate combination or bankruptcy resolution, implying a reasonably short duration for event-driven strategies. In contrast, value-driven positions lack the clear valuation realization triggers present in event-driven investing. To the consternation of fund managers, undervalued stocks frequently decline in price, while overvalued positions often rise in value, leading to poor performance relative to expectations. Even without adverse price moves, mispricings identified by long/short investors may be resolved over periods of years.

Although value-driven managers hold longer-term positions, well-constructed portfolios exhibit little correlation to comparable maturity debt instruments. To the extent that interest rates influence securities holdings, the impact of changes on long positions roughly offsets the impact on short positions, insulating the portfolio from the systematic influence of intermediate-term interest rates.

The short duration of absolute return strategies makes the short-term cost of funds a fair starting point for evaluating manager performance. The basic math of hedged positions implies that investors deserve a money market rate of return.* If managers add value or garner rewards for exposing assets to higher-than-market risk, returns will exceed short-term rates. If managers fail to add value or incur penalties for holding low-risk positions, returns will fall short of money market rates.

Asset Characteristics

Like other alternative assets, absolute return investments lack an investible benchmark, forcing investors to look elsewhere for defining characteristics of the asset class. Because of a limited institutional history, absolute return investing poses even greater challenges to the understanding of its quantitative attributes than do real estate, leveraged

---

*Absolute return strategies employing offsetting long and short positions (merger arbitrage and long/short investing) earn money market returns in the absence of manager value added (or subtracted). On one side of the portfolio, assume a manager invests contributed funds in long positions. On the other side, upon consummating a short sale, the manager receives cash proceeds from the transaction. Although the cash must be posted as collateral with the lender of the security, the short seller earns a "rebate," or money market rate, on the proceeds.

If both the long position and short position track the market precisely, gains (losses) from the long match losses (gains) from the short, eliminating the systematic market factors from performance. Under such circumstances, the investor earns a money market rate (the short rebate) on invested assets.

buyouts, and venture capital. Students of these more long-standing alternative investment approaches enjoy the benefit of more than two decades of data on active manager results, which provide important information about the experience of institutional investors in alternative investment vehicles and intriguing clues about the character of the portfolio investments underlying fund performance. The paucity of data regarding absolute return strategies requires investors to seek alternative means of estimating asset class attributes.

Survivorship Bias

Survivorship bias may be less of a problem for long-established illiquid investment approaches than for traditional marketable securities. Liquidity facilitates the hiring and firing of stock and bond managers, leading to churning in the universe of active managers. Poor performers leave and strong firms enter, constantly altering the standards implicit in the collection of returns used for assessing active managers.

Managers of private assets enter and exit the data pool with considerably less frequency than do their marketable security counterparts. Institutions tend to select real estate, venture capital, and leveraged buyout funds from an easily identified list of acceptable alternatives, suggesting a coherent definition of any given year's institutional cohort. The partnership vehicles through which investors conduct most private investing preclude easy departure from the business. Private investing results—good, bad, or indifferent—play out over the term of the partnership regardless of the degree of confidence that investors express in the fund managers.

In terms of survivorship bias, absolute return suffers from the combination of relative immaturity and fairly high degree of liquidity. Immaturity suggests a substantial amount of flux, as managers posting attractive risk-adjusted returns enter the realm of institutional acceptability, adding distinguished records to the store of absolute return knowledge. Liquidity allows easy entry and exit, creating instability beneath the surface of the pool used to evaluate manager returns.

The lack of an investible benchmark combined with relative youth and extreme survivorship bias create conditions promoting wildly unrealistic expectations regarding absolute return's risk and return character-istics. Managers posting extraordinary returns, as a result of skill and good fortune, garner institutional attention, implicitly setting the stan-dard for the asset class. Managers delivering poor, or even average, re-sults fail to rise above the crowd, depriving market observers of a full picture of the asset class. As time passes, the problem becomes less acute as those firms that first gained institutional attention begin to dominate the database. The increased scrutiny that comes with maturity, along with the forces of time and chance, causes results to mirror market op-portunities, not the hot hands of managers on a lucky streak.

Fundamental Attributes

Without useful historical data, investors turn to the underlying character-istics of the investment strategies that make up the asset class, hoping to develop a set of return, risk, and covariance attributes without guidance from a robust series of past performance numbers. Event-driven strategies tend to command expected returns three to four times the cost of capital, in this case a short-term money market rate. Since long-term nominal re-turns on cash average approximately 4 percent, the event-driven manager generally expects to earn 12 percent (three times cash rates) to 16 percent (four times cash rates). Value-driven managers earn two alphas (one on the long side and one on the short side) in addition to a money market return. Assuming a baseline 4 percent cash return along with excess re-turns of 3 percent each on longs and shorts, the value-driven manager expects to earn 10 percent gross (cash rate plus 3 percent alpha on longs and 3 percent alpha on shorts). After adjusting for fees and incentive compensation, investors employing a combination of event-driven and value-driven strategies might reasonably expect nominal returns of 10 percent to 12 percent, more or less equivalent to the long-term return to domestic equities, with lower risk and essentially no correlation.

The actual results of Yale's portfolio conform to the expectations generated by considering the fundamental investment attributes of absolute return strategies. Established as a separate asset class in 1990, the pioneering portfolio produced 13.4 percent per annum re-turns for the eight years ending June 30, 1998. With a remarkably low risk level of 4.6 percent standard deviation of returns, the risk-reward relationship indicates that managers exploited some interesting market anomalies.* The absolute return portfolio's diversifying power exceeded expectations, showing slightly negative correlation to domestic equities (−0.23 versus the Wilshire 5000 Index) and essentially no correlation to domestic fixed income (0.13 versus the Lehman Brothers Government Corporate Index) over the eight-year period.

Active Management

Without active management, absolute return does not exist. The fundamental notion of absolute return investing rests on identification and successful exploitation of inefficiencies in pricing marketable securities. In the absence of value added by active managers, investors receive money market rates of return, appropriate compensation for creating positions without material market exposure.

Event-Driven Investing

Event-driven opportunities exist because of the complexities inherent in business combinations and corporate reorganizations. Mainstream portfolio managers recognize that the forces that determine the merger end game and the bankruptcy resolution differ materially from the factors that predominate in day-to-day security valuation. The legal and regulatory environment changes upon announcement of a proposed combination or reorganization, giving the informed specialist an advantage over the competent generalist. Superior analytical skills create a meaningful edge for active event-driven investors.

The opportunity exploited by event-driven investors stems in part from sales of securities by investors unwilling to commit the resources to develop a thorough understanding of the circumstances surrounding complex corporate finance transactions. In the case of distressed securities, further selling pressure comes from investors unable or unwilling to hold securities of failing or failed companies. The sometimes massive supply of securities from holders uncomfortable with positions in com-

---

*The Sharpe ratio (see page 310 for a description of the ratio), a measure of excess return generated per unit of risk, for Yale's absolute return portfolio amounted to 1.8 over its eight-year life. In contrast, domestic equities and fixed income posted Sharpe ratios of 1.1 and 0.9, respectively, over equivalent periods.

**Figure 8.1 Merger Arbitrage Spread Narrows as Closing Date Nears
Merger Between Newell and Rubbermaid**
October 12, 1998–March 15, 1999

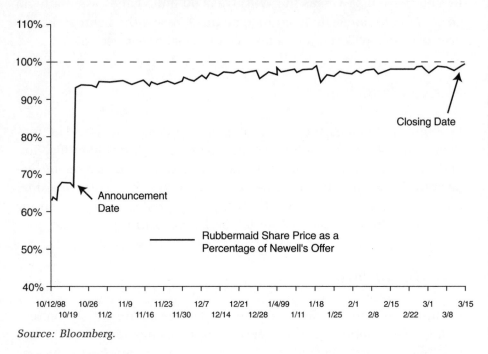

Source: Bloomberg.

panies undergoing basic structural change allows event-driven investors to establish positions with attractive embedded returns.

Newell Rubbermaid Merger Arbitrage. The March 1999 combination of Newell and Rubbermaid illustrates some of the market dynamics underpinning event-driven investment opportunities. After the
October 1998 announcement of the proposed merger, Rubbermaid
shares responded by rising nearly 25 percent, as shown in Figure 8.1.
Trading volume increased more than tenfold, from an average of
566,000 shares per day in the week prior to the announcement to
5,960,000 shares per day in the week following. Taking advantage of
the merger-induced price rise, investors exited the stock, creating an
opportunity for merger arbitrageurs to establish positions.

The terms of the definitive agreement called for a tax-free exchange
of shares in which holders of Rubbermaid would receive 0.7883 of a
share of Newell upon closing, expected in early 1999. By buying a
share of Rubbermaid at the post-announcement price of 31 13/16 and
selling 0.7883 of a share of Newell at 43 1/4, arbitrageurs generated

net proceeds of \$2.28 per share. If the companies were to complete the transaction on the originally proposed terms, arbitrageurs would have equivalent long and short positions at the closing, as the combining companies promised to exchange one share of Rubbermaid for 0.7883 of a share of Newell. Upon consummation of the deal, merger arbitrageurs closed out positions by delivering Newell shares received from the Rubbermaid exchange to cover the original Newell short sale.

Back-of-the-envelope calculations illustrate the return characteristics of the transaction. When the deal closed on March 14, 1999, merger arbitrageurs earned the \$2.28 post-announcement spread between the two stocks and a short rebate of about \$0.57, for a total of approximately \$2.85. Cash flow yield played essentially no role in the return calculation since the dividends earned on the Rubbermaid shares offset the dividends paid on the Newell shares. Based on an initial capital commitment of \$31 13/16 per share, the position delivered a gross return of about 9 percent over a five-month period, equivalent to an annualized return in the low 20 percent range.[1]

The Newell Rubbermaid combination proceeded without a hitch, as the spread between Rubbermaid and Newell shares narrowed week by week until the scheduled closing. Not all merger arbitrage transactions proceed as smoothly. The September 1998 combination of WorldCom and MCI Communications began in November 1996 as a proposal by British Telecommunications plc to acquire MCI in the largest cross-border transaction ever. Between the initiation of merger discussions and the ultimate resolution, merger arbitrageurs wrestled with a laundry list of problems: antitrust concerns, regulatory approvals, changes in company business strategy, corporate operating difficulties, international political issues, and competition from competing bidders.* Regardless of whether deals take a simple path from inception to resolution or follow a convoluted route, the returns to merger arbitrage investors depend far more on the specific event than on the general direction of the market.

•　•　•

*The story of Farallon Capital Management's handling of the MCI Communications/WorldCom combination appears in Harvard Business School Case Study N9-299-020, "Farallon Capital Management: Risk Arbitrage," by Robert Howard and Andre Perold (February 1999). The case study describes the ultimately successful efforts of Farallon's Tom Steyer, David Cohen, and Bill Duhamel in navigating the complexities of an extraordinary merger transaction.

Because event-driven investors strive to hit singles and doubles, creating a broadly diversified portfolio makes sense. In an environment without huge potential winners to offset inevitable costly mistakes, investors need to limit the costs that any one position might impose on the portfolio.

Event-driven portfolios benefit from engaging managers with a broad set of investment tools. Hiring a specialist focused on only one aspect of the business, say merger arbitrage, forces investors to ride a return roller-coaster. When opportunities abound, investors reap attractive returns from the niche strategy. If high returns attract capital to the activity or if the supply of investment opportunities wanes, specialized investors continue to commit funds, ultimately reaping poor returns from funds invested at inopportune times.

In contrast, if a manager develops expertise in more than one event-driven strategy, when returns appear sparse in one segment, more funds might be committed to another. The ability to target areas of relative opportunity dampens the inevitable fluctuations experienced by focused funds and creates the possibility of structuring higher-return portfolios.

Value-Driven Investing

Value-driven managers share much in common with active managers of traditional marketable securities. On the long side, concentrated portfolios of thoroughly researched securities provide the underpinnings for investment success. On the short side, the same bottom-up techniques of fundamental analysis used to evaluate long positions provide the basis for identifying overvalued securities. Adding the flexibility to exploit overvalued positions—through short sales—at least doubles the opportunity for a manager to add value. In fact, the general lack of capital dedicated to identifying and selling short securities may indicate the existence of a particularly broad set of overvalued companies for the short seller's evaluation. While short-selling investment disciplines share a common foundation with long investing, successful short portfolios represent more than a richly priced inverse of a long portfolio.

Short-Selling Challenges. The management of the short side of the portfolio poses several challenges peculiar to selling securities short. First, investors frequently underestimate the resilience of corporate management. Even when the facts and figures indicate that a company deserves classification as one of the "living dead," managers frequently find a way to escape the inevitable consequences of their circumstances. Second, the portfolio consequences of adverse price movements require greater diversification of short positions. If a stock moves against a short seller by increasing in price, the position increases in size. To take advantage of the now more attractively priced short-sale opportunity, the investor faces the uncomfortable prospect of further increasing the position. Starting with a modest allocation to a particular short idea allows an increase in position size without creating an uncomfortable concentration in a single stock. Contrast the dynamics of a losing short position with the behavior of a losing long position. As the long's price declines, it becomes a smaller portion of the portfolio, reducing its impact on returns and facilitating new purchases at the newly discounted, relatively more attractive price levels. The simple math of price behavior argues for running reasonably diversified portfolios of short positions. Short sellers face peculiar challenges from success, as well as from failure. When the stock price of a fundamentally troubled company crashes, the short seller benefits, but the short position disappears, requiring identification of attractive replacement candidates. While long managers often run with successful investments for years, short managers hope to operate on a treadmill, with frequent turnover of holdings caused by the exit of winning positions from the portfolio. The combination of price dynamics and high turnover causes successful short managers to follow and hold a large number of securities.

Aside from a peculiar set of investment challenges, short sellers face some unusual technical problems in managing portfolio positions. To execute trades, short sellers borrow securities to deliver to the buyer on the other side of the transaction. (Buyers purchasing shares, whether from a short seller or a natural seller, expect to receive securities on the trade's settlement date.) As long as short sellers maintain the "borrow," the position remains intact. If the short seller loses the "borrow" because the security lender recalls the security, the short seller must replace the "borrow" or lose the position. When the market for borrowing a particular security becomes tight, short sellers face a short squeeze. Security borrowers tend to have most trouble with small, less liquid companies, exactly the type of security most likely to present interesting short-sale opportunities.

The unusual set of problems confronting short sellers place an effective limit on portfolio size, forcing managers to constrain the level of assets under management. The resulting reasonable portfolio size augurs well for the potential to add value, as excessive levels of assets constitute a nearly insurmountable barrier to success. Although the aggressive assumption that value-driven managers might outperform the market by as much as three percentage points each on the long and short sides seems to fly in the face of traditional active manager experience, limits on portfolio size provide hope for significant outperformance by long/short managers.

•   •   •

Absolute return strategies require active management, since without accepting market risk or identifying security mispricings, investors earn only the risk-free rate. Since the very definition of absolute return rests on lack of correlation with traditional marketable securities, exploitation of individual security valuation anomalies forms the basis of the asset class. Event-driven managers generate returns by conducting thorough research in complex corners of the investment opportunity set often avoided by mainstream analysts. Value-driven managers attempt to add value by identifying undervalued and overvalued securities, creating portfolios with roughly offsetting long and short market exposures. Well-managed absolute return portfolios provide a high-return, low-risk source of diversifying returns.

ROLE OF REAL ESTATE

Real estate holdings play a special role in institutional portfolios, providing protection against unanticipated increases in inflation. Asset prices of high-quality, well-located, fully leased buildings respond directly to inflation as the cost of replacing properties increases along with rising price levels. Income flows rise as leases mature and new leases incorporate inflationary increases, insulating real estate owners from the debilitating effects of unexpected inflation on fixed payment streams.

Because of the benefits provided by real estate in environments of unanticipated inflation and by bonds under conditions of unexpected deflation, expected returns for both real estate and bonds fall below return requirements for marketable equities. By accepting lower expected returns from real estate, investors pay an insurance premium (in the form of opportunity costs) to protect the portfolio against times when prices rise more rapidly than expected, similar to the insurance premium paid by bondholders to protect against situations when the level of prices falls unexpectedly.

Under normal circumstances, real estate and bonds lend a measure of stability to portfolios, as high levels of current cash flow in the form of rent and interest payments moderate the fluctuations in price required to adjust for changes in expected returns. Over long periods of time, the provision of year-to-year volatility dampening comes at a substantial cost. If expectations regarding inflation and deflation were met year-in and year-out, real estate and bonds would play minor roles in portfolios of long-term investors. Only because inflationary or deflationary conditions occasionally surprise investors do diversifying assets play a major role.

Real estate investments span the continuum from pure debt to pure equity, with those assets combining debt and equity attributes providing the diversifying characteristics necessary to justify identifying real estate as a distinct asset class. At one extreme, real estate positions in the form of mortgages represent debt instruments, sharing characteristics with the fixed income asset class. None of the inflation-hedging benefits from holding real estate accrue to mortgage investors, since lenders receive only the promised stream of contractual payments (if borrowers perform as promised). At the other extreme, hotel investments represent equity participations, sharing characteristics with public or private equity asset classes. Because hotels rent rooms for very short periods—often one night at a time—lodging properties lack the stability of real estate subject to longer-term leases. The management intensity of hotels causes their investment character to resemble more closely the ownership of other operating businesses.

In the middle of the continuum resides real estate containing both debt and equity characteristics. The fixed nature of cash flows from a lease obligation resembles a coupon payment stream from a bond. The more fully leased the property and the longer the term of the leases, the more bondlike a real estate property becomes. In contrast, the variable nature of the residual value of a property gives real estate holdings equity-like attributes. Short-term leases and high vacancy rates contribute to equity risk in real estate positions. Real estate holdings combining debt characteristics from lease obligations with equity characteristics from residual value embody the capital markets characteristics central to identifying real estate as a distinct asset class, leading investors to seek core ownership positions in high-quality, well-leased properties located in healthy, growing markets.

The inflation-hedging characteristics of real estate depend on the asset class operating under reasonable conditions of equilibrium. Market observers frequently point out that real estate values fell precipitously from 1989 to 1994 in an environment of modest inflation. The dramatic decoupling of real estate values and inflation caused many investors to question the inflation-hedging capabilities of property investments. While changes in the general price level influenced real estate values in the early 1990s, the impact of excess supply of nearly every type of commercial real estate in nearly every major market overwhelmed all other factors. Because the decline in values stemmed from market adjustment to the dramatic overbuilding of the 1980s, inflationary levels played little role in determining prices in the 1990s. Real estate exhibits inflation-hedging attributes only when supply and demand show reasonable balance.

While real estate and bonds make qualitatively similar contributions to portfolios when financial conditions correspond to previous expectations, in the case where reality differs dramatically from earlier forecasts, real estate and bonds turn into polar opposites. Unanticipated inflation benefits real estate positions and damages bond holdings, while unexpected deflation helps bond positions and hurts real estate holdings. Well-diversified portfolios contain sufficient exposure to real estate and bonds to protect institutional assets from harm in economic environments where changes in the price level vary substantially from expectations. At the same time, investors limit holdings of bonds and real estate, because under normal circumstances the assets provide below-equitylike returns.

Asset Characteristics

Like all other private asset classes, real estate lacks a broad collection of properties defining an investible benchmark for investors. Unlike venture capital and leveraged buyouts, market observers benefit from access to information on the performance of large numbers of individual real estate properties. For the period 1978 to 1998, an unlevered portfolio of approximately 2,400 institutionally held real estate properties generated returns of 9.4 percent per annum with a risk level as measured by standard deviation of returns of 6.9 percent. The real estate performance nearly mirrored the results of intermediate-term bonds, which returned a marginally lower 9.3 percent with an identical risk level of 6.9 percent.* Both real estate and bonds fell short of equity returns of 15.8% with 12.9% volatility.

Observed real estate performance confounds expectations, as the results match those of bonds instead of falling between bonds and stocks. Perhaps the comparison suffers from an insufficiently long time period, excluding strong real estate results from the inflationary period of the 1970s and including weak real estate numbers from the disequilibrium of the late 1980s and early 1990s. Perhaps end-point sensitivity influences results by stopping the analysis in 1998 when real estate may be underpriced, causing the data series to understate the true return levels for the asset.[2] Or perhaps historical data accurately reflect underlying asset characteristics, contradicting the hypothesis that real estate return and risk levels fall between those for bonds and stocks.

In any event, true volatility of the real estate property index likely exceeds the observed standard deviation of returns, dampened by the appraisal-based means that investors employ to value real estate assets. Lacking a ready market for pricing assets, investors hire appraisers to assess market values, using discounted cash flows, comparable sales, and replacement cost as valuation metrics. Conducted infrequently, often by the same firm year after year, the appraisal process smooths the observed series of prices, understating true volatility.

Real Estate Investment Trusts

Contrast the behavior of stock market–traded real estate investment trusts (REITs) with the appraisal-valued real estate index. For the two decades ending 1998, REITs provided an 11.4 percent annualized return relative to a 9.4 percent result for a broad-based collection of privately held properties.[3] The superior REIT results, likely driven by the positive impact of leverage, came at the price of higher volatility of

*Data on private real estate returns are from the National Council of Real Estate Investment Fiduciaries (NCREIF).

16.4 percent standard deviation of returns relative to a 6.9 percent risk level for the unlevered property index. The higher volatility of REITs, along with a significant correlation to small-capitalization stocks, cause many investors to conclude that REITs share more characteristics with common stocks than with real estate.

The absurd notion that simply changing the form of corporate ownership alters fundamental investment attributes corresponds nicely to the idea of alchemy. The higher volatility witnessed in pricing of REIT shares reflects an appropriate upward adjustment of artificially dampened risk observed in appraisal-based data. While trading data for REITs may reflect the excess volatility generally found in pricing equity shares, the true risk of real estate no doubt lies closer to the volatility observed in pricing of REITs than to unrealistically low variability in appraisal-based return series.[4] Regardless of the observed differences in behavior between public and private holdings of real estate, in the final analysis REITs represent real estate.

Pricing differences in private and public markets for real estate create opportunities for investors to build portfolios using relatively attractively priced assets. When REITs fall from favor, research analysts explain why the publicly traded shares deserve a permanent discount to privately held assets, with justifications including illiquidity, management ineptitude, high overhead costs, and the inflexibility of REIT structures. When REITs ride high, the same analysts argue that public vehicles command a premium for good reasons, including liquidity, management expertise, economies of scale, and advantages of the REIT format. Regardless of the idea of the moment, long-term investors favor REITs when portfolios trade at a discount to private market value, avoiding high-priced private assets, and sell REITs when shares trade at a premium, pursuing relatively attractive private properties.

• • •

Further insight into real estate attributes comes from examining returns of active real estate managers as presented in a consultant's database with returns of 149 funds managed by institutional advisers.[5] Although a bottom-up assessment of risk places real estate between marketable equities and bonds, the dispersion of real estate returns indicates that active management opportunities exceed those in marketable securities, while falling short of other illiquid alternatives. The ten-year differential between first- and third-quartile returns of 4.7 percent for real estate overshadows comparable figures of 2.5 percent for large-capitalization stocks and 1.2 percent for bonds. In turn, the first- to third-quartile ranges for leveraged buyouts and venture capital of 13.0 percent and 21.2 percent, respectively, far exceed the real estate figure. Real estate investors face an opportunity to add significant value by selecting top-tier managers.

Active Management

Inefficiencies in the pricing and opportunities in the operation of real estate assets demand active management. Investors stand to increase return and lower risk by exercising careful judgment in selecting attractively priced assets and using diligence in managing properties.

Real estate lends itself to active management because mispricings create opportunities for nimble investors to take advantage of market anomalies. The task of identifying underpriced and overpriced properties poses surmountable hurdles, since valuations depend largely on readily observed variables. Calculation of replacement cost for an asset provides important information on the value of a well-located property. Data on leases in place, combined with projections of future lease rates and an estimate of residual value, throw off an easily analyzed stream of cash flows. Information on sales of comparable properties provides hard numbers reflecting the willingness of investors to pay for bricks and mortar, or a steam of expected cash flows. Active management decisions for real estate rest on the fundamental characteristics of replacement cost, discounted cash flows, and sales of similar assets, providing clear reference points unavailable for most other asset types.

Sony Building Acquisition

Douglas Emmett's 1993 acquisition of the Sony Building in Burbank, California illustrates some important valuation tools. Los Angeles ranked among the hardest-hit markets in the real estate debacle of the early 1990s, with vacancy rates reaching a staggering 24 percent for Class A office space in the metropolitan market. As a result, prices for office buildings declined dramatically. In a signature transaction, Sam Zell, known as the "grave dancer" because of his proclivity for distressed assets, bought Two California Plaza for $100 million, approximately one-quarter of what it cost to build a few years earlier.

Nearby Burbank, a distinctly different market with substantially stronger underlying fundamentals, experienced sympathetic price declines suffering by association with Los Angeles. Amid the tumult, as part of a corporate rationalization program, Coca-Cola decided to sell the Burbank property housing its former subsidiary, Sony Pictures. The sales price of $83 million compared favorably to the building's construction cost of more than $120 million, providing the purchaser a 30 percent discount to replacement cost.

Cash flow from lease payments further supported the acquisition. One hundred percent of the space was leased to Sony, at the time a credit rated single A by Standard & Poor's. If the investor received only those payments guaranteed by Sony, all invested capital would be repaid along with sufficient excess cash flow to generate annual returns of 12.3 percent. This return includes no payments from tenants other than Sony and no residual value for the building upon expiration of the lease. With reasonable assumptions regarding lease renewals and residual value, returns jump to the 20 to 25 percent range. In an interest rate environment where comparable maturity U.S. Treasury notes yielded about 6.5 percent, the relatively high-quality Sony payment stream represents a handsome return with little downside.

Comparable sales data tell less about the attractiveness of an acquisition than about the timing. The lack of bids for the Sony Building and other properties in the area signaled a contrarian opportunity to buy deeply out-of-favor assets, not a lack of value in the marketplace. Fortified by substantial discounts to replacement cost and high levels of investment-grade cash flow, investors move forward with confidence in the face of dismal market conditions. When the tone of the market improves to the point that real estate "experts" pronounce that asset irreplaceability justifies paying a meaningful premium to replacement cost and that a tight leasing environment presages transformation of low current cash yields into higher future cash flows, contrarian investors offer properties for sale.

The striking Sony Building, with its handsome tenant finishes,* provided a more than satisfactory baseline return, with the protection of a purchase price substantially below replacement cost. The combination of the reality of the hard work of asset management and the possibility of change in perception create a substantial potential profit opportunity. The limited downside of the Sony Building combined with meaningful upside possibilities create a positively skewed distribution of outcomes, providing extremely attractive investment characteristics.

Manager Specialization

Investors generally benefit from engaging specialists to manage portions of a fund's commitment to real estate. Experts in a particular property type—office, retail, industrial—enjoy a substantial edge over generalist managers, which suffer from spreading resources an inch deep and a mile wide. Subspecialization leads to greater focus on the particular dynamics of different markets, allowing separation of the relatively static mass of central business district office buildings from the ever-changing inventory of suburban office properties and division of the massive department store–anchored malls from the smaller infill community retail centers. By concentrating management resources on a fairly narrowly defined market segment, fund managers make better buys, better sells, and better day-to-day asset management decisions.

Investors choosing to select a group of specialist managers create more powerful portfolios, albeit at the price of a loss of diversification. By pursuing attractive investment opportunities, selected on a bottom-up basis, funds develop concentrations in the most out-of-favor asset types. For instance, valuation-driven investors may hold outsized positions in California retail properties or southeastern suburban office buildings, creating a profile with dramatic deviations from the characteristics of the general real estate market. Although idiosyncratic port-

---

*Peter Guber and Jon Peters, the former co-chairmen of Sony Pictures Entertainment, had lavishly appointed offices on the top two floors of the building. Rumored to have cost hundreds of dollars per square foot, the improvements were included as part of the purchase price.

folios tend to exhibit substantial tracking error relative to the market, a carefully chosen group of niche managers contains the potential to produce outstanding investment results.

•   •   •

To fulfill the core mission of hedging against unanticipated inflation, real estate investors hold high-quality, well-leased properties, avoiding both the bondlike mortgage and operating-intensive hotel ends of the property continuum. As with all other illiquid assets, real estate positions require active management. The easy availability of data on replacement cost and straightforward specification of cash flows from leases provide tools for investors to use in valuing real estate assets. Comparable sales data provide signals to contrarian investors, drawing attention to weak markets and highlighting the dangers of hot markets. Managers with a niche focus develop market-specific expertise, creating an edge that contributes to investment success. Well-managed holdings of real estate provide important diversification to institutional portfolios, with the potential to contribute handsome levels of return.

ROLE OF PRIVATE EQUITY

Properly selected investments in leveraged buyouts and venture capital contain the potential to generate high returns relative to other equity alternatives, providing a means to enhance overall portfolio results. The superior private equity returns come at the price of higher risk levels, as investors expose assets to greater financial leverage and more substantial operating uncertainty. Because of the strong fundamental links between private equity investments and marketable equity securities, private positions provide limited diversification to investors.

Public and Private Equity

Private equity investments tend to overcome the problems associated with divergence in aspirations of shareholders and management evident in many of today's publicly traded companies. Separation of ownership (by shareholders) and control (by management) often re-sults in a substantial gap between the interests of shareholders and the actions of management; without significant equity interests, managers might pursue a wide range of activities designed to improve their lot at the expense of outside owners. Fancy offices, excessive salaries, bloated fleets of airplanes, and other managerial perquisites rarely en-ter the picture in profit-oriented private investments. Moreover, pri-vate company managements tend to operate with longer time horizons and lower risk aversion, pursuing strategies that promote creation of enterprise value at the expense of personal job security. Because pri-vate deals generally require management to take material ownership stakes, interests of outside owners and operating management align.

In the venture capital world, entrepreneurial start-ups involve in-dividuals exhibiting a single-minded focus on building successful companies. Buyout transactions attract management devoted to im-proving the operation's bottom line, addressing the challenges of a highly leveraged capital structure with the goal of achieving a prof-itable exit. Managements in buyout and venture deals tend to share the goals and objectives of owners.

In spite of differences between the technology orientation of tradi-tional venture capital and the mature business bias of the leveraged buyout arena, discussions of private equity generally include both venture and buyout investments. In addition to the shared characteris-tics of illiquidity and high return potential, venture and buyout in-vesting embrace a scope of activities not dissimilar to that found in marketable equity asset classes.

Leveraged buyouts respond to many of the same factors that influ-ence marketable securities. In fact, buyouts often simply represent turbocharged equity, with leverage magnifying the results—good or bad—produced by a particular company. For example, when KKR took RJR private in a 1989 leveraged buyout transaction, the funda-mental nature of the company's consumer products business re-mained the same. Corporate valuation continued to respond to changes in consumer demand, commodity prices, and regulatory ac-tivity. While the same basic business factors determined the com-pany's financial results, dramatic increases in leverage magnified the response of equity prices to changes in fundamental conditions. The underlying similarity between the publicly traded RJR and the private

RJR suggests that investors should expect high levels of correlation between marketable securities and leveraged buyout transactions.

Although early-stage venture capital lacks the superficial similarities that leveraged buyouts share with marketable equities, strong links exist between venture investing and the stock market. Market action influences the price at which venture investors enter an investment and plays an even more critical role in the price at which investors exit successful positions.

When entrepreneurs start companies in an industry favored by the equity markets, venture capitalists pay handsome prices to participate. Conversely, less highly desired enterprises command lower entry valuations, providing outside investors with relatively attractive starting points. At exit, financiers hope to sell into strong equity markets, achieving premium prices for security offerings. Equity market conditions exert strong, albeit indirect, influence on venture capital valuations.

In their most basic form, venture and buyout investing represent a riskier means of obtaining equity exposure. The high leverage inherent in buyout transactions and the early-stage nature of venture investing cause investors to experience greater fundamental risk and to expect materially higher investment returns.

Strangely, historical results generally fail to reflect the hoped-for enhanced returns, while risk levels appear to fall below expectations. Unfortunately, poor returns from private investing probably reflect reality, while the low risk evident in data describing past returns from private investing constitutes a statistical artifact. By masking the relationship between fundamental drivers of company value and changes in market price, illiquidity causes private equity's diversifying power to appear artificially high. If two otherwise identical companies differ only in the form of organization—one private, the other public—the infrequently valued private company appears much more stable than the frequently valued publicly traded company. Although both companies react in identical fashion to fundamental drivers of corporate value, the less volatile private entity boasts superior risk characteristics, based solely on mismeasurement of the company's true underlying volatility. Not only does lack of valuation information reduce reported risk levels, the private company gains spurious diversifying characteristics based solely on lack of co-movement with the more frequently valued public company.

Value-Added Investing

While a fair portion of the observed "diversification" provided by private equity stems from the infrequent valuations accorded illiquid assets, some of the lack of correlation between marketable and private assets results from value-added strategies that private firms pursue. Consider the case of an idea, a garage, and an entrepreneur financed with venture capital. As the company develops its product, initiates sales, and becomes profitable, value creation takes place independent of the action on the floor of the stock exchange. Because results from company building activities loom large relative to results from the original corporate base, venture investments provide diversification relative to traditional marketable securities.

Similar value-added possibilities exist in the leveraged buyout arena, allowing adept private investors to improve returns by achieving operating improvements in portfolio companies. Because buyout transactions generally involve companies with a reasonably established corporate base, market influences tend to play the primary role in valuation, with firm-specific, value-added opportunities holding a secondary role. Although when compared to venture capital investments, the more mature companies typically targeted in buyout transactions offer less dramatic opportunities for business growth, value-added strategies contain the potential to offer a source of partially uncorrelated returns.

Pure financial engineering holds little interest for serious private equity investors, since providing financing represents a commodity-like activity with low barriers to entry. In the leveraged buyout business, simply adding leverage to a company increases expected returns and boosts risk levels, doing nothing to promote the goal of achieving risk-adjusted returns. In the venture capital arena, later-stage investors supply little more than cash, hoping to benefit from the work of early-stage investors and the prospect of achieving rapid liquidity through an initial public offering or sale. Private investors offering only capital operate in an extremely competitive market with reasonably efficient pricing mechanisms.

Private equity opportunities become particularly compelling when managers pursue well-considered value-added strategies. By seeking to improve the company's operations in the context of an appropriate financial structure, investors increase the scope of return-generating activity, allowing realization of superior results less dependent on marketable security valuations.

Asset Characteristics

Private equities differ from stocks and bonds in that no passive alternative exists for venture capital and leveraged buyouts. Investors desiring broad exposure to the stock market might purchase the S&P 500, while passive fixed income investors receive market-like results from a portfolio mimicking the Lehman Brothers Aggregate. Market observers describe the investment character of marketable stocks and bonds by citing historical return and risk data derived from public information on broadly defined collections of securities. Faced with a much less clearly defined market, private investors describe the investment environment by examining the returns produced by active investors.

Venture capital partnerships produced a surprisingly low median result of 8.1 percent for funds formed between 1980 and 1997.[6] As shown in Table 8.1, fund returns exhibited a wide dispersion, ranging from a stellar 498.2 percent to a much more terrestrial −89.7 percent, with a standard deviation of 30.0 percent. First-quartile results of 17.1 percent produced substantially greater-than-average rewards for venture investors, while the third-quartile result of 0.6 percent barely returned capital that had been exposed to substantial risk.

Leveraged buyout partnerships provide a similarly low 13.2 percent median return for funds formed between 1980 and 1997.[7] Although buyout partnerships report less extreme results than venture capital funds, the buyout distribution exhibits greater dispersion with a standard deviation of 35.7 percent. First-quartile returns of 23.8 percent produce materially more significant rewards than the poor third-quartile result of 1.1 percent.

Median results for venture capital and leveraged buyouts trail results for domestic equities over comparable periods. While the median venture partnership returned 8.1 percent and the median buyout partnership 13.2 percent over the eighteen years from 1980 to 1997, the median domestic equity manager generated a 15.5 percent annual

Table 8.1 Private Assets Underperform Marketable Securities
Investment Fund Returns, 1980–1997

	Real Estate	Venture Capital	Leveraged Buyouts	Domestic Equity	Foreign Equity
Maximum		498.2%	243.9%	18.1%	19.5%
First quartile	9.9%	17.1	23.8	16.6	16.1
Median	7.8	8.1	13.2	15.5	14.9
Third quartile	5.9	0.6	1.1	14.9	14.0
Minimum		-89.7	-65.9	13.2	11.1
First to third-quartile range	4.0	16.5	22.7	1.7	2.1
Standard deviation	2.5	30.0	35.7	1.3	2.1

Sources: Data for real estate are from Institutional Property Consultants (IPC). Data for venture capital and leveraged buyouts are from Venture Economics: 1998 Investment Benchmark Report: Buyouts and Other Private Equity and 1998 Investment Benchmark Report: Venture Capital. Data for domestic equity and foreign equity are from PIPER.

return. Marketable equity returns clustered tightly, exhibiting a 1.3 percent standard deviation, relative to the venture fund dispersion level of 30.0 percent and the buyout dispersion of 35.7 percent. Domestic stock managers appear to have generated higher returns than private equity funds, while exposing investors to lower likelihood of disappointment.

Head-to-head comparisons of historical risk and return data for marketable equities and private investments likely overstate the attractiveness of private assets by understating true risk levels. Infrequent valuations of private positions cause smoothing of results, reducing the observed volatility of private equity. Based on unrealistically low observed levels of historical risk, market participants incorrectly place private and marketable equity returns on more or less equal footing, unfairly favoring private assets relative to marketable alternatives.

In spite of a tendency for return data to understate the volatility of private equity returns, private fund returns show substantially greater deviation than do active marketable equity manager returns. Dramatic differences in return dispersion for managers of marketable and private equities underscore a fundamental difference between the two markets. Public security managers generate returns relatively tightly grouped around the market index, producing market-like outcomes less likely to lead to account termination. Private equity managers, lacking an index to mimic, produce portfolios exhibiting wildly disparate results. Without the alternative of aping the market, private investors forgo the benchmark-hugging game played by most stock market mavens, instead relying on higher risk levels and investment acumen to produce returns.

Risk-Adjusted Buyout Returns

Comparing returns of private funds with results from actively managed marketable equity portfolios produces conclusions akin to comparing a Porsche and a Beetle. Head-to-head comparisons stack the riskier activity of private investing against the less volatile alternative of marketable equity portfolios. To engineer a fair evaluation of public and private investment opportunities requires creation of a risk-equivalent portfolio of marketable assets. By adjusting the leverage of marketable securities positions to match the leverage of buyout investments, investors garner important insight into risk-adjusted returns for marketable and private assets.

Some interesting conclusions emerge from an examination of data on 542 buyout deals initiated and concluded between 1987 and 1998.[8] The group of transactions contains extraordinary survivorship bias, as the primary data source consists of offering memoranda submitted to the Yale Investments Office for investment evaluation. Obviously, only buyout groups meeting with reasonable degrees of success package their history into documents designed to solicit institutional backing, causing the sample to contain the cream of the buyout crop.

A further potential source of bias stems from consideration of only completed transactions, since more successful deals might achieve early liquidity, while the walking wounded might linger in buyout portfolios for years. Lacking reasonable valuations for private companies remaining in fund partnerships necessarily limits the study to the large number of investments that achieved liquidity through sale or public offering and a much smaller number of deals that resulted in failure through declaring bankruptcy.

As described in Table 8.2, the buyout sample produced a pooled rate of return of 48 percent per annum, apparently rewarding investors with the type of return expected from private equity investing. Over the same period, making similarly sized and similarly timed investments in the S&P 500 produced a 17 percent annual return, indicating that at least on the surface, the buyouts beat the stock market hands down.

A different story emerges when measuring returns on the S&P 500 with leverage equivalent to that employed in the buyout transactions. Matching each buyout transaction with a similarly sized, similarly timed, and similarly leveraged investment in the S&P 500 creates an equivalent risk standard against which to compare the buyout results. In the aggregate, the hypothetical borrowings move the leverage on the S&P 500 from the observed debt-to-equity ratio of less than one to the risk-equivalent level of more than five. The newly levered marketable security portfolio generates an 86 percent return, beating the buyout result by nearly 40 percent per annum!

Adjustment for fees worsens the relationship between returns for

Table 8.2 Buyout Managers Fail to Create Excess Returns

Completed Deals, 1987–1998

	Entire Sample		Yale's Portfolio	
	Return	Debt/ Equity Ratio	Return	Debt/ Equity Ratio
Buyout return	48%	5.2	63%	2.8
Risk-equivalent marketable security benchmark	86%	5.2	41%	2.8
S&P 500 benchmark	17%	0.8	20%	0.7
Number of deals	542		118	

Source: Yale University Investments Office.

leveraged marketable securities and private equities. The private equity return of 48 percent comes with a management fee of 1.5 to 2.0 percent, a profits interest of 20 percent, and a certain amount of cash drag. Back-of-the-envelope calculations estimate total fees at about twelve percentage points per annum, reducing net returns to investors to approximately 36 percent. Since the leveraged equity market returns come with minimal management fees, the risk equivalent marketable alternative beats the buyout result by a stunning 50 percentage points.

The telling comparison between buyout returns and equivalent-risk marketable security returns indicates that the vast majority of investors in buyout partnerships failed to earn results sufficient to compensate for risk. In aggregate, private equity managers did not even realize the results from financial engineering, as returns reflect value dimunition caused by poor investment choices or bad management decisions.

The limited partners providing capital to fund the transactions pay an enormous price. Net of fees, they receive lower-than-market returns with substantial levels of risk. In contrast, the general partners of buyout funds receive handsome rewards for rendering a disservice to investors. A contributing factor to the dramatic difference between the poor result for the limited partner and the happy outcome for the general partner lies in the inappropriate deal structure typical in private equity partnerships. Paying 20 percent of the profits to the general partner instead of 20 percent of the value added drives a meaningful wedge between the results for the general and limited partners. Poor incentive schemes cause buyout fund managers to benefit by placing limited partner assets at risk, creating an extraordinarily valuable option for the general partner that comes at the expense of the providers of funds.

Obviously, paying buyout managers only a portion of the incremental value created would wipe out staggering amounts of compensation "earned" by private fund managers. Since the majority of funds fail to match marketable equity returns, even when measured by the weakest standard, most managers create no additional value in which to share. If fair risk-adjusted returns set the hurdle for measuring value added, handsomely compensated private equity managers become an endangered species.

Investors backing funds that pursue pure financial engineering strategies face the unattractive prospect of accepting higher-than-market risk, realizing substandard risk-adjusted returns, and paying exhorbitant fees for the privilege. The alternative of engaging managers devoted to creating operating improvements allows for the possibility that investors might achieve superior returns relative to the risk inherent in private equity strategies.

Yale's Experience

Yale University attempts to invest only with firms that place central importance on enhancing the effectiveness of corporate operations. Company building strategies permit buyout fund managers to add value beyond the increase in returns expected from adopting higher-risk capital structures. By successfully identifying managers implementing operationally oriented strategies, Yale creates the possibility of earning risk-adjusted excess returns.

The data in the study provide evidence that the university identified a superior set of buyout funds. Yale participated in 118 of 542 transactions in the sample, generating gross returns of 63 percent relative to a risk-equivalent benchmark of 41 percent. If the risk adjustment appropriately captures the return expected from financial engineering, the premium return earned by Yale represents value added by the fund manager. Although fund manager fees take an estimated 15 percentage points of annual return, the university's net returns still comfortably exceed the risk-adjusted marketable securities bogey.

Yale's buyout results rely far less on leverage than do the results of the broad pool of buyout transactions. Contrast the broad pool's 69 percentage point difference between the unlevered S&P return and the risk-adjusted benchmark with the 21 percentage point difference for Yale's transactions. Less leverage and more attention to operations lead to superior risk-adjusted results.

In spite of evaluating a sample of buyout transactions known to contain a bias toward successful deals from successful firms, the pool of more than 540 completed transactions failed to generate returns even close to sufficient to compensate for risk. Exacerbating an already bad situation, private fund managers earn extraordinary compensation, deepening the divide between the equivalent-risk marketable security alternative and the private investment results. By employing an approach that emphasizes operating improvements and uses lower leverage, Yale's buyout portfolio manages to produce handsome absolute and risk-adjusted returns.

Mezzanine Finance

Many investors, attracted by high promised yield levels and apparently superior security, include mezzanine finance funds as part of private equity allocations. In highly leveraged capital structures, mezzanine debt occupies the position behind senior debt securities (often provided by banks) and ahead of equity risk capital. Because only a thin layer of equity protects subordinated bonds from the vicissitudes of corporate operations, mezzanine investors seek to balance risk by earning substantial margins over less risky fixed income alternatives.

The quest for superior returns on mezzanine securities faces formidable obstacles, since high coupon payments and costly equity participations come directly out of the pockets of equity owners. In the extraordinarily combative leveraged buyout environment, bondholders only rarely gain a competitive advantage.

The general risk and reward dynamics for junk bond financing fail to justify inclusion of mezzanine funds in portfolios. If investors finance successful deals, bondlike attributes of mezzanine securities limit upside potential. While equity participations provide a welcome kicker for winning transactions, fixed coupon payments dampen the ultimate appreciation of the securities. Call provisions, with the typical "heads I win, tails you lose" attributes favoring the issuer, frequently allow for fixed-price redemption of the bond issues of successful companies. Even when mezzanine investors back profitable transactions, the returns may not justify the risk.

When buyout deals fail, junk bond lenders frequently end up holding the bag. Without a deep equity base to absorb losses, in cases where equity owners take a hit, mezzanine lenders frequently face losses as well. The limited upside and substantial downside combine to create an investor-unfriendly, negatively skewed distribution of returns.

Historical returns on fixed income assets support the idea that investors receive inadequate rewards for exposing assets to the substantial risks of mezzanine lending. Table 8.3, covering the period from 1980 to 1997, indicates that the median return of actively managed bond portfolios nearly matched the median return of mezzanine funds, with the higher-quality, more liquid holdings posting a deficit of only 0.4 percent per annum. The return on an index of high-quality corporate bonds actually exceeded median results for mezzanine funds by a margin of 11.8 percent per annum to 11.7 percent per annum, providing yet another variation on the theme that relative to marketable security alternatives, private investors on average receive lower returns at higher risk.[9] Unless investors select top-quartile mezzanine funds, traditional high-quality bond investments provide ei-

Table 8.3 Mezzanine Funds Produce Unimpressive Risk-Adjusted Results

Investment Fund Returns, 1980–1997

	Fixed Income	Mezzanine Finance	Leveraged Buyouts
Maximum	15.1%	41.5%	243.9%
First quartile	12.4	17.1	23.8
Median	11.3	11.7	13.2
Third quartile	10.3	7.4	1.1
Minimum	9.3	0.0	-65.9
First- to third-quartile range	2.1	9.7	22.7
Standard deviation	1.8	9.6	35.7

Sources: Data for mezzanine finance and leveraged buyouts are from Venture Economics: 1998 Investment Benchmark Report: Buyouts and Other Private Equity. *Data for domestic fixed income are from PIPER.*

ther better absolute results (for the third and fourth quartiles) or superior risk-adjusted returns (for much of the second quartile).

An examination of top-quartile leveraged mezzanine results and top-quartile leveraged buyout fund returns indicates that successful buyout equity investments provide more handsome rewards than do successful buyout lending commitments. While a fair comparison requires appropriate adjustment for the marginally higher risk of the equity position, it appears that even after leveling the playing field, buyout funds generally fare better than mezzanine funds. Since traditional fixed income managers outpace the bottom three quartiles of mezzanine funds and buyout funds beat the top quartile, mezzanine funds end up squeezed between the low-risk alternative of high-quality bonds and the high-risk alternative of high-octane equity. Investors without skill fare better with traditional bonds, while investors with skill receive materially greater rewards by picking winners among equity funds.

Mezzanine and Equity Fund Comparisons

A comparison of subordinated debt and equity funds, managed by the same firm, illustrates the superiority of pure equity investing. Summit Ventures, a highly successful, Boston-based private equity firm pursuing acquisitions of technology-related enterprises, manages both mezzanine and equity funds. Summit's subordinated debt fund invests solely in the firm's deals but does not take positions in all of the firm's transactions.

The Summit Subordinated Debt Fund, begun in 1994, holds positions in fifteen companies, four from Summit Ventures III and eleven from Summit Ventures IV, two of the firm's equity investment vehicles, begun in 1992 and 1995, respectively. The mezzanine fund shows an internal rate of return of 28 percent net to limited partners, as of September 30, 1998, an extremely attractive result, particularly in comparison to other mezzanine finance vehicles. The high-risk lending results suffer only by comparison to the high-risk ownership results, as Summit's equity vehicles posted net returns to limited partners of 64 percent for the 1992 vintage fund and 42 percent for the 1995 vintage fund.

Individual transaction results further buttress the notion that owners do better than lenders. Summit's extraordinarily successful investment in Splash Technology Holdings produced an unusually high return on investment to subordinated debt holders of 105 percent per annum, multiplying the fund's original commitment of $7.8 million 2.4 times to $18.7 million. Although lenders received an eye-popping result, equity fund investors enjoyed an off-the-charts annualized return on invested capital of 335 percent, with the initial investment of $13.4 million multiplied 11.4 times to $153.1 million at the exit. Summit's wealth creation for equity investors in Splash Technology exemplifies the promise of private equity investing.

In contrast to the reasonably rewarding experience of Summit's subordinated debt investors, participants in the ML-Lee Acquisition Fund II, a mezzanine finance vehicle sponsored by Merrill Lynch and the Thomas H. Lee Company, received far from satisfactory results for the risk incurred. From its first closing in November 1989, the fund returned 7 percent per annum through the end of 1998. In spite of participating in the famed Snapple transaction, the subordinated debt–oriented ML-Lee Fund generated only 1.4 times invested capital over its life.

Equity commitments to Thomas H. Lee Equity Partners produced far superior returns, showing an internal rate of return of 55 percent from May 1990 through December 1998. The strong results of the equity fund created substantial amounts of investor wealth by returning 3.9 times the original invested capital.

While the dismal results of Tom Lee's mezzanine fund stem in part from investment in deals sponsored by other firms, the disparity in returns between Lee's debt fund and Lee's equity fund highlights the extraordinary difference in risk-reward relationships for lending and owning. The bulk of the ML-Lee Fund's participation in Snapple consisted of $24 million of 13 percent coupon debt, with a small prepayment penalty. Outstanding for about nine months, investors earned an estimated 18 percent annualized return on the junk bond position. The real excitement for the subordinated debt fund investors came from the much smaller $5 million equity participation in the popular beverage company. By combining the humdrum bond results with the red-hot equity returns, the Snapple position returned about seven times invested capital, boosting the aggregated Snapple results to an impressive 169 percent per annum.

In contrast, Thomas H. Lee Equity Partners' pure equity investment in Snapple created a 310 percent return over a thirty-two-month holding period, providing investors with a staggering twenty-seven times return of invested capital. Investors exposing assets to the risks inherent in Tom Lee's highly leveraged transactions received far greater rewards from making equity commitments than from holding subordinated debt positions.

Investors willing to take the risk of supplying funds to highly leveraged transactions find more attractive expected rewards in equity positions, as no structural constraints limit the potential price appreciation of successful investments. In contrast, the bondlike attributes of mezzanine finance dampen possible gains in winning transactions while providing little protection against losses in losing deals.

Limited Institutional Experience

The relatively short span of institutional private equity investment activity weakens any general conclusions drawn from the available data set. Venture capital and leveraged buyout returns beginning in 1980 represent samples drawn from an unusual capital market environment. Leveraged buyout transactions, for example, occur almost entirely under conditions of declining interest rates and rising equity valuations, fanning the wind at the back of private equity investors.

Market observers can only imagine the impact of the early 1970s on a buyout deal involving a highly leveraged capital structure. Beginning with extended equity market valuations, buyout investors would have experienced dramatic increases in interest rates and equally profound equity price declines. In the context of tough macroeconomic conditions, investors faced an environment with little margin for error in which leverage magnified the negative influences on company bottom lines and stock markets provided little opportunity for profitable exit, leading to extraordinarily bad investment outcomes. Since available data fail to include extended periods providing a poor backdrop for private investing, observed results paint an inflated picture of private equity potential, overstating likely future performance.

Similarly, structural changes in the venture capital market reduce the information value of data from the early period. Capital scarcity throughout the beginning years of the return series provided an artificial boost to results. By the mid 1980s eye-popping results attracted a flood of institutional capital to the venture industry, sowing the seeds for investor disappointment. Commitments made in the peak funding years of 1983 and 1984 provided lackluster results, as median funds returned 5.9 percent and 1.3 percent, respectively, in contrast to comparable ten-year returns of 16.2 percent and 14.9 percent per annum for simply investing in the S&P 500. The disappointing results from the 1983 and 1984 venture funds caused capital to withdraw from the arena, sowing the seeds for improved results as supply of capital ceased to overwhelm the investment opportunity. Investors might wonder about the results from venture investing in the context of another oversupply of capital or in less hospitable economic and financial conditions.

• • •

The characteristics of high risk and illiquidity separate private equity from otherwise comparable marketable securities, positioning private investments to increase portfolio returns without providing substantial diversification. Evaluated on an equivalent-risk basis, pure financial engineering approaches to private investing place investors at risk of paying enormous fees for disappointing net returns. In contrast, pursuing investment strategies designed to improve corporate operations provides opportunities to generate handsome risk-adjusted returns, while adding an uncorrelated element of incremental value to investment results.

Active Management

No sensible investor manages private assets passively. Even if participation in a broadly diversified market alternative were available, investors would face nearly certain disappointment. Burdened by staggering fees and characterized by well above marketable equity risk levels, a broad collection of private funds would likely produce returns far from sufficient to compensate for the risk incurred. Investors justify the inclusion of private equity in portfolios only by selecting top-quality managers pursuing value-added strategies with appropriate deal structures.

Due Diligence

The character of a private equity fund's investment principals constitutes the most important criterion in evaluating the merits of a buyout or venture investment. Driven, intelligent, ethical individuals operating in a cohesive partnership possess an edge likely to translate into superior investment results. On the other end of the spectrum, individuals willing to cut corners—operationally, intellectually, or ethically—place an investor's money and reputation at risk.

The central importance of choosing strong investment partners places enormous weight on the due diligence process. Concluding that a private equity firm consists of credible, professionally qualified individuals in pursuit of interesting investment opportunities serves merely as a starting point. Before making a commitment, careful investors determine that the fund's principals exhibit the characteristics necessary to justify entrusting them with institutional assets. Because of the long-term nature of private equity contracts, investors ultimately rely on the good faith of fund managers to behave in the best interests of the limited partners. While negotiating appropriate deal terms remains important, contractual arrangements invariably fail to deal with all of the important issues that ultimately arise. Good people can overcome bad contracts, but good contracts cannot overcome bad people.

Comprehensive due diligence requires substantial effort. Personal and professional references provided by the prospective fund managers provide an initial set of contacts. Because of the inevitable selection bias in a hand-picked reference list, sensible investors seek candid, confidential assessments from other individuals, including former business colleagues, professional relationships, and personal acquaintances. Over time, investors develop networks that facilitate reference checking, increasing confidence in the quality of decision making. Careful investors make skeptical calls, actively looking for potential issues. Going through the motions by conducting superficial checks adds nothing to the due diligence process.

Prospective investors must evaluate the fund manager's investment operation, spending sufficient time at the firm's offices to assess the character of the workplace. Firms develop personalities that influence the quality of operations in fundamental ways, allowing investors to favor those groups providing a comfortable fit. Spending time in informal social settings provides further perspective on a fund's principals, enhancing the data available to evaluate the decision makers. Selecting groups driven to produce superior results in a high-quality manner constitutes the central challenge of investing.

In spite of the enormous importance of conducting thorough due diligence, many investors fail to devote the time and energy necessary to make well-informed judgments. In 1999, an investment bank closed a $2 billion buyout fund, with only one investor taking time to meet the firm's full team before committing funds. By forgoing the opportunity to assess the quality of an investment operation's personnel, prospective investors fail to execute the most important task in selecting managers.

Long-Term Commitments

Private investment addresses Keynes's notion that the job of investment might be done better if decisions were "permanent and indissoluble, like marriage, except by reason of death or other grave cause."[10] While falling somewhat short of the gravity of the decision to marry, funding a private equity firm represents a long-term commitment. In contrast to the termination of a marketable securities manager where the vestiges of any relationship quickly disappear, traces of terminated private investment funds remain on the account books for years to come. Knowledge that private investment decisions represent long-term commitments forces sensible investors to establish high hurdles for initiating investment relationships.

The illiquid nature of private investing allows private equity managers to make the longer-term decisions necessary to pursue successful investment strategies. Marketable security managers know that clients possess little patience for performance shortfall, pulling the trigger quickly when the numbers fail to meet expectations. As a result, stock jockeys learn to overdiversify portfolios, holding small positions in securities selected as much to avoid disappointment as to generate exciting returns. In contrast, private fund managers lock in assets for long periods of time, often spanning a decade. While the typical fund-raising cycle of two to three years might pressure managers to shorten investment time frames, investors frequently accept the argument that "it's too early to judge the most recent fund," allowing private asset managers to make truly long-term decisions.

In fact, when evaluating private funds, investors tend to focus on the changes in corporate operations, not the market's minute-by-minute fluctuations in company valuation. By emphasizing an investment's intrinsic value, investors assess relevant data under the manager's control, liberating private fund managers from the frequently fickle judgments of the equity markets and allowing pursuit of more sensible investment strategies.

Strong private equity groups use the long-term investment horizon to pursue strategies that add substantial value to corporate activities. Fund managers providing only capital operate at a competitive disadvantage to groups that possess the ability to improve company operations in a fundamental way. In the venture capital arena, the ability to foster the development of early-stage ventures creates enormous reputational advantages, enhancing a firm's deal flow and improving its chances of success in bidding for hot deals. Over the years, a number of venture capital firms developed reputations as superior nurturers of developing companies. Consistent investment success translated into creation of a franchise that provides meaningful advantages in all aspects of managing the venture fund's activities.

Investors focused on late-stage venture capital lay claim to no such advantages. By coming into a company at the pre-IPO round of financing, a late-stage fund provides nothing more than money, operating in a competitive environment with low barriers to entry. Results for the pure financial engineer depend on the timing and pricing of the company's public offering, not on the fund's ability to improve company operations. Backing venture firms pursuing operationally-oriented strategies provides a superior investment strategy.

In the private arena, superior managers place value creation at the center of the investment process. By creating assets ultimately valued more highly than the sum of their parts, private equity managers generate returns independent of market forces. Value-oriented venture capitalists establish companies with significant products that address important, sizable markets. Serious venture capital firms provide more than money, contributing expertise, time, and energy to nurture start-up companies. In contrast, some players in the start-up market invest indiscriminately in the hottest areas, hoping to take companies public and realize returns before the temperature cools. Value-oriented venture capital represents a higher-quality, lower-risk approach to private investing.

In the leveraged buyout arena, supplying money to purchase a well-run company constitutes a commodity, as all major investment funds boast the financial skills necessary to complete plain vanilla transactions. Low barriers to entry allow former investment bankers to respond to midlife crises by abandoning the life of an agent to become investment principals, flooding the market with capital to pursue "clean" deals. In contrast, buyout firms that demonstrate the ability to deal with substantial operating issues carve out a special transactional niche, creating the potential for less competitive, proprietary deal flow. The combination of less competition for operationally oriented transactions and potential benefits from addressing business issues provides a compelling investment opportunity.

Buyout managers with a value orientation stress operating improvements as a means to generate superior returns. Building on the base created by financial engineering, value-added owners focus on creating better businesses. By taking an operations-oriented approach, firms benefit by driving returns through both increased profitability and leveraged capital structure.

Clayton Dubilier & Rice and WESCO

Clayton Dubilier & Rice (CDR), a firm with a long, distinguished track record, focuses its efforts on messy deals—transactions that require a high degree of intervention by the principals. The firm implements its value-added investment strategy by explicitly incorporating individuals with operating backgrounds into the partnership. These partners provide valuable perspective during the due diligence process, identifying acquisition candidates that might benefit from the firm's unusual skills. Once CDR acquires a company, operating partners take a hands-on approach to improving corporate operations. One subclass of transactions that CDR pursues involves corporate divestitures. Frequently the divested subsidiary lacks basic corporate organizational structure, having relied on the parent company to provide essential business services. Value creation results as CDR uses its combination of operational and financial expertise to create a stand-alone company from the erstwhile corporate division.

In February 1993, CDR principals began evaluating a spin-off of WESCO, Westinghouse's electrical equipment and supplies distribution arm. Within a short time, the buyout firm identified several major business issues: (1) transition from corporate subsidiary to market-driven business, (2) improvement of inventory and logistics management, and (3) reduction of corporate overhead. More than half of WESCO's 250 branches posted losses in 1993, contributing to firm-wide red ink totaling more than $3 million on a revenue base of $1.6 billion. On top of material business issues, WESCO required more aggressive management to instill a sense of corporate mission. Sleepy management had let the company drift, damaging morale and hurting performance.

After Westinghouse rejected CDR's initial bid as inadequate, the firm continued to work on the project. Operating partner Chuck Ames drove the process, identifying a management plan and preparing to run the company if necessary. By February 1994, when Westinghouse came back to CDR, Ames had identified a chief executive, Roy Haley, with the ability to create and manage the new company.

When CDR acquired WESCO for $330 million, the company lacked basic corporate infrastructure. Creating information technology, finance, and internal control divisions from scratch provided the basic building blocks necessary for corporate existence. Implementing the operating plan crafted prior to acquisition created substantial additional value, moving the company from losses to meaningful profits. By 1997, when a financial buyer purchased WESCO, the firm generated $90 million of operating income on $2.7 billion of revenue. The turnaround in performance produced great results for CDR. The buyout firm's original $83 million of equity generated proceeds of $511 million, providing annual returns of nearly 47 percent to the firm's limited partners. The extraordinary results stem from one measure of financial engineering and several measures of operating improvement.

Few firms possess the skill set required to address the severe operating problems and company-building challenges at WESCO. By combining operational and financial skills, CDR exemplifies the potential for unusual value creation.

Value creation in private equity takes transactions out of the commodity realm into an environment protected by barriers to entry. Venture capitalists providing only money and leveraged buyout specialists engaging in pure financial engineering face scores of well-financed competitors. In contrast, private equity managers with the ability to facilitate operating improvements possess unusual skills, for which they and their partners receive outsized compensation.

• • •

Strong alignment of interests marks most private equity arrangements, creating an appropriate set of incentives for fund managers. Significant co-investment by partners of buyout and venture funds moves investment decisions toward a principal orientation, away from a potentially damaging agency perspective. Side-by-side commitment of general partner dollars causes all parties to share in the gains and losses, forcing decision makers to consider the downside—as well as the upside—of corporate actions. The show of confidence inherent in a significant general partner co-investment sends a strong signal to potential investors.

At the company level, private investments in venture and buyout transactions usually engage bottom-line-oriented management with a substantial vested interest in the success of the enterprise. Because management typically owns a meaningful stake in the company, outside shareholders' interests align nicely with management's goals. In private investing, profit-seeking behavior on the part of both the fund managers and the portfolio company managers reduces the gap between investor interests and corporate behavior, providing an enormous advantage for private over public investment alternatives.

CONCLUSION

Nontraditional asset classes provide powerful tools for investors attempting to reduce risk by constructing well-diversified portfolios and augment return by pursuing profitable active management opportunities. Absolute return strategies and real estate holdings add diversifying power, while private equity investments improve portfolio return prospects.

Absolute return investments consist of event-driven and value-driven strategies that exploit mispricings in marketable securities. By offsetting market exposure with hedges, investors reduce systematic risk and cause results to depend on manager skill. Event-driven positions rely on evaluation of events associated with corporate mergers and bankruptcies, while value-driven positions depend on identification of inappropriately valued securities. Because absolute return strategies generate equity-like returns largely independent of market movements, the asset class contributes extremely attractive return and diversification characteristics to portfolios.

Real estate commitments protect investment portfolios against unanticipated increases in inflation, with investors paying a price for real estate's diversifying power by accepting expected returns below those of marketable equities. Under normal circumstances high levels of real estate cash flow provide a stabilizing influence, reducing the volatility of portfolio fluctuations.

Private equity positions increase portfolio returns at the price of meaningfully increasing portfolio risk, while producing little in terms of diversifying power. Investor experience over the past two decades failed to live up to expectations, as funds generally delivered below-marketable-equity returns at above-marketable-equity risk levels. Burdened by extraordinary fees in the form of substantial profit-sharing arrangements, investors face the difficult task of selecting top-decile funds to realize the promise of private investing.

Investors in nontraditional asset classes must engage in active management, seeking to identify the highest-quality people to manage investment funds. In selecting partners, due diligence efforts center on assessing the competence and character of the individuals responsible for portfolio decisions. Developing partnerships with extraordinary people represents the single most important element of alternative investment success.

By selecting high-quality partnerships pursuing value-adding strategies, Yale University achieved a nearly 30 percent per annum rate of return on private investments over the quarter-century from 1973 to 1998, highlighting the potential contribution to portfolio results provided by a well-managed private equity program. Even after adjusting for the higher risk inherent in venture capital and leveraged buyout participations, Yale's results stack up well relative to other investment alternatives.

Pure financial engineering holds little interest for serious private investors. Buyout firms that simply add debt to balance sheets and venture groups that provide only late-stage bridge financing operate in extremely competitive environments where money represents an efficiently priced commodity. Financial engineers merely expose assets to high levels of fundamental risk, doing nothing to justify the enormous fees represented by a profits interest.

Strategies for adding value to corporate operations make private equity an interesting investment activity, creating the possibility of exploiting less competitive deal-sourcing environments and identifying operations-enhancing opportunities. To the extent that private asset managers increase corporate value in a substantial way, investment results exhibit independence from the forces that drive valuation of marketable equities. Only by adding significant increments of value do private fund managers begin to earn the extraordinary fees common in private equity deals. Strong active management—at the investor level, the fund level, and the company level—forms the basis for successful private equity programs.

9
Investment Advisers

Pursuing active management involves competing in an extremely tough arena, since markets tend to price assets accurately. Enormous sums of money deployed by intelligent, motivated asset managers seek to exploit perceived mispricings at a moment's notice. Winning at the game of active management requires great skill and perhaps more than a little good fortune. Serious investors consider carefully the certain results of low-cost passive strategies before pursuing the uncertain returns from high-cost active management activities.

Significant costs raise the hurdle for active strategies. Identifying a portfolio that merely beats the market fails to define success, because managers must choose securities that generate returns sufficient to cover management fees, transactions costs, and market impact *and* beat the market. Because of the leakage of fees and costs from the system, more than half the money invested in marketable securities falls short of producing index-like returns. Overcoming the costs of active management presents a formidable problem.

In the context of an extraordinarily complex, difficult investing environment, fiduciaries tend to be surprisingly accepting of active manager pitches. Instead of examining critically the factors driving past performance, investors frequently simply associate superior historical results with investment acumen. Institutions all too often pursue the glamorous, exciting (and ultimately costly) hope of market-beating strategies at the expense of the reliable, mundane certainty of passive management.

Because of the nearly insurmountable hurdles in beating the market, prudent investors approach potential active strategies with great skepticism. Beginning with the presumption that markets price assets correctly places the burden of proof on the activity promising risk-adjusted excess returns. Only when compelling evidence suggests that a strategy possesses clear potential to beat the market should investors abandon the passive alternative.

Active managers worth hiring possess an edge that creates reasonable expectations of superior performance. This edge supplies an advantage stemming from a manager's personal attributes and organizational characteristics. In selecting external managers, investors attempt to identify individuals committed to placing institutional goals ahead of personal self-interest. Alignment of interests occurs most frequently in independent investment management firms run in an entrepreneurial fashion by energetic, intelligent, ethical professionals. Engaging investment advisers involves consequences beyond issues of financial returns, as fiduciaries entrust both the institution's assets and reputation to the external management firm.

Even after identifying a promising investment management firm, the job remains uncompleted until the investor and adviser negotiate satisfactory deal terms. The fundamental goal in establishing contractual arrangements consists of aligning interests to encourage investment advisory agents to behave as institutional fiduciary principals. Slippage between what the investor wishes and what the adviser does imposes substantial costs on institutions, reducing the likelihood of meeting basic goals and objectives.

THE GAME OF ACTIVE MANAGEMENT

Human nature clouds objectivity in assessing active management opportunities. Playing the game provides psychic rewards, generating grist for the mill of cocktail party conversation. Keynes likened active investment to children's entertainment:

> For it is, so to speak, a game of Snap, of Old Maid, of Musical Chairs—a pastime in which he is the victor who says *snap* neither too soon nor too late, who passes the Old Maid to his neighbor before the game is over, who secures a chair for himself when the music stops. These games can be played with zest

and enjoyment, though all the players know that it is the Old Maid which is circulating, or that when the music stops some of the players will find themselves unseated."[1]

Fiduciaries must ensure that active management leads to higher expected portfolio returns, not just higher investment manager job satisfaction.

The desire to believe that superior performance comes from intelligent hard work constitutes another factor clouding clear judgment. The investment world worships success, deifying the market seer du jour. Instead of wondering whether a manager at the top of the performance charts made a series of lucky draws from the probability distribution of security returns, the world presumes that good results stem from skill. Conversely, poor results follow from lack of ability. Market observers rarely consider whether high returns came from accepting greater than market risk, or whether low returns resulted from lower than market risk levels. This lack of skepticism regarding the source and nature of superior returns causes strange characters to be elevated to market guru status.

Joe Granville

Of all the individuals who moved markets with their predictions, Joe Granville may be among the strangest. In the late 1970s and early 1980s, the technical analyst made a series of on-the-money predictions. Strikingly, on April 21, 1980, when the market fell to a two-year low of 759, Granville issued a buy signal, anticipating a powerful rally that took the average over 1000 within three months. In January 1981, Granville's next major market call—a sell signal—prompted waves of selling, causing markets to decline sharply on record volume. The next day his picture appeared on the front page of the *New York Times,* while *Washington Post* headlines read "One Forecaster Spurs Hysteria—Markets Sink in Panic Selling." Granville predicted he would win the Nobel Prize, crowing that he had "solved the 100-year enigma, calling every market top and bottom."

Granville's technically driven forecasts came replete with costumes and props. His routine included dressing as Moses to deliver the Ten Commandments of investing, dropping his trousers to read stock quotations from his boxers, and appearing on stage in a coffin filled with ticker tape. Such antics did nothing to diminish his following. In late 1981, markets fell worldwide, sometimes in apparent response to Granville's calls. According to Rhoda Brammer of *Barron's,* "While Granville strutted across the investment stage, the market pretty much followed his bearish script."[2]

Unfortunately for Granville, he missed the turn of the market in 1982. Stubborn bearishness kept his followers out of the early stages of one of the greatest bull markets. In a cruel twist of fate, Granville turned wildly bullish prior to the 1987 crash. As a result, a 1992 study by *Hulbert's Financial Digest* concluded that Granville ranked last among an undistinguished group of investment newsletter writers, down 93 percent over the twelve-year period.

Joe Granville's one-time prominence in the investment world provides strong evidence of the investing public's desire to believe that superior returns stem from investment skill. Granville's methodology relied on technical factors with absolutely no predictive power. Yet he apparently moved markets, fooling large numbers of people into following his absurd predictions.

The Beardstown Ladies

More recently, the Beardstown Ladies captured the investing public's attention. Based on an impressive historical record of beating the S&P 500 by 8.5 percent per year for the ten years ending in 1993, the matrons of Beardstown parlayed their success into a lucrative writing and lecturing career. Their first book, *The Beardstown Ladies' Common-Sense Investment Guide: How We Beat the Stock Market—And How You Can Too,* sold more than 800,000 copies. The group followed with four more books: *The Beardstown Ladies' Pocketbook Guide to Picking Stocks, The Beardstown Ladies' Guide to Smart Spending for Big Savings: How to Save for a Rainy Day Without Sacrificing Your Lifestyle, The Beardstown Ladies' Stitch-in-Time Guide to Growing Your Nest Egg: Step-by-Step Planning for a Comfortable Financial Future,* and *Cookin' Up Profits on Wall Street.*

All of the hoopla surrounding the Beardstown Ladies met with relatively little skepticism. Superior performance provided prima facia evidence of the efficacy of their investment approach. No further analysis seemed necessary.

Unfortunately, the Beardstown Ladies possessed so little analytical ability that calculating investment returns challenged their capabilities. Because the investment club's treasurer erred when using a computer program, she reported a two-year return as applying to the ten-year period. In fact, upon critical examination, the extended record of apparently strong relative performance turned out to be worse than mediocre. Figures compiled by Price Waterhouse concluded that the Beardstown Ladies managed to produce returns of only 9.1 percent per annum, falling short of the S&P 500 return by 5.8 percent per year and failing to meet previously reported results by a staggering 14.3 percent per year. In short, the investment record merits not even a modest magazine article.

The fundamental lesson from the Beardstown Ladies saga relates to the uncritical attitude that many investors take toward performance records. Markets price securities efficiently enough that when presented with a superior performance record, the initial reaction ought to be that strong performance most likely resulted from good fortune, a series of favorable draws from the distribution of potential outcomes. Only when managers articulate a compelling coherent investment philosophy should fiduciaries begin to be drawn into evaluation of the active management opportunity.

•   •   •

Joe Granville and the Beardstown Ladies provide compelling evidence that many market participants uncritically accept superior results as proof of underlying sound investment strategy. The falls from grace suffered by the erstwhile market darlings should encourage investors to adopt skeptical attitudes in evaluating active management opportunities.

PERSONAL CHARACTERISTICS

Real estate investors invoke the mantra "location, location, location." Investors seeking to engage an active manager should focus on "people, people, people." Nothing matters more than working with high-quality partners.

Integrity tops the list of qualifications. Aside from the powerful fact that moral behavior defines a fundamentally important standard, acting in an ethical manner represents a pragmatic means of improving the probability of investment success. Choosing external advisers of high integrity reduces the gap between the actions of the advisers and the interests of an institutional fund.

Inevitable differences in interest exist between an endowment and an outside money manager. The more profound problems include time horizon, tax status, and various forms of business risk. Regardless of the structure of contractual arrangements, external advisers tend to respond to personal incentives. Employing individuals with high moral standards reduces the severity of conflicts of interest, as ethical managers consider seriously the interests of the institutional client when resolving conflicts.

Loyalty plays an important part in investment management relationships, allowing longer-term thinking to dominate decision making. Recognizing the mutual interdependence of institutional investors and external advisers creates a spirit of partnership, enhancing opportunities to create successful, lasting relationships.

Loyalty flows both ways. Investors owe external advisers the opportunity to pursue investment activities within a reasonable time frame. Firing a poorly performing manager simply to remove an embarrassing line item from an annual report fails to meet the test of reasonableness. Similarly an investment adviser abandoning reliable partners simply to pursue a lower-cost source of capital follows a short-sighted strategy.

Obviously loyalty does not require permanent maintenance of the status quo. Relationships between fiduciaries and external managers come to an end for a variety of compelling reasons. Far too frequently, however, investors abandon good partners for trivial reasons, imposing unnecessary costs and needlessly disrupting portfolio management activities. Investment advisers and institutional fund managers operating with a presumption of loyalty enhance opportunities for long-term success.

Top-notch managers invest with a passion, working to beat the market with a nearly obsessive focus. Many extraordinary investors spend an enormous amount of time investigating investment opportunities, continuing to labor long after rational professionals would have concluded a job well done. Great investors tend to pursue the game not for profit but for sport.

Markets fascinate successful investors. Diligence and hard work take an investment manager only so far; even the most carefully researched decisions ultimately face the vicissitudes of market forces. Because so much lies beyond a portfolio manager's control, superior investors seek to know as much as can be known, reducing uncertainty to the irreducible minimum stemming from unpredictable market and nonmarket variables.

Money provides an obvious motivation to investment managers, bringing enormous wealth to successful investment advisers. Yet money managers seeking to maximize income constitute a poor group from which to choose. Profit-maximizing business plans involve unbridled asset growth and unimaginative benchmark-hugging investment strategies, factors at odds with investment success. Appealing money managers limit assets under management and make aggressive unconventional security choices, incurring substantial risks for their money management business with the hope of generating superior investment returns.

Due diligence on the principals of an investment management organization provides critical input into the manager selection process. Spending time with manager candidates, in their offices and over a meal, allows assessment of whether the manager exhibits characteristics of a good partner. Extensive reference checking, questioning individuals on manager-supplied lists, confirms or denies impressions gathered earlier in the due diligence process. Contacts with people outside of an official reference list, including competitors, provide opportunities to evaluate the quality of a prospective manager's business dealings and integrity level.

ORGANIZATIONAL CHARACTERISTICS

The right people tend to create the right organization, reinforcing the centrality of selecting strong partners. However, finding good people, while necessary, marks only a starting point in the search for a money manager, for strong people in a poorly structured organization face the markets with a significant unnecessary handicap. In a world rich with alternatives, compromising on structural issues makes little sense.

Attractive investment management organizations encourage decisions directed toward creating investment returns, not toward generating fee income for the manager. Such principal-oriented advisers tend to be small, entrepreneurial, and independent.

Size

Appropriate size depends on the nature of the investment opportunity. In general, smaller tends to be better. Markets where amounts of assets under management pose little problem involve highly liquid securities such as U.S. Treasury bonds and large-capitalization domestic equities. Of course, such markets provide few opportunities to generate excess returns. Interesting active management situations tend to be situated in smaller, less liquid markets, requiring managers to exercise discipline in limiting assets under management.

Constraints related to the number of clients limit rational firm growth as severely as do constraints related to asset size. While routine communication might be conducted through broad-based mailings or by client service personnel, informed clients inevitably require meaningful amounts of an investment principal's time and energy. An investment adviser opting for less involved, less burdensome clients makes a potentially serious mistake. First, high-quality clients occasionally provide useful input into the investment process. Second, in the event that the firm experiences an explicable stretch of poor performance, well-informed clients tend to continue to support the manager's activities. Less sophisticated clients control unreliable money, which often exhibits procyclical tendencies, buying high and selling low.

A strong client base creates advantages for both the investment adviser and the clients themselves. If a money management firm's client roster contains many weak hands, poor relative performance might cause substantial asset withdrawals. Such withdrawals tend to harm other clients directly, in the case of transactions costs spread among participants in commingled funds, and indirectly, in the case of client defections, which lead to poor firm morale.

In contrast, intelligently supportive clients contribute financial and emotional support to investment managers experiencing a rough stretch of performance. By adding assets to a poorly performing manager's account, the client stands to profit from a future reversal of fortune, while the manager benefits from the client's vote of confidence.

Entrepreneurial Attitude

Small, independent firms reside at the opposite end of the spectrum from large subsidiaries of financial services conglomerates. Appropriate firm size and sensible ownership structures contribute to the probability of generating superior investment results. Moreover, the tendency of smaller, principal-oriented firms to behave in an entrepreneurial fashion provides critical context to the investment management process. Entrepreneurial environments emphasize people, putting plans and structures in a secondary position. By placing people first, investment organizations increase chances for success.

In entrepreneurial organizations, individuals drive decisions, placing great importance on selecting partners with attractive behavioral characteristics. Great people provide the core of a strong entrepreneurial operation, according to venture capitalist Len Baker, because they "execute better, respond better to surprise, and attract other great people." He suggests that managers "be out there, be obsessive, and be bottom up."[3]

Entrepreneurial capitalism constitutes a behavioral process with three driving forces: innovation, ownership, and adaptation. Each characteristic contributes to the core of successful money management organizations.

Innovation

Innovation requires new combinations. Although money managers do not create new products in the same sense as did Eli Whitney or Thomas Edison, by "see[ing] things which only subsequently prove to be true,"[4] investment advisers lay the groundwork for success. Excess returns stem from out-of-the-mainstream positions that achieve recognition in startling surprises to ordinary market observers. By identifying the unexpected consequence before it occurs, successful investment managers realize superior returns from exploiting superior insights. Without creative portfolio choices, investment managers face dismal prospects since the old combination represents the consensus view. Market efficiency drives returns on market-like portfolios to the average, causing conventional portfolios with conventional ideas to produce conventional results, a poor outcome for active investment managers.

In efforts to innovate, entrepreneurs encourage experimentation, accepting occasional shortfall as the price paid for potential gains. Repeated failure precedes success in most entrepreneurial endeavors, requiring an organizational culture that encourages experimentation and accepts mistakes. By explicitly permitting failure but holding down its costs, investment organizations create an environment allowing managers to construct truly novel investment portfolios.

Ownership

Financial and psychic ownership leads to superior results. Strong investment management firms reward contributions monetarily while engaging the hearts and minds of staff members. Widely distributed ownership enhances organizational stability, facilitating long-term thinking. Carefully structured financial incentives elicit appropriate behavior from investment personnel, discouraging fee-driven activity and encouraging managers to behave as owners. Psychic ownership provides a powerful complement to financial rewards. By causing investors to buy into the process, interests of manager and client come together.

Adaptation

Adaptation involves careful selection, amplifying the strong and eliminating the weak. In culling a portfolio of attractive positions from a large universe of potential opportunities, successful investors express unusual insights ahead of the herd. Strong ideas command meaningful portions of assets, magnifying the impact of high conviction positions, while weak positions disappear. When circumstances change, managers reconfigure portfolios to reflect new realities. Not only does adaptation influence the tactics of security selection, but as markets evolve, adaptation may lead to alternate investment strategies. If inefficiencies disappear in a particular market niche, the entrepreneur seeks new mispricings to exploit. Both tactically and strategically, adaptation plays an important role.

·   ·   ·

Contrast the flexibility of entrepreneurial organizations with bureaucracies. Bureaucratic structures deal effectively with repetitive, regular, slow-to-change environments. Control-oriented processes emphasize structure, subordinating the relative importance of people. Bureaucracies employ conventional wisdom and seek consensus, punishing failure quickly and ruthlessly. By pursuing safety and avoiding controversy, bureaucratic structures systematically screen out the market opportunities likely to yield superior returns. Bureaucracies deal poorly with the constantly changing market environment, failing to address even elementary active investment management problems.

Most fiduciaries pursue investment with "name brand" money managers, reducing career risk by choosing easily recognized firms blessed by an external consultant. "Safe" investment managers tend to be large, process-driven entities exhibiting consistency in results. These bureaucratic firms develop franchises, using their good name to attract and retain clients. In the realm of marketable securities, the franchise provides no benefit to portfolio management. The value of the franchise lies solely in the comfort level provided to clients.

Comfortable investment decisions frequently fail to generate exciting results. Discomfort when making commitments tends to be a necessary, albeit not sufficient, condition of success. Because entrepreneurial firms tend to be newer and smaller, track records may be harder to define and interpret. Less process-driven strategies and results depend heavily on individuals, reducing the fiduciary's ability to rely on the franchise for results. While backing an entrepreneurial group takes more courage than serving up a name brand recommendation, investment success may require funding managers without standard institutional credentials.

Unfortunately, when a fund manager identifies an attractive investment partner, making a commitment sows the seeds for future trouble. Schumpeter's concept of creative destruction takes hold as organizational evolution from a small, entrepreneurial craft shop to a large enterprise undermines the premise that supported forming the firm in the first place. As the organization grows, mutation "incessantly revolutionizes the economic structure *from within,* incessantly destroying the old one, incessantly creating a new one."[5] Achieving institutional acceptability threatens the very characteristics that made the firm interesting in the first place. As time and size erode the entrepreneurial enthusiasm that brought initial success to the firm, the fund manager needs to seek new partners to provide superior management capabilities. Fiduciaries must be wary of the process of creative destruction, which Schumpeter concluded is "the essential fact about capitalism."[6]

Investment Guerrillas

Miles Morland, general partner of Blakeney Management, captures the essence of the strengths of an entrepreneurial investment management organization in a letter describing why he did not proceed with a contemplated joint venture involving a much larger financial services conglomerate (Blakeney manages assets in Africa and the Middle East):

> I am afraid we are not going to go ahead with our merger .... Blakeney is a small group of guerrillas. Our success comes from our ability to fight and forage in places too small and too risky for people with more to lose. That is also what makes it such an exhilarating place to work. We are focused completely on getting and doing business with no thought for our supply lines or on whose territory we are trespassing. [Your firm] is a big and powerful uniformed army. Thanks to you it has retained its entrepreneurial spirit more than any other large American firm but that is like saying that the parachute troops are more entrepreneurial than the tank battalions. Big firms by their nature need disciplines and chains of command. Their sheer size means that when they venture overseas they build complex relationships with other powers in other lands who speak the same language. . . .
>
> Guerrillas cannot be integrated into the regular army without losing what it is that makes them effective. All the professionals at Blakeney have previously been officers in the regular army and have deserted to join the guerrillas. It is the thought that you

personally are a guerrilla at heart that has made us go on with the negotiations despite the warning signs. If we ask ourselves how will this deal help us do more and better business, and how will it make our lives more interesting and more fun, we cannot find an answer. Everything points in the opposite direction. This is no criticism of [your firm] or the excellent people we have got to know there. It is the reality of forming an affiliation with someone as big as you. Even if we don't have to put on uniforms we will have to run our business in a way that acknowledges the rules that are imposed on you and when we go foraging for business we will have to respect your existing alliances. We are rustlers by nature not herders. We want to make lightning raids in Zimbabwe and Ghana and Egypt while your partners . . . are holding meetings to decide . . . about how and where they are going to deploy their mighty troops. When they arrive we hope they will find a few of the local cattle are missing.

. . . I hope we can continue to do things together. All this only started because of the respect I have for you personally. I bear the blame for not realizing sooner what the implications of the deal were. At the end of the day, we might have been the majority shareholder and you the minority one, but if a majority mouse lies down with a minority elephant it is not the elephant who is going to end up as a pancake.

By selecting investment managers with an entrepreneurial orientation, fiduciaries improve the chances for investment success. Large, multiproduct, process-driven financial services entities face the daunting hurdle of overcoming bureaucratic obstacles to creative decision making. Small, independent firms with excellent people focused on a well-defined market segment provide the highest likelihood of identifying the intelligent contrarian path necessary to achieving excellent investment results.

Independent Organizations

Investors increase the degree of coincidence of interests with fund managers by choosing to work with focused, independent firms. Particularly severe conflicts between investor goals and money manager actions appear in "financial supermarkets"—large bureaucratic, diversified organizations offering a variety of investment management options. Employee turnover at such organizations appears to be substantially greater than at independent firms. The investment management subsidiary's revenues flow to the financial supermarket, which takes some as profit and returns some as salary to the subsidiary's principals. Successful portfolio managers employed by supermarkets simply move across the street, open up shop, and garner 100 percent of the revenues associated with their efforts. The profit objective of the financial supermarket creates instability at the investment management subsidiary, opening a gap between the interests of the firm and the client. Small, independent, entrepreneurial organizations provide greater coincidence of interest between firm and client.

Investment focus serves to improve the chances of satisfying client objectives. A narrow product line forces managers to live and die by investment results, creating an enormous incentive to produce superior returns. In contrast, a firm with a broad product line anticipates that hoped-for gains on winning products more than offset inevitable losses on losing strategies, reducing the cost of any single product failure. Even worse, in seeking steady streams of income, financial supermarket managers fashion broadly diversified portfolios, mimicking market benchmarks. Investors prefer that fund managers place all their eggs in one basket, watching that basket with great care. By selecting concentrated, focused managers, investors increase chances for success.

In pursuing flows of revenues, financial conglomerates generally seek income growth regardless of the consequences for investment performance. Investment managers soon recognize that rewards come primarily from attracting new cash flows, not generating superior investment returns. In the final analysis, client interests fail to be well served.

United Asset Management

United Asset Management (UAM), an acquisitive conglomerate of investment advisers, illustrates the problems with external ownership of investment managers. With equity interests in forty-five firms, managing in excess of $200 billion as of December 31, 1998, UAM ranks among the world's largest owners of investment management firms. While the firm boasts an impressive level of assets under management, UAM operates with a fundamentally flawed strategy.

The UAM investment manager roster includes a number of well-known, highly regarded groups, including Acadian Asset Management, Murray Johnstone Limited, and Pilgrim Baxter. While superior historical performance created UAM manager reputations, prospects for future excess returns appear dim. The emphasis on asset gathering, loss of entrepreneurial drive, and diversion of revenues to passive shareholders create conditions likely to lead to investment mediocrity.

Even though UAM's 1997 annual report lists the name, address, and investment strategy of each of the firm's affiliated managers, no performance data appear. Net client withdrawals of $16 billion in 1997, representing 9.4 percent of assets at the beginning of the year, point to the conclusion that managers produced generally unsatisfactory performance. The few textual references to investment performance do little to confuse the annual report's clear message: manager rewards stem from increasing assets under management, not from generating superior investment returns.

Board chairman Norton Reamer addresses the leakage of assets by identifying "improving our firms' net client cash flow [as] our top priority in 1998."[7] The report later outlines incentive programs to reach the goal, "which is clearly a function of improved client service and retention as well as product development and marketing." The annual report indicates that new acquisitions will "concentrate on firms with the highest growth potential," not on firms most likely to provide superior performance.

In spite of a roaring bull market, UAM failed in its marketing approach to increasing "net client cash flow." Throughout 1998, nearly $20 billion in assets left the money management firms under UAM's umbrella. While UAM continued to articulate a goal of increasing assets through improved client servicing, the firm announced several investment-oriented initiatives designed to improve performance.

Although attracting assets through superior investment performance satisfies client needs far better than efforts to attract funds through marketing pitches, UAM faces a difficult task as an external owner of investment firms. External ownership of investment firms inevitably alters the institutional culture, diminishing the entrepreneurial spirit so critical to successful money management organizations. When senior professionals cash out, the previous single-minded focus on generating strong results dissipates, sapping the vitality of the firm.

After the sale of a firm, junior professionals face a less rosy future. The diversion of resources to passive external shareholders reduces the size of the pie available for distribution to investment professionals, creating instability. Employees of professional services firms with substantial outside ownership enjoy the option of moving across the street, setting up shop, and garnering a greater share of the newly formed independent firm's profits.

Ultimately pursuit of investment excellence in the context of a conglomerate of investment managers proves futile, as the goals of external owners fail to coincide with the aspirations of investors. Asset gathering creates diseconomies of scale for investors, decreasing the possibility of achieving superior performance. The transformation of senior managers from owners to employees creates changes in firm culture that work to disadvantage investors. Finally, the necessity to compensate external shareholders impairs the money management firm's ability to pay portfolio managers at competitive levels, leading to high rates of turnover among the best personnel and posing obvious risks to investor assets. Significant external ownership of asset management firms creates enormous barriers to investment success.

Investment Banks and Investment Management

Conflicts of interest abound in the financial world, with large, complex organizations facing the widest range of issues. Investment banks frequently sponsor private equity funds, using access to proprietary deal flow as a selling point. But deals originated by the investment banking network come with built-in conflicts. When a company engages an investment bank to sell a division, alarm bells should ring when the banker suggests that the investment bank's private equity fund purchase the division. Is the investment bank serving the interest of a good corporate client by paying a rich price for the division? Or is it serving the interest of investors in the private equity fund by paying a low price? Under such circumstances, fairness opinions notwith-standing, no fair price exists.

Less subtle conflicts permeate the process. Investment banks frequently provide financial advisory and capital markets services to portfolio companies, for which the banks receive handsome remuneration. In an unusual public description of the bonanza created by captive private equity funds, the December 14, 1990, *Wall Street Journal* details fees generated by Morgan Stanley's investment in Burlington Industries.

Morgan Stanley and Burlington Industries. In 1987, Morgan Stanley's leveraged buyout fund invested $46 million of equity in the $2.2 billion purchase of Burlington Industries. Over the next three years, the investment bank charged the company more than $120 million in fees for services ranging from underwriting to advising on divestitures. Because Morgan Stanley controlled the board of Burlington Industries, decisions regarding financing and divestitures failed to be made at arm's length or subjected to competitive forces.

At best, all transactions benefited the company, with Morgan Stanley compensated at market rates for services rendered. At worst, unnecessary transactions generated above-market fees, disadvantaging the company and Morgan Stanley fund investors. When a fund sponsor profits by charging advisory fees at the direct expense of investors, serious conflicts of interest ensue.

Noting that "nearly every time Burlington needed advice, Morgan Stanley turned on the meter," *Wall Street Journal* reporter George Anders suggests that "the story of Burlington Industries raises troubling questions about Wall Street's foray into merchant banking."[8] Fees generated by Morgan Stanley "for everything from underwriting Burlington's high yield debt to overseeing a blizzard of divestitures" dwarf the equity investment made by the partners of Morgan Stanley in the Burlington transaction, providing handsome returns to the investment bank irrespective of the returns delivered to the firm's private equity investors.[9]

Goldman Sachs and the Water Street Corporate Recovery Fund. Goldman Sachs created an even more extensive web of conflicts when in 1990 it established the Water Street Corporate Recovery Fund, a $783 million "vulture fund" set up to make concentrated investments in distressed securities. Hoping to be viewed as a savior of bankrupt companies, Goldman instead stirred up a hornet's nest of conflicts.

One source of contention stems from conflicts between Goldman's financial restructuring advisory business and control investing in distressed situations. Investment banks generally rely on "Chinese walls" to contain sensitive data supplied by clients in the course of advisory assignments, keeping inside information away from securities analysts and traders. The term Chinese wall may be employed because such walls are easily removed at an assignment's end. A cynic (or realist) might argue that paper-thin permeability more aptly describes the defining characteristic of employing Chinese walls. Because Goldman partner Mikael Salovaara both ran the Water Street Fund and continued to advise clients on restructuring, any shred of separation between the businesses disappeared, causing "traders at other firms [to joke] that Mr. Salovaara had a 'Chinese wall' in the middle of his brain."[10]

The Water Street Fund investment in distressed bonds of toymaker Tonka illustrates several strands of the web of conflicts. After accumulating a position in Tonka's debt securities, Salovaara competed for an assignment to advise Mattel on a possible acquisition of Tonka, in the process picking up potentially valuable nonpublic information regarding the value and salability of Tonka's bonds. Goldman's advantage infuriated other junk bond investors not privy to the information, causing several to complain publicly and suggest they would reduce activity with Goldman's trading desk.[11]

Eventually Tonka agreed to be acquired by Hasbro, creating yet another problem for Goldman. The Water Street Fund owned more than half of Tonka's bonds, having acquired the position at less than 50 percent of face value.[12] Although Tonka's board of directors wished to sell the company to Hasbro, Goldman played hardball, holding out for more money for the firm's bond position. Although such tactics raise few eyebrows in the rough and tumble world of distressed debt, some clients saw Goldman's actions as inconsistent with the firm's avowal to avoid any participation in hostile merger activity. Ultimately the investment bank's tactics worked, increasing payments received for the Tonka bond position by reducing the value of other participants' Tonka and Hasbro shareholdings. Goldman's investment returns came at great expense, tarnishing the firm's reputation for putting clients first.

A final strand in the conflict web relates to Goldman's junk bond trading activity. To avoid competition, the firm limited the high-yield trading desk's activity in bonds that the Water Street Fund desired. Clients trading with Goldman, already concerned about the firm's possible informational advantages, faced market makers less able to take positions.

Goldman's advisory conflict troubles went beyond the Tonka case. According to an article in the June 4, 1991, *Wall Street Journal,* "Nine of twenty-one companies that the Water Street Fund selected for 're-structuring' are or were Goldman clients."[13] Perceptions mounted that Goldman invested the Water Street Fund with an unfair advantage.

Faced with a storm of controversy, Goldman shut down the fund in May 1991, several years ahead of schedule. Althrough the Water Street Fund generated handsome returns during its abbreviated life, the fund's enduring legacy may be its rich series of lessons on conflict of interest.

• • •

Although investors cannot avoid conflicts entirely, fewer differences in interest exist when investing with independent investment management organizations. Some reasonably high-quality opportunities may be missed by eliminating affiliates and subsidiaries of financial services firms from the universe of eligible managers; nevertheless, sufficient numbers of independent investment managers exist to provide a rich set of active management choices.

DEAL STRUCTURE

Appropriate deal terms play an important role in producing satisfactory investment results. After identifying independent management firms likely to add value to the investment management process, investors face the issue of evaluating (or negotiating) fair compensation arrangements. The degree of efficiency in asset pricing determines in part the nature of the compensation scheme, with passive management of efficiently priced securities demanding different treatment from active exploitation of anomalously priced assets. All aspects of investment management fee structures contain potential for conflict between the interests of investors and investment managers, forcing fiduciaries to pay close attention to explicit and implicit incentives embodied in contractual arrangements with money managers.

Co-investment

Although agency issues pervade the relationship between investors and external advisors, co-investment provides a powerful means of aligning fiduciary and fund manager interests. To the extent that a manager becomes a principal, issues regarding agency behavior diminish. With substantial co-investment, new issues arise regarding possible differences in goals between mortal, taxpaying money managers and perpetual, tax-exempt institutions, but incentives for investment advisers to profit at the expense of clients decrease dramatically.

While any level of co-investment encourages fund managers to act like principals, the larger the personal commitment of funds, the greater the focus on generating superior investment returns. Managers cease to benefit from attracting new capital at the point where the return diminution on the manager's personal stake caused by increasing assets under management exceeds the opportunity costs of fees forgone by limiting asset growth. Because the easily measured level of fees forgone generally eclipses the fuzzy estimate of size-induced performance drag, only the wealthiest managers confront a clear trade-off favoring asset growth limitations. Although the numbers might favor asset-gathering strategies for most managers, substantial levels of co-investment send strong signals to investors regarding the principal orientation of fund managers. The idea that a fund manager believes strongly enough in the investment product to put a substantial personal stake in the fund suggests that the manager shares the investor's orientation.

Investment of fund manager personal assets side by side with investor capital creates a powerful alignment of interests. While profit participations help to focus manager attention on the investor goal of generating handsome investment returns, a profit-sharing arrangement in which managers share only in gains creates an option that encourages risk-seeking behavior. By making a substantial co-investment, managers participate directly in gains and losses, leading to more balanced assessment of investment opportunities. To realize the hoped-for behavior modification, the commitment must be large relative to the manager's net worth, even though the co-investment might be modest in absolute terms. When writing a check representing a material portion of personal assets, the investment manager steps into the role of a principal.

While co-investment generally improves the investor's position by aligning investment interests, differences in goals bear careful scrutiny. Taxpaying fund managers in partnership with tax-exempt institutional investors face different after-tax return scenarios. Mortal decision makers operate with time horizons shorter than appropriate for an organization's permanent funds. Individuals with large fund investments frequently desire greater diversification than required by most institutions, which hold an already well-diversified collection of assets. Although differences in tax status, time horizon, and risk tolerance drive wedges between the unconstrained behavior of individual fund managers and institutional investors, the benefits of substantial co-investment far outweigh any potential costs.

Compensation Arrangements for Marketable Securities

The character of sensible compensation arrangements for investment managers varies with the degree of efficiency in asset pricing. Passive management of government securities demands fee arrangements different from those appropriate for intense active management of private equity positions. For most asset classes, investors face well-entrenched fee arrangements, ranging from asset-based fees for management of relatively efficiently priced marketable securities to a combination of fees and incentive payments for less efficiently priced asset types. Because marketplace practices frequently deviate from ideal compensation structures, price-taking investors generally take the pragmatic approach of choosing the best option from a set of bad alternatives, with the hope of reducing the likelihood that money managers engage in agency activities.

Passive Strategies

Issues confronting passive asset managers differ fundamentally from problems facing active fund managers. Size, the enemy of active investors, often works in favor of index fund managers. For example, passive funds with large numbers of investors frequently offer crossing opportunities, in which some portion of exiting investor demand for funds matches entering investor supply of funds, allowing nearly costless exit from and entrance to the investment pool.* Scale improves tracking of benchmarks, as large size facilitates full replication of the investment universe, reducing the need for tracking-error-inducing sampling procedures. Experience shows that funds with billions of dollars track benchmarks with little or no slippage.

Barclays Global Investors, one of the world's largest Index fund managers, offers a wide variety of products designed to mirror various marketable security benchmarks, segregated into distinct pools for different types of investors. The largest pool of assets designed to track the S&P 500 contained $120 billion on December 31, 1998. Before fees, the fund returned 19.20 percent for the trailing ten years relative to 19.19 percent for the S&P 500 index.† The much smaller bond pool, with $3.7 billion on December 31, 1998, showed similarly impressive results, with ten-year returns of 9.36 percent relative to 9.33 percent for the Lehman Brothers Government Corporate Index.

The commodity-like nature of passive investing commands commodity-like compensation. Index fund managers compete with the alternative of internally managed passive portfolios, forcing fees to less than a single basis point per year for large accounts. By choosing passive alternatives for efficiently priced assets, investors expect superior results at a bargain price.

Two factors argue for passive management of bond portfolios. First, to satisfy the required deflation hedging role of fixed income, investors must hold long-term, high-quality, noncallable bonds, suggesting the creation of stable-duration government bond portfolios. Second, the extraordinary degree of efficiency in pricing government

---

*Barclays Global Investors reports that from 1993 to 1996, more than 90 percent of the firm's S&P 500 Index Fund transactions represented crossing trades. Such internal trades create no market impact and require no commission payments.

†Barclays Global Investors' fee schedule for the S&P 500 Index Fund starts at 15 basis points on the first $15 million, moving to 10 basis points on the next $35 million, and 1 basis point on the next $450 million. For amounts over $500 million, the firm charges 8/10 of 1 basis point.

bonds makes active security selection decisions a costly exercise in futility. The combination of needing a stable maturity structure and avoiding individual security bets requires that investors manage bond portfolios passively.

While domestic equity investors enjoy more flexibility than bond investors in structuring portfolios, the difficulty of identifying material mispricings in the stock market, particularly among large-capitalization securities, leads many investors to index common stock exposure. By avoiding high fees and substantial transactions costs, index funds provide long-term results that represent a formidable challenge to investors hoping to outperform the most efficiently priced portions of the marketable securities universe. Nevertheless, in spite of clear difficulties in realizing risk-adjusted excess returns, most investors pursue active management strategies.

Active Strategies

Given the important role of management costs in dampening returns, careful active investors pay close attention to fee arrangements, recognizing that the drag on performance from fees represents a substantial obstacle to market-beating performance. Active managers of marketable securities generally receive asset-based fees in exchange for portfolio management services. On one level, interests coincide. To the extent that a manager increases assets through superior investment performance, both the manager and the investor win as the manager's income increases and the investor benefits from strong returns. On other levels, interests conflict. The manager may pursue a staying-in-business strategy of closet indexing, holding a market-like portfolio unlikely to produce results that would lead to termination. Perhaps even more damaging, the manager may conclude that gathering assets provides greater fee income than does generating superior returns.

In growing assets, managers respond to economic incentives. With asset-based fees, income increases as assets under management increase. Frequently managers find it easier to add assets by attracting new accounts than by creating excess returns. With distressingly few exceptions, fund managers aggressively pursue marketing activities, attempting to gather as many assets as possible. Retaining assets requires avoiding disastrous performance, causing money managers to create marketlike portfolios that all but eliminate the chance for superior performance. Investment management represents at best a secondary consideration for most institutional fund managers.

Creating appropriate deal structures allows investors to mitigate many of the conflicts inherent in the investment advisory relationship. Sensible fee arrangements contain two elements: base compensation covering reimbursement of reasonable overhead costs, and incentive compensation providing a sharing between the parties of a manager's value added. The incentive compensation, or profits interest, represents a share of the returns generated in excess of a benchmark appropriate to the investment activity. For example, large-capitalization domestic equity managers might be rewarded for returns generated in excess of an index of security prices, such as the S&P 500, while foreign equity managers might receive a profits interest in returns above the Morgan Stanley Capital International EAFE Index. Fair deal structures, rare in the investment management arena, encourage appropriate behavior on the part of money managers.

Unfortunately, the overwhelming majority of marketable security managers employ asset-based fee schemes, causing market gains or losses and portfolio inflows or outflows to overwhelm the impact of value added or subtracted on manager compensation. Although a number of managers offer superficially attractive incentive compensation arrangements, three factors diminish the appeal of most schemes. First, the vast bulk of marketable security funds subject to active management generate asset-based fee revenues, encouraging managers to emphasize increasing asset totals. In other words, incentive arrangements fail to influence fund manager behavior because investment firms continue to depend almost exclusively on fee income expressed simply as a percentage of assets under management. Second, investment managers tend to offer terms on incentive schemes that involve modest levels of risk to the firm's existing income flows. Instead of taking a blank slate approach to determining baseline fees calculated to cover reasonable overhead, money managers try to structure incentive arrangements that ensure continued income flows even with mediocre performance, protecting the profit margins implicit in existing fee structures. Finally, investors choosing between a manager's traditional asset-based fee and alternative incentive-oriented structure encounter cognitive dissonance, as the performance expectations implicit in hiring an active manager cause expected costs of incentive compensation to exceed anticipated payments from asset-based fees. While the concept of incentive compensation structures for active managers of marketable securities carries a great deal of theoretical appeal, the limitations of real-world arrangements reduce the effectiveness of incentive schemes in causing fund managers to behave as principals.

Investment management fees, whether asset based or incentive oriented, represent a heavily scrutinized term in most contract negotiations, with investors seeking the lowest possible fee burden along with a most-favored-client clause ensuring advantageous treatment in the future. Beneath the open, honest discussion concerning marketable equity fee arrangements lie hidden soft dollar payments, representing old-fashioned kickbacks designed to increase investment adviser cash flow at the direct expense of clients.

Soft Dollars

Investors in marketable equities almost invariably pay a hidden tariff in the form of soft-dollar payments to the investment advisory community. The odious practice of managers receiving rebates from Wall Street drives a wedge between the interests of investors and investment advisers. While most aspects of investment management agreements result from explicit understandings between fund managers and investors, soft-dollar arrangements lurk beneath the surface, hiding transactions from open view and allowing managers to impose charges on clients in an opaque fashion. A powerful group of industry participants benefits from soft-dollar activity, implicitly conspiring to preserve a means of generating profit at the expense of the vast majority of investors.

According to a 1998 Securities and Exchange Commission (SEC) report, "Almost all advisors obtain products and services (both proprietary and third party) other than pure execution from broker dealers and use client commission to pay for those products and services."[14] Investment advisers use the portion of commission costs above the cost of pure execution, known as soft dollars, to obtain research-related products and services produced directly by the brokerage house, or by a third party receiving cash payments from the executing firm. A variant on soft dollars, client-directed brokerage, allows clients to direct money managers to send orders to a specific broker, with the client, not the manager, receiving a cash rebate or research services.

Soft dollars trace their origin to the 1950s when fixed commission rates precluded brokers from competing for business on the basis of price. In order to attract customers, brokers offered "discounts" in the form of research services or even direct payments. When the SEC abolished fixed rates in 1972, some argued that price competition would drive commissions so low that brokers would no longer be able to provide managers with research. In addition, concerns were raised that soft-dollar practices were inconsistent with a manager's obligation under the Investment Advisers Act of 1940 to act in the best interest of the client. A manager could be deemed to have violated this duty if clients paid anything but the lowest commission rate consistent with best execution.

In response to these concerns, Congress in 1975 enacted section 28(e) of the Securities Exchange Act of 1934, which provides a safe harbor for certain soft-dollar arrangements. Section 28(e) provides that a manager with investment discretion over an account will not be deemed to have acted unlawfully or to have breached its fiduciary duty by causing the account to pay a higher commission to a broker providing research benefiting the adviser's accounts. To rely on the section 28(e) safe harbor, an adviser "must determine in good faith that the commissions paid are reasonable in relation to the value of the brokerage and research services provided."

The scope of practices falling within the section 28(e) safe harbor depends on the definition of research. The current standard, articulated in a 1986 SEC release, states, "The controlling principle to be used to determine whether something is research is whether it provides lawful and appropriate assistance to the money manager in the performance of his investment decision-making responsibilities." When a soft dollar service has a mixed use, the component that provides assistance to a money manager in the decision-making process may be paid for in commission dollars, while those services that provide administrative or other nonresearch assistance must be paid for by the money manager.

At best, soft dollars used to pay for third-party services creates modest inefficiencies. The silly practice of the first party (the client) paying the second party (the broker) a high rate so a portion can be transferred to a third party for provision of services to the first party sounds like an Alice in Wonderland arrangement. In general, soft dollars move beyond generating minor frictions to thwarting client interests, with the payments representing an opaque method of increasing investment manager income. At worst, soft dollars serve as a means by which investment managers use client assets to pursue nefarious ends, providing a mechanism to divert resources for private use or to pay off the investment consulting industry.

SEC chairman Arthur Levitt described soft-dollar conflicts in a February 15, 1995 *Wall Street Journal* article: "Soft-dollar arrangements can create substantial conflicts of interest between an adviser and its clients. For example, advisers may cause their clients to pay excessive commission rates, or may overtrade their clients' accounts simply to satisfy soft-dollar obligations. Soft-dollar arrangements may also result in inferior executions when advisers direct trades to the wrong broker to satisfy a soft-dollar obligation."[15]

Hidden charges inherent in soft dollar arrangements prove even more worrisome than the dangers Levitt outlined. When investment advisers use soft dollars to pay for subscriptions to newspapers, research services, and electronic media, those managers divert client funds to pay for expenses that ought to be covered by management fees. The management fee represents a transparent, often highly negotiated means to compensate investment advisers. Investors expect that (handsome) fees cover operating expenses and provide managers with a (substantial) income. Soft dollars represent a means through which investment managers cause client portfolios to bear a portion of ordinary business expenses through payment of excessive commissions. A classic agency problem results, with a manager improving its lot at the expense of the client.

Abuses of Soft Dollars. The most outrageous "legitimate" use of soft dollars stems from what amount to payoffs to consulting firms made by investment advisers in the form of purchasing unnecessary services. According to the 1998 SEC report, performance attribution services constitute "a significant portion of the total commission dollars used in soft dollar transactions."[16] Obviously any competent investment manager develops internal capabilities to understand sources of investment returns, creating evaluation mechanisms specific to the firm's particular approach to markets. Purchasing performance attribution from consultants serves simply to line the pockets of the consulting firm at the expense of the investment manager's clients. Presumably the consulting firm receiving the payoff places the investment management firm in a favored position when making manager recommendations. While investment advisers may wish to improve their standing by purchasing useless information from consulting firms, using client assets for the purpose turns inanity to ignominy.

Some investment managers need so much assistance in understanding performance that they purchase multiple reports. The SEC study cites a large institutional adviser that "directed $882,000 in client commissions to pay for 13 separate performance analyses." According to a report in *Pensions and Investments,* J&W Seligman & Co., a money management firm with $24.3 billion under management, engaged seven consulting firms to provide performance attribution reports, using client assets to fund the purchase through soft dollars.[17] By paying Callan Associates ($79,000), Evaluation Associates ($100,000), Frank Russell ($26,789), Madison Portfolio Consultants ($17,500), SEI Corporation ($10,000), Wellesley Group ($52,500), and Yanni-Bilkey Investment Consulting ($25,000), J&W Seligman no doubt expects favorable treatment in the consulting firms' next search recommendation. Such egregious abuse of client funds ought to lead to dismissal of the manager.

Beyond the "legitimate" use of soft dollars to "curry favor with the consultant in his rankings and recommendations of advisors," nearly 30 percent of investment advisers employ soft dollars for "non-research products and services." The purchases, which fall outside the safe harbor, include use of soft dollars for office rent, equipment, marketing expenses, telephone services, and salaries. The SEC observed that "virtually all of the advisers that obtained nonresearch products and services had failed to provide meaningful disclosure of such practices to their clients."[18] Aside from using an illegitimate source of funds for legitimate business expenses, many advisers stepped over another line by diverting funds for personal use, including purchase of travel, entertainment, theater tickets, limousine services, interior design, Internet web site design and construction, and computer hardware and software. In the most flagrant abuse of soft dollars, one investment adviser stole money from clients by directing "funds ostensibly for verbal 'regional research' and 'strategic planning' to family members of the adviser's principal," by transferring soft dollars through a daisy chain of companies controlled by the adviser's president, and by paying "round trip airfare to Hong Kong for the principal's son." Although soft dollars did not cause the theft, the opacity of the arrangement facilitated the crimes.

Directed Brokerage. Some clients benefit from a different aspect of the current system of commission-related activity, taking advantage of the murky character of directed brokerage. With directed brokerage, plan sponsors cause trades to be executed by specified brokers, paying higher-than-market commission rates. A portion of the above-market rate flows back to the plan sponsor in the form of cash rebates or investment-related goods and services. Two factors drive directed brokerage activity: investors gain an advantage by pursuing such activity at the expense of clients not directing brokerage, and fund sponsors use rebates from directed brokerage to purchase goods and services otherwise unavailable through normal procurement channels.

Investment advisers commonly aggregate trades for a number of separate account clients, allocating shares to accounts on a pro rata basis. If one client requests that brokerage be directed to a particular securities firm, receiving a cash rebate, that client accrues an unfair benefit relative to other clients. In fact, the client that steps out of the aggregated trade likely benefits implicitly from all of the brokerage conducted by the investment adviser at the designated firm. Such arrangements exist only as long as they remain hidden; when they become known, disadvantaged clients demand fair and equitable treatment.

Some investors, particularly in political or corporate environments, fail to obtain sufficient direct support for investment management operations. As a result, investment offices receive inadequate resources to create the necessary infrastructure and hire appropriate numbers of qualified staff. To augment direct appropriations, investments staff sometimes employ directed brokerage and soft dollar programs, generating resources outside regular appropriations or operational channels.

Appearing before a Department of Labor Working Group on Soft Dollars and Commission Recapture, the former director of the New Jersey Division of Investment openly testified that "he utilizes soft dollars to pay for needed administrative expenses," since "he does not receive sufficient funding from the New Jersey State Legislature." In fact, the former director urged that "the current interpretation of 'research' should be expanded to include travel and hotel expenses."[19] Soft dollars provide a convenient mechanism for the New Jersey Division of Investment to circumvent constraints imposed by the state legislature, allowing the investment operation to thwart the intent of New Jersey's elected representatives.

SEC Proposals. To ameliorate conflicts surrounding brokerage activity, in February 1995, the SEC proposed a new rule under the Investment Advisers Act of 1940 that would require investment managers to disclose the services they receive for brokerage commissions. The report would list the twenty brokers to which the adviser directed the largest amounts of commissions during the previous year, the top three execution-only brokers, the aggregate amount of commissions directed by the adviser to each broker, and the average commission rate paid to each broker. The disclosure would permit a client to assess the costs and benefits of the soft dollar services that the adviser receives and, consequently, whether the client should attempt to limit the adviser's use of soft-dollar brokers. Unfortunately, no action resulted from the 1995 SEC rule proposal.

The 1998 SEC report proposes more guidance, more record keeping, more disclosure, and more controls. While the SEC attempts to bring greater transparency to soft-dollar practices, the question remains: Why do soft dollars exist? Powerful market participants in the brokerage community benefit from the inherent murkiness of soft-dollar transactions. Third-party providers of soft-dollar-eligible goods and services maintain a strong vested interest in supporting the current system. Investment advisers employing soft dollars increase net income by transferring a portion of investment management costs to clients. And, in fact, even a number of fund fiduciaries wish to keep the current soft dollar infrastructure in place to garner operating funds, unobtainable through normal channels.

• • •

Soft dollar activity flies in the face of reasonable governance. Investment advisers employ soft dollars to pay off consulting firms and increase investment management revenues, relying on the technique's opacity to hide activity from view. Fund managers incur frictional costs to pursue initiatives with directed commissions for which hard dollars are unavailable, perhaps frustrating the intentions of fund fiduciaries. Soft dollars and directed brokerage, the slimy underbelly of the brokerage world, ought to be banned.

Compensation Arrangements for Nontraditional Assets

Deal structures in the alternative arena often encourage investment managers to expose investor assets to risk, as the managers typically receive compensation in the form of an option-like profits interest. Facing a "heads I win, tails you lose" arrangement, managers respond by adopting an agent's perspective, focusing on achieving personal gains that may or may not correspond to generating risk-adjusted investment returns for the providers of capital.

A particularly troublesome problem results from granting investment managers a profits interest without specifying an appropriate benchmark or hurdle rate. By paying 20 percent of gains after return of capital, investors give asset managers a windfall in the form of a "profit" participation in gains stemming from a strong tailwind. In neglecting to create structures incorporating a reasonable measure of the opportunity cost of funds, investors nearly guarantee the economic success of alternative asset managers and almost ensure the failure of nontraditional vehicles to deliver superior risk-adjusted returns.

In spite of important limitations, when compared to typical marketable security deal terms, alternative asset deal structures tend to do a better job of aligning the interests of fund managers and providers of funds, as the profits interest focuses manager attention on generating investment gains. Large co-investment by managers provides the strongest force for creating parallel interests, causing the manager to share in investment losses as well as in investment gains. Forcing managers to pay attention to the downside of an investment mitigates investor concerns about the one-way nature of the profit-sharing options.

Alternative asset compensation arrangements consist of fee income, generally calculated on portfolio value or committed capital, and incentive schemes, generally calculated as a portion of investment gains. In the rarely achieved ideal world, fees offset ordinary costs of pursuing the investment business, while profits interests create incentives for adding value to the process. All too frequently, fees exceed the level required to cover costs, becoming a profit center, and profit participations cover more than value added, rewarding (or penalizing) managers for results beyond their control.

Fee Income

Reasonable fee income provides sufficient revenue to cover a firm's overhead, allowing investors to run the business comfortably. Investment principals deserve fair salaries, nicely appointed offices, and sufficient resources to structure and manage the portfolio. Ideally investors would discuss with fund managers the level of resources required to operate the firm, setting a budget sufficient to meet the agreed-upon needs. In practice, as fund sizes grow and fee percentages remain stable, fund managers generate enormous cash flows simply from raising ever larger funds.

Deal fees, paid to private fund managers upon consummation of an acquisition, serve to line the pockets of fund managers at the direct expense of investors. Typically found in the leveraged buyout arena, such fees motivate firms to do deals providing an unnecessary addition to the more-than-generous compensation package represented by fund management fees and carried interests. Fees in excess of those required to run the business drive a wedge between the interests of investors and fund managers, subtly shifting the manager's focus to maintaining fees at the expense of generating returns.

Profits Interests

Incentive compensation in the form of a share of gains generated by fund investments provides a powerful tool to motivate fund managers. A fair and effective arrangement splits the value added by the fund manager between the manager and the investor. Both parties deserve to share in incremental gains, since without the manager's work, there would be no value added, and without the investor's capital, there would be no deal. Achieving a hurdle rate reflecting the investor's opportunity cost of capital represents the point at which a fund manager begins to add value. By paying only asset-based fees or providing profits interests after return of capital, investors compensate fund managers inappropriately. Structuring incentive compensation in the form of sharing excess returns causes managers to pursue the active investor's goal of beating the market.

A particularly egregious deal structure causes investors to pay incentive compensation to fund managers before the return of invested capital. Under some private equity arrangements, the investor's capital account declines by the amount of management fees paid. When "gains" are calculated off the reduced base, investors actually pay incentive compensation before receiving a return of their original investment, raising the possibility that fund managers receive a "profits interest" on a fund that fails to return investor capital. At the very least, fund managers ought to return investor capital before reaping the significant rewards of incentive compensation

Fairness demands that investors earn hard hurdles before profit sharing begins. Hard hurdles represent rates of return that investors realize before fund managers participate in gains, with only profit above the hurdle rate subject to sharing. Soft hurdles, a popular marketing scheme, constitute preferred return schemes that allow fund managers to "catch up" after exceeding the hurdle rate, providing little value for investors.

Identifying an appropriate hurdle rate poses a tricky problem, since illiquid markets lack a ready benchmark such as the S&P 500 for domestic equities. In the case of absolute return, since absolute return managers generally take short-duration positions, measuring investment success relative to short-term interest rates makes sense. In the case of real estate, where expected returns fall between bonds (representing a low-risk measure of an institution's opportunity cost of funds) and stocks (representing a higher-risk measure of opportunity cost), rates representing some premium over intermediate-term fixed income returns provide an appropriate hurdle. When forming new funds, investors and fund managers revisit the question of an appropriate hurdle rate in the light of changes in market conditions. For instance, as interest rates continued to move downward throughout the 1990s, appropriate real estate hurdle rates declined from the high single digits to mid single digit levels.

In contrast to reasonable deal structures sometimes available to investors in the absolute return and real estate markets, investors in venture capital and leveraged buyouts face generally unattractive partnership terms. By compensating private equity managers with 20, 25, or 30 percent of every dollar generated after return of capital, standard profit-sharing arrangements fail to consider the opportunity cost of capital. At the very least, private managers ought to return a money market rate before collecting a profits interest. The return on a marketable equity benchmark provides a hurdle rate more closely approximating the risk characteristics of private equity. In fact, the higher risk inherent in venture capital and leveraged buyout investments suggests using a multiple of returns from marketable equity as a threshold for benchmarking private equity funds, compensating managers only for returns generated in excess of a fair risk-adjusted benchmark.

Use of a risk-adjusted marketable security hurdle rate for private investments avoids the problem of compensating (or penalizing) fund managers for market moves that they cannot control. In the bull market of the 1980s and 1990s, buyout managers "earned" 20 percent of the profits on gains largely attributable to stock market–induced valuation increases. Unfortunately, employing a marketable security hurdle rate for private investments creates complexities arguing for a simpler solution. In a reasonable world, investors might compensate private managers with a profits interest in returns exceeding some premium over long-run historical results from marketable equity investments, implying a mid-teens hurdle rate.

Fair incentive compensation schemes for alternative asset managers face nearly insurmountable obstacles. Under the current conditions of overwhelming demand for high-quality groups, investors lack power to influence terms, facing the choice of accepting the standard deal or walking away. Investors hoping to encourage fund managers to behave as principals look to other aspects of deal structure.

Absolute Return Investment Vehicles

Private fund managers usually lock-in a pool of funds, benefiting from having a firm call on the monies necessary to support investment activities and avoiding the midcourse correction problems associated with interim contributions or withdrawals. In contrast, absolute return managers, operating in a marketable securities environment, usually allow existing investors to withdraw assets and new investors to make contributions. Although partnership terms generally restrict the timing and size of inflows and outflows, stable investors face the possibility of incurring costs created by other investors' cash moving in and out. Cash contributions to an existing partnership dilute the interest of existing investors. By buying into an existing commingled fund, new investors participate in an established portfolio without paying transactions costs to establish positions. Cash withdrawals pose the same free-rider problem as departing monies fail to bear the burden of trading costs required to raise the cash necessary to compensate departing investors.

A more significant problem arises when cash outflows disrupt a manager's investment strategy. During the market panic in late 1998, many hedge fund managers wondered whether year-end withdrawals might exceed normal levels, requiring generation of substantial cash reserves. The threat of potentially large withdrawals posed a dilemma, as managers needed to prepare to accommodate departing investor demands while asset sales at depressed prices might harm the entire portfolio. The not surprising confluence of tough market conditions and concern regarding client withdrawals caused many managers to raise cash by selling assets trading at temporarily depressed prices, impairing results for the manager and steadfast investor alike.

Fund managers solve the free-rider problem by allocating costs appropriately to entering and exiting investors. In the case of easily measured transactions costs, managers simply assess entry and exit fees, resulting in a fair allocation of costs. To meet the objective of forcing investors to bear appropriate charges, fees must be paid to the fund, not to the manager, as the charges offset costs incurred by the fund.

More complicated procedures address the issue of allocating less predictable costs, particularly charges from transactions conducted in markets exhibiting poor liquidity. A rough approximation of fairness results from segregating new investor contributions, investing the funds, and contributing the resulting assets to the general portfolio at cost. Although the package of securities purchased by the entering investor may not bear precisely the same level of transactions costs as would trades in existing portfolio securities, if the manager makes new purchases in markets similar to the existing holdings, the new entrant bears a fair burden. Upon exit, the departing investor receives a pro rata share of the general portfolio in a segregated account, incurring the associated transactions costs during the liquidation process and insulating continuing investors from any adverse impact. By causing entering and exiting investors to absorb costs related to purchases and sales, fund managers avoid unfair treatment of core investors. Most important, the process allows managers to invest assets without regard to concerns regarding extraordinary withdrawal requests, since departing investors simply receive the proceeds of their proportionate share of the fund.

Private Equity Investment Vehicles

Private equity managers best serve investor interests by focusing undivided professional attention on a single investment vehicle. With only one place to conduct business, managers avoid the inevitable conflicts that arise when managing multiple funds with noncoincident goals. For example, if a buyout firm accepts responsibility for an equity pool and a mezzanine debt pool, tensions arise in pricing transactions. Better pricing on the mezzanine debt leads to worse results for the equity holders, and vice versa. Some firms attempt to deal with pricing issues by creating a formula for determining the terms of mezzanine finance. By prespecifying the relationship between the mezzanine coupon level and U.S. Treasury rates, as well as prespecifying the size of the equity kicker for the bondholders, fund managers hope to avoid the tricky issues involved in dividing expected returns between competing sets of investors.

Because dynamic market conditions constantly alter terms of trade for various investment tools, formulaic approaches almost inevitably fail to reflect the current market. If the formula determines worse-than-market terms for mezzanine investors, fund managers fail to discharge fiduciary duties to mezzanine lenders. If the formula results in a better-than-market deal, equity investors suffer. The convenience of controlling a captive mezzanine fund comes at the cost of dissonance caused by pursuit of conflicting goals, attempting to serve simultaneously the interests of lenders and owners.

In the event of financial distress, as members of the same firm attempt to wear mezzanine hats and equity hats, problems become even more painfully obvious. If equity owners seek forbearance from lenders, fund managers find themselves in a hopelessly conflicted position. The best course for bondholders frequently differs dramatically from the path preferred by equity owners, posing a nearly insolvable dilemma for even the best-intentioned fund manager. In the case of bankruptcy, the problems worsen as interests clash in the zero-sum game of allocating value to debt and equity. By creating and managing multiple funds, managers invite exposure to the crossways pull of competing interests.

While debt and equity funds provide a dramatic example of tensions arising from management of multiple funds, complementary activities create similar types of issues. Decisions regarding which fund receives a particular transaction, carefully delineated in the fund-offering documents, tend to involve unforeseen factors, creating messy allocation issues for fund managers. Perhaps even more important, fund managers face the daily problem of deciding which particular activity will receive the benefits of time and attention. Because multiple funds contain different sets of investors with different proportional interests, in choosing which prospects to pursue the fund manager decides which set of investors to serve.

Fund manager investment outside investment pools deserves careful scrutiny. Investment principals must avoid doing private deals for their own account, even if the transactions seem too small, too funky, or otherwise inappropriate for the institutional fund. Investors deserve the complete dedication of fund manager investment efforts in exchange for providing handsome levels of compensation for investment principals. Structuring a vehicle to focus all professional energies on the management of a single investment pool forms an important starting point in creating a sensible deal structure.

KKR's Deal Structure Flaws. Poorly structured private investment deals often produce dramatically misaligned interests. The well-known buyout firm Kohlberg Kravis & Roberts (KKR) negotiated partnership terms in its 1993 fund that enrich the principals regardless of the results for the limited partners. Like most other managers of private equity funds, KKR received a carried interest of 20 percent of the partnership's profits. Unlike most other funds, KKR did not aggregate investments when calculating the profits interest. That is, KKR collected 20 percent of the profits on successful deals, with no offset for losses incurred in failed transactions, creating an incentive to "roll the dice." KKR owns a share of the profits of big wins but suffers none of the pain of big losses. In essence, deal structure encouraged the firm to take enormous risk, creating option-like payoffs for the general partners through use of extreme financial or operating leverage.

KKR's agreement with the limited partners called for a management fee of 1.5 percent of assets, typical of leveraged buyout partnerships. Such fees, designed to cover the cost of running a buyout fund's business, became a profit center for KKR because of the enormous multibillion-dollar size of funds under supervision. Not satisfied with excessive management fees, KKR collected deal fees for consummat-

ing transactions, monitoring fees for managing positions, and investment banking fees for subsequent capital market transactions. The
combination of overly generous management fees, deal fees, monitoring fees, and investment banking fees drives a wedge between the interests of the general partners (more is better) and the limited partners
(less is more). Contrast this with the terms of Warren Buffett's original
partnership, in which he charged no management fee, believing that
he should profit only if his co-investors profited![20]

KKR's August 1995 purchase of Bruno's illustrates the misaligned
interests. The $1.2 billion transaction, which included an equity in-
vestment of $250 million, involved the acquisition of a chain of super-
markets headquartered in Mississippi. KKR charged an acquisition fee
of $15 million, which exceeded the general partners' investment by a
significant margin. Pro-rated management fees, charged on committed
capital, amounted to $3.75 million on an annual basis. The monitor-
ing fee consumed an additional $1 million annually. Moreover in
1997, KKR charged Bruno's investment banking fees of $800,000. In
exchange for financing the purchase and paying tens of millions of
dollars of fees, the limited partners lost their entire investment in February 1998, when Bruno's declared bankruptcy, filing for Chapter 11.

Properly structured deals cause general partners and limited partners to share in both profits and losses. If a managing agent shares
only in profits, incentives to take excessive risk abound. Management
fee income ought to be sufficient to cover overhead, forcing dealmak-
ers to perform before receiving extraordinary profits. Fees above the
basic overhead level represent a completely undeserved transfer from
limited partners to general partners. The combination of high levels of
fee income and option-like payoff structure allowed KKR to profit unreasonably on the Bruno's deal, while the firm's investors wrote off
substantial sums invested in the transaction.

Some aspects of the unusually egregious fee structure employed
by KKR disappeared in 1996, when the firm raised its most recent,
staggeringly large $5.7 billion fund. Pressured by substantial institu-
tional investors, the buyout firm agreed to aggregate the results of all
deals in the fund, offsetting deficits from losers before taking profits
on winners. While KKR's investors expect to benefit from the pooling
of transaction results, the firm continues to benefit from extraordinary
levels of fee income, ensuring general partner success regardless of
limited partner investment results.

In spite of KKR's removal of the deal-by-deal incentive compensation clause, investors generally exercise little influence over deal terms, as investment managers hew to an industry standard scale that provides higher levels of income at lower risk than would a fair compensation structure. Consider an environment where managers receive base fees to cover reasonable overhead and earn a portion of excess returns to provide incentive. Since a majority of market participants fail to beat a fair risk-adjusted benchmark, most fund managers would face a substantial decline in income under a fair deal structure.

Because profits interests begin to accrue after return of capital, private managers "earn" incentive compensation after investors receive a zero rate of return. If private manager compensation depended on generating returns in excess of marketable investment opportunities, most would fail to receive a profits interest as results for the majority of private funds fall short of traditional equity alternatives. If private managers received a profits interest in gains above a risk-adjusted benchmark, based on historical results the overwhelming portion of managers would fail to earn incentive compensation. Because the investment management industry receives compensation far in excess of levels justified by the degree of value created, investors encounter enormous resistance to reasonable deal structures.

Unfortunately, when altering the terms of the trade, investors face the challenge of making industry-wide changes, since manager-by-manager change introduces the potential for instability. If a single private equity manager promoted a fair deal structure, compensation for that firm's principals would fall far short of industry standards. Personnel at the firm could cross the street and work for a private fund operating under the old profit-sharing regime, thereby increasing personal income dramatically. The innovative private fund, offering a fair deal, retains only those principals without other alternatives.

Negotiating Change

While long-established practices limit the ability of investors to negotiate fair deal terms, the real estate industry in the early 1990s presented an opportunity for radical restructuring. After recklessly throwing staggering amounts of capital into real estate in the 1980s, institutions withdrew almost completely from the market after the turn-of-the-decade collapse in prices. Those few investors interested in committing funds to exploit opportunities created by the debacle faced a host of unattractive investment management alternatives.

Large fee-driven advisers dominated institutional real estate activity in the 1980s. Firms such as AEW, Copley, Heitman, JMB, LaSalle, RREEF, and TCW amassed billions of dollars in assets, driven by the steady stream of acquisition fees, management fees, and disposition fees. Not surprisingly, the real estate advisory community adopted a laser-like focus on initiating, maintaining, and enhancing flows of fee income, often neglecting even to consider the notion of generating investment returns for clients.

JMB's Fee Bonanza. Headquartered in Chicago and named for Robert Judelson, Judd Malkin, and Neil Bluhm, JMB typified the fee orientation of the 1980s advisory crowd. Not content to collect flows of income based on the fair value of client assets, the firm went to extraordinary lengths to collect its fees even as portfolio assets withered in the 1990s real estate collapse.

Exhibiting nearly unbelievable greed, JMB retained underwater positions simply to collect fees from clients. In July 1986, the firm acquired Argyle Village Square, a retail property in Jacksonville, Florida, for $22 million as part of a portfolio of properties held in a commingled fund, Endowment and Foundation Realty–JMB II. Encumbered by a mortgage of $12.4 million, the property generated fees for JMB of 1.25 percent on the gross value of the asset, equivalent to nearly 2.3 percent on the original equity investment.

By 1992, Argyle Village Square had declined in value to the extent that the property's mortgage exceeded its market price. The anchor tenant, the discount department store Zayre's, vacated its space, dramatically impairing the property's future prospects. Instead of turning the shopping center over to the lender, JMB held the asset on its books at zero equity value, continuing to collect fees from investors based on the gross value of the property. With a cash return of 1.1 percent (after debt service and before fees), Argyle Village Square's fee of 1.25 percent exceeded the property's income. To add insult to injury, JMB used investor cash flow from other assets to make up the difference, ensuring the continued flow of fees to the firm. In spite of repeated requests from investors to dispose of Argyle Village and stop the diversion of portfolio cash flow to pay fees, JMB retained the shopping center and piggily fed at the trough of investor assets.

In the "largest real estate acquisition ever," JMB's 1987 purchase of Cadillac Fairview, a collection of Canadian retailing properties, generated a fee bonanza for the firm on a stupendous scale.[21] Continuing its practice of assessing fees on the gross value of transactions, JMB's initial fee amounted to 1 percent of the C$6.8 billion deal, representing a load of 3.4 percent on original equity contributions of approximately C$2.0 billion. JMB included in the gross transaction value a portfolio of assets worth approximately C$560 million already under contract for sale, causing the firm to "earn" C$5.6 million for acquiring and immediately selling assets with absolutely no potential to benefit investors.

JMB's "feeing" frenzy continued with annual asset management fees of 0.5 percent per year on gross fair market value (equivalent to 1.7 percent of initial equity), participation fees of 1.75 percent per year on cash flow and capital proceeds, and disposition fees of 1.0 percent on gross proceeds (with a parenthetical reminder in the offering memorandum that gross proceeds "include indebtedness," in case the investor forgot).

In addition to initial fees, annual fees, participation fees, and disposition fees, JMB retained the right to provide property management, leasing, insurance brokerage, and other services with compensation negotiated on an "arms-length" basis. Not satisfied with the staggering array of fee-generating opportunities, JMB contracted to receive incentive fees of 15 percent of profits after providing a 9 percent simple annual return to investors.

Unfortunately for JMB and its co-investors in Cadillac Fairview, in the tough environment of the early 1990s, the overpriced, overleveraged buyout suffered. Notwithstanding an additional 1992 equity contribution of C$700 million, by 1994 interests representing the C$2.7 billion of equity contributed by investors traded at twenty cents to twenty-five cents on the dollar. As pension investors from California, Massachusetts, Illinois, and Iowa watched the relentless decline in asset value, JMB continued to collect its management fees.

Responding to investor outrage over the real estate adviser's insulation from the failure of the Canadian megadeal, JMB voluntarily reduced its annual fee from $30 million to $25 million, while noting that the fee compensated the firm for advising Cadillac Fairview, not the investors! Judd Malkin highlighted the lack of coincidence of interest with his investors, observing that "if I cut my fees by one-half, it still doesn't change their return."[22]

Succumbing to the inevitable consequence of too much debt and too little cash flow, Cadillac Fairview filed for protection from creditors in December 1994 in Canadian bankruptcy court. In spite of the failure of the company and massive losses by its investors, JMB aggressively sought to retain the gravy train, suing Cadillac Fairview for C$225 million, of which C$180 million represented the future stream of fees for advising the company on its Canadian properties. JMB settled the fee claim for $22.5 million in 1995.

While JMB may represent the worst of the fee-driven excesses, in the 1980s all major real estate advisers focused on collecting fees, not generating investment returns. Institutions hoping to exploit real estate opportunities in the early 1990s faced a collection of discredited advisers operating with fundamentally flawed deal structures. Fortunately, an almost total withdrawal of capital from the real estate market provided great negotiating leverage to investors willing to commit funds to the cash-starved asset class.

• • •

The capital drought of the early 1990s placed investors and real estate fund managers on equal footing, allowing negotiation of fair deal terms. Providers of funds negotiated management fees sufficient to cover overhead but insufficient to create a profit center. Investors obtained a hard hurdle, forcing managers to provide a fair return before earning a profits interest. In cases where real estate managers enjoyed a substantial net worth, general partner commitments to funds amounted to tens of millions of dollars, often exceeding the contributions made by many of the limited partners. When managers exhibited more modest means, recourse loans from the partnership provided funds for the managers' co-investment.

The dearth of capital in the early 1990s created an unusual opportunity for investors to alter the compensation arrangements for real estate investing. Moving from the dysfunctional fee-driven agency structure of the 1980s to a principal orientation in the 1990s promoted the interests of investors and fund managers alike.

While the return of capital to real estate investing in the late 1990s eroded some of the deal structure gains, many managers chose to continue employing principal-oriented structures even when presented with rich fee-driven opportunities. Aside from purely economic considerations, the loyalty engendered by previous successful pursuit of mutually rewarding investment activities contributed materially to the decision to continue working with the existing structure. The dislocations in the real estate markets contributed to long-lasting changes in institutional deal terms.

Currently, investors find terms of trade in the private equity arena moving away from fairness. Fees on multibillion dollar buyout funds generate tens of millions of dollars per annum, far in excess of amounts necessary to fund reasonable levels of partnership operating expenses. Buyout fund profits interests take 20 percent of returns created by the bull market's gale force wind, not to mention 20 percent of returns attributable to use of highly leveraged capital structures. After adjusting for fees, profits interests, and the risk to which buyout managers expose investor assets, no value added remains for the overwhelming number of buyout fund participants.

Investors in today's venture capital partnerships fare little better. In the past, the venture community fell into a neat three-tier structure, with Kleiner Perkins atop the hierarchy earning a 30 percent profits interest, a handful of superb firms receiving a 25 percent carry, and the rest of the industry taking home 20 percent of gains. The late 1990s Internet mania turned many solid venture capitalists into bull market geniuses, causing them to demand an increase in compensation from 20 percent of profits to 25 percent or even 30 percent. While a few firms making the move deserve inclusion in the elite ranks of the industry, most firms simply say, "It's the market," or, "We need to do it for competitive reasons." Such top-of-the-market increases in compensation will likely persist through the next period of weak venture returns, creating a pattern of one-way ratcheting of deal terms against investor interests.

CONCLUSION

Market efficiency creates substantial hurdles for investors pursuing active management strategies, causing most to fail even to match results of market benchmarks. Although trying to beat the market proves tough and costly, fiduciaries frequently accept active manager claims at face value, attribute investment success to skill (not luck), and fail to adjust results for risk. In the face of active management obstacles, market players respond to the thrills and excitement generated by a game with scores tallied in the millions, and even billions, explaining the nearly universal pursuit of active strategies by institutional investors.

Thoughtful investors approach active management opportunities with great skepticism, starting with the presumption that managers exhibit no skill. Historical performance numbers deserve careful scrutiny, mindful of the part that good fortune plays in successful track records. Odds of winning the active management game increase when committing funds only to managers possessing an edge likely to produce superior performance in extremely competitive markets.

Selecting the right people to manage assets poses the single biggest challenge to fiduciaries, since the integrity, intelligence, and energy with which the outside adviser approaches investing influences portfolio outcomes in the most fundamental manner. The actions of external managers contribute not only to investment performance, but also to the reputation and public perception of the institution itself, forcing fiduciaries to enforce extremely high standards in manager selection.

Appropriate organizational structure plays a part in successful execution of investment programs, by ensuring sufficient alignment of interests between the institutional fund and the external adviser. Independent investment advisers with carefully structured economic incentives stand the greatest chance of producing high risk-adjusted returns, placing institutional goals ahead of personal agendas. While thoughtful deal terms and sensible organizational attributes contribute to the likelihood of success, even the most carefully constructed arrangements fail when implemented by the wrong people.

Entrepreneurial firms provide the greatest likelihood of dealing successfully with ever changing market dynamics, ultimately increasing the chances of delivering superior investment returns. Unfortunately, successful firms contain the seeds of their own destruction, as size and time sap the energy essential to the investment process. Fiduciaries must stand ready to cull the old and tired, while identifying the new and energetic.

In all aspects of investment management, deal structure plays a critical role in shaping the behavior of investment managers and determining the fairness of investment gain and loss allocations. By encouraging asset managers to behave as principals, appropriate deal terms cause investors to seek investment gains, deemphasizing return-reducing streams of fee income.

Typical compensation arrangements cause asset manager income to depend on factors beyond the investment adviser's control. As bull market gains inflate marketable security portfolios and increase private fund assets, managers benefit through high management fees and profits interests. Bear market losses impose costs unrelated to investment manager activity. In the case of both marketable and private deal structures, investment advisers' compensation waxes and wanes with the market's fortunes, resulting in earnings streams not directly tied to the level of value created.

By operating under asset-based compensation arrangements that fail to consider value-added measures, investment managers lose focus on return generation, emphasizing instead a staying-in-business strategy designed to protect streams of fee income. Partly as a consequence of poor deal structure, standard compensation arrangements allocate investment gains and losses unfairly, frequently enriching the investment manager while generating substandard risk-adjusted returns to providers of funds.

Appropriate deal terms generally serve to encourage fund managers to behave as principals, causing them to pursue gains while avoiding losses. Structural points that play an important role in aligning investment manager and investor interests include the character of the investment vehicle, level of fees, nature of incentive compensation, and size of manager co-investment. By establishing investment arrangements that motivate managers to pursue high levels of risk-adjusted portfolio gains, investors operate in a framework conducive to generating satisfactory investment results.

Investors hoping to beat the odds by playing the game of active management face daunting obstacles ranging from the efficiency in pricing of most marketable securities to the burden of extraordinary levels of fees in most alternative asset investment vehicles. Only by identifying extremely high-quality people operating in an appropriately structured organization do active investors create an opportunity to add value to the investment process. Painstaking identification, careful structuring, and patient implementation of investment management relationships provide essential underpinnings to an active management program.

10
Performance Assessment

Effective management of relationships between fiduciaries and investment advisers provides opportunity to add substantial incremental value to the portfolio. Strong relationships, based on mutual trust and understanding, allow money managers and clients to behave in an informed contrarian manner. In the absence of well-grounded relationships, clients run the risk of making ill-timed cash flow decisions, damaging the portfolio by buying high and selling low.

Successful portfolio management depends on client comprehension of the investment adviser's decision-making process. Without intimate knowledge of a firm's investment principles, clients simply react to performance, a no-win proposition. If fiduciaries chase performance, funding a manager on a hot streak, disappointment results when the wind at the manager's back inevitably dissipates. When contrarian instincts cause fiduciaries to back a poorly performing manager, mediocre returns follow if poor performance persists because the manager lacks skill. Distinguishing between good fortune and expertise demands thorough understanding of the manager's approach to investing.

Informed relationship management requires ongoing performance evaluation, incorporating qualitative and quantitative factors important to successful investing. Monitoring the quality and commitment of a firm's principals plays a central role in assessing the ability of an organization to achieve excellence. Other significant issues include fidelity to investment principles and maintenance of an appropriate organizational structure. Regular face-to-face meetings between fund managers and external advisers constitute the most important tool for performance evaluation.

Portfolio return data provide essential hard input into the performance assessment process. By comparing manager returns to market benchmarks and appropriately constructed universes of active management returns, investors measure the past successes and failures of an investment program. Beyond the glare of the spotlight on return numbers lie the less-well-understood risks associated with the portfolios that generated the returns.

Quantitative measures dominate performance evaluation exercises, reducing the complex web of portfolio construction decisions to a precise presentation of return data. The stark clarity of a set of historical performance numbers causes many investors to overemphasize hard quantitative tools at the expense of fundamentally important soft factors. Striking an appropriate balance between quantitative and qualitative factors poses a challenge for fund fiduciaries.

Many fiduciaries attempt to expand the fund's breadth of expertise by employing external experts to assist in portfolio decisions. When used appropriately, outside consultants and "fund of funds" managers add significant value to the investment process. Under other circumstances, intermediaries interfere with portfolio management, imposing a dysfunctional filter between the investment manager and the ultimate client.

Ultimately sensible fiduciaries impose their limitations on a portfolio. By limiting commitments to transparent, well-understood strategies, the universe of appropriate managers for a fund coincides with the scope of that institution's expertise. While investors need not be able to replicate an external adviser's investment management process, clients must obtain a complete understanding of portfolio strategies. Without a firm grasp of the process, the client's role is reduced to passive monitoring of performance, with the dangers inherent in placing investment results foremost in manager evaluation.

PERFORMANCE EVALUATION

Assessing the viability of manager relationships requires continuous monitoring, employing a combination of qualitative and quantitative factors. Strong investment performance alone fails to justify maintaining a manager relationship. If the sense of partnership diminishes because of changes in people, philosophy, or structure, then fiduciaries must reevaluate the relationship. Similarly, weak performance fails to be sufficient cause for considering fundamentally changing an investment management contract. If an appropriately structured firm pursues an intelligent approach to markets, implemented by strong people, then elements critical to investment success remain in place. While understanding the causes of poor performance provides important insights for investment oversight, bad results in isolation present no fundamental threat to investment relationships.

Qualitative Factors

As in hiring decisions, qualitative considerations dominate performance evaluations. If investment decisions simply involved retaining managers with strong performance and firing managers with weak performance, life would be simple. Because the numbers provide only part of the story, qualitative factors play a central role.

Just as the quality of people drives manager-hiring decisions, monitoring the people involved in the investment process constitutes the core of relationship management. Short-run issues concern the enthusiasm, motivation, and work ethic of investment advisers. Responsible fiduciaries monitor the degree of an adviser's engagement, looking for warning signs of diminished interest or commitment.

In the long run, generational transition issues loom large. While thoughtful planning by investment management organizations increases the likelihood of successful transfer of responsibility from one generation to another, the process poses significant challenges, particularly for smaller organizations. The idiosyncratic nature of entrepreneurial firms causes people to be far less interchangeable than would be the case at larger bureaucratic money managers. People dominate process at smaller firms, causing significant uncertainty regarding the outcome of the old guard's retirement. Transferring responsibility to younger colleagues inevitably alters the nature of the firm as the new decision makers express their individual approach to markets. In short, the more attractive the investment manager, the greater the challenge posed in passing the baton.

The venture capital community exhibits an unusual number of entrepreneurial firms that succeed in spanning generations. By transferring responsibility seamlessly, early market participants Sutter Hill (founded in 1962), Greylock (1965), Mayfield (1969), Venrock (1969),

Sequoia (1972), and Kleiner Perkins (1972) each created and sustained leading positions in the venture capital community. As a result of smooth general partner transitions and investment success, a number of well-established venture firms have created franchise value, favorably positioning the premier partnerships relative to the rest of the venture community. Outside the private equity world, few examples exist of small entrepreneurial investment firms retaining their character through several generations of control. Some grow large, abandoning investment goals to focus on asset gathering. Others, dependent on one or two individuals, fade away with diminished interest from those who drove the investment process. Perhaps dependence on the idiosyncratic brilliance of a successful investor decreases the likelihood of transmission of essential skills to younger associates. In any event, assessing the energy, commitment, and enthusiasm of the individuals responsible for managing assets takes priority in monitoring relationships.

Changes in investment approach raise yellow and red flags for fiduciaries. Increases in assets under management provide a common reason to alter investment methods. As assets increase, small-capitalization managers purchase more and larger securities, reducing the likelihood of producing superior returns. Some hedge funds, beginning as focused stock pickers, evolve into shops making macro bets, as increases in size dictate playing in broad, deep, and liquid markets.

Managers of all stripes face the temptation to become closet indexers. Running a market-like portfolio guarantees market-like results, reducing the likelihood of being fired for poor performance. When value managers report positions in Coca-Cola or Microsoft, fiduciaries must pose skeptical questions.

Disappointing results sometimes lead managers to alter approaches to portfolio management. Investment advisers may take greater risk, hoping to hit the long ball to recoup earlier losses. At the extreme, pursuit of risk to remedy past losses poses grave danger to portfolios, exposing assets to potentially significant losses as managers speculate in a desperate attempt to recover lost ground.

The Feshbach Brothers

Poor results occasionally cause investors to undergo radical change, leading to bizarre transformations. The Feshbach brothers, Matt, Joe, and Kurt, developed a high profile in the 1980s based on impressive investment returns and controversial short selling techniques. Using L. Ron Hubbard's theory of dianetics as an integral part of their investment strategy, the Feshbach brothers focused on identifying overvalued companies headed for a tumble. Using traditional securities analysis and private detectives to uncover fraudulent business practices, the Feshbachs were widely rumored to "talk down" stocks in their portfolio. In at least one instance by using "naked shorting" to establish illegal short positions when they were unable to access securities through legitimate channels, the brothers surrounded themselves with controversy.[1] Surprisingly, many investors, including the Frank Russell Trust Company, ignored the controversy, chased the Feshbachs' strong performance numbers, and committed funds to the brothers' pool, which peaked at nearly $1 billion in 1990.

In the early 1990s the Feshbach wizardry disappeared, as the strategy of shorting securities in a bull market produced the nearly inevitable disastrous results. After a spell of horrendous performance, losing 55 percent of assets in 1991 alone, the Feshbach brothers reinvented themselves.

In 1993, according to short seller David Rocker, the Feshbachs "publicly disavowed their short selling activities . . . to focus on a strategy of small capitalization growth stocks."[2] The change in strategy, by the "world's most notorious short sellers," akin to switching sides in the middle of a battle, attracted more interest in the press than with investors. By 1998, the firm managed $50 million, primarily in traditional long strategies, representing less than 5 percent of peak assets under management.

Organizational Change

Not all changes in approach bode ill for portfolio managers. Sensible managers adapt, altering strategy to exploit opportunities within the adviser's area of competence. Many absolute return managers began their businesses by focusing exclusively on merger arbitrage transactions. Recognizing the complementary analytical and legal skills required to assess reorganizations and bankruptcies, some firms started pursuing investments in the realm of distressed securities. By adding a fundamentally related activity, managers create a powerful tool for portfolio improvement. When merger and acquisition activity proceeds apace, portfolios hold significant positions in risk arbitrage. In less robust economic times, when workouts and defaults litter the investment landscape, firms increase exposure to distressed investments. In contrast to investors expert in only one discipline, managers with more than one arrow in the quiver create the potential to mitigate the cyclicality inherent in market activity. The manager with a narrowly focused skill set rides the investment roller coaster, rising when opportunity abounds and plunging when deals dry up.

Gradual, incremental changes in investment approach provide opportunity to expand the scope of activity without abandoning the base on which the firm's success rests. Natural, evolutionary improvement creates potential for enhancing portfolio results, benefiting external adviser and client alike. Radical change poses extreme danger to client assets, demanding an immediate, dramatic response by fiduciaries.

Change in organizational structure, particularly the sale of a firm, requires careful evaluation. In a small, independent partnership, economic fortunes of the principals correspond directly to the success of the firm. The rewards associated with strong performance, and the penalties related to poor results, accrue to the decision makers.

When an investment management organization sells out, incentives change radically. Concern regarding superior investment performance may be subordinated to behavior focused on retaining assets by moderating investment bets, increasing net client cash flow by enhancing marketing activities, and diversifying the income stream by expanding product offerings. On top of concerns regarding changes in corporate strategy, the degree of commitment of investment professionals frequently wanes.

Senior partners of successful independent investment managers face a dilemma. On the positive side of the ledger, equity owners receive a handsome payday by selling the firm, walking away from the transaction with a small fortune. On the negative side, pursuing a sale sows the seeds of the firm's denouement. Selling shareholders retire to focus on managing personal assets. The most talented young people leave to pursue opportunities to create wealth, just as their now retired mentors did. Those who remain tend to be less adept investors with fewer alternatives. No advantage accrues to clients from a sale.

By not selling the firm, senior partners fail to maximize the value of their stake. In what amounts to a partial act of charity, younger principals receive equity interests for less than true economic value, creating the potential for the firm to continue as an independent entity. No guarantee of longevity exists, however, as the new owners now face the same dilemma their erstwhile senior partners did.

If sales of entire firms raise red flags, partial sales raise yellow flags. Taking external equity causes fiduciaries to wonder about the continuing commitment of senior principals to the business. Minority external ownership poses the same issues as a total sale, moderated only in degree.

Qualitative assessments of people, strategy, and structure lie at the core of relationship management. Sensible fiduciaries regularly revisit the premises on which original hiring decisions rest, reviewing initial assumptions and subsequent behavior. Changes in an investment advisory firm's circumstances require particularly careful evaluation, causing prudent clients to underwrite once again the adviser's suitability.

Qualitative Tools

Regular face-to-face meetings between investment advisers and clients constitute the most important tool for relationship management. Meetings allow challenges to existing processes and exploration of new ideas. Frank discussion of adviser and client concerns contributes to early resolution of problems. Letters and telephone conversations provide important input, but nothing duplicates the benefits of sitting down with an investment manager for an in-depth review of portfolio activities.

Client responsibilities include being well-informed and engaging without being intrusive. Respecting the boundary between adviser and client requires avoiding behavior that makes investment decisions difficult. Pushing advisers to take positions, or discouraging specific investments crosses the line. Challenging a manager's thought process or encouraging a contrarian play contributes to successful relationships.

Investment adviser responsibilities include being open and honest regarding portfolio activity. Complete transparency in portfolio matters provides an essential foundation for client understanding of the investment process. Occasionally investment managers refuse to identify positions, expressing concerns regarding public disclosure on ability to trade or manage a position. If a manager refuses to trust a client (or potential client) with portfolio information, the client should not entrust the manager with a portfolio. Advisers benefit from better-informed clients, who tend to remain faithful during stretches of poor performance and facilitate sometimes difficult contrarian tactics.

Openness regarding business issues allows adviser and client to understand the present and anticipate change. Many business issues help to shape the character of a money management firm. Compensation practices influence motivation and retention of investment professionals. Succession planning affects the character of an investment firm in fundamental ways. Partial or full sales of investment firms alter incentives and increase instability. Firms that engage clients in discussion regarding sensitive business issues face stronger prospects of successfully overcoming the difficulties inherent in running an investment management operation.

Continuing due diligence checks on investment advisers contribute to effective relationship management. Fiduciaries should take advantage of opportunities to discuss with third parties the business approach and ethical standards of existing managers, always attempting to gain insight into adviser characteristics. While less formal than the round of reference checks undertaken before hiring a manager, ongoing due diligence provides important insight into external adviser activities.

Regular interaction between client and adviser constitutes the most important tool for relationship management, providing a stream of input for qualitative assessment of manager activity. Constant reevaluation of the investment rationale contributes to effective oversight of external money managers, causing fiduciaries to maintain healthy skepticism regarding active management activities.

Quantitative Factors

Beating the market, as described by a fair benchmark, constitutes the foremost objective of an investment manager. Mature, liquid marketplaces have a host of well-structured benchmarks from which to choose. For example, U.S. equity markets boast a variety of broad-based indexes, including the S&P 500, the Russell 3000, and the Wilshire 5000. The benchmark represents the passive alternative, a portfolio that faithfully replicates asset class performance. Active managers attempt to beat the benchmark, net of fees, in an effort to add value to the portfolio.

In contrast to marketable securities, illiquid assets tend to have less well-defined performance measurement benchmarks. Private investments come from a wide variety of sources, ranging from divisions of publicly traded companies to family-owned energy assets to entities in bankruptcy. Almost by definition, inefficiently priced assets reside in markets without benchmarks since an investible benchmark constitutes a characteristic of well-established, liquid markets.

Investors pursuing private opportunities jerry-rig benchmarks, generally using a derivative of a marketable securities metric, either explicitly as in the S&P 500 plus 500 basis points, or implicitly as in a real return of 12 percent (based, perhaps, on an expectation of 7 percent real returns for equities plus a 500-basis-point premium).

Each manager requires a clearly articulated benchmark, defining the investor's objective. A fair benchmark encompasses all investment opportunities from which an active manager chooses. The more liquid markets provide the best-defined benchmarks, leading to the irony of precise measurement in the markets least likely to produce something worth measuring. Managers focusing on specific niches and investors pursuing activities in less efficient markets present benchmarking challenges. Ultimately the index against which fiduciaries assess performance constitutes the manager's most important quantitative measure.

Benchmark Specialization

In recent years, investment consultants created impressive numbers of specialized benchmarks, providing apparently precise tools to measure performance of a broad range of strategies and substrategies. Ranging from a reasonably standard matrix of style and capitalization indexes, to a somewhat motley collection of esoteric measures, investors obtained tools to assess even the most unusual approach to portfolio management.*

Specialized benchmarks occasionally provide valuable insight that

---

*A few of the more esoteric indexes include the Handelsbanken All-Nordic Combined Bond Index, an index tracking Scandinavian bonds, the Bloomberg Football Index, an index of companies that own or operate English and Scottish football clubs, and the Themis FTSE Fledgling Index, a U.K. micro-capitalization index.

is unavailable from broader measures of market activity. Consider the 1993 results for value managers focusing on large-capitalization stocks. Median returns of 14.6 percent bested the S&P 500 return by a full 4.5 percent, on the surface a more-than-satisfactory result. When compared to a value benchmark, however, the managers' results fall short of the passive alternative by 4.8 percent, a far less impressive performance. In recent years, value managers generally failed to exceed returns of a value benchmark. For the five years ending December 31, 1997 the value benchmark placed in the second decile of value manager results, an extraordinary showing for a passive portfolio.[3]

Why did the value index pose such a tough challenge for managers? The value index, created by a mechanistic screen to select low price-to-book and low price-to-earnings ratio stocks, includes a number of unattractive, washed-out companies. Because active managers often avoid obviously risky, distressed companies, the resulting portfolio contains dampened value characteristics. When value stocks perform well, active managers frequently fail to match passive results, as markets reward the riskier profile of the mechanistically chosen portfolio. Only in times of severe market stress do outcomes favor the higher-quality actively managed value portfolios.

Fiduciaries must compare manager results to appropriate benchmarks. Examining value manager returns relative to the S&P 500 tells only part of the story. Adding a specialized passive benchmark provides a richer comparison, allowing more direct evaluation of style-specific portfolios. When using specialized benchmarks, fair comparisons require understanding possible differences in risk profile between the active portfolio and the benchmark.

Peer Comparisons

Peer comparisons provide another quantitative metric for performance assessment. While certain asset classes present less-than-satisfactory passive benchmarks, nearly every investment category contains a group of managers among which results can be compared.

Survivorship bias plays an important role in peer comparisons, particularly in less efficient asset classes. Because benchmarks provide so little short-term guidance for private assets and absolute return strategies, peer comparisons tend to take on more significance.

Unfortunately, survivorship bias dramatically influences the composition and character of inefficient asset class peer groups.

Consider long/short investing, an absolute return strategy in which investors construct portfolios without market exposure by holding long and short positions of roughly equivalent value. Historical data support the notion that such hedged positions provide 20 percent annual returns with little correlation to traditional marketable securities. Yet 20 percent per annum returns imply a staggering increment of added value. If the cost of funds approximates 5 percent, then superior security selection provides 15 percent excess returns. In the domestic equity world, where beating the benchmark by 2 percent on a consistent basis constitutes heroism, double-digit value added defies imagination.

What explains the impressive historical record? Part of the answer lies in the nature of the peer group. Only those long/short managers with sufficient skill and luck to generate extraordinary returns rose high enough to register on investors' radar screens. The strong historic success embodied in less efficient market peer groups leads to unfair comparisons and unrealistic expectations.

In the case of long/short equity managers, more realistic investors expect low double-digit returns. A cost of funds of 5 percent and excess returns of 3 percent for both long and short positions result in an 11 percent return with no market risk. Examining the fundamental nature of the investment activity leads to realistic goals, avoiding some of the unreasonably high expectations incorporated in manager groups suffering from survivorship bias.

Risk Adjustment

Adjusting portfolio returns for risk plays at best a supporting role in performance evaluation. Managers tend to avoid discussing risk, unless explaining poor relative performance, as in "We did worse than the market, but we did it with less risk." Perhaps the poor picture of risk provided by quantitative tools justifies the low level of discussion.

Standard deviation of returns, the measure of dispersion most commonly used to assess risk, fails to capture much that concerns fiduciaries. Simply understanding the historical volatility of returns provides little useful information regarding the efficacy of a particular investment strategy. Did returns more than justify the level of risk assumed, or did results fail to compensate for the degree of volatility experienced? In spite of its limitations, historical volatility constitutes the most widely employed quantitative measure of risk.

Nobel laureate William Sharpe developed an analytical tool to assess the relationship between risk and return. By evaluating returns above (or below) the risk-free rate, the Sharpe ratio focuses on the excess returns that investors hope to generate by accepting risk. Dividing the excess return by the standard deviation of returns produces a ratio describing the productivity of risk, quantifying the excess return generated per unit of risk incurred. Sharpe's ratio suffers from the same obvious shortcomings as do other measures of historical volatility.

American Government Securities Fund. Consider the results of the Piper Jaffrey American Government Securities Fund (AGF), a mortgage bond investment vehicle, for the five years ending December 31, 1993. As shown in Table 10.1, AGF returned 19.3 percent per annum, representing a 13.7 percent annual premium over treasury bills. Since volatility of 8.8 percent accompanied the excess return, AGF delivered a Sharpe ratio of 1.6 units of return for each unit of risk assumed.

From an investment perspective, AGF's 19.3 percent return appears at first glance to overshadow the 11.2 pecent return of the Salomon Brothers Mortgage Index. However, because the mortgage index produced excess returns of 5.5 percent with substantially lower volatility than AGF, the bond fund and the index sport nearly identical Sharpe ratios for the period. In other words, AGF's higher returns appear to stem from accepting higher risk, not from generating superior risk-adjusted returns.

Although the Sharpe ratio illuminates historical relationships between risk and return, backward-looking quantitative measures fail to capture fundamental risk factors other than those in the numbers. When the future differs in material ways from the past, investment choices based on quantitative analysis frequently disappoint investors.

The 1994 bond market debacle crushed the Piper Jaffrey mortgage fund, causing losses of nearly 29 percent with a risk level of nearly 15 percent. The Salomon Brothers Mortgage Index fared substantially better, as returns of −1.4 percent came with a risk level of 4.0 percent. AGF's Sharpe ratio of −2.2 for 1994 indicates risk-adjusted performance dramatically inferior to the index with its ratio of −1.4.

**Table 10.1 Unsettled 1994 Mortgage Market Conditions
Alter Bond Fund Characteristics**
Mortgage-Backed Security Returns, 1989–1995

		Return	Excess Return	Risk	Sharpe Ratio
Five years ending December 31, 1993	AGF	19.3%	13.7%	8.8%	1.6
	Salomon Mortgage Index	11.2	5.5	3.5	1.6
1994	AGF	-28.8	-32.7	14.9	-2.2
	Salomon Mortgage Index	-1.4	-5.3	4.0	-1.4
Five years ending December 31, 1994	AGF	8.5	3.7	12.3	0.3
	Salomon Mortgage Index	7.8	3.0	3.5	0.9
1995	AGF	25.9	20.3	5.8	3.5
	Salomon Mortgage Index	16.8	11.1	3.2	3.5
Five years ending December 31, 1995	AGF	11.3	7.0	12.2	0.6
	Salomon Mortgage Index	8.9	4.6	3.3	1.4

Sources: Bloomberg and Yale Investments Office.

Quantitative characteristics of AGF's mortgage strategy change dramatically as the trailing five-year assessment period moves forward to include 1994. By including 1994's poor performance and volatility, returns drop from 19.3 percent for the five years ending December 31, 1993, to 8.5 percent for the five years ending December 31, 1994, even as volatility increases from 8.8 percent to 12.3 percent. Suddenly the double-digit return opportunity with single-digit risk becomes a single-digit return strategy with double-digit risk.

The Sharpe ratio story reads even worse. Annualized returns for AGF of 8.5 percent over the five-year period ending December 31, 1994, generate excess returns of 3.7 percent at a risk level of 12.3 percent. The resulting Sharpe ratio of 0.3 compares unfavorably to the ratio of 1.6 for the five years ending December 31, 1993. Although the investment strategy remained firmly in place, market conditions transformed what appeared to be a reasonably efficient high-risk strategy into a low-return, high-risk technique.

In contrast, the five-year mortgage index return of 7.8 percent for the period ending December 31, 1994, along with excess returns of 3.0 percent and risk of 3.5 percent provides a superior set of characteristics. Although the risk-adjusted attributes of the mortgage index deteriorate with the addition of 1994's data, the index's Sharpe ratio of 0.9 indicates a material advantage over AGF's 0.3 level.

While quantitative risk assessment helps investors take a disciplined, analytical approach to assessing investment opportunities, the limitations of backward-looking number crunching frequently become apparent when markets produce surprises. Based on data for the five years ending December 31, 1993, Piper Jaffrey's AGF and the Salomon Mortgage Index garnered identical Sharpe ratios, indicating roughly equivalent efficacy in translating risk into excess return. Moving forward one year makes the turtle-like index appear much more attractive than the hare-like mortgage fund.

In the case of the Piper Jaffrey mortgage fund, investors focusing on historical return and risk characteristics might make poor timing decisions. In late 1993, attracted by high returns and index-like efficiency, investors saw ample reason to purchase shares of the fund. In late 1994, disappointed by terrible returns and poor relative efficiency, investors easily find justification to sell shares. Of course, in 1995, in spite of poor trailing five-year quantitative characteristics, the fund returned 25.9 percent, with a Sharpe ratio of 3.5, matching index delivery of excess return per unit of risk.

The only defense against chasing the excellent 1993 numbers and avoiding the dismal 1994 returns lies in a fundamental understanding of the nature of the investment activity producing the results. Investors making decisions based only on historical numbers focus exclusively on what has been, ignoring what will be. While looking into the future poses challenges fraught with peril, investors armed with a thorough grasp of the forces driving valuations face a higher probability of success. At the very least, investors cognizant of the nature of AGF's mortgage portfolio recognize the contribution of leverage to 1993's strong performance, and the danger of an extreme reversal in a 1994 type of environment.

•   •   •

Yale economist Robert Shiller argues that markets exhibit excess volatility.[4] That is, security prices tend to fluctuate more than necessary to respond to the fundamental factors, such as earnings and interest rates, that determine intrinsic value. In other words, "if price movements were rescaled down . . . so as to be less variable, then price would do a better job of forecasting fundamentals." Shiller's self-described "controversial claim" provides "evidence of a failure of the efficient markets model."[5] Anyone attempting to understand October 1987's market crash from a fundamental perspective sees merit in Shiller's position.

In a world with excess volatility, investors care about the direction of security price fluctuations. Price declines might provide buying opportunities, and price increases opportunities to sell. Under some circumstances, following a significant decline in price, an asset actually becomes less risky, since it can be acquired more cheaply. The common-sense conclusion of bottom-fishing investors contrasts with the statistician's conclusion that a dramatic drop in price increases observed (historical) volatility, implying a higher risk level for the asset. Of course, price volatility creates opportunity only when prices change more than necessary to reflect changes in underlying fundamentals.

Risk adjustment matters. Unfortunately, reducing risk assessment to a single statistical measure fails to capture the essence of the concept. Prudent investors employ risk measures with care, supplementing the science with careful interpretation.

Quantitative Tools

The most basic financial tools measure returns either weighted by dollars or linked across time. Dollar-weighted returns or internal rates of return (IRR) assess results considering the magnitude and timing of dollars invested. IRR calculations best measure returns for investors controlling cash flow decisions, such as private equity investors who determine when and how much to invest in particular opportunities.

Time-linked returns derive from a series of periodic returns, without considering portfolio size at any point in time. Time-linked returns best measure results for managers that do not control cash flow decisions, such as marketable securities managers who accept client decisions regarding contributions and withdrawals.

Barr Rosenberg's Value Added

The experiences of investors in Rosenberg Institutional Equity Management's (RIEM's) core equity product provide an interesting example of differences in dollar-weighted and time-weighted returns. As illustrated in Table 10.2, RIEM began corporate life with extremely strong returns on relatively small amounts of money. Following a pattern typical in the investment management industry, impressive results attracted large new accounts, with assets peaking at more than $8,100 million in 1990. As asset size created a headwind and as good fortune dissipated, poor investment performance followed, exposing large amounts of money to substandard management.

Over the firm's roller-coaster history, time-linked investment performance remained consistently positive. For the twelve years ending December 31, 1997, RIEM's core equity portfolio returned 17.3 percent per year, eking out a 30-basis-point advantage relative to the S&P 500.

Dollar-weighted returns tell a less inspiring story. IRR calculations show a return of 11.8 percent per annum. Had RIEM's cash flows been invested in the S&P 500, the resulting IRR would have been 13.1 percent per annum. Over the life of the core portfolio, RIEM's clients lost

Table 10.2 Rosenberg Fails to Deliver Value to Clients
Portfolio Returns and Value Added, 1985–1997

Date (Year End)	Core Equity Assets (millions)	Excess Return (RIEM Return—S&P 500 Return)	Value Added (millions)
1985	$ 188	6.2%	$12
1986	1,037	-0.4	-4
1987	2,037	6.6	134
1988	4,222	-0.6	-23
1989	8,020	-4.8	-386
1990	8,157	-3.7	-304
1991	6,608	-0.8	-52
1992	3,692	3.9	143
1993	3,692	1.1	42
1994	1,838	-1.0	-19
1995	2,225	0.8	17
1996	2,023	-2.9	-58
1997	1,644	1.2	20

Source: Nelson's Directory of Investment Managers, *1985–1997*.

1.3 percent annually relative to the market, translating into approximately $480 million of opportunity costs.

In evaluating marketable security performance, both time-linked and dollar-weighted returns prove helpful. Time-linked returns provide evidence regarding a manager's investment acumen. Dollar-weighted returns shed light on a client's cash flow timing decisions. When evaluating private investment performance, dollar-weighted returns provide the most appropriate measurement tool, as private investors control cash flow decisions.

Risk Measurement

Quantitative measures of risk for individual portfolios leave much to be desired. Even if in isolation a particular investment strategy appears risky, as measured by standard deviation, when combined with somewhat uncorrelated assets, the resulting diversified portfolio may produce reasonably stable results. Unfortunately, assumptions regarding correlation between various portfolios tend to be quite unreliable, providing little guidance to investors. The fiduciary faces a situation in which a difficult-to-assess variable—correlation between individual portfolios—mitigates a less useful but more easily forecast variable—individual portfolio risk.

The Sharpe ratio, a quantitative risk measure, provides interesting insights, attempting to measure the efficiency of actively managed portfolios. By measuring the excess return generated per unit of risk assumed by a manager, the Sharpe ratio indicates the benefit received (excess return) for cost incurred (volatility).

Aside from the fact that investors seek high Sharpe ratios, the number holds little intuitive appeal. To increase user friendliness, Morgan Stanley's Leah Modigliani joined with her Nobel laureate grandfather, Franco Modigliani, to create M-squared (M^2), an easier-to-interpret variant of the Sharpe ratio.

Beginning with risk levels of specific portfolios and market risk levels, M^2 creates portfolios with market-like risk by either borrowing to increase risk or lending to reduce risk. The resulting risk-adjusted portfolio returns now compete on a level playing field, providing an easily understood, fair comparison to the market and to other managers' risk-adjusted returns. While the Sharpe ratio and M^2 provide identical rank orderings of portfolios, M^2's expression of risk-adjusted results in the form of returns allows a more intuitive grasp of the conclusions.

•   •   •

Successful portfolio management combines art and science, requiring qualitative and quantitative assessment of investment strategies. Quantitative measures provide essential data for decision makers, yet fiduciaries must guard against placing too much emphasis on the easily quantified at the expense of less "scientific" qualitative factors. Successful relationship management demands placing soft factors in a place of primary importance. The numbers, while important, play a supporting role.

USE OF PERFORMANCE ASSESSMENT

Investors employ performance assessment conclusions in structuring portfolios through account sizing and firing decisions, with the choice of time frame providing a critical variable in the evaluation process.

Thoughtful application of performance conclusions creates opportunities to add substantial incremental returns, while misdirected actions easily destroy value.

The appropriate time frame for performance assessment depends on the asset class involved and the management style employed. Feedback mechanisms operate over different cycles. Money market investments provide nearly immediate feedback, as assets mature (either successfully or not) within a matter of months. The short cycle provides fiduciaries with substantial amounts of round-trip data. Unfortunately, in the highly efficient money markets, the information generates little value.

Private investing resides at the opposite end of the spectrum. Holding periods for assets span as much as a decade, forcing fiduciaries to make manager retention decisions well before meaningful feedback comes from past investment activity. The long private investing cycle causes investors to focus on factors other than near-term investment performance.

Between the money market and private equity extremes lie other asset classes. The time necessary for feedback mechanisms to operate corresponds roughly to the degree of market efficiency. The more efficient the market, the shorter the time needed to assess manager skill. Efficient markets provide fewer mispricings to exploit, and those mispricings tend to be fleeting. In degree of efficiency, following the ultraefficient money markets would be fixed income and large-capitalization domestic equities, with small-capitalization stocks and foreign equities lying further out the efficiency continuum. The time required to gather meaningful performance data ranges from one to two years for more efficiently priced securities to three or four years for less efficient markets.

Portfolio turnover influences the time necessary to evaluate a manager's strategy. High-turnover portfolios presumably reflect manager buy and sell decisions in a short period of time. Two hundred percent turnover corresponds to an average six-month holding period, allowing assessment of portfolio decisions in a reasonably short time frame. In contrast, 20 percent turnover corresponds to a five-year average holding period, leading to a much longer assessment period for patient investment strategies.

Performance evaluation ultimately determines the fiduciary's degree of confidence in an external money manager. Reassessing manager relationships places investors in an uncomfortable position, as reasonable investors engage investment advisers with a view toward establishing long-term relationships. Questioning the validity of the original hiring decision and examining the continued viability of the investment relationship causes some measure of cognitive dissonance. Fiduciaries must seek stable long-term arrangements, even while evaluating their dissolution.

The degree of confidence in particular managers influences portfolio allocations, with high-confidence managers receiving greater funding levels. Periodic reviews of manager account sizes allow portfolios to reflect opinions regarding relative manager skill levels. Obviously manager allocations incorporate factors other than confidence levels, including the appeal of the manager's particular strategy as well as the number of managers available to exploit a specific type of opportunity. Performance evaluation shapes portfolios in important ways through short-run manager allocation decisions.

Rebalancing Activity

With a clear grasp of a manager's approach to markets, clients obtain opportunities to add value through the portfolio rebalancing process. If manager account sizes generally reflect fiduciary preferences, recent performance might be used as a secondary indicator for rebalancing contributions and withdrawals. Even the most skilled managers experience periods of underperformance, attributable to positions that, once established, continue to perform poorly in the marketplace. If, in the face of poor results the original investment case remains intact, by adding funds to an out-of-favor strategy, clients increase exposure to a now even more attractively priced set of assets. Managers tend to react positively to the vote of confidence implicit in client cash flows arriving after a period of poor results.

In contrast, following periods of greater-than-expected performance, clients ought to consider reducing account size. Extraordinarily strong performance likely stems from a combination of manager skill and fortuitous market conditions. Reducing the account of an outperforming manager and reallocating funds to weaker performers will likely improve performance. While managers enjoy receiving cash flow, particularly when their investment style lacks favor in the marketplace, managers dislike disgorging funds. The market gets the blame for poor results; skill completely explains strong performance.

In any event, clients must avoid costly disruptive cash flow requests. Withdrawals require particularly great care, since incurring unnecessary transactions costs dampens portfolio returns. Contributions to poor performers and withdrawals from strong performers might be made as part of a fund's rebalancing activity, generating only transactions already required for risk control purposes. In and of themselves, periods of strong or weak relative performance generate signals insufficiently strong to justify significant portfolio moves.

Manager Termination

When considering firing a manager, fiduciaries must focus on two broad categories of potential problems. First, the initial hiring decision may have been a mistake. Regardless of the thoroughness of due diligence efforts, the true nature of an investment relationship emerges only after adviser and client work together for a period of time. Constant reexamination of initial assumptions causes fiduciaries to continue to learn about the manager's process, either reinforcing the hiring decision or exposing shortcomings missed earlier. Second, changes in people, philosophy, and structure require reassessment of manager relationships. When significant changes occur, fiduciaries ought to take a fresh look at the manager, subjecting the relationship to a thorough reevaluation.

Perhaps the most difficult part of managing a portfolio of external advisers involves termination of unsatisfactory relationships. The unpleasant nature of firing a manager causes many investors to stay with dysfunctional manager-client relationships far longer than prudent. Rationalizations for maintaining the status quo abound, providing superficial justification for avoiding the unpleasant task at hand.

In short, either the investor made a mistake in hiring the manager, or changes in circumstance cause the manager to be unfit for duty. In the final analysis, fiduciaries must ask the question, "Would this manager be hired today?" If the answer is no, investors must consider seriously the firing of the manager in question.

Role of Staff and Committee

Since relationship management involves a broad range of issues close to the heart of the investment process, clear definition of the respective roles of investment staff and committee serves as a prerequisite for effective portfolio implementation. Hiring and firing decisions carry significant import, requiring committee involvement. If circumstances demand immediate action, staff could be authorized to fire a manager without prior committee approval. Under normal conditions, however, both engaging and terminating managers would follow full investment committee deliberation.

Portfolio sizing and rebalancing moves demand quick action, allowing flexibility to respond to market opportunities identified by staff and external managers. Requiring prior committee approval delays time-sensitive decisions, potentially causing investors to miss opportunities. Seeking committee approval for rebalancing or account sizing decisions involves the oversight body too deeply in tactical issues, possibly interfering with the relationship between external managers and staff. After the-fact review provides an adequate forum for discussion of staff-initiated cash flows.

USE OF INTERMEDIARIES

Frequent interaction between fiduciaries and external managers provides the strongest foundation for investment success. Employing a "fund of funds" manager or engaging a consultant places a filter between those entrusted with responsibility for the assets and those making security selection decisions. Without the confidence engendered by thorough understanding of a firm's approach to market opportunities, investors judge competence primarily by the performance numbers, an unreliable, and sometimes perverse, indicator of investment attractiveness. Risks associated with distancing fiduciaries from investment managers dictate that fund-of-funds arrangements receive especially skeptical scrutiny.

Fund of Funds

Fund-of-funds managers provide the service of selecting investment advisers for fiduciaries. By pooling assets, usually from smaller investors, economies of scale allow professional staff to manage monies in institutional fashion. Fund-of-funds firms range from multiproduct concerns, such as the Common Fund and The Investment Fund for Foundations, to entities focused on specific niches, including venture capital, managed futures, and absolute return strategies.

By providing manager selection and monitoring expertise, broad-based funds of funds allow smaller organizations to tap into sophisticated investment strategies. Larger organizations sometimes hope to benefit by employing fund-of-funds managers to gain exposure to unfamiliar market niches.

In spite of the obvious benefits gained from employing fund-of-funds managers, substantial risks stem from imposing a filter between the investment manager and the ultimate client. Regardless of the level of disclosure provided by the fund-of-funds manager, transparency in the investment management relationship declines dramatically. Clients unable or unwilling to understand the underlying manager fundamentals tend to rely on performance to evaluate investment strategies. When results disappoint, clients wonder not only about the investment advisers but also about the competence of the fund-of-funds manager.

Faced with poor performance, the client loses the benefits associated with delegating responsibility to the fund-of-funds manager. Understanding the source of poor results requires investigation of the underlying investment management organizations, a task that the fiduciary hoped to avoid. Short of a thorough underwriting of the constituent managers, clients respond based primarily on performance, exposing the portfolio to the attendant dangers.

When employing fund-of-funds managers, investors must search for firms with compatible professional and ethical standards. Delegating authority to engage investment managers carries enormous import.

Large, reputable fund-of-funds managers occasionally make staggeringly inappropriate judgments. Several years ago, a private equity vehicle launched by a multibillion dollar fund of funds considered engaging an individual to manage an oil and gas program. Aside from the fact that the individual's resumé showed little direct relevant experience, a criminal history clouded his past. The purported energy manager had been convicted of drug dealing and had been arrested and convicted for spousal abuse. Most investors, when confronted with this set of facts, would move on to the next opportunity. Under the best of circumstances, investing poses significant challenges. Starting with an inexperienced partner with a criminal past increases the difficulties immeasurably.

What motivates the staff to propose backing a poorly qualified manager of dubious character? While the full story likely contains a complex set of reasons, one obvious answer stands out. Fund-of-funds managers justify their role in part by making nonstandard choices. Investing in the usual suspects provides less value added than does identifying emerging managers unavailable to most market participants.

Ultimately the fund of funds decided to put the former drug dealer in the energy investment business. Not content simply to back this individual in the firm's standard format as one of a number of managers in a pool, the organization decided to devote the entire energy fund to this single manager. Life is too short to waste time making a concentrated bet on an individual with a checkered past, when the world provides countless superior alternatives.

In another extraordinary incident, Paloma Partners, a multibillion-dollar fund of funds, engaged John Mulheren's Buffalo Partners to manage a risk arbitrage portfolio. Mulheren gained notoriety in February 1988, when he packed his trunk with a .233 caliber Israeli Galil assault rifle, 9-millimeter semiautomatic pistol, .357 Magnum pistol, 12-gauge pistol-grip shotgun, and 300 rounds of ammunition, intending to shoot Ivan Boesky. Alerted by Mulheren's wife, New Jersey State troopers arrested Mulhern, preventing a possible tragedy.[6]

Since Paloma Partners refuses to disclose names of underlying investment managers, even to clients, most of the firm's investors were unaware of the relationship. Upon learning of the involvement with Mulheren, a potential client challenged the fund manager, arguing that the investment did not meet institutional standards. "Mulheren's a great investor when he's taking his lithium," replied the manager.

• • •

Adding a layer to the investment management process decreases transparency, posing serious problems for fiduciaries. Instead of relying on someone's judgment in making investment decisions, the fiduciary relies on someone's judgment about someone's judgment in making the ultimate decisions. While backing convicted drug dealers and funding would-be assassins represent extreme examples of poor judgment, the incidents highlight the risk of using intermediaries to make decisions. The greater the number of layers there are, the greater is the likelihood that outcomes deviate from the fiduciary's preferences.

In spite of the challenges, many fund-of-funds managers offer important services, particularly valuable to small institutional investors. For example, The Investment Fund for Foundations (TIFF), with its broad range of multimanager products, provides access to investment expertise otherwise unavailable to small foundations. Perhaps part of TIFF's appeal results from its not-for-profit charter, causing the cooperative to be motivated to represent client interests, not maximize profits.[7]

Consulting Firms

Consultants present an interesting set of related questions. Seeking to supplement inadequate internal resources, many institutions engage consulting firms to augment their efforts. In some situations, consultants decrease the transparency of the process and drive clients to poor investment decisions; in others, consultants provide valuable advice.

Consulting firms maximize profits by providing nearly identical advice to as many clients as possible. In the investment world, which demands portfolios custom tailored to institution-specific risk and return preferences, a cookie-cutter approach fails. Clients must either identify a consulting firm that cares about goals other than profit maximization or manage the consulting relationship to achieve appropriately tailored advice.

Consultants tend to express conventional views and make safe recommendations. Selecting managers from an internally approved recommended list serves as a poor starting point for identifying managers likely to provide strong future results. While consultants rarely espouse unconventional market-beating tactics, they provide more than adequate cover when dealing with investment committees. Decision makers rest comfortably, knowing that a recognized consulting firm blessed the chosen investment strategy.

Unfortunately, the economics of consulting drives an unusual wedge between the interests of the consultant and the interests of the client. Continuing demand for consulting services requires that clients remain dependent on outside help, reducing incentives for consultants to move clients toward self-sufficiency. In extreme cases consultants recommend programs that are ostensibly in the client's interest yet simply serve to ensure a continued stream of income for the consultant. For example, private equity consultants, also known as gatekeepers, sometimes recommend direct co-investment programs to clients who are obviously ill-equipped to handle the program. (The client cannot even make a partnership decision without assistance. How could the client make an even more difficult direct investment decision?) Along with the co-investment recommendation, gatekeepers offer selection and monitoring services. If successful, the gatekeeper creates an annuity stream lasting the life of the investment program.

In spite of the dangers associated with use of consultants, properly managed relationships provide advantages to fiduciaries. Collegial advice, focused on institution-specific characteristics and issues, serves as a supplement to the work done by internal staff. As long as consultants do not drive the investment process, fiduciaries have the potential to realize benefits from the relationship.

CONCLUSION

Sensible investors assess investment advisory relationships with a balance of soft qualitative attributes and hard quantitative characteristics. Qualitative factors play a central role in manager evaluations, placing people issues at the core of portfolio structuring decisions. Critical variables include the quality of investment professionals, the strength of the investment philosophy, and the character of the organizational structure. Regular face-to-face meetings constitute the most important manager monitoring tool.

Quantitative portfolio management tools include return data on individual managers, market benchmarks, and active manager universes. Overreliance on the neat precision of numerical results frequently leads to poor decisions. Investors looking only at the numbers face the prospect of buying high and selling low, making commitments based on chasing strong results and bailing out when the inevitable patch of poor performance appears.

Successful investment programs require open, honest relationships between institutional clients and external money managers. Direct, frequent communication allows investors to take advantage of market opportunities. When declining prices allow the purchase of assets on attractive terms, fund managers ought to be able to access incremental funds, if necessary, to exploit the opportunity. Conversely, money managers with relatively few attractive opportunities should be willing to return funds to clients. Such activity takes place only when a high degree of confidence and trust exists between money managers and clients.

Fund-of-funds managers block communication between institutional clients and money managers, potentially interfering with the investment process. One rationale for using a fund of funds rests on the client's inadequate knowledge of a particular field. Lack of understanding may lead to poor investment results, as investors react to the numbers by abandoning strategies that disappoint, even when the fundamental investment case remains intact. In such situations, neither the client nor the fund manager succeeds, as the client posts needlessly poor results and the manager loses assets at an inopportune time. While third parties frequently create dysfunctional filters, unusually strong intermediaries provide opportunities for fiduciaries to expand the scope of investment activity.

Performance evaluation drives portfolio allocation decisions, as conclusions regarding manager ability influence the confidence of fiduciaries in particular firms. In many respects, the investor faces a binary decision. If confidence exists, fiduciaries muster the courage necessary to behave in a contrarian manner, supporting managers experiencing a spell of poor results. If a fiduciary lacks the confidence to increase exposure to an underperforming manager, either the manager or the fiduciary should go.

11
Investment Process

An effective investment process facilitates structuring of a portfolio consistent with the philosophical tenets of an organization. Most aspects of investment philosophy embody an intuitive appeal, allowing groups to adopt and follow sensible principles without great difficulty. Among the less challenging principles are maintaining an equity bias, adopting appropriate diversification policies, and structuring investment relationships to align interests. Other, more problematic principles include recognizing opportunities in illiquidity and avoiding active management in efficiently priced markets. In spite of modest challenges, were these principles sufficient to manage a portfolio effectively, establishing appropriate governance structures would pose little problem.

Two important tenets of investment management—contrarian thinking and long-term orientation—create great difficulties for governance of endowment funds. Because large, bureaucratic organizations invariably use groups of people (investment committees) to oversee other groups of people (investment staff), the investment process becomes greatly influenced by consensus-building behavior. Unless carefully managed, group dynamics frequently thwart contrarian activities and impose shorter-than-optimal time horizons on investment activity. Creating a governance process that encourages long-term, independent, contrarian investing poses an enormous challenge to endowed institutions.

J. M. Keynes, in *The General Theory*, describes the difficulties inherent in group investment decision making:

Finally it is the long-term investor, he who most promotes the public interest, who will in practice come in for most criticism, wherever investment funds are managed by committees or boards or banks. For it is in the essence of his behavior that he should be eccentric, unconventional, and rash in the eyes of average opinion. If he is successful, that will only confirm the general belief in his rashness; and if in the short run he is unsuccessful, which is very likely, he will not receive much mercy. Worldly wisdom teaches that it is better for reputation to fail conventionally than to succeed unconventionally.[1]

The challenges facing an institution attempting to structure governance processes lie in exercising appropriate fiduciary oversight, while encouraging "eccentric, unconventional, and rash" behavior in a long-term investment program.

DECISION-MAKING CHALLENGES

Effective endowment management processes encourage long-term investing. The universality with which investors proclaim themselves long term in orientation matches only the startling degree to which short-term thinking drives investor decisions. Perhaps human nature dictates that short-term issues overwhelm long-term considerations. Time horizons shrink with the desire for immediate gratification and the competitive need to win.

The human desire to make a visible contribution often contributes to short time horizon investment. Because investment staff and trustees desire to leave their marks on the portfolio, potential problems exist if the investment fund's horizon exceeds a staff member's expected tenure or trustee's term. In the management of perpetual life assets, explicit recognition of the discontinuity between personal and institutional time frames and adequate continuity in management and governance provide the only practical response.

Investors seeking short-term success will likely be frustrated by markets too efficient to offer much in terms of easy gains. Even if managers find short-term opportunities to exploit, they put themselves on a treadmill. As investors successfully exploit one short-term inefficiency, it must be replaced by another attractive position followed by another, and yet another, ad infinitum. Creating wealth through a series of short-term investments is difficult, risky work. Moreover, by avoiding mis-pricings unlikely to resolve themselves in the near term, managers hoping to beat the market every quarter create opportunities for those few who attempt to invest based on considered long-term estimates.

True long-term investing dramatically broadens the investment opportunity set, allowing investors to profit from the irrationality of short-term players. Yet because long-term investing creates an intrin-sically higher risk profile, successful organizations develop mecha-nisms to cope with the associated risks.

Short-Term Thinking

The competitive atmosphere surrounding investment management ac-tivities encourages short-term thinking. Mutual funds provide a case in point. *The New York Times Mutual Funds Report*, a quarterly fea-ture of the paper's Money and Business section, prominently displays "Winners and Losers: Best—and Worst—Performing U.S. Diversified Stock Funds for the Second Quarter." In the July 5, 1998 edition, Gretchen Morgenson's front-page article focuses on trailing three-month underperformance of actively managed funds. Page four of the section (following a two-page advertisement for Charles Schwab) dis-plays a chart showing twenty leaders and laggards, starting with quar-terly performance, but finally including one-year and five-year data as well. On the opposite page, complete with pictures, three fund man-agers with strong quarterly numbers explain through reporter Carole Gould how they were able to "land at the top of the lists." Throughout the special section, reporting focuses on short-term performance.[2]

Aside from the fundamental irrelevance of such a short period of trailing performance data, the publishing of these rankings causes managers to respond to the incentive of appearing at the top of the list. Anecdotal evidence abounds that most mutual fund managers favor investment ideas that promise to pay off in three or six months. At the same time, fear of failure makes the portfolio manager hug the bench-mark to avoid potentially disastrous falls to the bottom of the rank-ings. Mediocre performance inevitably results as managers incur high transactions costs pursuing second-rate ideas within the context of an index-like portfolio.

Similar problems exist in the world of endowment management.

Annual investment performance comparisons create (or reflect?) a horse race mentality. An audience of trustees, alumni, and faculty waits with great anticipation for the year-end results, comparing asset allocation and performance numbers among the peer group within which the institution competes. Short of beating an archrival at football, posting the highest one-year investment result ranks near the top of the list of institutional aspirations. Obviously, judging long-term pools of assets by trailing twelve-month performance numbers induces the wrong kind of thinking, emphasizing short-term, consensus-oriented investing.

Performance competition causes some institutions to engage in bizarre behavior, inflating published endowment values and reporting returns gross of fees. While secrecy surrounding overreporting of endowment levels prevents accurate measurement, a distressingly large number of institutions follow the practice of reporting gross returns. In the most recent endowment return survey, 134 institutions, or 28 percent of those participating, reported results before fees.[3] Of what possible use are such numbers? From a budgetary perspective, net returns provide useful data since institutions consume investment income after fees. From an investment perspective, net returns allow the measurement of true value added relative to benchmarks. Barring a reasonable explanation, it appears that institutions report gross returns to gain advantage in the annual investment derby.

Consensus-Driven Behavior

Endowment managers engage in behavior similar to mutual fund benchmark hugging, with peer group investment policies providing the stake to which an institution's asset allocation is tethered. Varying too far from the group consensus exposes the manager to the risk of being labeled unconventional. If the institution fails in its unusual approach, the policy will likely be abandoned and the investment staff will likely be looking for new positions. In contrast, had the institution failed with a standard institutional portfolio, policies may still be abandoned, but investment professionals would likely remain gainfully employed.

Concern regarding peer behavior rests in part on a rational basis. Educational institutions operate in a competitive environment, vying with one another for faculty, students, administrators, and financial support. Endowment size helps define an institution's competitive position through direct financial support and reputational capital. If dramatically different investment policies cause one university's endowment to decline precipitously, that institution may join a new, less prestigious peer group, losing not only financial support but also the confidence of important institutional constituencies. Obviously unusual investment success enhances an institution's financial and reputational position. Trustees, generally a risk-averse lot, may conclude that the potential costs of failing with an unusual portfolio exceed the potential benefits of unconventional success.

However rational concern regarding peer behavior might be, if market participants weight heavily the consensus portfolio in asset allocation deliberations, change becomes quite difficult. In the extreme, fear of being different has everyone looking over their shoulder at their neighbor's portfolio—and no one looking at fundamental portfolio structure. Sensible portfolio management processes encourage creation of portfolios appropriate for the institution, not replication of other institutional asset mixes.

Contrarian Opportunity and Risk

The attitude of portfolio managers contributes to the success or failure of an investment program. Significant differences between successful investment operations and other well-run business activities cause the application of standard corporate management techniques to fail in the investment world. Most businesses grow by feeding winners. Putting resources behind successful products generally leads to larger, increasingly impressive gains. Ruthless cuts of failed initiatives preserve corporate resources for more attractive strategies.

In contrast, investment success generally stems from contrarian impulses. Winners should be viewed suspiciously, with consideration given to reducing or even eliminating previously successful strategies. Losers should be eyed hopefully, seen as potential sources of future gains for the portfolio.

Contrarian investing represents more than a reflex action, causing investors to buy the dips. Immediate gratification should not be expected. In fact, going against the grain will likely appear foolish in the short run as already cheap assets become cheaper, causing the true contrarian to appear fundamentally out of sync with investors more successfully in tune with the market.

Establishing and maintaining positions out of the mainstream requires decision making by individuals or relatively small groups. As groups increase in size, consensus thinking increasingly dominates the process. Behavioral studies illustrate the tendency for group think in startling ways. Most people so desire conformity that they embrace obviously wrong positions to avoid being at odds with the crowd.

Contrarian, long-term investing poses extraordinary challenges under the best of circumstances. In an institutional environment with staff and committees and boards, nearly insurmountable obstacles exist. Creating a decision-making framework that encourages unconventional thinking constitutes a critical goal for fund fiduciaries.

Unfortunately, overcoming the tendency to follow the crowd, while necessary, proves insufficient to guarantee investment success. By pursuing ill-considered, idiosyncratic policies, market players expose portfolios to unnecessary, often unrewarded risks. While courage to take a different path enhances chances for success, investors face likely failure unless a thoughtful set of investment principles undergirds the courage.

New York University and Bonds

Even the most well-meaning fiduciaries, motivated by altruistic intentions, sometimes pursue out-of-the-mainstream policies which cause substantial economic and reputational damage. The story of NYU's endowment management over the past two decades vividly illustrates the dangers of implementing poorly founded investment strategies.

In the late 1970s and early 1980s, motivated by concerns regarding the fragility of the university's finances and the riskiness of the stock market, NYU allocated an average of 66% to bonds, 30% to stocks, and 4% to other assets. NYU differed materially from its sister institutions by holding roughly double the average proportion of bonds and roughly half the average proportion of stocks.

Between 1981 and 1982, at the bottom of the equity market, NYU dropped its already low equity allocation from 33 percent to 7 percent of the portfolio, increasing the already high bond commitment from 62 percent to 90 percent of assets. Bonds continued to maintain a share in excess of 90 percent of assets through 1985, according to public reports on asset allocation, while stocks languished at single-digit levels, falling as low as 3 percent of the endowment. Even though after 1985 annual reports ceased to provide information on portfolio allocations, it appears that NYU persisted with its unusual portfolio structure throughout the late 1980s and early 1990s. After a nine-year disclosure hiatus, in 1995 the university reported holding 86 percent of assets in bonds, and 9 percent of assets in stocks, indicating a continuing extraordinary commitment to bonds. Only in 1997 did NYU begin to make a modest move away from fixed income to assets with a higher expected return.[4]

Unfortunately, the bond-dominated portfolio left NYU on the sidelines during one of the greatest bull markets in history. From 1978 to 1998, stock returns exceeded bond returns in sixteen of twenty years, with stocks enjoying a 6 percent per annum advantage over bonds. Only in the aftermath of the 1987 crash did the fixed income strategy appear sensible, causing NYU board chairman Larry Tisch to receive a standing ovation at a NYU investment committee meeting. Market activity supported only a brief huzzah as the S&P 500 ended the 1987 calendar year 5.2 percent above the level recorded at the beginning of the year. Even when viewed from the perspective of a time frame as short as twelve calendar months, NYU's strategy failed to make sense.

As the bull market continued apace, Tisch turned away questions regarding the lack of equity exposure by responding that "the train has left the station."[5] Meanwhile, the opportunity costs for the NYU endowment mounted. From 1982 to 1998, an endowment wealth index for colleges and universities increased nearly eightfold, while NYU's endowment grew 4.6 times.[6] Had the institution's results simply mirrored college and university medians, NYU's endowment in 1998 would have been nearly $1 billion larger than the actual level of $1.3 billion. By failing to understand the relationship between the permanent nature of endowment funds and equity investments, NYU's endowment sustained long lasting, if not permanent, damage.

Boston University and Seragen

Boston University's investment in Seragen, championed by the institution's former president, John Silber, posed a fundamentally different threat to the health of the university's finances. By funneling as much as $90 million of operating and endowment funds into a single biotechnology-based start-up company, Boston University made an unreasonably large bet on an extremely high-risk investment.[7]

Silber first became interested in Seragen's "fusion toxins" at a 1986 lecture by Boston University scientist and Seragen founder John R. Murphy. In 1987, the university plowed $25 million of its $175 million endowment into the venture, buying a controlling interest from a Norwegian pharmaceutical company. Over the years, through further equity investments, operating support, and asset purchases, Boston University's exposure to Seragen went from excessive to irresponsible. In exchange for massive injections of funds, the university obtained control of the board, with Silber among the designated directors.

The institution's unusually concentrated, controlling position in Seragen attracted the attention of the Massachusetts attorney general, who caused the university to dilute its ownership stake by pursuing public offerings. Although share issuance raised more than $50 million in 1992 and 1993, Seragen's burn rate managed to outpace the cash inflows. By 1996, cumulative losses amounted to $200 million, causing Murphy to disassociate himself from Seragen, citing "business problems."

In spite of successes on the scientific front, Seragen's finances faltered, leading to delisting from the Nasdaq in September 1997. The stock, which went public in April 1992 at $12 a share and reached a high of $15 in January 1993, traded at 5/8 upon delisting. At the time, Boston University's stake amounted to little more than $5 million.

Desperate to salvage value, Boston University in December 1997 infused a further $5 million into Seragen by purchasing money-losing assets, allowing provision of ongoing support from the university's operating budget. By buying time, the institution managed to arrange an exit from the financially troubled company through a sale to Ligand Pharmaceuticals in August 1998. On September 20, 1998, the *New York Times* reported that the value of Boston University's position ultimately amounted to approximately $8.4 million, representing a loss of more than 90 percent on cost. Had the university's Seragen stake been invested in a diversified portfolio of stocks, the endowment would have benefited by avoiding the disastrous Seragen loss, as well as by appreciation of tens of millions of dollars on the equity positions.

Ironically, Silber's positive assessment of Seragen's science appears well founded. The firm's major drug, Interleukin-2, received an approval recommendation from an FDA advisory panel in June 1998. Yet even if the drug becomes a commercial success, the university stands to accrue little benefit, as its economic interest in the project diminished greatly with the Ligand takeover. Seragen's progress came too late and cost too much to reward the firm's shareholders.

By rolling the dice with endowment investments, Boston University violated fundamental investment principles, providing a disservice to the institution's constituents. Haunted by its failure to invest in Alexander Graham Bell's invention of the telephone, the university vowed not to repeat the mistake with Seragen. Unfortunately, spectacular investment success stories become clear only after the fact, forcing sensible investors to avoid outsized bets. A high-risk concentrated investment in Seragen, in the words of one faculty member, allowed Silber a shot at leaving "as a legacy a gigantic endowment."[8] Fiduciary requirements, no matter how liberally interpreted, fail to accommodate actions inconsistent with constructing a reasonably diversified portfolio.

In pursuing investment policies motivated by a desire to make an impact, NYU and Boston University inflicted serious damage on their portfolios of permanent assets. By playing a futile market timing game, NYU missed the benefits of one of the greatest bull markets ever. In an ill-considered attempt to swing for the fences, Boston University suffered a dramatic direct loss and incurred even greater opportunity costs. Responsible fiduciaries best serve institutions by following basic investment principles, avoiding the temptation to pursue policies designed to satisfy specific individual agendas.

DECISION-MAKING PROCESS

Reasonable decision-making processes give appropriate emphasis to the range of issues facing committee and staff. Charley Ellis describes a useful framework for categorizing various portfolio management decisions. Policy decisions concern long-term issues that inform the basic structural framework of the investment process. Strategic decisions represent intermediate-term moves designed to adapt longer-term policies to more immediate market opportunities and institutional reali-

ties. Trading and tactical decisions involve short time horizon implementation of strategies and policies.

In his wonderful book, *Winning the Loser's Game,* Ellis bemoans
the fact that decision makers spend too much time on relatively exciting trading and tactical decisions at the expense of the more powerful,
yet more mundane policy decisions.[9] A decision-making process designed to place appropriate emphasis on policy decisions increases an
investor's chances of winning.

Policy Target Focus

In many ways, establishing policy asset allocation targets represents
the heart of the investment process. No other aspect of portfolio management plays as great a role in determining a fund's ultimate performance, and no other statement says as much about the character of a
fund. Establishing a framework focused on policy decisions represents the most fundamental obligation of investment fiduciaries.
Without a disciplined, rigorous process for setting asset allocation targets, effective portfolio management becomes impossible.

Asset allocation targets ought to be reviewed once (and only once)
per year. An annual review allows managers to make changes necessary to move portfolios in desired directions. Perhaps more important,
limiting policy discussions to the assigned meeting diminishes the
possibility of damage from ill-considered moves made in response to
the gloom or euphoria imbuing current market conditions.

Yale and the 1987 Market Crash

Stresses and strains placed on decision-making processes exhibited
themselves after the October 1987 crash in stock prices. Yale was not
immune from the pressure. Although the university had followed a
quarterly meeting schedule since the Investment Committee was established in 1975, two extraordinary meetings were held, in late 1987 and
early 1988, to deal with the crash. Although at the time of the meetings
stock prices were substantially lower and bond prices measurably

higher than at the time of the most recent policy review conducted only a few months earlier, the question on the agenda was whether to increase the policy allocation to bonds at the expense of stocks.

The committee also wished to review a late October rebalancing purchase of tens of millions of dollars of equities funded by a corresponding sale of bonds. In the context of the gloom of late 1987, Yale's action appeared rash. Other institutions not only allowed equity positions to drift downward by the amount of the relative stock market decline, they further reduced equity exposure through net sales in November and December 1987. Such sales seemed prudent in an environment where the *New York Times* published a weekly chart that superimposed 1987 stock prices on a chart of prices for 1929 through 1932.

Yale's internal committee dynamics proved difficult. One member characterized Yale's asset allocation as "super aggressive" and on the "far edge of aggressiveness." Citing bleak short-term prospects for equities, he commented that if Yale was right in having an aggressive equity posture, the university would get "little credit," but if Yale was wrong there would be "all hell to pay." Believing that "events of the past six months have diminished long-term prospects for equity markets," he concluded that the university's assumptions regarding expected returns were overly optimistic. Hence, he suggested that both short-term and long-term considerations required downward adjustment of Yale's equity target. A more analytically inclined member wondered if increases in historical volatility made stocks less attractive on a relative basis.* By questioning—after the fact—assumptions that had been examined recently as part of the annual policy target review, four months earlier, committee members exposed Yale to the risk of an untimely reversal of strategy.

Ultimately Yale maintained policy targets, reaping attractive returns on its postcrash rebalancing trade. In spite of the university's success, discussions at the extraordinary meetings illustrate the potential danger of revisiting policy target levels too frequently, particularly in the midst of a market crisis. While the 1987 stock market crash caused the university to violate past practice of limiting policy alloca-

---

*The 1987 stock market crash was a 25-standard-deviation event. Backward-looking estimates of volatility would naturally increase if the extraordinary data from October 1987 were included in historical estimates.

tion discussions to one meeting per year, reasonably disciplined implementation of a sensible policy framework contributed to the pursuit of effective policies in a difficult environment.

While in retrospect the committee's actions appear innocuous, in other states of the world, the positions taken by the investment committee members could have had severe repercussions for Yale's investment staff. In particular, the extraordinary memo containing a committee member's criticism of the policy allocation targets had dangerous overtones. Had the market not recovered within a relatively short time frame, staff members closely identified with the rebalancing trade might have suffered serious damage to their careers.

Strategic and Tactical Issues

While the committee meeting on policy asset allocation represents the focal point of the investment process, other meetings deal with important strategic issues. Following the close of the fiscal year, a meeting devoted to portfolio evaluation discusses in detail overall endowment and individual asset class characteristics. Portfolio review memoranda describe performance in the context of recent market conditions, focusing on factors that influence significant investment opportunities. The positioning of an asset class relative to benchmark with respect to fundamental characteristics, such as size, sector, and style, defines significant portfolio bets, which are evaluated retrospectively and prospectively. Active management efforts receive grades in the form of detailed report cards for each manager. Analysis of strengths and weaknesses of portfolio strategies and tactics leads to an outline for future projects to improve portfolio management. In essence, the portfolio evaluation meeting provides a backward-looking assessment and a forward-looking strategic plan.

The remaining two quarterly meetings generally have a topical focus, frequently involving an in-depth analysis of a specific asset class. Meetings centered on individual asset classes provide a detailed look at a particular portfolio, allowing committee and staff to understand the strengths and weaknesses of asset class management. One particularly effective exercise involves a decision-making assessment that goes beyond traditional metrics of performance evaluation. For instance, by evaluating returns of terminated managers relative to benchmarks and actual portfolio results, investigators gain insight into the effectiveness of firing decisions, a topic often comfortably ignored after completing the difficult task of severing ties.

Asset class reviews provide a chance for external investment managers to engage investment committee and staff members in discussion of significant asset management issues. While sensible investors avoid the all-too-prevalent beauty contest hiring pageant, creating a forum for lively interaction between existing managers and committee members adds value to the investment process. Rather than allowing managers to present canned portfolio appraisals, structured panel discussions stimulate candid discussion of manager-specific approaches to asset class pitfalls and opportunities.

Occasionally committee meetings deal with market issues that cut across individual asset classes. For example, the savings and loan debacle of the late 1980s generated opportunities for private equity, real estate, and absolute return asset classes. Focusing attention on the breadth of options associated with a particular economic event enhances the ability of an investment organization to identify and pursue attractive strategies.

Effective investors maintain focus on long-term policy targets, making the annual asset allocation review the centerpiece of an investment fund's agenda. Devoting the meeting after the close of the fiscal year to a thorough review of portfolio characteristics and performance provides a report card for the past and a road map for the future. The two interim meetings allow in-depth examination of a particular asset class or interesting investment opportunity. Hewing to a well-defined schedule of meetings reduces the opportunity for committee and staff to make undisciplined moves that might put long-term goals at risk.

OPERATING ENVIRONMENT

Effective investment committees provide appropriate oversight, while taking care not to infringe on staff responsibilities. Limiting committee meetings to four per year prevents trustees from becoming too involved in day-to-day portfolio management decisions, yet allows staff to receive appropriate guidance from the committee. By presuming that initiatives come from staff, not from committee members, responsibility for the nature and direction of the investment program rests squarely on the shoulders of the investment office. In short, the investment committee should play the role of a board of directors for the fund management operation.

Investment Committee

A strong investment committee brings discipline to the endowment management process. By thoroughly and thoughtfully vetting investment recommendations, the committee inspires staff to produce ever more carefully considered proposals. Ideally committees rarely exercise the power to reject staff recommendations. If a committee frequently turns down or revises investment proposals, the staff encounters great difficulty in managing the portfolio. Investment opportunities often require negotiation of commitments subject to board approval. If the board withholds approval with any degree of regularity, staff loses credibility in the eyes of the investment management community. On the other hand, the committee must provide more than a rubber stamp for staff recommendations. In a well-run organization, committee discussion of investment proposals influences the direction and nature of future staff initiatives. Effective portfolio management requires striking a delicate balance between respect for the ultimate authority of the investment committee and delegation of reasonable responsibility to the investment staff.

Committee members often provide assistance between meetings, suggesting strategies to pursue or providing feedback on past actions. Informed give and take brings investment dialogue to a higher level, challenging staff and committee to improve the quality of investment decision making.

Investment committee members should be selected primarily for good judgment. While no particular background qualifies an individual to serve on the committee, broad understanding of financial markets often proves useful in overseeing the investment process. On the other hand, specific expertise occasionally poses dangers, particularly when committee members attempt to manage the portfolio, not the process. Successful businesspeople bring a valuable perspective to the table provided that they suspend their natural inclination to reward success and punish failure. The sometimes deep-rooted instinct to pursue winners and avoid disasters pushes portfolios toward fundamentally risky momentum-driven strategies and away from potentially profitable contrarian opportunities. The most effective investment committee members understand the responsibility to oversee the investment process and support the investment staff, while avoiding actual management of the portfolio.

Investment Staff

Strong investment staffs drive the portfolio management process. Whether dealing with broad issues of asset allocation and spending policy or specific issues of manager selection, the staff needs to make a rigorous, compelling case for adopting a particular course of action. Advocacy must not compromise disclosure; actual and potential weaknesses need to be fully described and discussed. Intellectual dishonesty ultimately proves fatal to the investment process.

In the absence of a disciplined process for articulating investment recommendations, decision making tends to become informal, even casual. A rigorous evaluation of all aspects of an investment opportunity, including thorough due diligence on the quality of the investment principals, serves as an essential precondition to committing investment funds.

Written recommendations provide a particularly useful means of communicating investment ideas. The process of drafting memos often exposes logical flaws or gaps in reasoning. Knowledge that a critical audience of colleagues and committee members reviews investment memos stimulates careful, logical exposition of proposals. Comprehensive written treatments of investment issues provide a common background for staff and committee members, elevating the quality of dialogue at meetings.

Regardless of staff size, decision-making groups must be small, consisting of no more than two or three people. As the number of people involved in a decision increases, the likelihood of a conventional, compromising consensus increases. Obviously, with a large staff, the same two or three people need not be responsible for all decisions. For example, different small groups might make recommendations for different asset classes. Spreading power and delegating responsibility improve both performance and professional satisfaction.

Organizational Characteristics

Strong investment management groups share a number of characteristics, with great people constituting the most important element in building a superior organization. Hank Paulson, Chairman and Chief Executive Officer of Goldman Sachs, in an October 1997 speech at Yale's School of Management, suggested that high-quality individuals gravitate toward firms that operate on the cutting edge in a global environment, provide opportunities to benefit from focused mentorship and encourage delegation of early responsibility.

Organizations on the cutting edge choose from a broader opportunity set. By examining nontraditional asset allocations, investors improve the chances of finding a portfolio mix well-suited to the institution's needs. By considering alternatives outside the mainstream, investors increase the likelihood of discovering the next big winner well before it becomes the next big bust. By evaluating managers without the requisite institutional characteristics, investors might uncover a highly motivated, attractive group of partners. Operating on the periphery of standard institutional norms increases opportunity for success.

A global perspective facilitates understanding of investment alternatives, providing valuable context for consideration of even the most parochial domestic opportunity. Aside from improving an investor's decision-making framework, global reach increases the investment opportunity set, magnifying the possibility of identifying superior options. Along with the expanded range of possibilities comes the increased potential for failure. Overseas commitments entail inherently higher levels of risk, as availability of information and depth of understanding compare unfavorably to knowledge of domestic market alternatives.

Focused mentorship provides essential training for new staff as individuals assimilate investment management principles through experience, not academic training. Aspiring investors learn through serving an apprenticeship, benefiting from day-to-day exposure to the thoughts and actions of experienced colleagues.

Giving junior members of the team early responsibility challenges all members of an investments organization to spread critical skills throughout the group. Transmitting key principles to younger colleagues magnifies the impact of more senior players, broadening the scope of an organization's reach and the range of its accomplishments. As a corollary benefit, the training process reinforces and freshens the commitment of all participants to the group's core investment beliefs.

Independent thinking contributes to strong investment decision making. Behavior at large, bureaucratic plan sponsors provides a counter-example to good practices. Standard investment manager search techniques exclude nearly all interesting managers from consideration. By widely circulating requests for proposals on seemingly endless questionnaires, and establishing criteria for minimum levels of historical performance, asset size, and years of experience, plan sponsors ensure conventionally unimaginative, and ultimately unsuccessful, management. While the bureaucratic process practically guarantees poor relative returns, the fund manager's job proves secure, as massive stacks of paper protect every investment decision. The courage to pursue nonconventional paths proves essential to building a successful investment program.

Self-awareness plays a critical role in investment analysis. Understanding and exploiting strengths make an obvious contribution to performance. Recognizing and dealing effectively with weaknesses represent a less obvious contribution to the portfolio management process. Ruthlessly honest evaluation of absolute and comparative advantages increases the likelihood of backing winners and avoiding losers.

While self-examination contributes to the investment process, second-guessing and finger pointing prove counterproductive. Frank, open discussion of previous failures and successes provides essential feedback for improved decision making. By understanding past failures, investors create the opportunity to avoid old mistakes when seeking new investments. Analysis of previous winners provides keys for unlocking future successes. In contrast, assigning blame engenders an atmosphere that discourages risk taking, impairing the investment process in a fundamental fashion.

Collegiality plays a critical role in creating and sustaining an appropriate investment environment. Frequent failure marks even the most successful investment management programs. Supportive, understanding colleagues take some of the sting out of mistakes, facilitating continued pursuit of risky investment opportunities.

Providing an environment with low costs of failure encourages experimentation, allowing investors to take well-considered, intelligent risks knowing that losses do not threaten careers. The type of unconventional behavior necessary for meaningful investment success produces its share of abject failures. Encouraging experimentation represents a necessary precondition for investment success.

Successful investing requires operating outside the mainstream. In institutional settings, where conformity is prized, pursuit of potentially rewarding investment opportunities requires strong intellectual leadership. Without strong leadership, investment management decisions fail to rise above normal bureaucratic standards, leading to predictably mediocre results. By establishing a decision-making framework that encourages unconventional, controversial actions, leaders provide the foundation for a successful investment program.

ORGANIZATIONAL STRUCTURE

Many foundations, colleges, and universities face the complexities of running substantial investment portfolios. At June 30, 1997, 339 educational institutions and 711 foundations boasted endowment assets in excess of $50 million.

Decades ago, trustees generally chose individual securities at regularly scheduled quarterly meetings. Simple portfolios contained relatively few positions, allowing full review in a period of several hours. Finance committees populated by titans of industry frequently contributed direct, useful knowledge regarding individual security holdings.

In the 1960s and 1970s, portfolios managed by a handful of external managers typically pursued balanced mandates, placing modest demands on fiduciaries. Governance issues remained similar to those confronting trustees managing portfolios out of their back pockets. Instead of monitoring dozens of individual securities, investment committee members tracked and evaluated a limited group of outside managers. Because the managers invested in securities and markets with which committee members were familiar, the process proved comfortable for trustees and staff alike.

Since then, demands placed on investment staff and trustees have multiplied along with increases in the number of institutional asset classes and the corresponding explosion in the number of specialty investment managers. Along with the greater complexity of the investment world, equally dramatic increases in the breadth and seriousness of issues faced by trustees of educational institutions serve to limit the time and attention devoted to investment management.

The structure of nonprofit investment organizations generally failed to keep pace with changes in the external world. In many cases, institutions devoted insufficient resources to financial asset management, with the treasurer frequently spending part time supervising hundreds of millions of dollars of endowment. Failing to provide adequate staff support may be penny wise and pound foolish. If diligent work adds only 1 percent per annum to investment returns, a half-billion-dollar endowment generates an incremental $5 million annually for institutional support.

Compensating qualified investment staff poses a particular challenge for nonprofit institutions. In the private sector, financial services professionals earn staggering amounts of money. In contrast, most employees in not-for-profits generally earn somewhat less than their for-profit counterparts. The combination of a below-market nonprofit pay scale and extraordinary compensation for investment professionals creates potential for divisive tension regarding compensation issues in the nonprofit community.

Separate Management Companies

To deal with compensation issues, a number of universities established distinct management companies to invest endowment assets. The fundamental problem with this organizational (and in some cases, physical) separation lies in the tendency to treat the management company solely as an investment entity. Proper stewardship of endowment assets requires consideration of both spending and investment policies, with particular attention to the ways in which they interact. The job is not likely to be well done if the management company takes responsibility for investment decisions, while others determine spending policies.

In fact, stewardship of endowment assets improves when the investment operation constitutes part of the fabric of the institution. The greater the degree of professional interaction that exists between endowment managers and the rest of the educational enterprise, the more credibility investment professionals have in discussing and recommending spending policies. At universities, common avenues of interaction include teaching by investment staff, seeking portfolio advice from faculty, and working with development office staff. Aside from enhancing effectiveness, engaging others in the institution increases professional fulfillment.

Ironically, establishing separate investment management companies to facilitate increased compensation for professionals sometimes exacerbates the problem. Greater separation leads to less identification with the institution, reducing the psychic income garnered from supporting the not-for-profit's eleemosynary mission. Psychic income forgone must be replaced with hard cash, further straining the bond between the management company and the rest of the institution.

While compensation of university investment professionals appears to drive the establishment of separate management companies, desire for improved governance may be a contributing factor. As the breadth and complexity of investment alternatives increases, so do the demands on trustees responsible for overseeing investment operations. Establishing an independent management company addresses the issue of institutional focus by providing a dedicated staff and board of directors. Unfortunately, increased separation of the investment operation from the institution appears to be a consequence of establishing an independent management company.

Compensation and governance issues can be addressed without creating a separate management company. Since its establishment in 1975, Yale's investment committee included nontrustee advisers to assist in governance. The use of outside advisers, who bring valuable insights and perspective to the process, obviates the need to establish a separate investment company to draw from a broader pool of governance talent.

Compensation levels for investment staff need not be limited by the standard university framework. Exceptions might be made to pay reasonably competitive salaries, including the use of incentive-based compensation, without causing the radical break implied by the creation of a separate management company. Dealing with the inevitable tensions within the context of the university lessens the magnitude of the problems associated with separate treatment of investment compensation and governance issues.

• • •

Establishing appropriate governance and compensation structures for endowment management organizations poses a difficult set of issues, as radical differences between the private and nonprofit markets create inevitable tensions. While establishing distinct subsidiaries to manage endowment funds addresses oversight and pay issues, the accompanying physical and psychological separation imposes subtle costs on the entire organization. Addressing compensation and governance concerns within the context of the broader institution provides a solution more likely to produce results consistent with the organization's needs.

Internal Control Environment

Back office operations represent a significant yet often overlooked source of risk. Operational controls do not even begin to appear on the radar screens of most institutional fund managers, as investors prefer to deal with issues surrounding relatively exciting active portfolio management strategies. Fund managers ignore control environment issues at their peril, creating the possibility of generating high levels of unwelcome excitement following the event of a major operational failure.

Endowment fund investors face internal and external control risks. Internal control risks consist of exposures created at fund headquarters in the course of day-to-day portfolio management. Conventional audit procedures focus on internal practices, examining the efficacy and integrity of systems designed to support investment activity. External control risks consist of exposures created at outside managers. Traditional audit activities rarely assess directly the control systems of external investment managers, relying instead on work conducted by other professional service firms. Since a chain is only as strong as the weakest link, both internal fund and external manager back office operations require careful examination and oversight.

Inadequate control environments provide fertile breeding grounds for problems ranging in severity from continual imposition of small costs to sudden, headline-grabbing disasters. Pain avoidance requires careful planning. Poorly conceived controls expose investors to the possibility of fraud and malfeasance, occasionally resulting in dramatic losses. Widely publicized investment debacles at Barings, Daiwa, Piper Capital, and the Common Fund raise questions about appropriate policies without providing clear answers. Unfortunately, institutions tend to be complacent, focusing on mundane back office operations only after incurring significant losses.

Investment organizations benefit from regular, independent, intensive external review of operational practices. For simple portfolio structures, internal and external auditors provide a comprehensive look at investment office activity, examining relatively basic issues related to safekeeping portfolios of standard marketable securities. As increasingly esoteric portfolio management activities add layers of complexity, generalist auditors face a dramatically more difficult task. To deal effectively with more sophisticated investment programs, engagement of high-quality specialists to assess back office practices provides fiduciaries with an important tool for evaluating an often ignored aspect of investment management.

A strong audit team from a first-class firm constitutes the first line of defense against internal control problems. While a thorough audit represents an important starting point, in today's investment management world, routine annual reviews no longer constitute an adequate assessment of portfolio practices. Occasional special audits by a team of experts provide important strategic insights into risks facing fund fiduciaries. No-holds-barred intensive reviews identify potential sources of risk, allowing understanding and mitigation of existing issues and potential problems.

Effective special audits engage high-quality experts in an unrestricted, independent review of control practices. By bringing a fresh perspective to the oversight process, the investigative team provokes staff members to revisit comfortable assumptions regarding internal operations, challenging individuals to improve existing procedures. Identification of best practices provides a standard against which to measure current activities and future efforts.

In the past decade, Yale twice employed Coopers & Lybrand to undertake top-to-bottom examinations of the university's investment operations. The first review provided a substantial amount of useful feedback, including several findings highlighting risks in security lending activities. Prompted by the Coopers & Lybrand report, the university took a fresh look at the security loan program, concluding that structural changes in the market created an unattractive risk-and-reward relationship. As a result, the university discontinued its internal lending operations, a move that appeared prescient when the Common Fund's security lending debacle became public sometime later.*

In a second special audit of Yale's investment operations, Coopers & Lybrand concluded that while industry best practices characterized the university's monitoring of external manager back offices, room for improvement existed. Standard industry practice involves relatively superficial investigation of internal controls at external managers, if such controls receive any attention at all. Since external manager control processes determine in part the integrity of the overall control framework within which the endowment operates, the university's risk exposure depends on the quality of these sometimes superficially evaluated manager operations.

Coopers & Lybrand concluded that Yale had an opportunity to redefine industry standards by dedicating resources to understanding and improving the financial control environment, internally and externally. The basic mission involves evaluating regulatory and internal compliance activities, accounting and trading systems, legal and

---

*Yale's security lending operation, managed much more conservatively than the Common Fund's, pursued a matched book strategy. That is, maturities of security loans matched maturities of investments, with the university generating returns by accepting credit risk in the reinvestment vehicle. Prompted to examine the issue by the Coopers & Lybrand study, Yale concluded that spreads were too thin to justify continuing the security lending operation.

auditing professional support, as well as valuation, risk, derivative, and soft-dollar policies. Yale's compliance evaluation efforts create direct opportunities to improve operations by introducing superior practices identified in one investment operation to the university's other managers, thereby improving control processes across the entire portfolio. Not only does the university benefit from evidence gathered when examining the control environment at outside managers, the evaluation process communicates the importance Yale attaches to strong internal operations. Such attention prompts managers to focus increased time and energy on back office activities.

CONCLUSION

Structuring a disciplined framework for decision making constitutes a necessary precondition for investment success. Clear definition of the respective roles of staff and committee ensures that staff members drive the process, while committee members provide effective oversight. Without a rigorous process that is informed by thorough analysis and implemented with discipline, investment portfolios respond to natural human instinct, tending to follow the whims of fashion. Casually researched, consensus-oriented investment positions provide little prospect for producing superior results in the intensely competitive investment management world.

An effective investment process reduces the inevitable gap between the needs of the institution and the actions of the portfolio's stewards. Trustees desire to create an impact during their tenure, while staff members seek job security, pursuing aspirations potentially at odds with institutional goals. By establishing and maintaining investment operations as part of the fabric of the institution, fiduciaries increase the likelihood of placing institutional needs ahead of personal interests.

Appropriate investment proceedures contribute significantly to investment success, allowing investors to pursue profitable long-term contrarian investment positions. By reducing pressures to produce in the short run, liberated managers gain the freedom to create portfolios positioned to take advantage of opportunities created by short-term players. By encouraging managers to make potentially embarrassing out-of-favor investments, fiduciaries increase the likelihood of investment success.

Long-term success requires individualistic contrarian behavior based on a foundation of sound investment principles. Establishing a framework that overcomes the handicap of group decision making encourages well-considered risk taking and increases the opportunity to add value to the portfolio management process. Engaging a motivated investment staff, with appropriate oversight from a strong committee, provides the underpinnings for a successful investment program.

Notes

Foreword

1. Sure that socialism and communism were anathema, but unable to argue convincingly for capitalism in the face of the Depression, the Harvard faculty were opposing Keynes and his *General Theory* "as a matter of principle" if nothing else. In 1936, the Harvard faculty voted to bring East from Minnesota Alvin Hansen, who had written negative reviews of Keynes' theories. Unbeknownst to his new colleagues, Hansen had "come around" to Keynes' new ideas, and he would soon become the principal American advocate of Keynes' theory and its ability to rescue capitalism from intellectual—and political—perdition. Economics at Harvard was soon being shaped by the Keynesian theories previously opposed.
2. Tobin left Yale for two years to serve JFK as a member of a remarkably effective Council of Economic Advisors.
3. Yale has invested over $1 billion this decade in a spectacular revitalization of the campus and in major academic programs that will assure its continuing leadership among the world's great universities.
4. For example, in 1987's sharp market break, when others were frightened into caution and buying bonds, Yale was a bold, reasoned buyer of stocks—at what proved to be bargain prices.

Chapter 2: Endowment Purposes

1. Brooks Mather Kelley, *Yale: A History* (New Haven: Yale University Press, 1974).
2. The governor and lieutenant governor continued to serve ex officio as

fellows of the corporation, although in the modern era they have not participated actively in Yale's governance.

3. Merle Curti and Roderick Nash, *Philanthropy in the Shaping of American Higher Education* (New Brunswick, N.J.: Rutgers University Press, 1965); Frederick Rudolph, *The American College and University: A History* (Athens: University of Georgia Press, 1962).

4. Hugh Davis Graham and Nancy Diamond, *The Rise of American Research Universities* (Baltimore: Johns Hopkins University Press, 1997).

5. Ibid.

6. Howard R. Bowen, *The Costs of Higher Education: How Much Do Colleges and Universities Spend per Student and How Much Should They Spend?* (New York: McGraw-Hill, 1980). See also Graham and Diamond, *Universities,* 97.

7. Denise LaVoie, "School Year Begins with New Unification Church Affiliation," Associated Press, 28 August 1992.

8. Joseph Berger, "University of Bridgeport Honors Reverend Moon, Fiscal Savior," *New York Times,* 8 September 1995.

9. Ibid.

10. Lynde Phelps Wheeler, *Josiah Willard Gibbs* (New Haven: Yale University Press, 1951): 91–92.

11. Leonard Curry, "Congressional Hearing Puts Stanford Officials on Hot Seat," *Orange County Register,* 14 March 1991.

12. The 0.5 percent increment was designated "to support renewal of campus buildings and infrastructure." See *Stanford University Annual Financial Report,* 1995.

13. The unpublished survey of endowment size and institutional quality relies on research conducted by Paula Volent at the Yale investments Office.

14. "The Fortune 1,000 Ranked Within Industries," *Fortune,* 28 April 1997.

15. "Best Colleges 1998," *U.S. News & World Report,* 1 September 1997. USNWR ranks twenty-eight of the twenty-nine Carnegie universities. Rockefeller University, because it does not grant degrees, is excluded from the study.

16. National Center for Education Statistics, *Directory of Post Secondary Institutions, 1987–1997,* vol. 1. (Washington, D.C.: National Center for Education Statistics, 1997).

17. The National Association of College and University Business Officers (NACUBO) has published an annual survey of college and university endowments since 1971. The NACUBO Endowment Study (NES) is prepared by Cambridge Associates, a consulting firm that provides investment and financial research services to nonprofit endowed institutions.

Chapter 3: Investment and Spending Goals

1. James Tobin, "What Is Permanent Endowment Income?" *American Economic Review* 64, no. 2 (1974): 427–432.
2. Harvard University, *Managing Harvard's Endowment* (Cambridge, Mass.: Harvard University, 1990).
3. Even though Harvard's 1974 spending policy rationale contains flaws, in practice the university spends at prudent levels, producing payouts similar to those of comparable institutions.
4. Yale University, *Report of the Treasurer, 1965–66,* ser. 62, no. 19 (New Haven, 1966): 6–7.
5. National Association of College and University Business Officers (NACUBO). Data are from various *Endowment Studies,* prepared by Cambridge Associates.
6. In the 1997 NACUBO survey, 335 institutions reported using target spending rates.
7. See pages 18–23 for analysis of Carnegie Foundation Research Universities.
8. Karen W. Arenson, "Q&A. Modest Proposal. An Economists Asks, Does Harvard Really Need $15 Billion?" *New York Times,* 2 August 1998.
9. Henry Hansmann, "Why Do Universities Have Endowments?" *PONPO Working Paper,* no. 109 (New Haven: Program on Non-Profit Organizations, Institution for Social and Policy Studies, Yale University, January 1986): 21.
10. Ibid., 23.
11. Tobin, "Endowment Income," 427.

Chapter 4: Investment Philosophy

1. Gary P. Brinson, Brian D. Singer and Gilbert L. Beebower, "Determinants of Portfolio Performance II: An Update," *Financial Analysts Journal* 47, no. 3 (1991): 40–48. The Brinson, Singer, and Beebower article builds on Gary P. Brinson, L. Randolph Hood and Gilbert L. Beebower, "Determinants of Portfolio Performance," *Financial Analysts Journal* 42, no. 4 (1986): 39–44.
2. Charles D. Ellis, *Winning the Loser's Game: Timeless Strategies for Successful Investing,* 3d ed. (New York: McGraw-Hill, 1998): 11.
3. See, for example, William N. Goetzmann and Philippe Jorion, "Global Stock Markets in the Twentieth Century," *Journal of Finance* 54, no. 3 (1999): 953–980.
4. Stephen J. Brown, William N. Goetzmann, and Stephen A. Ross, "Survival," *Journal of Finance* 50, no. 3 (1995): 855.
5. Goetzmann and Jorion, "Global Stock Markets," 978.

6. Robert Lovett, "Gilt-Edged Insecurity," *Saturday Evening Post,* 3 April, 1937.
7. Cambridge Associates, *1998 NACUBO Endowment Study* (Washington, D.C.: National Association of College and University Business Officers, 1998).
8. John Maynard Keynes, "Memorandum for the Estates Committee, King's College, Cambridge, May 8, 1938," in Charles D. Ellis, ed., *Classics: An Investor's Anthology* (Homewood, Ill.: Business One Irwin in association with the Institute of Chartered Financial Analysts, 1989): 79–82.
9. Gilbert Burck, "A New Kind of Stock Market," *Bank Credit Analyst* (April 1998): 22. First published in *Fortune,* March 1959.
10. Ibid.
11. Endowment asset allocation figures come from Cambridge Associates.
12. Burton Malkiel and Paul Firstenberg, *Managing Risk in an Uncertain Era: An Analysis for Endowed Institutions* (Princeton, N.J.: Princeton University Press, 1976).
13. The Pension and Investments' Performance Evaluation Report (PIPER) rankings for managed accounts are compiled and published quarterly by *Pensions and Investments,* a trade publication for the investment management industry.
14. The eight managers that disappear produce results falling in the eighth decile for the three years preceding exit from the investment scene. The dramatic underperformance supports the hypothesis that client defections prompted dissolution or sale of the hapless investment management firms.

   The eleven managers discontinuing small-capitalization growth products represent a mixed bag, with returns falling in the sixth decile for the three years prior to termination. Some investment vehicles disappear because a critical manager jumps ship, as when Carlene Murphy Ziegler left Strong Corneliuson Capital Management to found her own firm, Artisan Partners. Other products appear to lose independent identity in a wave of corporate rationalization or reorganization, as might be the case with products once managed by industry giants Equitable, Prudential, and AIG. Occasionally disappearances arouse suspicion, as when investment firms drop the poorer performing of a number of small-company growth products. In 1994, one of two Dawson-Samberg funds disappeared, with the sixth-decile performer dropping out of the contest, while the top-decile fund continued to compete. Did the weak performer simply merge into the strong, causing the mediocre record to vanish?

   Twelve investment firms stopped reporting results, but continued to offer small-stock growth products, reporting returns that fall in the seventh decile for the three years before data flows cease. Reasons for failing to continue to provide PIPER with information prove difficult to uncover. As a result of a bank merger, Security Pacific's investment management subsidiary combined with Bank of America Investment Management. The record of Security Pacific's strong-performing Pacific Century Advisors small stock fund continued (under a new name in the Bank of America fund organization) without being included in the PIPER database. Perhaps the lack of an institutional relationship between Bank of America and PIPER led to interruption of the data flow. Aside from changes in corporate structure, managers might stop reporting out of frustration. The relatively low ranking of many funds in the nonreporting category suggests that poor results caused some firms to seek a lower profile by withholding data, perhaps awaiting improvement in the product's performance.

While the funds that left PIPER's small-capitalization growth universe over the five-year period posted generally poor results, some strong products departed as well. Departure of a key manager caused Strong/Corneliuson to drop a third-decile fund, and a bank merger resulted in another third-decile fund's departure from the pool. From the perspective of the pool of investment managers, the dampening influence of the departing handful of strong performers failed to offset the inflationary impact of the much larger exiting group of mediocre products, causing survivorship bias to boost overall reported results.

15. Brady Commission, *Report of the Presidential Task Force on Market Mechanisms, January 1988* (Washington, D.C.: GPO, 1988): 53.
16. John Maynard Keynes, *The General Theory of Employment, Interest and Money* (New York: Harcourt and Brace, 1964): 155.
17. Ibid., 160.
18. Benjamin Graham, *The Intelligent Investor* (New York: Harper Business, 1973): 279.
19. See Eugene Fama and Kenneth French, "Size and Book-to-Market Factors in Earnings and Returns," *Journal of Finance* 50, no. 1 (1995): 131–155, and Eugene Fama and Kenneth French, "The Cross-Section of Expected Stock Returns," *Journal of Finance* 47, no. 2 (1992): 427–465.
20. Graham, *Intelligent Investor.*
21. Keynes, *General Theory,* 157.
22. Ibid., 151.

CHAPTER 5: ASSET ALLOCATION

1. Moody's Investor Service, *Moody's Transportation Manual* (New York: Moody's Investor Service, 1973): 358–370.
2. Richard Michaud, "The Markowitz Optimization Enigma: Is 'Optimized' Optimal?" *Financial Analysts Journal* 45, no. 1 (1989): 31–42.

3. Richard Bookstaber, "Global Risk Management: Are We Missing the Point?" (presentation given at the Institute for Quantitative Research in Finance, October 1996, and at a conference on Internal Models for Market Risk Evaluation: Experiences, Problems and Perspectives in Rome, Italy, June 1996).
4. Keynes, *General Theory,* 155. The full quote from Keynes is: "The social object of skilled investment should be to defeat the dark forces of time and ignorance which envelop our future."
5. Jeremy Grantham. "Everything I Know About the Stock Market in 15 Minutes," internal memo. Grantham, Mayo, Van Otterloo & Co., 1997.
6. Vijay Kumar Chopra and William T. Ziemba, "The Effect of Errors in Means, Variances, and Covariances on Optimal Portfolio Choice," *Journal of Portfolio Management* 19, no. 2 (1993): 6–11.
7. Roger G. Ibbotson and Rex A. Sinquefield, "Stocks, Bonds, Bills, and Inflation: Year-by-Year Historical Returns (1926–1974)," *Journal of Business* 49, no. 1 (1976): 11–47.
8. A more complete discussion of the relationship between stock returns and inflation is included on page 181.
9. Paul M. Firstenberg, Stephen A. Ross, and Randall C. Zisler, "Real Estate: The Whole Story," *Journal of Portfolio Management* 24, no. 3 (1988): 31. Apparently the article continues to be highly regarded; it appears in Peter L. Bernstein and Frank J. Fabozzi, eds., *Streetwise. The Best of the Journal of Portfolio Management,* (Princeton, N.J.: Princeton University Press, 1997).

CHAPTER 6: PORTFOLIO MANAGEMENT

1. Linda Sandler, "Endowments at Top Schools Bruised in Market," *Wall Street Journal,* 13 October 1998.
2. John R. Dorfman, "Report on Common Fund Cites Warning Signs," *Wall Street Journal,* 17 January 1996, C1.
3. Andrew Bary, "Paying the Piper: Star Mutual Fund Gets Hamstrung," *Barron's,* 11 April 1994, 15.
4. Jefferey M. Laderman and Gary Weiss, "To Win It, You'll Have to Take a Few Calculated Risks," *Business Week,* 12 December 1996, 140.
5. Bary, "Paying the Piper," 15.
6. Laura Jereski, "Mortgage Derivatives Claim Victims Big and Small," *Wall Street Journal,* 20 April 1994.
7. Bary, "Paying the Piper," 15.
8. PIPER: Pensions and Investments' Performance Evaluation Reports, *Managed Accounts Report, December 31, 1995.* (New York: Pension & Investments, 1995).
9. Keynes, *General Theory,* 157.

CHAPTER 7: TRADITIONAL ASSET CLASSES

1. Ibbotson Associates, *Stocks, Bonds, Bills, and Inflation 1998 Yearbook* (Chicago: Ibbotson Associates, 1998). The bond return series describes long-term government bonds with an approximate maturity of twenty years, while the cash returns consist of thirty-day treasury bills. Inflation is based on the consumer price index for all urban consumers, not seasonally adjusted.
2. For a fascinating rendering of the RJR buyout saga, read Bryan Burrough and John Heylar, *Barbarians at the Gate* (New York: Harper & Row, 1990).
3. Tom Herman, "How Bond Buyers Can Avoid an LBO Hit," *Wall Street Journal,* 24 October 1988.
4. *Los Angeles Times-Mirror,* 18 November, 1988.
5. The Government National Mortgage Association (GNMA—"Ginnie Mae"), the Federal Home Loan Mortgage Corporation (FHLMC—"Freddie Mac"), and the Federal National Mortgage Association (FNMA—"Fannie Mae") represent by far the largest share of the mortgage pass-through market.
6. The Lehman Brothers Aggregate Index and Lehman Brothers Government/Corporate Index sometimes contain a very small percentage of issues rated BB or lower due to downgrades of issues during the monthly holding period.
7. Results are measured against the SEI Large Plan Universe.
8. Data are from Ibbotson Associates, *Stocks, Bonds.*
9. Data are from Morgan Stanley Capital International.
10. Burrough and Heylar, *Barbarians at the Gate,* 93.
11. Ibid., 93–96.
12. Keynes, *General Theory,* 156.
13. Jeremy J. Siegel, *Stocks for the Long Run* (New York: Richard S. Irwin, 1994).
14. Ibid., 210.
15. Putnam, Lovell, de Guardiola & Thornton, and Wechsler Ross & Partners, "Alliance Capital Management L.P. Acquires Cursitor-Eaton Asset Management," *Mutual Fund Café,* on-line database, 25 November 1995.
16. Ibid.
17. Alliance Capital Management L.P., *1998 Annual Report* (New York: Alliance Capital Management L.P., 1998), 69.
18. Data on international equity rankings come from PIPER: Pension and Investments' Performance Evaluation Reports, *Managed Accounts Report, December 31, 1998* (New York: Pension & Investments, 1998).
19. See pages 78, 182–185 for a discussion of the exceptional case of Japan.
20. Morgan Stanley Capital International, *Methodology and Index Policy March 1998* (Los Angeles: Morgan Stanley Capital International, 1998).

21. Malkiel, *A Random Walk Down Wall Street,* 140.
22. Cambridge Associates, *U.S. Common Stock Managers. Executive Summary* (Washington, D.C.: Cambridge Associates, 1998): 5.
23. Keynes, *General Theory,* 151.
24. Ibid., 155.
25. Ibid., 151.
26. Ibid., 149.
27. Ibid., 157.
28. Ibid., 155.
29. Julie Rohrer, "Inside the Alpha Factory," *Institutional Investor* 23, no. 9 (1989).
30. Shoba Narayan, "Is Less More?" *Institutional Investor* 32, no. 8 (1998): 135.

CHAPTER 8: ALTERNATIVE ASSET CLASSES

1. The amount of the capital required to execute the Newell Rubbermaid trade ranges from an aggressive value of the Rubbermaid price less the net proceeds from the short sale of Newell (31.8125 − 2.28 = 29.5325), to a conservative value of the Newell short position (.7883 × 43.25 = 34.09). Choosing the value of the Rubbermaid share (31.8125) represents a middle-of-the-road position.
2. At December 31, 1998, the ratio of real estate yields to ten-year treasuries stood at 1.68, representing the highest level since February 1975. The relationship between yields on real estate investment trusts (REITs) and intermediate-term bonds provides a rough indication of comparative value. The high ratio of REIT yields to bond yields suggests that real estate might be attractively priced relative to bonds.
3. The NCREIF Property Index held approximately 2,400 properties valued at $65 billion on September 30, 1998.
4. For a discussion of excess volatility, see page 307.
5. The Institutional Property Consultants (IPC) database consists of 149 pooled fund portfolios, which contain approximately 2,330 properties with an aggregate value of $43 billion on September 30, 1998.
6. Venture Economics, *1998 Investment Benchmarks Report: Venture Capital* (Newark, N.J.: Venture Economics Investor Services, 1998). The analysis includes the longest period for which reasonable data are available. Although the venture capital series began in 1969 and the leveraged buyout series began in 1976, the analysis excludes data prior to 1980 because the buyout database includes only one fund for the period 1976 to 1979.
7. Venture Economics, *1998 Investment Benchmarks Report: Buyouts and Other Private Equity* (Newark, N.J.: Venture Economics Investor Services, 1998).

8. The data were compiled and analyzed by Yale's director of investments Timothy Sullivan, and summer associate Daniel Levin.
9. The corporate bond data come from Ibbotson Associates, *Stocks, Bonds.*
10. Keynes, *General Theory,* 160.

CHAPTER 9: INVESTMENT ADVISERS

1. Keynes, *General Theory,* 155.
2. The information on Granville is drawn from Rhonda Brammer, "10 Years After He Peaked, Will Joe Granville Rise Again?" *Barron's,* 24 August 1992.
3. The discussion of entrepreneurial capitalism draws heavily on a 1997 essay by G. Leonard Baker, General Partner of Sutter Hill Ventures, "How Silicon Valley Works: Reflections on 25 years in the Venture Capital Business," 1997.
4. Joseph A. Schumpeter, *The Theory of Economic Development,* trans. Redvers Opie (Cambridge: Harvard University Press, 1934): 66.
5. Joseph A. Schumpeter, *Capitalism, Socialism, and Democracy* (New York: Harper & Brothers, 1950): 83.
6. Ibid.
7. United Asset Management, 1997 *Annual Report* (Boston: United Asset Management, 1997): 2.
8. George Anders, "Captive Client: Morgan Stanley Found a Gold Mine of Fees," *Wall Street Journal,* 14 December 1990, sec. A.
9. Ibid.
10. Randall Smith, "Hasty Retreat: How Goldman Scored with a 'Vulture Fund' Yet Decided to Kill it," *Wall Street Journal,* 4 June 1991, 6.
11. Ibid.
12. Ibid.
13. Ibid.
14. U.S. Securities and Exchange Commission, Office of Compliance, Inspections and Examinations, *Inspection Report on the Soft Dollar Practices of Broker-Dealers, Investment Advisers and Mutual Funds* (Washington, D.C.: September 1998).
15. Jeffrey Taylor, "SEC Wants Investment Managers to Tell Clients More About 'Soft Dollar' Services," *Wall Street Journal,* 15 February 1997, 5, 21.
16. See *Inspection Report,* 40.
17. Barry B. Burr, "Soft Dollar Managers Pay," *(Chicago) Pensions and Investments,* 10 August 1998, 10.
18. SEC, *Inspection Report,* 3.
19. Advisory Council on Employee Welfare and Benefit Plans, *Report of the Working Groups on Soft Dollars/Commission Recapture* (Washington D.C.: November 1997): 5, 21.

20. Roger Lowenstein, *Buffett: The Making of an American Capitalist* (New York: Random House, 1995): 62.
21. Susan Pulliam, "JMB Realty Hits Discord with Funds Over Investments," *Wall Street Journal,* 15 July 1992.
22. Ibid.

CHAPTER 10: PERFORMANCE ASSESSMENT

1. Staff Reporter. "Shortselling in America: To have and have not," *The Economist,* 22 October 1988.
2. David A. Rocker, "Refresher Course. Short Interest: No More Bullish Bellow," *Barron's,* 1 May 1995, 43.
3. PIPER: Pensions and Investments' Performance Evaluation Reports, *Managed Accounts Report, December 31, 1997* (New York: Pensions & Investments, 1997).
4. Robert J. Shiller, *Market Volatility* (Cambridge: MIT Press, 1989).
5. Ibid., 2–3.
6. James B. Stewart, *Den of Thieves* (New York: Touchstone, 1992): 421.
7. I am a director of The Investment Fund for Foundations, a post for which I receive no compensation.

CHAPTER 11: INVESTMENT PROCESS

1. Keynes, *General Theory,* 157–158.
2. Gretchen Morgenson. "As Indexes Boom, Funds Fizzle," *New York Times,* 5 July 1998, 27; Carole Gould, "Indexes Make for Stiff Competition," *New York Times,* 5 July 1998, 32.
3. Information comes from the 1997 survey of investment returns sponsored by the National Association of College and University Business Officers.
4. New York University, *New York University Financial Report, 1977–1997,* 20 vols. (New York: New York University, *1977–1997);* New York University, *New York University Annual Report, 1977–1985,* 9 vols. (New York: New York University, 1977–1985).
5. Roger Lowenstein, "How Larry Tisch and NYU Missed the Bull Market's Run," *Wall Street Journal,* 16 October 1997.
6. The NACUBO (National Association of College and University Business Officers) Endowment Wealth Index reflects median annual changes in the aggregate endowment market value of institutions participating in the group's annual survey. Year-to-year change in wealth includes the impact of investment returns, gifts, and spending.
7. David Barboza, "Loving a Stock, Not Wisely But Too Well," *New York Times,* 20 September 1998, sec. 3.
8. Ibid.
9. Ellis, *Winning.*

Index

Absolute return investment, 114–16, 204, 205–16
  active management of, 114, 216
  compensation for, 281–83
  event-driven, 205–7, 210, 212–14
  fundamental attributes, 210–13
  historical data on, 115
  hurdle rate for, 280
  return assumptions for, 114–16, 208, 210
  risk assumptions for, 114–16, 210
  survivorship bias in, 209–10
  value-driven, 207–9, 210, 214–16
Academic research, federal support for, 12–13
Active management, 55–57, 138–41. *See also* Investment advisers
  of absolute return, 114, 216
  of bonds, 76–77, 167–71
  challenges of, 6–7
  compensation arrangements for, 270–72
  costs of, 248
  dollar-weighted evaluation of, 87
  of equity, 77–78, 178–79
  game of, 249–52
  market efficiency and, 56, 74–76
  market illiquidity and, 87–88
  portfolio biases and, 138–39
  of private equity, 87, 239–45
  of real estate investment, 76, 77, 221–24
  survivorship bias and, 79–87
Adaptation, entrepreneurial, 257–58
Administrators, on endowment purposes, 9
Advisers. *See* Investment advisers
Agency issues, 4–6, 197. *See also* Investment advisers
  in bond investment, 163–69
Ahrens, Kent, 146

Alliance Capital, 184
Alpha (excess return), 115n
Alternative asset classes. *See* Absolute return investment; Private equity investments; Real estate investment
American Government Securities Fund (AGF), 304–7
Ames, Chuck, 244
Arbitrage, 147–48
  convertible, 147–48
  merger (risk), 205–7, 212–13, 298
Arbitrage pricing theory (APT), 104
Argyle Village Square, 287
Asian financial crisis (1998), 89–90, 158
Askin, David, 143–44, 154
Asset allocation, 52, 52n, 53–54, 57–67, 100–131
  analysis of. *See* Qualitative analysis; Quantitative analysis
  diversification, 62–67
  drift in, 134
  equity bias in, 56–62
  global, 185
  policy targets of, 4, 329–31
  portfolio management and, 132
  rebalancing, 70–73
  results of disciplined portfolio management, 128–30
  tactical (TAA), 68–69
  testing, 123–30
  top-down and bottom-up factors in assessing, 3
Asset classes. *See also* Absolute return investment; Bonds; Private equity investments; Real estate investment; Stocks
  definition of, 12–4
  fashion and, 100–102

Asset classes *(continued)*
  reviews of, 331–32
Audits, 341–43
Avon Products, 63–64

Back office operations, 340–43
Baker, Len, 256
Baldwin, Simeon, 62
Bankruptcy, 206
Banks, investment, 263–66
Barclays Global Investors, 269*n*
Barings, 341
BARRA, 194
Base compensation, 271
Beardstown Ladies, 251–52
Beebower, Gil, 53
Benchmarks, 300–301
  active management of bonds and, 168–71
  specialized, 301–2
Berkeley Fellowship, 15
Biases, portfolio, 138–40
  equity, 57–62
Bills, treasury, 58, 59
Blakeney Management, 259
Bloomberg Football Index, 301*n*
Bluhm, Neil, 287
Bok, Derek, 13
Bonds, 102–3, 156–72
  active management of, 76–77, 167–71
  agency issues, 163–69
  asset characteristics, 160–67
  call options, 162, 163, 167–68, 234–35
  corporate, 5, 59, 163–67
  deflation and, 103, 119, 155, 158, 171,
    216, 217, 218
  diversifying role of, 155, 156–57, 160
  duration (maturity) of, 161–62
  foreign, 103, 163, 168
  government, 58–59, 103
  inflation and, 118, 119, 157–58
  inflation-indexed, 103
  junk, 102–3, 234–35
  NYU overinvestment in, 325–26
  panic of 1998 and, 158–60
  passive management of, 269–70
  quality of, 162
  railroad, 101
  returns on, 111, 112, 118, 160
  risks of, 111, 112
  spending implications of different types
    of, 32, 33
  timing purchase of, 68
  treasury, 88, 159–60, 162, 163–64, 171
Bookstaber, Richard, 106
Boston University, 326–28
Bottom-up investment, 179
Brainard, Provost Bill, xii, 30, 98
Brammer, Rhoda, 251
Brewster, Kingman, 13

Bridgeport, University of, 13–14
Brinson, Gary, 53
Broker dealers, 272
Brown Bros. & Co., 101
Bruno's, 285
Bruntjen, Worth, 150–52
Buffalo Partners, 316
Buffett, Warren, 77, 285
Bureaucracies, 258, 336
Burlington Industries, 264
Buyouts. *See* Leveraged buyouts

Cadillac Fairview, 288–89
Call options, 162, 163, 167–68, 234–35
Call risk, 59*n*
Cambridge Associates, Inc., 79, 189
Capital asset pricing model (CAPM), 104
Capital market assumptions, 109–23, 128.
    See also Returns; Risk
  alternative asset characteristics, 114–18
  correlation matrix assumptions, 118–19,
    120–21
  historical data and, 109–10, 112
  marketable security characteristics, 110–13
  simulations and, 125
Carnegie Foundation for Advancement of
    Teaching, 18
Carnegie Institution of Washington, 43
Cash, 69, 160–61
Cash collateral, 145, 147, 150, 208*n*
Chairs, endowed, 15–16
Chieftain Capital, 198
Chinese walls, 265
Citron, Robert, 149
Clap, Thomas, 11
Clark Foundation, 63–64
Clayton Dubilier & Rice (CDR), 243–45
Client-directed brokerage, 272–73
Coca-Cola, 222
Cohen, David, 213*n*
Co-investment, 267–68, 278, 318
Collateral, 145, 147, 150, 208*n*
Collegiality, in investment environment,
    337
Collins, George, 164
Committee. *See* Investment committee
Common Fund, 146–50, 342
Company size, public scrutiny and, 91, 92
Compensation arrangements, 268–90
  hard hurdles, 280
  incentive, 271–72, 278, 279–81
  for marketable securities, 268–77
  for nontraditional assets, 278–90
  soft hurdles, 280
Completeness funds, 139–40
Concentrated portfolios, 62–64, 197–200
Conflicts of interest, 263–66. *See also*
    Agency issues
  consultant-client, 318

with external investment managers, 5
   in soft-dollar arrangements, 274
Consensus-driven behavior, 320, 323–24
Consultants, 294, 318
Consulting firms, 317–18
Consumer stocks, 140–41
Contracts, 18–19, 21, 163
Contrarian investing, 5, 7, 187, 293, 300,
   319, 320
   opportunities and risk of, 324–28
   value-oriented, 95, 96–98
Control environment (back office operation),
   340–43
Control risks, 340–41
Convertible arbitrage, 147–48
Cooper, Richard, 30
Coopers & Lybrand, 342–43
Corporate bonds, 5, 59, 163–67
Corporate profitability, 176
Correlations, 105, 118–19, 120-21
Creative destruction, 258–59
Credit risk, 59, 103, 145, 147, 159, 162, 167,
   169–70, 171, 201
Creedon, John, 165
"Crossing" opportunities, 269
Currency exposure, 175
Cursitor Eaton, 183–85
Custodian banks, 145
Cyclical stocks, 140–41

Daiwa Bank, 149, 341
Dana, Professor James Dwight, 15
Day, Jeremiah, 63
Deal fees, 279
Deal structure, 149–50
Debt. *See also* Bonds
   emerging market, 89–90
   sovereign, 89
   subordinated, 234, 236, 237, 238
Decision making
   consensus-driven behavior, 320, 323–24
   contrarian opportunity and risk, 324–28
   policy target focus, 329–31
   within rigorous investment framework, 3
   self-interest in, 4–5
   short-term thinking, 322–23
   strategic and tactical issues in, 331–32
Deflation, 157
   bonds and, 103, 119, 155, 158, 171, 216,
      217, 218
   overseas, 168
   real estate and, 217, 218, 269
   stocks and, 119, 202
Degree of opportunity, 74–76
Derivatives, 142–43, 151
"Determinants of Portfolio Performance"
   (Brinson, Singer, & Beebower), 53
Diamond, Graham and Nancy, 12
Directed brokerage, 276–77

Diversification, 54, 62–67
   through bonds, 155, 156–57, 160
   at Clark Foundation, 63–64
   Great Crash of 1929 and, 64–67
   at Yale, 62–63
Divestitures, corporate, 243–45
Dividends, 32, 68, 161, 182n
Dollar-weighted returns (internal rates of re-
   turn), 87, 308–9
Domestic bond and stock managers, sur-
   vivorship bias in, 84–86
Domestic bonds. *See* Bonds
Domestic stocks. *See* Stocks
Donors, 9, 10, 14–15, 27, 42, 43, 51, 124
Douglas Emmett, 221
Due diligence, 240–41, 300
Duhamel, Bill, 213n
Duration, 161–62

Eagle Bank of New Haven, 62–63
Edna McConnell Clark Foundation, 63–64
Educational excellence, endowments to
   achieve, 17–23
Educational institutions, 17, 42, 45
Efficiency. *See* Market efficiency
Efficient markets hypothesis, 188–89
Ellis, Charles, 55, 328
Emerging markets, 89–90, 113, 156
   risk and returns in, 174, 175
   top-down investing opportunity in,
      185–87
Endowment management, 2–3
Endowment purposes, 8–24
   academic excellence, 17–23
   debates over, 9
   income stream, 8, 17
   independence, 8, 10–14
   stability, 8, 14–17, 45–46
Entrepreneurs, 98, 226, 227, 256–60
Equities. *See* Private equity investments;
   Stocks
Equity bias, 54, 56–62
Event-driven investing, 114, 205–7, 210,
   212–14
Excess return (alpha), 115n
External managers, 5, 341, 342
Extreme spending policies, 46–50

Faculty, on endowment purposes, 9
Fair value, 192
Farallon Capital Management, 213n
Federal regulation, cost of compliance with,
   12–13
Federal Reserve, 111
Fees, 274, 278, 279. *See also* Compensation
   arrangements
   asset-based, 27
   deal, 279
   entry and exit, 282–83

Fees *(continued)*
  excessive, 176–77, 274, 279, 284–85, 286,
    289, 290
  incentive oriented, 271–72
Feshbach brothers, 296–97
Financial crisis, 155, 156–57, 171, 206
  Asian, 89–90, 158
Financial engineering, 227, 232, 233
Financial supermarkets, 261
First Capital Strategists, 146, 149–50
Firstenberg, Paul, 122
Fixed income assets. *See* Bonds; Cash
Florida, portfolio management in state of,
  150–52
Foreign bonds, 103, 163, 168
Foreign equities, 77, 82, 113, 174
  active management of, 77–78, 178–79
  currency exposure associated with, 175
Forward currency market, 89–90, 163
Forward-looking investment, 192
Foundations
  investment goals of, 41–44
  undiversified portfolios of, 63–64
Franklin, Benjamin, 25
Frank Russell Trust Company, 297
Free-rider problem, 281–82
Fundamental analysis, momentum invest-
  ing and, 189, 191, 214
Fundamental risk, value investing and,
  189–91
Fund-of-funds manager, 314, 315–17
Futures contracts, 142

Gatekeepers (private equity consultants),
  318
General Assembly of Connecticut, 11
General Theory, The (Keynes), 93, 98,
  320–21
Generational transition in investment orga-
  nizations, 44, 295–96
Gibbs, Josiah Willard, 15–16
Gifts, 8, 27–28
  impact on foundations, 43–44
  purchasing power and, 36–37
  restricted and unrestricted, 10
"Gilt-Edged Insecurity," 65
Global asset allocation, 185
Global perspective, 335
Gold, 60
Goldman Sachs, 264–67
Gould, Carole, 322
Governance issues, 339–40
Government bonds, 58–59, 103
Graham, Benjamin, 94
Graham, Hugh, 12
Granite Capital, 143–44
Grantham, Jeremy, 95, 96, 109, 182, 190–91
Grantham, Mayo, Van Otterloo (GMO),
  182–83

Grants, 8, 10, 18–19, 21
Granville, Joe, 250–51, 252
Great Crash of 1929, 64–67, 190
"Greater fool" concept, 191
Greenberg, Glenn, 198
Greylock, 295
Growth (momentum) strategies, speculative
  excess and, 191–92
Growth stocks, 96, 189
Guaranteed Student Loan Program, 90
Guber, Peter, 223*n*
Guerrillas, investment, 259–60

Haley, Roy, 244
Handelsbanken All-Nordic Combined Bond
  Index, 301*n*
Hansmann, Henry, 44–45
Harvard University, 13, 28, 43, 128–30,
  141–42
Hasbro, 265
Hedge funds, 296
Hedging, 148, 217, 218
Higher Education Price Index (HEPI), 35
Hillhouse, James, 62
Historical data, 109–10
  on absolute return, 115
  inappropriate use of, 119–23
Hoadley, George, 63
Hotel investing, 217
Hurdle rates, 280–81

Ibbotson, Roger, 58
Ibbotson-Sinquefield data series, 111
IFC Global Emerging Markets Index, 187
Igushi, Toshihide, 149
Illiquid assets, performance benchmarks
  for, 301
Illiquidity
  acceptance of, 56, 57
  attractions of, 91–92
  rebalancing and, 136–38
Incentive compensation, 271–72, 278,
  279–81
Independent investment organizations,
  260–67
  investment banks and investment man-
    agement, 263–66
  United Asset Management (UAM),
    261–63
Indexes, 169, 170, 187, 228, 269, 271, 301,
  301*n*, 304
Index fund managers, 268–70
Index funds, 138
Inflation
  bonds and, 118, 119, 157–58
  gifts to offset, 28
  measurement of, 35
  real estate as hedge against, 216–17, 218
  stocks and, 118–19, 176, 181

Inflation-hedging, 217, 218
Inflation-indexed bonds, 103
Innovation, entrepreneurial, 256–57
Integrity of investment advisers, 252
Interest-only strips, 143
Interest rate risk, 147
Interest rates, 69, 157
Intergenerational equity, 27, 33, 44
Interleukin-2, 328
Intermediaries, performance assessment of,
    314–18. *See also* Investment advisers
  consulting firms, 317–18
  fund-of-funds manager, 314, 315–17
Internal controls, 340–41
Internal rates of return (IRR), 308–9
International equity, *See* Foreign equities
International equity managers, survivorship
    bias in, 82–83
Investment advisers, 248–92. *See also* Ac-
    tive management; Performance assess-
    ment
  co-investment by, 267–68, 278, 318
  compensation arrangements, 268–90
  due diligence checks on, 300
  entrepreneurial attitude among, 256–60
  independent organizations, 260–67
  organizational change in, 297–99
  personal characteristics of, 252–54
  size issues, 255–56
Investment Advisers Act of 1940, 273, 277
Investment banks, 263–66
Investment committee, 331–34
  defining role of, 314
  meetings of, 331–32
Investment framework, rigorous, 3–4
Investment Fund for Foundations (TIFF),
    317
Investment goals, 26–30, 41–44
  gifts and, 27–28
  purchasing power preservation vs. oper-
    ating support tradeoffs, 25–27, 28–30
Investment guerrillas, 259–60
Investment management firms, 263–66
Investment philosophy, 52–99, 320
  asset allocation, 52n, 53–54, 57–67
  market timing, 52n, 53, 55, 57, 67–73
  security selection, 52, 52–53, 53n, 55–57,
    74–99
Investment process, 320–43
  decision-making challenges in, 321–28
  decision-making process, 328–32
  group dynamics in, 320–21
  operating environment, 332–37
  organizational structure, 337–43
Investment staff, 314, 334–35

J.P. Morgan, 64
Japan, top-down investing in, 181–85
Japanese market, 78

JMB, 287–89
Johnson, F. Ross, 176–77
Judelson, Robert, 287
Junk bonds, 102–3, 234–35
J&W Seligman & Co., 275

Kelley, Brooks Mather, 11
Keynes, J.M., 67, 93, 97, 98, 153, 180, 190,
    191, 192, 249, 320–21
Kleiner Perkins, 290
Kohlberg Kravis Roberts (KKR), 164, 165,
    225–26, 284–86
Korea, 186–87

Large-capitalization stocks, 156, 178
Leeson, Nicholas, 149
Lehigh Valley Railroad, 101
Lehman Brothers Aggregate Index, 169,
    170, 228
Lehman Brothers Government Corporate
    Index, 269
Leverage, 133–34, 141–52
  Common Fund case, 146–50
  explicit and implicit, 133–34, 141–44
  Granite Capital case, 143–44
  security lending, 144–50
Leveraged buyouts, 117, 172, 225–26, 227
  active management opportunities in, 76,
    77
  fees for, 279, 290
  limited institutional experience with,
    238–39
  median results for, 78–79
  mezzanine funds vs., 235–38
  partnership terms in, 280–81
  returns on, 228–33
  of RJR Nabisco, 164–67
  survivorship bias in, 231
  value-added possibilities in, 227
  value-oriented, 243
Levin, Richard C., xiii
Levitt, Arthur, 274
Liquidity, 87–94. *See also* Illiquidity
  of absolute return, 209
  emerging market debt, 89–90
  ephemeral nature of, 93–94
  full faith and credit obligations, 88–89
  mean-variance optimization and, 107
  noncash sources of, 161
  Sallie Mae stock, 90–91
Long-short investing, 303
Long Term Capital Management, 158
Long-term orientation, 320
Lovett, Robert, 65
Loyalty of investment advisers, 253

M^2, 310
Macaulay, Frederick R., 161n
Macaulay duration, 161n

Malkiel, Burton, 73, 188–89
Malkin, Judd, 287, 288
Management
    self-interest of, 176–78
    shareholders' interests vs., 224–25
Management companies, separate, 338–40
Management fees, 274
Managers
    external, 5, 341, 342
    fund-of-funds, 314, 315–17
    index fund, 268–70
    senior partners of, 298–99
    specialists, 223–24
    termination of, 313, 332
Managing Risk in an Uncertain Era
    (Malkiel), 73
Margin of excellence, 17–23
Margin of safety, 94–96
Marketable securities, 100–13, 300. *See also*
    Bonds; Securities; Stocks
Market efficiency, 74–87
    active management and, 56, 74–76
    degree of opportunity, 74–76
    forms of, 188–89
    returns and, 76–79
    survivorship bias and, 79–87
Market timing, 52n, 53, 55, 57, 67–73
    rebalancing and 1987 market crash,
    70–73
Market volatility. *See* Volatility
Markowitz, Harry, 62, 104
Mayfield, 295
MCI Communications, 213
Mean reverting behavior, 109
Mean-variance optimization, 104–7, 110
    capital market assumptions, 109–23, 128
    choosing portfolio and, 123
    correlation matrix, 118–19
    gradualism in, 108
    limitations of, 105–7, 125–28
    misuse of, 119–23
Mentorship, focused, 336
Merger and acquisition activity, 298
Merger arbitrage, 205–7, 212–13
Metropolitan Life Insurance Company, 165
Mezzanine finance, 234–38, 242, 283
    equity funds vs., 236–38
    returns on, 235–36
Michaud, Richard, 105–6
ML-Lee Acquisition Fund II, 237
Modern portfolio theory (MPT), xiv, 104
Modigliani, Franco, 310
Modigliani, Leah, 310
Momentum (growth) strategies, speculative
    excess and, 191–92
Money managers. *See also* Investment
    advisers
    conflicts with investment goals and, 261
    differences with endowment, 253

performance evaluation of, 311–12
    search for, 254–55
    soft dollar expenses of, 273
Money market investments, 311
Moon, Sun Myung, 14
Morgan Stanley, 264
Morgan Stanley Capital International All
    Country World Index, 187
Morgan Stanley Capital International Eu-
    rope Australia Far East (MSCI EAFE)
    Index, 113n, 174, 184
Morland, Miles, 259
Morningstar, 151, 200
Mortgage-backed securities, 151, 162, 167,
    169–70, 171, 305
Mortgage derivatives, 151
Mortgage investing, 217
Mulheren, John, 316
Murphy, John R., 327
Mutual funds, short-term focus on, 322

NACUBO Endowment Study (1998), 34n
Newell Rubbermaid merger arbitrage,
    212–13
New Jersey Division of Investment, 276–77
New York University (NYU), 325–26
Nifty Fifty, 64n
Nippon Telephone & Telegraph (NTT),
    182–83
Nonnormally distributed variables, 106
Nontraditional assets. *See* Absolute return
    investment; Private equity invest-
    ments; Real estate investment
Nordhaus, William, 30
Normally distributed variable, 72n
Normal portfolios, 139–40

October 1929 crash, 64–67, 190
October 1987 crash, 70–73, 93, 106,
    329–31
Off-the-run treasury bonds, 88
On-the-run treasury bonds, 88
Operating environment, 332–37
    investment committee, 314, 331–34
    investment staff, 314, 334–35
    organizational characteristics, 335–37
Operating support, 25, 26, 27, 124
    purchasing power preservation vs.,
    25–27, 28–30
Opportunity, degree of, 74–76
Organizational change, 297–99
Organizational characteristics, 335–37
Organizational structure, 337–43
    internal control environment, 340–43
    separate management companies,
    338–40
Overseas Private Investment Corporation,
    88–89
Ownership, entrepreneurial, 257

Palladas, 134
Paloma Partners, 316
Panic of 1998, 158–60
Partnerships, 118, 209, 228–29, 240, 268, 280–81, 298
Passive management, 268–70
Paulson, Hank, 335
Peer comparisons, 302–3
Pension funds, 145
Performance assessment, 293–319
  outside consultants for, 294
  by intermediaries, 314–18
  qualitative factors in, 295–99
  qualitative tools for, 299–300
  quantitative factors in, 294, 300–308
  quantitative tools for, 308–10
  use of, 310–14
Performance attribution services, 274–76
Performance chasing, 293
Performance competition, 323
Peters, Jon, 223n
PIPER, 86, 115n, 235
Piper Capital, 150–52
Piper Jaffrey American Government Securities Fund (AGF), 304, 306
Policy asset allocation targets, 4, 329–31
Porter, Noah, 15
Portfolio
  concentrated, 62–64, 197–200
  diversified, 197–200
  drifting, 70, 134
  efficient, 104–5
  normal, 139–40
  sizing of, 310, 314
  turnover in, 311
Portfolio management, 132–54. *See also*
  Active management
  asset allocation at center of, 132
  completeness funds, 139–40
  Florida example, 150–52
  leverage, 133–34, 141–52
  opportunity and risk in, 133–35, 140–41
  rebalancing, 132–33, 134–38
Princeton University, 128–30
Private equity consultants (gatekeepers), 318
Private equity investments, 204, 224–45.
  See also Leveraged buyouts; Venture capital
  active management of, 87, 239–45
  alignment of shareholder and management interests in, 224–25
  asset characteristics, 230–39
  compensation for, 283–86, 290
  hurdle rate for, 281
  information on, 91
  infrequent valuation of, 226–27
  investment bank sponsorship of, 263–64
  limited institutional experience with, 238–39

  mezzanine finance funds, 234–38, 242, 283
  performance assessment in, 301, 311
  rebalancing activity for, 136–37
  risk and return assumptions for, 117–18, 226, 228–33
  value-added investing in, 227–28
  value creation in, 244–45
  Yale's experience with, 233–34
Professors World Peace Academy, 13–14
Profitability, corporate, 176
Profits interests, 146, 246, 267, 278, 279–81
Public universities, 18
Purchasing power
  evaluation of, 35–38
  gifts and, 36–37
  preservation of, 25–30, 124
  of Yale, 35–38

q, 98
Qualitative analysis, 108
Qualitative performance assessment tools, 299–300
Quality ranking, endowment size and, 19–21
Quantitative analysis, 104–8. *See also*
  Mean-variance optimization
  capital market assumptions, 109–23, 128
  historical capital markets data as starting point for, 109–10, 112
  identifying efficient portfolios, 104–5
  of performance, 308–10
Quantitative models
  data specification techniques for, 119
  Rosenberg's Black Box, 194–97

Railroad bonds, 101
Random Walk down Wall Street, A (Malkiel), 188
"Real Estate: The Whole Story" (Firstenberg, Ross & Zisler), 122–23
Real estate investment, 204, 216–24
  active management of, 76, 77, 221–24
  asset characteristics, 218–19
  compensation structure for, 286–89
  debt and equity characteristics of, 217–18
  deflation and, 217, 218, 269
  hurdle rates for, 280
  as inflation hedge, 216–17, 218
  overinvestment in, 119–23
  portfolio stability and, 216–17
  risk and return assumptions for, 116–17, 122–23
Real Estate Investment Trusts (REITs), 220
Real estate markets, 116–17
  in 1990s, 97–98
Reamer, Norton, 262
Rebalancing, 132–33, 134–38
  frequency of, 135–36

Rebalancing *(continued)*
   illiquidity and, 133, 136–38
   market crash of 1987 and, 70–73
   performance assessment for, 312–13
   return-chasing, 150
   risk control by, 71, 72
Recapitalization, 164
REITs, 220
Report of the Presidential Task Force on
   Market Mechanisms, 93
Research University
   contributions, 21
   Federal support for, 12–13, 16
   income, 18–23
   student charges, 21
Research analysts, 91, 199
   soft dollar payments for, 273
   Wall Street, 198–99
Resolution Trust Corporation (RTC), 97
Returns, 52
   on absolute return investing, 114–16, 208,
     210
   by asset class, 58
   assumptions of. *See* Capital market as-
     sumptions
   on bonds, 111, 112, 118, 160
   in developed foreign markets, 174
   dollar-weighted (internal rates of return),
     308–9
   in emerging markets, 174, 175
   on equities, 112, 113, 117–18
   market efficiency and, 76–79
   on mezzanine finance funds, 235–36
   nonnormal distributions of, 105, 106
   on private equity, 226, 228–33
   on real estate, 116–17, 122–23
   Sharpe ratio and, 304
   time weighted, 308–9
Risk
   in absolute return investing, 114–16, 210
   adjusted, 303–7
   asset allocation and, 54
   assumptions. *See* Capital market assump-
     tions
   in bonds, 111, 112
   call, 59n
   of contrarian approach, 325–28
   credit, 59, 103, 145, 147, 159, 162, 167,
     169–70, 171, 201
   in developed foreign markets, 174
   diversification to reduce, 62–67
   in emerging markets, 174, 175
   in equities, 112, 113, 117–18
   interest rate, 147
   internal and external control, 340–41
   market timing and, 55
   measurement of, 309–10
   in real estate, 116–17, 122–23
   rebalancing to control, 71, 72

   Sharpe ratio and, 304
   value investing and, 189–91
Risk arbitrage, 298
RJR Nabisco, 164–67, 176–77, 225–26
Rockefeller Foundation, 143, 195
Rocker, David, 297
Rogue traders, 146, 149
Rosenberg, Barr, 194–97, 308–9
Rosenberg Institutional Equity Management
   (RIEM), 194–97, 308–9
Ross, Stephen, 122
Rubbermaid, 212–13
Rudolph, Frederick, 12
Russian default, 158

Safety, margin of, 94–96
Sallie Mae, 90–91
Salomon Brothers Mortgage Index, 304
Salovaara, Mikael, 265
Samsung, 89–90
Savings and loans debacle (1980s), 332
Schumpeter, Joseph, 258–59
Schuyler, Eugene, 15
Section 28(e) of Securities Exchange Act of
   1934, 273
Securities. *See also specific instruments*
   compensation arrangements for, 268–77
Securities and Exchange Commission
   (SEC), 272, 273, 275, 277
Security lending, 144–50
   deal structures in, 149–50
   trading intensity in, 148–49
Security selection, 52, 52–53, 53n, 55–57,
   74–99. *See also* Active management
   liquidity and, 87–94
   market efficiency and, 74–87
   value orientation, 94–99
Self-awareness, in investment analysis,
   336–37
Semi-strong form of market efficiency, 188
Seragen, 326–28
Shapiro, John, 198
Shareholders, 176–77, 224–25
Sharpe, William, 304
Sharpe ratio, 304, 306, 310
Shiller, Robert, 307
Short selling, 90n, 214–16
Siegel, Jeremy, 60, 110, 181
Silber, John, 326–28
Simulations, 124–28
   capital market assumptions and, 125
   mean-variance optimization limitations
     mitigated by, 125–28
   one-year investment periods and, 127
   results interpretation, 125
   tradeoffs between critical goals exposed
     by, 125–27
Singer, Brian, 53
Sinquefield, Rex, 58

Small-capitalization growth managers, sur-
vivorship bias in, 80–82
Small-capitalization stocks, 64–65, 77–78,
156, 178
Small-capitalization value managers, sur-
vivorship bias in, 83–84
Snapple, 237–38
Soft dollars, 272–77
abuses of, 274–76
conflicts of interests and, 274
directed brokerage, 276–77
legitimacy of, 273–74
SEC proposals regarding, 277
Sony Building, acquisition of, 221–23
Sovereign debt, 89
S&P 500, 53n, 72, 113n, 142, 158, 173, 196,
231, 280, 326
Specialization, manager, 223–24
Speculative excess, momentum (growth)
strategies and, 191–92
Spending, evaluation of sustainability of,
39–41
Spending policy, xii, 30–35, 41–42
on appreciation in market value, 32–33
extremes in, 46–50
to insulate operating budget from market
fluctuations (smoothing mechanism),
30–31, 40–41, 45–46
purchasing power evaluation, 35–38
simulations for evaluating, 124–25
target spending rate, 33–35, 38
Spending rate, 30, 33–35, 51
Splash Technology Holdings, 237
Staff. *See* Investment staff
Stanford University, 16–17, 128–30
Start-up companies, 118
Steyer, Tom, 213n
Stock options, 177
Stocks
active management opportunities in, 76,
77
consumer, 140–41
cyclical, 140–41
deflation and, 119, 202
foreign, 77–82, 113, 174
foreign, currency exposure associated
with, 175
Great Crash (1929) and, 64–67
inflation and, 118–19, 176, 181
large-capitalization, 156, 178
returns on, 118
risk and return assumptions for, 112–13,
117–18
Sallie Mae, 90–91
small-capitalization, 64–65, 77–78, 156,
178
value, 189, 190
Stocks for the Long Run (Siegel), 60, 110–11
Strategic issues, 331–32

Strong form of market efficiency, 189
Student Loan Marketing Association ("Sallie Mae"), 90–91
Students, on endowment purposes, 9
Subordinated debt, 234, 236, 237, 238
Summit Subordinated Debt Fund, 236
Summit Ventures, 236–37
Survivorship bias, 59n, 61, 79–87
in absolute return investing, 115–16,
209–10
in domestic bond and stock managers,
84–86
in international equity managers, 82–83
in leveraged buyouts, 231
overinclusion, problems of, 79–80, 82
in peer comparisons, 302–3
in small-capitalization growth managers,
80–82
in small-capitalization value managers,
83–84
underinclusion, problems of, 80–82
Sutter Hill, 295

Tactical asset allocation (TAA), 68–69
Tactical issues, 331–32
Taiwan, 186–87
Takahashi, Dean, vii
Target spending rate, 33–35, 38
Taxes, 11, 25, 42, 165, 268
Technical analysis, 188
Tenure, 9
Termination of managers, 313, 332
Themis FTSE Fledgling Index, 301n
Thomas H. Lee Company, 237
Thomas H. Lee Equity Partners, 237–38
TIFF (Investment Fund for Foundations),
317
Time horizon of investor, mean-variance
optimization and, 107
Time weighted returns, 308–9
tactical asset allocation (TAA), 68–69
Timothy Dwight Professorship Fund, 27
Tisch, Laurence, 326
Tobin, James, xi–xii, 26–27, 30, 98
Tobin-Brainard *q*, 98
Tonka, 265
Top-down investment, 179, 180–81
in emerging markets, 185–87
in Japan, 181–85
Trading activity, 146, 148–49
Traditional asset classes. *See* Bonds; Stocks
Treasuries
bills, 58, 59
bonds, 88, 159–60, 162, 163–64, 171
Treasury Inflation-Protection Securities
(TIPS), 103
Trustees, 9–14, 17, 42, 45, 337–39
agency issues, 4
of Common Fund, 150

Trustees *(continued)*
  of Edna McConnell Clark Foundation, 64
  institutional direction by, 10, 13
  long-term vs. short-term goals of, 9, 34–35
  portfolio decision-making and, 321, 324,
    332–33, 337–38
  Tobin on, 26
Tuition, 10, 18
Turnover, portfolio, 311

Unification Church, 13–14
United Airlines, 150
United Asset Management (UAM), 261–63
U.S. News and World Report, 19
Unrestricted gifts, 10
Utility function, 123, 126

Value-driven investing, 56–57, 94–99, 114,
    115, 207–10, 214–16
  contrarian investing and, 95, 96–98
  fundamental risk and, 189–91
  margin of safety and, 94–96
  short selling, 214–16
  Tobin's *q*, 98
Value stocks, 189, 190
Venrock, 295
Venture capital, 117, 172, 225, 226, 227
  active management opportunities in, 76,
    77
  fees on, 290
  generational transition issues in, 295–96
  limited institutional experience with,
    238–39
  median results for, 78–79
  partnership terms in, 280–81
  returns on, 228, 229
  value-added possibilities in, 227
  value-oriented, 242–43
Volatility
  excess, 307

historical, 303–4
  smoothing mechanism to dampen, 30–31,
    40–41
  spending rates and, 38

Wall Street research, 198–99
Water Street Corporate Recovery Fund,
    264–67
Weak form of market efficiency, 188
WESCO, 243–45
Wheelock, Eleazer, 15
Whitney, Eli, 62
"Why Do Universities Have Endowments?"
    (Hansmann), 45
Winning the Loser's Game (Ellis), 329
Woolsey, William, 62, 63
WorldCom, 213

Yale—A History (Kelley), 11
Yale Corporation, 11
Yale endowment, xii–xiii
  distributions of, 39–41
  Eagle Bank investment, 62–63
  purchasing power of, 35–38
  quantitative portfolio management in,
    128–30
Yale Investment Committee, 339–40
Yale University
  Gibbs and, 15–16
  October 1987 crash and, 329–31
  private equity investment experience,
    233–34
  security loan program, 342
  support during colonial period, 11–12
Yield curves, 69*n*

Zack's investment research, 199
Zell, Sam, 222
Zisler, Randall, 122

About the Author

David Swensen, Yale University's Chief Investment Officer, manages the university's seven-billion-dollar endowment as well as several hundreds of millions of dollars of other investment funds. Prior to assuming his position at Yale in 1985, Mr. Swensen spent six years on Wall Street—three years at Lehman Brothers as Senior Vice President responsible for the firm's swap activities and three years at Salomon Brothers as Associate in Corporate Finance. His work on Wall Street focused on developing new financial technologies, or, as he characterizes them, "products that people love to hate."

Mr. Swensen serves as a leader and important critical thinker in the field of endowment management. Employing a rigorous, disciplined, yet unconventional approach to portfolio management, Swensen uses active management for large parts of the portfolio, searching for excess return in inefficient, under-researched areas of the market. During his tenure at Yale, superior investment management added more than two billion dollars to Yale's coffers. In addition to his work with the endowment at Yale, Swensen teaches at Yale College and the Yale School of Management.

Mr. Swensen holds a B.A and a B.S. from the University of Wisconsin at River Falls and a Ph.D. in economics from Yale University. His dissertation, "A Model for the Valuation of Corporate Bonds," was directed by Nobel laureate James Tobin and former Yale provost William Brainard. Swensen has previously published articles on endowment management under the auspices of the Association for Investment Management and Research and the Institute of Chartered Financial Analysts. He serves as a Trustee of the Carnegie Institution of Washington, Director of The Investment Fund for Foundations, Member of the Hopkins Committee of Trustees and Member of the Investment Advisory Committee for the Howard Hughes Medical Institute.